A Natura:

John Love was born and brought up in Inverness. He studied zoology at Aberdeen University, including three years' postgraduate research, before going to the Isle of Rum National Nature Reserve in 1975 to work for the Nature Conservancy Council managing the re-introduction of the white-tailed sea eagle. His books include a monograph on the sea eagle, and a human history of Rum. He later took up a position with Scottish Natural Heritage as Area Officer for Uist, Barra and St Kilda. He first reached St Kilda in 1979 and through his job has been able to return many times since. He retired from SNH in 2006 to concentrate on writing, drawing and lecturing.

By the same author:
The Return of the Sea Eagle (1983)
Eagles (1989)
Sea Otters (1990)
Penguins (1994)
A Salmon for the Schoolhouse (1994) [with Brenda McMullen]
Penguins (1997)
Rum: A Landscape without Figures (2001)

A Natural History
of St Kilda

John A. Love (signature)

John A. Love

with ink drawings by the author

BIRLINN

First published in 2009 by
Birlinn Ltd
West Newington House
10 Newington Road
Edinburgh
EH9 1QS

www.birlinn.co.uk

ISBN: 978 1 84158 797 4

The publishers gratefully acknowledge the support of Scottish Natural Heritage
towards the publication of this book.

Line illustrations are by the author unless otherwise specified.

British Library Cataloguing-in-Publication Data
A catalogue record for this book is available on request from the British Library

Typeset by Carnegie Book Production, Lancaster
Printed and bound in Britain by MPG Books Ltd, Bodmin

The human inhabitants of St Kilda possess many primitive traits which make them well worth study, but others have followed this enticing path, and the inhabitants we have in mind as we write, are the wild creatures of the little group of islands of which St Kilda is the heart. There is always a possibility of unusual interest in an island fauna, especially when, as in St Kilda, it has long been isolated from other land, without the possibility of natural communication. And St Kilda certainly does not betray expectation. In its isolation it has bred new races and species, and what will happen to these when man deserts its shore?

Professor James Ritchie 1930

Descriptions of countries without the natural history of them are now justly reckoned to be defective.

Martin Martin 1698

In memory of my elder brother
James Quintin (Jim) Love
1943–2006

Contents

List of plates   vii

List of figures   x

List of tables   xii

Preface   xiii

Introduction   1

1 Martin and ministers   8

2 Geology   24

3 Vegetation   43

4 Invertebrates   65

5 Seabirds 1   84

6 Seabirds 2   109

7 The Great Auk   121

8 Fowling   137

9 Land birds   164

10 The St Kilda wren   184

11 St Kilda mice   199

12 St Kilda sheep   219

13 Marine life   238

14 Visitors   255

15 Conservation   294

Bibliography   321

Index   335

Plates

Plate section 1

1   Hirta and Dun, St Kilda, from the air.

2   A bathymetric diagram of the sea floor around St Kilda in July 2000 – yellow, red and purple lie above the surface indicating the positions of Boreray (left) with Dun, Hirta and Soay at the top right.

3   SNH marine survey boat braves a storm on the way to Boreray.

4   Jewel anemones underwater.

5   A mosaic of marine creatures on an underwater rock face off St Kilda.

6   An orca family in waters off St Kilda in June 2008.

7   Looking across Village Bay, Hirta, in 1956, before the Army base was built.

8   The smoky village street on Hirta.

9   Tan-coloured ewe with dark twins on Hirta.

10   A young Soay lamb.

11   The extinct St Kilda field mouse as painted by Archibald Thorburn.

12   St Kilda field mouse.

13   A yellow morph of the rare weevil *Ceutorhynchus insularis*.

14   St Kilda wren on Hirta.

15   A Manx shearwater taking off at night.

16   A Leach's petrel caught under licence for ringing.

Plate section 2

17 Stac Biorach and Soay Stac in Soay Sound with Stac an Armin, Stac Lee and Boreray behind.

18 An aerial view of The Gap, Conachair and Mina Stac.

19 Stac Lee from above, during the ten-year gannet count.

20 A pair of gannets fighting.

21 Gannets on Boreray, with Stac Lee, Hirta and Soay beyond.

22 Off-duty puffins on a rock.

23 A puffin with thrift or sea pink.

24 Lofoten puffin dog or Lundehund in Bodø, northern Norway.

25 A group of guillemots (one bridled) with their young almost ready to fledge.

26 A great skua (bonxie) divebombing the camera.

27 A pair of fulmars calling.

28 A flock of Boreray sheep on Boreray.

29 Passengers landing from the NTS cruise ship *Meteor* in 1963.

30 An army landing craft begins Operation Hardrock in 1957.

31 The supply vessel MV *Elektron* aground in Village Bay on 14 October 2000.

Figures

Fig. 1. Martin Martin's map of St Kilda 1698.   9

Fig. 2. Fulmar and storm petrel as illustrated in Martin Martin's book.   12

Fig. 3. Evelyn Heathcote climbing.   36

Fig. 4. A St Kildan boat sailing through a natural arch.   37

Fig. 5. Stac Biorach.   39

Fig. 6. Cleits in the village meadows from a house window.   50

Fig. 7. John MacGillivray.   69

Fig. 8. James Fisher.   86

Fig. 9. John Alexander Harvie-Brown.   93

Fig. 10. Charles Dixon (1858–1926).   101

Fig. 11. Flying puffins on Dun in 1979.   106

Fig. 12. Euphemia MacCrimmon.   124

Fig. 13. John Wolley.   131

Fig. 14. Cartoon of tourists and great auks.   134

Fig. 15. A fowler, Alex Ferguson, poses on a rope to have his
photograph taken.   140

Fig. 16. Women and children with the fulmar crop.   156

Fig. 17. Plucking the fulmar catch.   158

Fig. 18. Eagle Clarke on St Kilda.   171

Fig. 19. A sea eagle in flight.   179

Fig. 20. Neil Gillies finds a snipe nest.   182

Fig. 21. St Kilda wren eggs in Kelvingrove Museum.   192

Fig. 22. Richard Kearton.   193

Fig. 23. Robert Atkinson with Finlay MacQueen, Neil Gillies
and Mrs Gillies.   197

Fig. 24. Alasdair Alpin Macgregor.   207

Fig. 25. Probably the only photograph of a St Kilda house mouse.   208

Fig. 26. Spanish fishing boat *Spinningdale* on the rocks of Village Bay,
February 2008.   216

Fig. 27. A Soay ram casting its fleece.   223

Fig. 28. Calum Macdonald, Neil Gillies and Finlay MacQueen rowing
to Soay for sheep in 1932.   228

Fig. 29. Sheep counts on Hirta, Boreray and Soay.   234

Fig. 30. Boreray sheep.   235

Fig. 31. A diver with the Scottish Natural Heritage survey team.   243

Fig. 32. Sowerby's beaked whale.   250

Fig. 33. A party of tourists on St Kilda.   258

Fig. 34. An advertisement for weekly tours on the *Dunara Castle*.   265

Fig. 35. Finlay MacQueen with a stuffed puffin.   271

Fig. 36. The Duchess of Bedford.   283

Fig. 37. A bird collector on St Kilda.   286

Fig. 38. St Kildan boys blowing eggs with Alex Ferguson to sell to
tourists.   287

Fig. 39. Annual visitor numbers on Hirta 1986–2006.   288

Fig. 40. The *Dunara Castle*.   296

Fig. 41. Jean and Niall Rankin, Lord Dumfries, Lady Dumfries (?),
Alex Ferguson, Mrs McWilliam (?), Rev. McWilliam,
Neil Gillies, Calum Macdonald.   297

Fig. 42. Michael Powell and Seton Gordon.   299

Fig. 43. Operation Hardrock.   309

Fig. 44. J. Morton Boyd and David Boddington on Stac an Armin,
1959.   311

Tables

Table 1. Some species lists for St Kilda.   68

Table 2. Numbers of seabirds breeding on St Kilda.   110

Table 3. Comparison between island races of wren.   189

Table 4. Sightings (days) of cetaceans from St Kilda (usually May to
August; 1973–2000).   251

Table 5. Whales killed between St Kilda and Rockall and processed in
the Harris Whaling Station.   252

Table 6. St Kilda's conservation designations.   318

Preface

The zoology of archipelagoes will be well worth examination ...

Charles Darwin 1835

THE HUMAN HISTORY of the St Kildans has been told admirably by many authors over the last few centuries. This book makes no attempt to recount that story; instead it focuses on the non-human inhabitants of St Kilda, and the people who took an interest in them over the centuries, including the St Kildans themselves of course – whose very survival depended upon these natural resources.

It is, however, through visitors to the island – many of whom were naturalists – that we learn much of what we know about the islanders themselves. So it is understandable that this particular account of naturalists and natural history should be woven around the St Kildans' own story. At the outset I chose three pioneering and well-informed personalities to introduce the island and its people; two of them were ministers, one of whom lived on Hirta for many years, but all were gifted observers with a strong interest in the world around them and thus they feature prominently in subsequent chapters.

But who were those other naturalist visitors whose names are so familiar to any student of St Kilda's human history? Most are dead and gone and, I feared, risked fading to obscurity as real people. Many were well known to each other so together they seem to offer a nice continuity through the last couple of centuries. Along with a brief background of their lives we will also consider their efforts and achievements. I do not delve too deeply into modern researchers; at least we can still seek them out and learn first-hand of their valuable work.

Sources are not inserted into the text to the extent that they disrupt its flow, but they can be traced easily by name in the bibliography at the back. In the text the date associated with each author is not the year they published, however, but the year they visited St Kilda – which is after all more relevant to the narrative. Neither is the bibliography intended to be complete. To save space I have included those references where a more comprehensive list of sources can be found.

Research at St Kilda is ongoing, and fresh insights are being delivered every day. Thus it would be pointless to strive for completeness. Nevertheless, if we arrive at a position where we have a deeper understanding of St Kilda, its natural environment and its people past and present, then the journey will have been worthwhile.

In the preparation of this book I have relied upon the considerable corpus of material published over several centuries and displayed in the bibliography. David Wilson has tirelessly made available vital material for me, especially the detailed notes and researches of James Fisher, who was robbed of his own opportunity to write this book by his untimely death in a car accident in 1970. To David and to the Fisher family I owe an immense debt of gratitude. In compiling the text I have expanded my contributions to the World Heritage Site resubmission (and freely dipped into those of my co-authors), also my St Kilda booklet published by Scottish Natural Heritage, together with a few other articles I have written recently. Dr Geoff Hancock of the Hunterian Museum in Glasgow kindly read and commented upon Chapter 4 (Invertebrates) and Susan Bain of the National Trust for Scotland upon Chapter 15 (Conservation).

I met Stuart Murray on my very first visit to St Kilda in 1979, when he was studying puffins, and we have remained firm friends ever since. No one today, I venture, knows St Kilda as intimately as Stuart, so it is with my gratitude (and relief) that he undertook to read, comment upon and improve the entire manuscript. I have used many of my own photographs and drawings, but Scottish Natural Heritage, the National Trust for Scotland, the School of Scottish Studies, David Wilson, Geoff Hancock, David Maclennan, Stuart Murray, Alasdair MacEachen, David Clugston, Catriona MacGeoch and John Macdonald (son of the St Kildan Calum who assisted in the transfer of sheep from Soay to Hirta in 1932) have all kindly made other photographs available to me. The publishers and I have made every effort to trace the copyright on the remaining photographs without success. To all who assisted in the final publication of this book my grateful thanks.

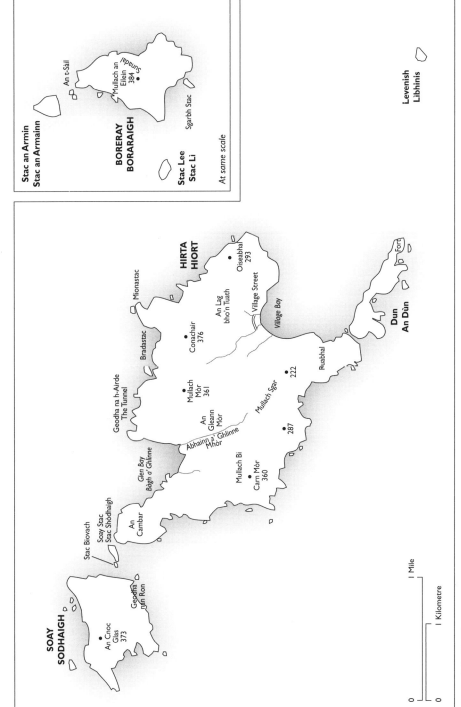

SOAY
SODHAIGH

An Cnoc
Glas
373

Geodha
nan Ron

Stac Biovach

Soay Stac
Stac Shodhaigh

An
Cambar

Glen Bay
Bàgh a' Ghlinne

Geodha na h-Airde
The Tunnel

Bradastac

Mionastac

HIRTA
HIORT

Conachair
376

Mullach
Mòr
361

An
Gleann
Mòr

Abhainn a' Ghlinne
Mhòr

Mullach Bi

Carn Mòr
360

287

Mullach Sgar

222

Ruabhal

Oiseabhal
293

An Lag
bho'n Tuath

Village Street

Village Bay

Dun
An Dùn

Fort

STAC AN ARMIN
STAC AN ARMAINN

An t-Sàil

Mullach an
Eilein
384

Sunadal

BORERAY
BORARAIGH

Stac Lee
Stac Li

Sgarbh Stac

At same scale

Levenish
Libhinis

0
0

1 Mile

1 Kilometre

Map of St Kilda

Introduction

There is something in the very name of St Kilda which excites expectation. Remote and solitary, the spirit of romance appears still to dwell in the clouds and storms that separate this narrow spot from the world; but like other spirits, it vanishes at the rude touch of investigation. Still, this island will be interesting to him whose amusement it may be to study [it].

So JUDGED THE GEOLOGIST John MacCulloch in 1815, one of the first scientists ever to set foot on the islands. St Kilda is still a charismatic place and a name to conjure with. Many early writers used the name for the main inhabited island of Hirta – *Hirte* or *Hiort* in Gaelic. Nowadays it is usually applied to the whole archipelago.

There never was a saint called St Kilda and 'Kilda', some think, came about from a printing error on early maps. The 'St' was an afterthought, an affectation perhaps. The Old Norse word for a well is *Kelda* and in St Kilda there is a well called *Tobar Childa*. *Tobar* is the Gaelic word for well. Well, well? Who knows? But perhaps, more convincingly, the name 'Kilda' arose from the islanders' habit of pronouncing 'R' in their native Gaelic like an 'L'. So, they spoke *Hirte* as *Hilte*, enunciating the 'e' at the end. We may never know the real derivation of the name 'St Kilda', just as discussions continue as to what the word *Hirte* may mean.

Hirta is the largest (1567 acres/639 hectares) in the archipelago, the only island that was ever permanently inhabited and the one that, in Gaelic, also gives its name to the whole archipelago – *Hirte* or sometimes *Hiort*. There are three other main islands, all difficult of access – Dun (*an Dùn*), Soay (*Sodhaigh*) and Boreray (*Boraraigh*), with numerous isolated stacs just offshore – Levenish (*Libhinis*), Stac an Armin (*Stac an Armainn*), and Stac Lee (*Stac Li*) amongst others.

The archipelago of St Kilda is the most remote inhabited place in the British

Isles, lying 40 miles (64 km) west of the Monach Isles in North Uist, the nearest land. True, its native inhabitants opted to move to the mainland in 1930, but several islanders chose to return for several months each summer, until the onset of World War II. Thereafter, a few scientific expeditions came to St Kilda for short periods until the establishment of a military radar base in 1957. This has resulted in permanent settlement again and, with a ranger on the island every summer, now constitutes St Kilda's modern community. It may be something of an artificial one, but it still ranks as the most remote in Britain.

In effect then, the island has never been without inhabitants since 1957 when the first contingent of soldiers overwintered. St Kilda now enjoys benefits and services the original islanders never could have dreamt of – running water, electricity, telephones and computer access, a supply ship several times a year and a twice-weekly helicopter to transport staff. What services the St Kildans would now enjoy if only they had been able to endure their island for three more decades . . .

In 1954, the Swedish artist Roland Svensson published *Lonely Isles*. His son Torbjorn is a good friend of mine who, like his father, and as a captain of a cruise ship, has visited St Kilda several times. Ten years later Roland summed up the tragedy of the St Kildans so perceptively:

> The people were evacuated in 1930, partly because they were unable to maintain communications with the mainland. About eight years ago (in 1957) I saw the Forces move into that island. They brought bulldozers, tractors, big lorries, diesel generators, helicopters, and so on, and regular communications were established with the mainland ... Who paid for all these wonderful modern implements, tractors and lorries? The British paid for them. And we ought to be able to invest the far smaller sum necessary to assist island populations, building what would be of lasting importance.

Hundreds of accounts have been published about the original community of Hirta. The stimulus for these came largely from their unique way of life, which was largely based upon hunting seabirds. As the Reverend Kenneth MacAulay recognised in 1758:

> The island of St Kilda may be ranked among the greatest curiosities of the British Empire.

It is a sad fact, however, that virtually none of these erudite works were written by islanders themselves. Contrast this with the Blasket Islands in south-west Ireland. By the early 20th century – just like St Kilda – their worth too was recognised, but as a last bastion of Irish Gaelic, attracting scholars from afar to study the ancient language and oral tradition. This contact with men of learning imparted a certain confidence in some of the islanders, whose minds, less educated perhaps, were every bit as sharp as their academic visitors. Firstly, and most notably, was a remarkable old man called Thomás Ó'Criomhthain who penned his own life, as *An tOileánach (The Islandman)* – but in his native tongue. Others were to follow, resulting in some two-score works of Gaelic literature – the Blasket Library. Many have since been translated into English. Sadly, in 1953 this community of only 30 souls opted to abandon its native home – just as had the St Kildans – for a more secure living on the mainland (Love 2007).

It will always be an abiding tragedy that no home-spun 'library' exists for St Kilda. Virtually everything that was ever written about it was by outsiders, many of whom – such as the advocate George Seton in 1877 – spent no longer than a few hours on Hirta. One or two accounts have been taken down from islanders after the evacuation, such as that of Malcolm MacQueen (1828–1913), one of the 36 islanders who emigrated to Australia in 1852 (sadly half of them did not survive the voyage). MacQueen's story was taken down by his son, just before the old man died. Calum Macdonald has also written his own story, while a few other even briefer accounts have been collected from exiled islanders. David Quine (1988) has done more than most in bringing these accounts to a wider audience. I know of only one book in Gaelic, by Calum Ferguson, from Lewis although of St Kilda stock. *Hiort; far na laigh a'ghrian* was published by Acair in 1995, and translated into English as *St Kilda Heritage* in 2006.

Fortunately, however, a few visitors did spend weeks, months, even years there, such as various ministers of the Church – some of whom were Gaelic-speakers – and intrepid Sassenach souls like John Sands and the Heathcotes who will figure prominently later. It is not surprising that these should prove the most insightful accounts we have. Very few casual visitors could speak Gaelic to converse with the islanders themselves in their native tongue. One of the first was Martin Martin from Skye who visited in June 1697. As a native Gaelic-speaker not only did he learn much about the community and its way of life, but he even detected fragments of a much earlier pagan tradition. Importantly, from the point of view of my own interests, he was the first to record anything of the islands' natural history, all of which would have been told to him by the islanders themselves – and at a time when few outsiders were taking any interest.

While others who came after could not ignore the wildlife – for that was what the islanders' economy relied upon – most written accounts concentrate upon human history. Detailed descriptions of the natural history are only to be found in scientific journals. I have been unable to identify any other full-length book dedicated solely to the natural history.

At least one writer, quite recently, has even gone as far as condemning naturalists for having ignored the islanders' story altogether, concentrating too much on their own chosen field. This is quite unfair. On the contrary, one popular synthesis of island tradition was an oft-forgotten book *St Kilda Summer*, written by two fine naturalists J. Morton Boyd and Ken Williamson and published as recently as 1960. Indeed, Ken's own book *The Atlantic Islands*, published in 1948, dealt with folklife in the Faroes where he was posted during World War II and it remains a recognised classic to this day, even in the Faroes. So, it is quite untrue, and indeed quite preposterous, to claim that visiting naturalists were focused only upon natural history. They were in fact largely restrained from including much background in their published accounts, for scientific journals require that papers keep strictly to the subject in hand.

It is also true that naturalists who wish to collect and describe flora and fauna would wish to spend as long as practicable in their study area. And so it was on St Kilda. Many visiting scientists, from John MacCulloch in 1815 and John MacGillivray in 1840 right up to and just after the evacuation, stayed just long enough to get to know and interact with the St Kildans, in a way that casual visitors could not. Indeed, naturalists depended upon the islanders to reach some of the more remote islands in the archipelago. It is not surprising to discover just how many of the classic accounts about St Kilda and its people were written by men who were naturalists, if not by profession then by inclination – Martin, MacAulay, Mackenzie, G. C. Atkinson, Wilson, etc. Only a few such were to write books on their experiences. Notable amongst them is Robert Atkinson's *Island Going*, still one of my favourite island books. Other serious naturalists confined their observations to their personal diaries, which can prove valuable yet largely inaccessible sources, and hitherto largely ignored. I have endeavoured to consult as many as I could in the preparation of this book.

It will become obvious in the following chapters just how long St Kilda has been recognised as a place of great biological and conservation value. After the evacuation in 1930, its next owner, Lord Dumfries, later the Marquis of Bute, continued to employ an islander Neil Gillies (1895–1989), as a nature warden until World War II put a stop to regular summer visits by any of the islanders. Atkinson was one of the last to experience this epilogue to the St Kildans' story, sharing the island in 1938 with old Finlay MacQueen, Neil Gillies and his mother.

In 1949 – the year Atkinson's book was published – the Nature Conservancy was set up as the government conservation body. It considered St Kilda well enough protected then, under Bute's stewardship, to necessitate designating the archipelago as a National Nature Reserve.

It was only when Bute's estate offered St Kilda to the National Trust for Scotland in 1956 that the Nature Conservancy became involved as a major player in the future management of the islands. St Kilda became a National Nature Reserve in 1957. Indeed, as new owners, the Trust could not have achieved as much as it did without that input from the Nature Conservancy. As a government agency, the Conservancy was also a sufficiently powerful lobby to help the Trust mitigate against the intentions of the Ministry of Defence to construct a radar base in St Kilda. The first Conservancy warden, Ken Williamson, and his immediate line manager, Morton Boyd, were to be prominent in this regard, preventing the demolition of the old buildings to build a road.

The highly successful partnership between the National Trust for Scotland and the Conservancy (later the Nature Conservancy Council, and now Scottish Natural Heritage) continues to the present day. Together the two bodies achieved World Heritage status for St Kilda in 1987. At first, this only included the natural history interest since the cultural case had been insufficiently argued. Eventually, however, in 2005, the islands joined an élite group of World Heritage Sites (WHSs) that possess both natural and cultural status; there are currently only 25 out of 878 worldwide. At the same time the marine interest was added to the terrestrial natural heritage.

St Kilda might well be considered the Galapagos of the British Isles. Ever since Darwin, the Galapagos Islands have been considered a biological treasure. They too were accorded World Heritage status, in 1978. Not only did this volcanic archipelago inspire Darwin to formulate his monumental thesis on the origin of species through natural selection, but it has informed scientists on how animals and plants first colonised such a remote spot, 600 miles out in the Pacific. Nowadays not only are the Galapagos Islands at the forefront of evolutionary and biogeographical research, but they also pioneer conservation management against alien species invasions.

It would be decades after Darwin that science finally realised that St Kilda too had evolved its own unique wildlife. It possessed distinct races of both house and field mice, and of wren. Perhaps there are other examples yet to be discovered in its invertebrate or plant populations.

But that is not all. Questions have been posed as to how remote islands like St Kilda were originally colonised. Take the wren for instance – as long ago as 1758 the Reverend Kenneth MacAulay pondered:

... how these little birds ... could have flown thither or whether they went accidentally in boats, I leave undetermined.

Early studies of island mice by Professor 'Sam' Berry offered suggestions as to how and when these rodents might have reached St Kilda, 45 miles west of the Outer Hebrides – as stowaways aboard Viking ships. Modern DNA studies appear to confirm this original thesis. Then, in 1963, a new island of Surtsey erupted from the sea, 12 miles south of the Westmann Islands in Iceland.

Icelandic scientists quickly recognised a unique opportunity to study how the bare lava of Surtsey came to be colonised by plants and animals. One of their many insights into this process was the identification of a tiny weevil now living on Surtsey that had only ever been identified before from St Kilda! A few years ago, as I flew round Surtsey, I pondered its parallels with St Kilda's own story. It too had erupted from the ocean floor, albeit some 55 million years previously. Whatever wildlife St Kilda might have supported since then was wiped out when its surface was effectively swept clean again a few hundred thousand years ago during the Ice Ages. So the saga of life on ancient St Kilda we are now to consider here lies somewhere between the 5-million-year-old story of Galapagos and the 5-decades-old story of Surtsey.

In this book, the scene is set with short introductory narratives about Martin Martin's visit in 1697 – one of the very first visitors to write about the islands – and then by two ministers of the Church, also Gaelic-speakers, who were to assemble equally important and informative accounts that included natural history. We then consider the geology which created the archipelago all these millions of years ago. Geomorphological processes during the last Ice Age, only thousands of years ago, then eliminated virtually all life on St Kilda. As to what lived on St Kilda in ages past we may never know.

And so the assembly of life on these islands had to begin afresh. We ponder how St Kilda came to be recolonised by plants and animals since then, tapping into what we know of other islands, especially Surtsey. The current situation of its wildlife is described, and, of course, the role seabirds came to play in the establishment and maintenance of a human population on St Kilda.

Subsequent chapters reveal St Kilda's natural history, how visitors and scientists came to study the archipelago, and the part that they have played in its story – from Martin Martin to modern research projects into the Soay sheep. Despite its isolation, at the end of the 19th century, St Kilda supported a significant tourist industry, upon which the islanders came to rely. Thus tourists – and naturalists – were to play their part in the ultimate demise of the human interest of the islands that they had come to experience for themselves. Finally, we reach modern times, to consider the conservation history of St Kilda, from private wildlife reserve, through military base to World Heritage status.

St Kilda may only be an isolated speck on a map of Great Britain but its very existence out in the North Atlantic continues to invoke fascination. Everyone who comes to hear of it wants to go there. Those who are fortunate enough to do so – even if they never make a return visit – will never forget it. Clearly these islands have an attraction that far exceeds their size.

As the naturalist James Fisher (1948) concluded:

> Whatever he studies, the future observer of St Kilda will be haunted the rest of his life by the place, and tantalised by the impossibility of describing it, to those who have not seen it.

Perhaps it is indeed an impossible task to describe St Kilda. But for those who might never get there, and even for those who do, this book will take up the challenge. I first visited St Kilda in 1979, for ten days. I have since returned many times, firstly leading small parties on charter boats. In 1992, I took up a post as Area Officer for Scottish Natural Heritage in South Uist in the Outer Hebrides, so St Kilda came within my remit. I supervised the National Nature Reserve and line-managed the summer wardens, while also liaising between the army (on St Kilda and in Uist) and the National Trust for Scotland on the mainland (Love 2004). My position entitled me to tap into helicopter transport. One of my final tasks before retirement from Scottish Natural Heritage was to assist the Scottish Executive in compiling the World Heritage submission in 2003. This included accounts by various experts in their fields thus providing a good modern synthesis of the current state of knowledge; it is available on-line. A year later, I wrote a short booklet for Scottish Natural Heritage entitled *St Kilda – a world apart*, a precursor to this more detailed book. Most recently, in 2008, I was lecturer on the National Trust cruise that landed some 300 passengers for a brief time before circum-navigating the entire archipelago. As we departed southwards we could view the entire collection of islands and stacs against a spectacular sunset.

Ever since boyhood I have been fascinated by islands, especially remote ones. My obsession began first with Handa in 1964 and continued with the first of several expeditions to North Rona back in 1971. With Sulaisgeir, Rona is a National Nature Reserve like St Kilda and also came within my jurisdiction until I left Scottish Natural Heritage in August 2006. A third National Nature Reserve in my patch – the Monach Islands or Heisgeir – lies only 4 miles west of North Uist, but in many ways is much less accessible than St Kilda with its defence facilities, 40 miles further west. Every island group has its own story to tell, of human occupation, vegetation and seabirds. St Kilda, however, has a longer and more detailed history of research and still remains a spectacular outdoor laboratory. It is, in effect, Britain's very own Galapagos.

Martin and ministers

IN 1697, a British buccaneer named William Dampier published a remarkable book entitled *A New Voyage Round the World*. Amongst his many, exciting global adventures, Dampier had been one of the first Englishmen ever to set foot on the Galapagos, that remote uninhabited and little-known archipelago on the equator, 600 miles west of Peru. His book not only contained the first published account of these islands, but also the first chart of them made by one of his shipmates, Ambrose Cowley. William Dampier's book proved an instant success and gained him a considerable reputation for scientific enquiry and the sobriquet 'a pirate of exquisite mind'. No detail of botany, zoology, hydrography or meteorology escaped Dampier's interest. He was an accomplished naturalist/explorer and, indeed, his book earned him more money than buccaneering ever did.

In that same year – 1697 – a whole world away – a gentleman/traveller called Martin Martin first set foot on St Kilda. The following year he too published a remarkable book entitled *A Late Voyage to St Kilda* that, like Dampier's, was to prove something of a bestseller. In it he explained how:

> ... a description of some remote corner in the Indies shall be sure to afford us high amusement, whilst a thousand things much nearer to us might engage our thoughts to better purpose ... The author ... by a laudable curiosity was prompted to undertake the voyage and that in an open boat, to the almost manifest hazard of his life.

His destination had been an archipelago only 45 miles west of the British Isles, but in many ways it was every bit as remote and unknown as Dampier's Galapagos Islands. Martin's book was one of the first and certainly the fullest account of St Kilda and its inhabitants ever published; like Dampier, its author even included one of the first-ever maps of these islands.

A year later, in 1698, he published his *Description of the Western Islands of Scotland* about the wider Hebrides, a territory which was:

> ... but little known or considered, not only by strangers but even by those under the same Government and climate ... it is become customary in those of quality to travel young into foreign countries, whilst they are absolute strangers at home ...
>
> ... Foreigners sailing through the Western Isles have been tempted, from the sight of so many hills that seem to be covered all over with heath and faced with high rocks, to imagine the inhabitants, as well as their places of residence, are barbarous; and to this opinion, their habit as well as their language have contributed.

Indeed, the Highlands and Islands were still a forgotten and rather lawless outpost of the Empire. The clans had not yet been subdued and, only a decade before Martin's St Kilda voyage, those remaining loyal to the deposed Stuart king had defeated government troops at Killicrankie. In 1692, five years before Martin's voyage, the shameful Massacre of Glencoe was perpetrated. It would be ten years before the union of England and Scotland. Three more Jacobite

Fig. 1. Martin Martin's map of St Kilda 1698.

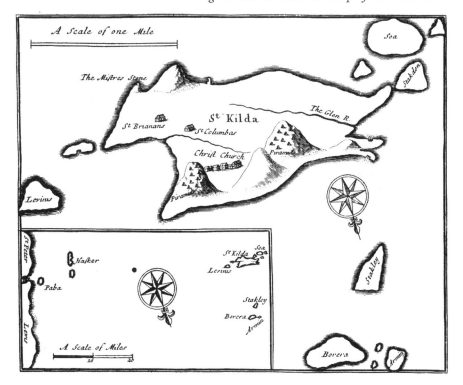

Rebellions had yet to occur, the last of which culminated in the Battle of Culloden in 1746, after which the Highlands and Islands were never the same again (Love 2008).

Undeterred, Martin embarked upon his hazardous journey throughout the Hebridean Isles, even to St Kilda.

Born around 1660 and brought up at Duntulm in the north of Skye, Martin studied at Edinburgh University before returning to his native island first as tutor to the Macdonalds of Sleat and then to the Macleods of Dunvegan. In 1708, he was to study medicine at Leiden whose records claimed that he had been born in 1669. But this would have made him only 12 years old when in 1681 – according to Scottish records – he graduated from Edinburgh University! While it was not unusual in those days for gifted and privileged children to embark upon higher education quite early in life, Martin's case does seem a bit improbable.

Although a Gaelic-speaker, he wrote in English, for he was writing for a southern population who still considered anything north of the Highland line as a foreign country. Martin himself was quick to point out how these islands were:

> ... never described till now by any man that was a native of the country, or had travelled them.

Although under the patronage of the naturalist Sir Robert Sibbald and other London men of science, Martin died in 1718 in London in relative obscurity.

Martin had been particularly intrigued by:

> ... the most remote and remarkable St Kilda ... Providence having distinguished [its islanders] in many things both as to their naturals as well as morals from the rest of mankind ... a race of men so truly happy and contented with their lot.

Given the historical importance of his account, he may be forgiven for romanticising about the lot of the St Kildan. Few who encountered this curious race after Martin's time seemed to have been immune to this viewpoint.

As owners of St Kilda, the Macleods of Dunvegan sent a Factor or Steward at least once a year to collect the rents. Martin tried several times to accompany him to St Kilda without success. Finally, at 6 o'clock in the evening of 29 May 1697, Martin was able to join the minister from Rodel, the Reverend John Campbell, and set out from the island of Ensay in the Sound of Harris in an open boat. The strengthening south-east wind did not bode well for the crossing so they rowed all night trying to seek shelter off the Hasgeir rocks. In the event, they determined to make for Hirta after all. The passage out into the Atlantic took 16 hours, after which the small party could take heart from the sight of 'several Tribes of the Fowls of St Kilda'. Their first view of Boreray, three leagues to the south of Hirta:

> ... gave new vigour to our men, who being refreshed with victuals, lowering mast and sail, rowed to a miracle. While they were tugging at the oars, we plied them with plenty of Aqua Vitae to support them.

They then had to shelter for two nights under the brooding north cliffs of Boreray with the clamour of seabirds all around, where:

> ... the heavens were darkened by their flying over our heads, their excrements were in such quantity, that they gave a tincture to the sea, and at the same time sullied our boat and cloaths.

At last, on 1 June, they reached Hirta, the only inhabited island of the group, three days after they had first set out from Harris! As they approached the shore:

> [The islanders] welcomed us with a God Save You, the usual salutation, admiring to see us get thither contrary to wind and tide; ... some of their number coming by pairs into the sea received Mr Campbell and me upon their shoulders and carried us to land, where we were received with all the demonstrations of joy and kindness they were able to express ...
>
> We all walked to the little village, where there was a lodging prepared for us, furnished with beds of straw; ... [and] bread, butter, cheese, mutton, fowls, eggs, fire, etc, all of which was to be given in at our lodging twice every day.

With the Factor and his motley entourage of assistants and friends, the visitors numbered some 50 folk. Martin mused on the strain this must have imposed on their own resources. The population of St Kilda at that time comprised only 27 families, or 180 souls, a peak – and, indeed, heyday – the community would never again achieve. The village, however, was not the Village Street so familiar today, but a cluster of beehive-like dwellings further inland.

Martin saw cattle feeding on Dun, the island separated from Hirta by a narrow passage. He noted how the islanders still saw the ancient ruined fort there as a useful retreat in times of danger. Martin described the dress of the inhabitants and was particularly fascinated by their ancient customs, folklore and cures. He was told of the Amazon warrior in Gleann Mor who was:

> ... much addicted to hunting in days when St Kilda was joined by dry land to Harris ... Some years ago a pair of large deer's horns were found in the top of Otterveaul Hill [Oiseval], almost a foot under ground, and a wooden dish full of deer's grease. 'Tis said of this warrior that she let loose her grey-hounds after the deer in St Kilda.

Fig. 2. Fulmar and storm petrel as illustrated in Martin Martin's book.

This is a curious tale, for there is no evidence that St Kilda deer ever reached there. Indeed, it would also be remarkable if there was ever a foot depth of soil on the rocky, windswept summit of Oiseval. Martin went on:

> The whole Island is one hard rock, ... the grass is very short but kindly, producing plenty of milk; the number of sheep commonly maintained in St Kilda and the two adjacent Isles, does not exceed two thousand ...

The islanders had 18 small red horses for carrying turf and corn, as well as 90 small cows with black and white foreheads which produced a fat and sweet beef. The soil was:

> ... very grateful to the labourer, producing ordinarily sixteen, eighteen or twenty fold; their grain is only bear [barley], and some oats ... They use no plough but a kind of crooked spade ... The chief ingredient in their composts is ashes of turf mixed with straw; with these they mix their urine ... they join also the bones, wings, and entrails of their Sea-Fowls to their straw.

He noted how fish were plentiful, naming cod, ling, mackerel, congers, braziers, turbot, graylords, sythes, also laiths, podloes and herring. As bait the islanders used limpets, also the flesh of seabirds they called *bowger* (puffin) which they caught on hooks.

Fortunately, for our purposes, Martin was adamant that:

Descriptions of countries without the natural history of them are now justly reckoned to be defective …

In the course of my travells … any thing that was remarkable fell under my observations … Our Isles afford a greater variety of natural as well as moral observations, than I expected; of both these I have amassed a considerable number.

The 'large cargoe of natural curiosities' he was said to have accumulated on his travels included 'Skins of fowls, Minerals, Coral, Talk, Nitre, Ambergriece, Shells, etc'. He noted the only 'Amphibia' to be seen on St Kilda were otters and seals, but there were no trees, shrubs nor bees.

We will see in succeeding chapters just how important his detailed descriptions of the wildlife of St Kilda have turned out to be. He concluded his little book, only 70 pages in length, with no fewer than 11 pages about a young bard called Roderick the Impostor, a religious fanatic whose unorthodox ideas seemed to have held much sway in his community. Martin did not dwell upon his leaving St Kilda except that it took place at the end of June and, against the wishes of the St Kildans, he and the Reverend Campbell took the Impostor away with them to face trial and ultimate exile. One can only hope the return voyage was less eventful than had been the journey to reach Hirta.

In an account published nine years after his own visit to St Kilda in 1815, the geologist John MacCulloch was rather dismissive of Martin and his book:

… a most provoking fellow. He was a native of Skye, and had therefore ready access to information, he was not illiterate; he was a scientific man, because he was a physician or a surgeon acquainted with natural history; and he was employed by Sir Robert Sibbald to investigate that of all the islands. But his propensities seem to have been directed rather to supernatural history.

Dr Samuel Johnson had been even less charitable in 1772, although conceding that Martin had been fortunate to be born at a time when:

… the chiefs of the clans had lost little of their original influence. The mountains were yet unpenetrated, no inlet was opened to foreign novelties and the feudal institutions operated upon life with their full force.

As a youth Johnson had read Martin's book and carried a copy with him on his own travels through the Hebrides in 1773. He was nonetheless critical of its literary content. He dared suggest that it was inaccurate in parts, even in the descriptions of Martin's native island! Johnson was also disappointed that the book did not reveal more. His companion, James Boswell, however, admitted:

I cannot but have a kindness for [Martin], notwithstanding his defects.

Despite alleged deficiencies in his narrative, Martin presented vivid insights into traditions which at that time still retained elements of ancient pagan rituals, not just on St Kilda but throughout the Highlands and Islands. Indeed, Gaelic culture was so removed from the rest of the kingdom as to repeatedly rebel against Establishment for decades to come. Martin even elevated St Kilda's isolated community to be something to which the rest of society should aspire. Undermining his scientific integrity perhaps, he then went on to consider the St Kildans:

> ... much happier than the generality of mankind, as being almost the only people in the world who feel the sweetness of true liberty.

This was a strange conclusion about a community trapped on the most remote inhabited island group in the United Kingdom! By 1815, even the hard-nosed geologist MacCulloch was drawn into the same trap:

> ... if happiness is not a dweller in St Kilda, where shall it be sought?

A truer picture could only be revealed by those who actually lived there, enduring the harsh and precarious life-style for themselves. Since the St Kildans were illiterate, it fell to the Reverend Alexander Buchan (c 1645–1729) to provide the first such account in 1727. Three-quarters of his modest little book, *Description of St Kilda, the Most Remote Western Isles of Scotland*, seems to have been copied from Martin, but he did contribute some observations of his own, not least one at odds with – and probably closer to the truth than – Martin's more romantic notions:

> They are in a manner prisoners, yea worse, all things considered; prisoners in other places have the advantage of visits from friends and converse with them, which that poor people have not for the greatest part of the year, except when the Steward and his followers come among them to demand his rents ... They very much grudge what he carries away with him, and that they must all the year be toiling for others.

Martin had seen the island from a visitor's perspective a privileged friend of the Factor, while Buchan – as a resident – saw the hardships to be suffered long after the Factor had left. Buchan was a Gaelic-speaker from Caithness. He had been sent to St Kilda as catechist by the Church of Scotland in 1705. Subjected to miserable treatment from his employers, Buchan finally, 'for want of subsistence', had to go to the mainland twice to try to win some remuneration for all his efforts. Ordained at last in 1710 but not in the best of health, he returned to St Kilda as official catechist and schoolteacher for the newly founded Society in Scotland for the Propagating of Christian Knowledge (SSPCK).

In 1728, the Reverend Daniel MacAulay, minister in Bracadale, Skye, was sent to St Kilda to report on the Reverend Buchan for the SSPCK, the first such visit for many years. MacAulay concluded:

> He is fitter for this place than any other person I know ... But it would be a great hardship upon the poor people now in their dismal circumstances to take Mr Buchan from them. The said person is getting very old, and not everyone will go there to succeed him.

MacAulay returned from St Kilda in July 1728 with the first news of a tragic disaster that had befallen the community the previous year. On his arrival he had been given:

> ... a lamentable account of the depopulation of that place by the small pox, for, of the twenty one families that were there, only four remain, ... the escape of some of the few who live, is owing to a remarkable act of Divine providence; For, about the fifteenth of August last, three men and eight boys were left in the rock called Stackriarmin, in order to catch a loadning of young Solan Geese ... untill the thirteenth of May at which time they were relieved by the Baillie's brother but before I went to Hirta. They were sent to the Isle Soa, where they remained while I was at Hirta so that I could see none of them ...

A century later, the Reverend Neil Mackenzie added more detail:

> [Smallpox] broke out [in Hirta] just after a party had been left on Stac an Armin to collect feathers ... Death after death followed. At last there were scarcely sufficient left to bury the dead ... Out of twenty five families only five could keep a fire. There were ninety four deaths. When the factor came next summer he found those who had been left on Stac an Armin all well. They lived on fish and fowls, but at times suffered much from cold and hunger. They made fish hooks of a few rusty nails, and also contrived to stitch together their clothing with feathers and patch them with the skins of birds. They returned mostly to empty houses, crops generally never reaped, and the cattle roaming about half wild.

The Reverend Buchan's family had been away on the mainland at the time. Alone on Hirta, remarkably, he himself had escaped the disease. However, his health might well have suffered in some other way whilst ministering to the sick, for he died the next year (1729). As he himself had admitted:

> The Island of Hirta has been much upon my heart and I have denied myself the ease and other worldly accommodations I might have had elsewhere to serve the interest of the Gospell in that place, and I bless the Lord not without some success.

Having preached the gospel on St Kilda for 24 years on little stipend, Buchan left his widow aged 60 and six children all but destitute. The SSPCK reluctantly gave up £25 that was still owing to the Buchans in order to support the education of one of the sons. It would be five years before a replacement for Buchan was found in St Kilda, one Roderick Maclennan. That same year too (1734) the unfortunate Lady Grange was exiled to the island by her husband for threatening to expose his Jacobite sympathies to the authorities. Initially, for two years, Lord Grange had incarcerated her on the Monach Isles or Heisgeir, and then on St Kilda, where she is said to have written how 'I was in great misery in the Husker, but I am ten times worse and worse here.' In 1742, she was finally removed to Skye, where she died three years later.

From an acute bottleneck following the smallpox epidemic, the population had recovered to 88 by 1758, mainly due to the arrival of more families from Skye. For the first half of the 19th century the number of inhabitants then hovered around 100. Thirty-six were to emigrate in 1852 to Australia and the population never recovered after that, infant tetanus probably being the main limiting factor (see Chapter 8).

New genes from sporadic immigrants to St Kilda may have accounted for a change from Martin's observation that the menfolk there had limited facial hair since, latterly, many sported big beards. Fresh blood would also have precluded any possibility that the islanders – in common with the mice and wrens – were themselves evolving into a race apart. It was often claimed that they possessed large, powerful feet and ankles with toes that were almost prehensile. In 1896, the Keartons attempted to demonstrate this in a photograph, but it merely showed a characteristic easily acquired by cragsmen constantly exercising on the steep rocky cliffs. A characteristic lisp in their Gaelic speech persisted however, as mentioned by Martin (1697), MacAulay (1758) and Mackenzie (1830s).

The Church was always to exert a huge and powerful influence upon St Kilda and its inhabitants, but the clergy contributed much to the early natural history. It is worth digressing a little at this juncture to provide some background to one or two more men of the cloth who will be quoted frequently hereafter. Michael Robson's monumental book *St Kilda: Church, Visitors and 'Natives'* (2005) provides a very full synthesis.

The Reverend Buchan's *A Description of St Kilda* had been disappointingly brief and dipped liberally into Martin's narrative, but it was soon to be overshadowed by an account from the Reverend Kenneth MacAulay – not to be confused with the Reverend Daniel MacAulay mentioned earlier.

Having graduated from Aberdeen University in 1742, Kenneth MacAulay had succeeded his father, Aulay MacAulay, as minister in Harris in 1752. Here, he would have been in a good position to gather information about St Kilda. In 1756, he was asked by the SSPCK to go out to report on their catechist in St Kilda, a man called Alexander Buchanan. It would in fact be two years before MacAulay achieved this.

He was finally 'loosed from Harris' (as he put it) on 6 June 1758, when his six-oared open boat immediately had to seek shelter off Hasgeir. His crew of ten amused themselves by collecting birds' eggs, a strange activity and, according to MacAulay himself, an 'unnecessary acquisition' for a vessel headed to St Kilda. Indeed, the operation smacked of the proverbial coals to Newcastle! Notwithstanding, they set off, battling through stormy seas for hours 'without either being overset or dashed to pieces' until they finally sighted Levenish and at long last entered Village Bay. MacAulay's early impressions are of considerable interest and provide a useful portrait of St Kilda half a century after Martin:

> As the wind blew with all its fury into the bay, and as the waves dashed themselves with excessive violence against the rock, just now described, it was impossible to attempt a landing ... The people of St Kilda, upon the first notice they had of our arrival on their coast, flew down from the village to our assistance, men, women and children ... After having divided and formed themselves into two lines ... [they] marched forward into the sea ... got hold of the boat ... The consequence is, the boat and everything contained in it, are with surprising quickness and dexterity hauled on beyond the reach of the sea ... our little vessel, ourselves, and all the luggage that belonged to us, to a dry part of the strand ...

Having endured the voyage, MacAulay then endeavoured to describe the scene laid out before him:

> Their arable land hardly exceed eighty acres [all within the precincts of the village while Gleann Mor had] some choice spots of ground, where one may see intermixed with the more common kinds of grass, a great and beautiful variety of the richest plants, clover, white and red; daisies, crowfoot, dandelion, and plantains of every sort ... The cattle of St Kilda ... yield, it may be naturally expected, more than ordinary quantities of milk ... the cream it gives is so luscious, or rather so strong that some of my people sickened upon drinking it.
>
> ... The people of St Kilda sow and reap very early [compared to west coast of Scotland] ... I saw the barley of this island about the beginning of June ... The harvest is commonly over in this place before the beginning of September; and should it fall out otherwise, the whole crop will be almost destroyed by the equinoctial storms ... Potatoes have been introduced among that people only of late, and hitherto they have raised but small quantities of them.
>
> Cattle [are] stalled all winter in one of the two rooms of each house near the door, the other serves for kitchen, hall and bedroom ... All the cows in the principal isle ... hardly exceed forty including the young ones ...

The few cows they have are very pretty, though quite small; they are generally red or speckled, and would be thought curiosities, I fancy, in other parts of Britain.

All the horses of St Kilda are only ten, including foals and colts, they are of a very diminutive size, but extremely well cast, full of fire and very hardy ... Their turf they bring down from the tops of the hills, which hang above the village in wicker baskets or hampers ...

The St Kildians owe a great part of their felicity to sheep and wild fowl. They have considerable flocks of sheep; it is hardly possible to ascertain the precise number of them in the main isle ...

MacAulay's report was completed by the spring of the following year, 1759, but then had to be sent to the more scholarly Reverend John Macpherson at Sleat on Skye for editing. Macpherson moaned constantly about the effects of this task on his health, but he was resolved not to 'confine himself to the text of St Kilda' so as to incorporate it into his own *Critical Dissertations on the Ancient Caledonians*.

Not surprisingly, MacAulay resented this idea and, mercifully, two years later, in 1761, managed to retrieve a copy of his manuscript to submit to the SSPCK, albeit, perhaps, retouched by Macpherson. A week later MacAulay took up a new post in Ardnamurchan and, by November 1772, was in Cawdor, near Nairn, where he would ultimately end his days, seven years later, aged 56.

It had been a 'voyage of amusement' in the Highlands and Islands by the naturalist Thomas Pennant (1726–98) that had stimulated two eminent literary gentlemen, Samuel Johnson and James Boswell, to embark on their own fact-finding tour of the Hebrides in 1772. Both Boswell's and Johnson's accounts of the journey were to be highly acclaimed. Unfortunately, neither they – nor Pennant himself – reached St Kilda.

Nonetheless, they were familiar with the Reverend Kenneth MacAulay's *History of St Kilda*, which had been published in 1764. MacAulay had invited Boswell and Johnson to his Manse at Cawdor where Johnson thanked him for his book, saying 'it was a very pretty piece of topography'. Although Boswell found their host kindly and generous, Johnson clearly thought otherwise. Indeed, Boswell began to fear the two men might quarrel. From their conversation Dr Johnson was persuaded that MacAulay was not capable of writing the book on his own. Later, on Skye, Johnson met the Reverend Dr John McPherson of Skye and became even more convinced that the *History*, although based on materials collected by MacAulay, had been largely rewritten by Macpherson. The geologist John MacCulloch went even further, suggesting that MacAulay had written about a voyage that he never undertook!

The controversy, more imagined than real, remains to this day, so MacAulay has never quite received the recognition that he most probably deserved. Literary ability may have run in the family. After all, it would be a great nephew of the good Reverend, the historian Lord MacAulay (1800–59), who would write the classic *History of England*. But, as Michael Robson observed in his book *St Kilda: Church, Visitors and 'Natives'* (2005), it is not difficult to distinguish the essential MacAulay from the rather superfluous additions by Macpherson. It was, in the end, the Reverend Dr Macpherson who was writing about a journey he never undertook and he rather gave himself away by dipping too freely into the pages of Martin Martin.

Later, back in London, Johnson and Boswell mused about the fabled island of St Kilda:

> ... Johnson then spoke of St Kilda, the most remote of the Hebrides. I told him I thought of buying it.
>
> JOHNSON: 'Pray do, Sir. We will go and pass a winter amid the blasts there.

Of course, this was all a flight of fancy.

Notwithstanding, and fully in the tradition of Martin Martin, MacAulay had given a useful account of St Kilda, of the St Kildans and of their way of life – despite the fact that he was only on St Kilda for ten days. As will unfold throughout this book, he also provided a wealth of natural history information.

At first, replacement missionaries chose only to spend short periods out on St Kilda, mindful of any firm commitment from the SSPCK and understandably reluctant to endure the privations and ultimate fate of their unfortunate predecessor, Alexander Buchan. It was not until May 1830 that Neil Mackenzie (1795–1879) from Arran was persuaded to give up a missionary position in Kintyre – and indeed an alternative job opportunity in Labrador, Canada. He would initiate a whole new approach to religious conviction amongst the islanders, and a new standard of scientific inquiry.

At dawn on the last day of June 1830, Mackenzie stepped ashore at Village Bay, with his wife and baby, her sister and mother. Not a dog barked, but the islanders soon awoke to give the new family a traditional welcome. Tragically, however, only a few days later, Mackenzie's infant son died 'of cold'. His in-laws returned home that autumn, leaving his wife (having no Gaelic) with no one to converse with – other than her husband of course.

In common with many other earlier ministers, Mackenzie was a native Gaelic-speaker, able to converse freely with the islanders, and so included much first-hand material in his account. Thus Mackenzie will figure prominently in the chapters which follow.

As his son was later to conclude:

The good work he did in the island has left a deep and lasting impression on the people, and his name is still mentioned with the greatest reverence and respect. His efforts, it will be seen, were by no means confined to ordinary ministerial work. He acted as a sort of Governor of the island, presiding at their weekly meetings for settling the work they were to engage in during the week, and arranging all kinds of petty disputes ...

Though very strictly orthodox in his religious practices and beliefs, he was by no means a fanatic or ascetic, and he encouraged the people during the long winter nights to cultivate the art of reciting their ancient stories and of singing their pathetic Gaelic songs. Of these he made a collection, which, along with most of his papers, was lost at the time when in his own absence his effects were despatched from the island to the parish on the mainland to which he had gone, with the exception of a few fragments which were printed in the *Celtic Review*.

In this good work he was greatly assisted by my mother, who taught the female population something of the art of housekeeping, of the management of their young children, of the importance of proper cooking and other sanitary matters, and of the virtues of soap and starch.

After three years labouring to his flock, Mackenzie began to sense that the island was changing him. One fine day he found himself on the summit of Conachair:

The lowing of a solitary cow, the bleating of sheep at the fold, the barking of dogs in the village below me, and the ceaseless screaming of the various tribes of sea-fowls feeding their young, seem to give life to the scene around me, and draw my attention from contemplating the vast expanse of water, and the ample dome above me, and to fix it on the little spot of earth to which I am attached.

By the time that Mackenzie had begun his pastoral duties, St Kilda was attracting a new type of visitor. They came not to collect rents or to check upon the spiritual or scholastic welfare of the islanders, but to experience St Kilda as what today we would call 'a tourist destination'. It all began perhaps with the appearance of George Clayton Atkinson and his brother in June 1831 (see Chapter 5). Then the steamer *Glenalbyn* and its 60 passengers announced their arrival on 21 July 1834 with cannon fire, much to the consternation of the islanders. In September of that same year, *The Lady of St Kilda* dropped anchor. Aboard were her owner, Sir Thomas Dyke Acland, and his wife, Lady Lydia (after whom the vessel was named).

Mackenzie recounted:

Sir Thomas and his lady, willing to confer a more lasting mark of their favour on the inhabitants of this island, or rather his benevolent mind being excited by their miserable home, left me with twenty sovereigns, to help them to build new houses, as soon as they could get their ground lotted ...

After the houses were finished we next set to work at clearing the ground, draining it, and deepening and straightening the natural water courses. When this was completed we built a ring fence round the whole of the arable land ...

Lastly we built a massive stone wall around the burial ground. It was built oval in form and was rather troublesome to keep exactly in shape owing to the great inequalities in the levels of the foundation. It was the portion of our work in which I took the greatest personal interest, as there I buried three of my children who died in infancy.

And so, with further improvements in the 1860s, the now familiar landscape of Village Bay was configured.

Some of these early tourists took a deeper interest than most in the islands and their wildlife. The Reverend Mackenzie met the naturalist John MacGillivray (see Chapter 4) in 1840 and then, the following year, the Reverend James Wilson (1795–1856) from Paisley aboard the government cutter *Princess Royal*, reporting on behalf of the SSPCK. Wilson was also a keen naturalist and enjoyed Mackenzie's company around Boreray and Stac Lee.

Happily, Mackenzie liked nothing better than showing visitors and naturalists alike round the islands of St Kilda, and he always proved a mine of information, not just on natural history but also on island traditions. Some of Mackenzie's visitors and naturalists populate the pages of this book, alongside the islanders themselves. Some have remained shadowy figures since they, like the Reverend Mackenzie himself, did not see fit to publish accounts. The fruits of their endeavours often lie buried in their own private journals, or in inaccessible scientific journals. Thus many do not feature much in the popular literature of St Kilda. Martin, MacAulay and, fortunately, even Mackenzie himself, are notable exceptions.

Mackenzie's own, highly informative account – written at various times and on all sorts of scraps of paper – was ultimately edited by his son, Reverend J. B. Mackenzie of Kenmore, and published as 'Notes on the birds of St Kilda' in the *Annals of Scottish Natural History* in 1905, and then privately printed in 1911. An invaluable and oft-quoted resource it has since proved to be.

Accompanying the Reverend James Wilson in 1841, who recounted the voyage the following year, was SSPCK secretary Sir Thomas Dick Lauder. Impressed by Mackenzie, Lauder eventually found him a charge in Duror, Argyll, so, after 12 years, the Reverend Neil Mackenzie finally quit St Kilda in 1844. Lauder commented:

My only regret in this matter is for the poor people of St Kilda, for I cannot conceive how they can do without you ... this last trip ... a tremendous gale of wind and awful sea prevented my landing, for if I had landed I don't know what I could have said to them, conscious as I felt that I had been the cause of depriving them of their much-loved Archbishop!

It is normally said that Mackenzie left St Kilda in 1843, a date which is also given in the memoir by his son. But in his scrutiny of SSPCK papers in *St Kilda: Church, Visitors and 'Natives'* (2005) Michael Robson ascertained that it was in fact 1844. Neil Mackenzie was to die in Glasgow, in his 82nd year.

Although Martin had collected tales of ancient inhabitants on St Kilda, Neil Mackenzie might well have been the first to ponder more seriously about where they might have come from:

Scattered about here and there, and very numerous, were green mounds called Gnothan sithichean, which were looked upon as the abodes of the fairies. These were all removed in the course of agricultural improvements ... In a few of them bones were found, and in nearly all of them pieces of earthen vessels ... In clearing the glebe I removed a mound in a little field, and found in it a long and narrow whetstone, an iron sword, a spear head, and various other pieces of iron, mostly of irregular shape, and the use of which was not obvious ... All the place names are derived from modern Gaelic, so that it is probable that the more ancient inhabitants were exterminated by the Norwegians when they frequented the island. From their language, traditions and surnames, the present inhabitants must have come from the long island [the Outer Hebrides] in comparatively recent times.

The Keartons were to photograph an assortment of similar archaeological finds in 1896 (see Chapter 14). The arrival of humans has of course impacted heavily upon the arrival of so many plants and animals at the same time. Although T. S. Muir, John Mathieson and others had offered crude descriptions of the antiquities, it is only with modern excavation that the prehistory of St Kilda is becoming clearer.

It is not the intention here to describe the later human story of St Kilda, since there have been many others who have already and more admirably achieved this task. Tom Steel's popular *Life and Death of St Kilda* (1965) is both readable and informative and remains in print to this day. Mary Harman's *An Isle called Hirte* (1997) contains considerable historical and original ethnographic detail. Andrew Fleming's *St Kilda and the Wider World* (2005) begins as a work of archaeology, but is a worthy and up-to-date successor to Tom Steel.

Seven or eight thousand years ago the climate of the Outer Hebrides would have been a lot more pleasant than nowadays, with plenty of woodland scrub of birch and hazel for example. The sea level was lower than today and the distances between islands not so great. While evidence of hunter-gathering peoples has been found in the Inner Hebrides, little has yet been discovered within the Outer Hebrides chain. While Mesolithic peoples could 'island hop' relatively short distances, this might suggest that they were reluctant to cross larger bodies of open sea. Thus they are unlikely ever to have reached St Kilda.

Five thousand years ago, however, the first farming communities were well established, even in the Outer Hebrides, and the archaeologist Andrew Fleming found evidence of their presence on St Kilda:

> Our discoveries suggest that this island was occupied by an energetic, viable community in later prehistory, cultivating an extensive area of land at Village Bay ... Gleann Mor was evidently occupied too. The pre-Iron Age occupation of these islands is surely not now in doubt; the number, variety and quality of the stone tools left behind bear witness to that.

There are a host of structures all over St Kilda such as the Amazon's House in Gleann Mor, and Tigh Stellar on Boreray that, although first described by Martin, have yet to be adequately investigated or dated. The ruinous fort on Dun could well date from Iron Age times. As the Reverend Mackenzie had appreciated, the Norsemen also reached St Kilda. There is a mention in the Icelandic sagas of a cleric taking shelter in 1202 'on the islands that are called Hirtir, after being blown off course in a storm'. As we shall discuss, it may well have been the Vikings who brought the field mice with them to St Kilda.

So it seems that St Kilda – or at least Hirta as the most hospitable of the archipelago – has been occupied continuously for some 5,000 years. Like any island community of plants and animals, the human occupants may have suffered bottlenecks in numbers, such as during the smallpox epidemic of 1727, or they may have even experienced periods of extinction in the more distant past. Suffice it to say that the human presence has been a long one. But in the 50 million years of St Kilda's existence, its plants and animals as we know them today, along with human inhabitants, are very recent arrivals indeed.

.2.
Geology

Surtur fares from the south
With the scourge of branches,
The sun turns black,
Earth sinks into the sea.
The hot stars down from Heaven are whirled.
Fierce grows the steam and the life-feeding flame.
Till fire leaps high about Heaven itself.

'Voluspa', 10th-century Icelandic poem

JUST BEFORE DAWN on 14 November 1963, a boat was fishing 20 km south of the Westmann Islands in southern Iceland. Suddenly the sea began to heave and to boil. The startled fisherman was about to witness the first stirring of a volcanic eruption. A rift had opened up 130 m below on the seabed. From a submerged cone of black tephra or volcanic ash, explosions of hot lava and steam thrust skywards. By the next day the cone was protruding above the surface and a new island was born; it came to be known as Surtsey after the mythical Norse god of fire.

Soon a column of ash and steam reached 9,000 m into the atmosphere and could be seen as far away as Reykjavik, Iceland's capital. Activity slowly diminished until, in early February 1964, a second, larger eruption began.

Once Surtsey's vent was raised clear of the sea, the eruptions became less explosive; and a hard glassy lava could exude over the crumbling slag to protect it from wave erosion. By the end of May the island was nearly 3 km² in extent, with a lava crater 90 m above sea level.

It would be another three years before the eruption ceased altogether, having produced about a cubic kilometre of ash and lava, although less than 10 per cent of it protruded above sea level.

St Kilda probably arose under somewhat similar circumstances, but around 55 million years ago when, of course, there would have been no people around to witness the event – only dinosaurs perhaps! It was just at this time – known as the Tertiary Period – that the Atlantic began to split apart, separating the ancient rocks of Greenland from their slightly younger counterparts in the Hebrides. The youngest of Britain's rocks were created amongst the oldest – amongst Lewisian gneiss some three billion (3,000 million) years old. This sparked a turbulent period of volcanic activity centred around Antrim in Northern Ireland, Arran, Mull and Staffa, Ardnamurchan, Skye, the Small Isles of Rum, Eigg, Muck and Canna, the Shiant Isles, Rockall and – St Kilda.

The Hebrides probably saw the most violent episodes, as the northern part of the ancient continent of Pangea was rent apart. Volcanic events still occur along the length of the mid-Atlantic ridge, deep under the sea. So the ocean continues to widen to this day, albeit imperceptibly to the human eye – at a rate equivalent to the growth of a human fingernail. Sitting astride this central rift, Iceland is one of the most active volcanic zones in the world. Nowadays, just south of Reykjavik, tourists can stride across a short bridge which spans the actual contact between the continental plate of Europe and that of America.

In 1689, when Martin Martin landed on Boreray, he was told of an earthquake felt by the St Kildans three years earlier, which lasted but a few minutes:

> It was very amazing to the poor people, who never felt any such commotion before or since.

Volcanic eruptions still occur along the mid-Atlantic Ridge, however, including one in Iceland in 1946, one in the Azores in 1957, another on Tristan da Cunha in 1961, Surtsey in 1963, Jan Mayen in 1970, Hecla in Iceland again the same year, and in the Westmann Islands near Surtsey in 1973.

On St Kilda, erosion has long since removed the ash deposits and lava flows produced by those Tertiary volcanic events millions of years ago, so that only the hard, resistant rocks remain – gabbros, granites and breccias – from deep within the very hearth of the volcano. Mere fragments now make up the archipelago of St Kilda, which cannot boast the spectacular lava columns of the Giant's Causeway or Staffa. However, recent bathymetric surveys offshore have revealed the remnants of the original collapsed crater or caldera on the seabed, indicating how the scattered, craggy islands of Hirta, Dun, Soay and Boreray link up along its perimeter (Plate 2). The whole structure has collapsed inwards – in a process known as 'cauldron subsidence' – leaving a circular platform 60 m below the present sea surface. Beyond the outer edge of the caldera the seabed is some 140 m deep.

The mineralogist Edward Daniel Clarke (1769–1822) visited St Kilda in July and August 1797 (see Chapter 14), but it was the Guernsey-born geologist, John MacCulloch (1773–1835), who, in 1815, made an initial assessment of St Kilda's geology – the first visitor for a whole year. Indeed, he was probably the very first scientist to reach the islands. He was met ashore by the minister's wife, and a host of islanders eagerly pulled his boat up the beach. MacCulloch discovered that if the islanders' 'curiosity was great, their civility and good humour were still greater', but added 'I know of no place where people can have such a plentiful supply of food with so little exertion'. Being a violinist, he was interested in their music and devoted several pages to it in his verbose accounts; but he was disappointed to find neither fiddle nor Jew's harp. Professionally, too, he found little to inspire him on his visit:

> The geological history of St Kilda may be contained within a very narrow space, yet it is not without interest.

MacCulloch recognised the volcanic nature of the rocks and their similarity to other Tertiary areas in Scotland, such as Skye and Rum. He sketched a line of contact between 'syenite', now known as granophyre, against the dark 'trap' rocks, i.e. the more basic gabbros and dolerites poor in the mineral silica.

He was not far off the mark when he added:

> He that has no other means of clambering up to the temple of fame, may come to St Kilda: he will assuredly be remembered in its archives; and some future Martin or Macaulay shall record him in calf well bound, as I myself trust to be recorded.

And so crusty old MacCulloch has indeed come to be remembered in the annals of St Kilda, and of the Hebrides in general. He wrote several useful volumes describing the geology, landscape and people of the western islands of Scotland. He found a fossil tree on the Isle of Mull which is named after him (although nowadays only the impression of its giant trunk in the lava rock remains). When Professor Archibald Geikie was roaming the Highlands half a century later, he met several old people who recalled MacCulloch – not as a geologist however. Wherever he had stayed, even on remote St Kilda, MacCulloch had unashamedly enjoyed nothing but the finest hospitality, but in his books he was quite outspoken and less than flattering about his hosts and their humble dwellings. Thus, not surprisingly, they remembered him for his haughty, mocking attitude. One Skye landowner went as far as to commission a set of porcelain chamber-pots depicting MacCulloch's portrait!

The geologist's name yet looms large in the annals of the earth sciences, however. He was to go on to produce the first geological map of Scotland, his life's work, which was published posthumously in 1836, MacCulloch having died the previous year, aged 62, while on his honeymoon, by being dragged along in the wheel of his carriage. It would be many years before a geologist of his calibre again took interest in St Kilda.

In June 1884, Alexander Ross (1834–1925) paid a visit to St Kilda. Born in Brechin, Alexander moved when he was eight years old, to Inverness where his father James was to be an architect. He took over the family firm when his father died in 1854 and came to be considered by many as the 'Christopher Wren of the North'. He was responsible for designing many churches, schools and schoolhouses throughout the Highlands and Islands, but notably for Inverness Cathedral, Duncraig Castle and Skibo Castle. He served as Provost of Inverness from 1889 to 1895. As an architect, historian, naturalist and writer, Ross was awarded an honorary doctorate from the University of Aberdeen.

In 1875, Ross had helped found the Inverness Scientific Society and Field Club. Nine years later he was able to deliver to the Field Club an excellent account of St Kilda and its geology which was published in their *Transactions* later that year. He illustrated his lecture with glass slides taken on the trip by Mr D. Whyte, an Inverness photographer. (There seems to be confusion here with a G. G. Whyte, a photographer who also visited St Kilda and whose initials, David Quine has suggested, may well be being confused with those of yet another, more celebrated photographer of the day, George Washington Wilson.)

Immediately upon their arrival at St Kilda, Ross's party picked up an islander as pilot and took advantage of fine weather to sail around the island:

> On rounding the south point we had a slight roll ... Mr Whyte began to experience the mal-de-mer and seemed attracted by the scenery at which he gazed with a somewhat vacant expression rather than at his apparatus.

Undeterred, the photographer cleverly rigged the camera on his tripod, by a system of ball-joint and weights, in order to overcome the motion of the steam yacht.

Although Ross concluded that 'the geological history of the island is by no means complicated', he recognised that the volcanic rocks had crystallised at considerable depth below the earth's surface. He criticised MacCulloch for misreading the evidence and concluding that trap rocks and syenite 'belonged to a common deposit' of comparable age. Instead, Ross astutely recognised that the granophyre was younger than the gabbros and dolerites and he spotted the interesting contact between gabbro and breccia in Glen Bay (see below). To wrap up his talk in Inverness that winter, Ross exhibited the rock samples that he had collected. Throughout the evening he ably held his own in front of the Club President, no less than John Horne from the Geological Survey. Professor John Wesley Judd of the Royal School of Mines at Imperial College,

London and President of the Geological Society later used Ross's samples to publish a short paper on the geology of St Kilda – even though the professor himself had never been there!

A few years later, an Orcadian, Professor Matthew Forster Heddle (1828–97) of St Andrews University, paid a brief visit to St Kilda with gentleman/naturalist John A. Harvie-Brown aboard the steamer *Dunara Castle*. Heddle began life as a botanist but went on to study medicine, then chemistry. It was when a friend accidentally dropped Heddle's vasculum into a stream that he turned from botany to geology. Indeed, he has been described as 'one of the most dedicated, ruthless and successful mineral collectors who ever lived'.

He was a man of great stamina, often wielding a 28-lb geological hammer, and not averse to using dynamite to acquire specimens. Fortunately, he did not resort to this in St Kilda! In 1889, Heddle included a short account of St Kilda's geology in Harvie-Brown and Macpherson's classic volume *A Vertebrate Fauna of the Outer Hebrides*:

> The St Kilda group much resembles the partially submerged circlet of cliff-faced eminences which cincture a volcanic crater; broken away, however, at one side in great part, as is ever the case with presently existing volcanoes.

Here he was unwittingly anticipating modern bathymetric studies. Heddle recognised only two varieties of rock: one rich in feldspar and weathering into rounded hills of a pale colour similar to the syenite of Skye, Mull and Rum; and a second type – hard, rough-surfaced and dark in colour – which he called augite. Also referred to as trap rocks, these are the gabbros and dolerites that have produced the serrated peaks of the Skye and Rum Cuillins. By now Professor of Chemistry at St Andrews University, Heddle related the nature of these rocks to their differing mineral content and noted dark basalt dykes intruding into the paler syenite. However, none of this added much to Ross's account. Heddle went on to write *Mineralogy of Scotland*, published posthumously in 1901.

Professor Sir Archibald Geikie (1835–1924) was born in Edinburgh, the son of a local businessman and composer. He set out on a career in banking but abandoned it for a university degree, encouraged by none other than the celebrated geologist Hugh Miller. He joined the Geological Survey as a mapping assistant in 1855 and, just over a decade later, was appointed its Scottish Director. After six years, however, he took the first Murchison Chair of Geology and Mineralogy at the University of Edinburgh and in 1873 founded its museum for the teaching of geology. Author of a classic text on the scenery of Scotland, he was also an acknowledged expert on glaciation and volcanic geology. There is an igneous seamount lying on the ocean floor between Scotland and Faroe which came to bear his name, and even a feature on the surface of the moon, *Dorsa Geikie*, has been named in his honour. In 1881, Archibald became Director General of the Geological Survey for the whole of the United Kingdom, while his younger brother succeeded to his Chair at Edinburgh University.

Knighted a few years before, Sir Archibald visited St Kilda several times in 1895 and 1896 in a boat called the *Aster* from Loch Roag in Lewis:

> On one of our visits we were fortunate in finding the weather calm and sunny, so that it was possible to pull in an open boat round the base of the cliffs. And such cliffs and crests! It is as if a part of the mountain group of Skye had been set down in mid-ocean ... But it is the bird life which most fascinates a visitor. In the nesting season, the air is alive with wings and with all the varied cries of northern sea-fowl ... We could watch the sure-footed natives making their way along ledges which, seen from below, seemed impracticable even to goats ... In passing between the main island and Boreray, we sailed under a vast circle of those majestic birds, the gannets, wheeling and diving into the sea all around us ... While watching this magnificent meteor-like bird-play, we were surprised by the appearance of three whales, parents and son, which slowly made their way underneath the swarm of gannets.

His St Kilda field notes in Edinburgh University and his published papers describe a series of gabbros, dolerites and basalts which dip north-eastwards on Hirta and Soay, but from the opposite direction in Boreray, which suggested to him that the vent of the volcano lay in between. All this was then invaded at a later date by a mass of granophyre. Even younger still are abundant dykes and veins of basalt which intrude through both these basic and acid masses. Although Geikie wrote a popular book called *Scottish Reminiscences* in 1904 (quoted above), the style of his geological textbooks was very much that of the day, and not necessarily easy reading nowadays, for example:

> The testimony of the rocks of St Kilda to the posteriority of the granophyre to the gabbros and basalts is thus clear and emphatic. It entirely confirms my previous observations regarding the order of sequence of these rocks in Mull, Rum and Skye. But the St Kilda sections display, even more strikingly than can be usually seen in these islands, the intricate network of veins which proceed from the granophyre, the shattered condition of the basic rocks which these veins penetrate, the remarkable liquidity of the acid magma at the time of its intrusion, and the solvent action of this magma on the basic fragments which it enveloped.

There are 65 words in that last sentence!

No one matched his treatise on St Kilda's geology until in 1927 Alexander Cockburn took a fresh look. It would be Cockburn who in 1932 catalogued

Geikie's original geological collection in Edinburgh University, and with more recent additions, formed what is now called the Cockburn Geological Museum.

This new interest in St Kilda was initiated by John Mathieson (d. 1945), also of Edinburgh University. Mathieson, born in Durness, Sutherland, was an adventuring surveyor who in 1909 had accompanied the eminent Scottish polar explorer W. S. Bruce to map part of Spitzbergen. Mathieson was to return there on three more expeditions 1919–21. On his retiral from the Ordnance Survey he at last found time to fulfil his greatest ambition, to survey the St Kilda group, the only corner of the British Isles yet to be officially mapped. It was Mathieson who was to suggest to the film producer Michael Powell that his epic *On the Edge of the World* (1937) could equally be staged on Foula, after the Marquis of Bute refused permission for it to be made on St Kilda (see Chapter 15).

Extracts from Mathieson's diary appear in David Quine's *St Kilda Portraits* (1988):

> We are going to make the first topographical survey of the island on a scale of 6 inches to the mile, giving place names, antiquities and topographical features. It is intended to make a contour map of 100 ft so that physical features will be clearly traced ... The geological survey is being done by Mr Cockburn, and we hope that a botanist will join us later, so that the geological, topographical and botanical survey will be complete.

Mathieson (who was accompanied some of the time by his wife) left Fleetwood on 19 April 1927. He would work alongside the young geology research student Alexander M. Cockburn (1902–59). The fishery steamer *Robert Murray* also carried a month's accumulation of mail for St Kilda. In November 1951 in a radio broadcast, Cockburn recalled the experience:

> The survey of St Kilda was a difficult, physically trying, and sometimes a dangerous job. But my old friend, John Mathieson, was never one to be daunted by anything that came between him and his chosen tasks. In 1926, he invited me to accompany him on a topographical survey of St Kilda, when he was laying his plans for an assault on what I think was then the only unsurveyed island of any size in Britain. He had been for many years an officer of the Ordnance Survey in Scotland and had more than passed the allotted span when he set out to accomplish one of the surveys he had planned for years. His energy and enthusiasm often put to shame the efforts of younger men.

Just before leaving to complete the team on 15 June, the botanist, 19-year-old history student John Gladstone, received a less than encouraging communication from Mathieson:

Today we are experiencing the worst storm we have had since we came here and if the steamer comes it will be impossible to land either stores or passengers ... I am making good progress with the survey of the islands.

When Gladstone did finally arrive in St Kilda, Mathieson and Cockburn were bivouacked in the bothy on Boreray, where he finally met them a few days later. With the islanders Finlay MacQueen and Ewen Macdonald, they were sleeping in one of the old stone bothies.

On Hirta, Mathieson had based himself upstairs in the Factor's House until he eventually quit the island in mid-September aboard a whale catcher from Harris. His departure had been delayed by some of the worst gales in living memory. Cockburn remained for several more weeks.

The 25-year-old Cockburn lived in a tent behind the Factor's House for five wet and windy months of 1927, returning for a further two months the next summer. His field work and thesis gained him a PhD from Edinburgh University in 1929. His major paper on *The Geology of St Kilda* was published in 1935 in which he apologised for the incompleteness of his observations. He pointed out, for the benefit and welfare of future workers, the necessity of using a rope:

> Great caution must be exercised, particularly after rain, on the grassy slopes facing seawards. These slopes are generally very steep, inclinations up to 40° and over being common.

Cockburn found a friend and willing helper in Ewen Macdonald, whose native skills as a cragsman greatly facilitated field work. (In later years Cockburn was to name his son Ewen as a tribute to his friend.) Cockburn noted how the islanders were always very cautious and, although they reached some dangerous situations, they were never reckless. They always ensured they had a rope, with another man at the end of it. In 1927, Cockburn and Mathieson visited Soay with the islanders, when an ornithologist, Seton Gordon, was able to accompany them. In the BBC broadcast of November 1951, Cockburn recalled another memorable visit with the islanders, to Stac an Armin:

> I think the day I can never forget was the day in August 1928 when Finlay MacQueen, Donald Gillies, and Ewen Macdonald took me to the top of Stac an Armin. I can still remember the long arguments we had before we set out. It was a slightly misty day, dead calm, and the sea like black oil. But Finlay argued it was safe, he bossed and off we went rowing the five miles to Stac an Armin in our little lifeboat in about two hours. The landing place was on the north side of the stack, beyond a blow-hole called Am Biran ... I refused the first suggestion to land. Finlay kindly and encouragingly jeered at me: 'Och, you are no good' and led the landing in the usual St Kildan fashion, with a rope round

his waist, in bare feet, jumping on to a tiny step of rock a foot or two above the wet, wave-mark, jumping from the bows of our boat when right on top of a four or five foot swell. Ewen followed, and the jeering began again, and for very shame I jumped ashore too, and was lugged over several feet of dry but smooth rock. A nasty little piece of crack-walking, performed by me in a state of prayerful panic, took us round a rock-corner and life became suddenly all interesting again. There was nothing now but a scramble of 600 feet to the summit of the great stack, in a series of steps, like what I think climbing the pyramids must be. One of the most amazing things we encountered were half a dozen sheep grazing quietly on small patches of rich grass growing at different levels. We walked through the gannetry to the top of the stack . . . It felt all of its 627 feet. Stac Lee a mile to the south-west and a hundred feet lower was a marvellous sight.

Cockburn collected rock samples. On the way home, however, they had to forego landing on Stac Lee, something he always regretted.
Cockburn continued:

The islands represent, perhaps, the peripheral remnants of a much more extensive complex of igneous rocks having an original diameter of some 6 or 7 miles and a centre situated between Boreray and [Hirta] . . . The intrusion of three granophyres has been accompanied by widespread crushing, brecciation, and granulitisation of the walls of the acid masses and by close net-veining and consequent acidification of the older, finer-grained basic rocks.

Although the rounded nature of the inland hills indicated ice action, Cockburn failed to find any definite features that could inform the glaciation story. In addition, back in the Geology Department, he carried out extensive chemical and thin-section analyses of the rock-types.

Alexander Cockburn had shown a great interest in everything about St Kilda, taking many photographs that remain classics to this day. Another Alexander, the son of the missionary John Macleod, remembered as a schoolboy how:

My clearest and fondest memory of Sunday school is of the period when it was conducted by the geologist Alick Cockburn – in English of course, as Mr Cockburn had no Gaelic. He was a delightful young man, very devout, and we worshipped him. He was equally popular with the adults, a remarkable young man . . .

On his return home in October 1927, Cockburn conveyed a message to the *Sunday Post*:

One thing the St Kildans were anxious that I should tell people on the mainland when I got home was that a very bad storm, following the wet summer, had completely ruined their potato crop . . . The storm . . . was tremendous. I saw spray six hundred feet high coming over the island – a sight one could never forget.

Cockburn served as Senior Lecturer in Geology at Edinburgh University from 1951 until he died in February 1959. In an obituary for the *Scotsman* his Professor, Sir Arthur Holmes, wrote:

> All who knew him will remember with gratitude and affection the help and advice he gave so readily, and his unfailing kindness, wisdom and good humour. As a lecturer he was unusually inspiring ... Thoughtless of self-advancement and never seeking geological fame, yet his beneficent influence has already spread far and wide across the world, wherever geologists trained in Edinburgh are to be found.

Cockburn's work was not to be bettered until the British Geological Survey visited in 1978 and 1979. This new survey involved mapping, extensive rock sampling and magnetic analysis. On my own first visit to Hirta in 1979 I recall watching two field geologists removing pairs of cylindrical samples with a heavy rock drill, the empty twin cavities remaining to puzzle observant visitors to this day. Their efforts culminated in a meticulous geological report with accompanying colour map (1984). Subsequently, there have been shorter field surveys in 1998 and 1999 by W. Robson and Fiona MacTaggart for Scottish Natural Heritage, and their reports (2001) make easy reading. This work also contributed to the account by John Gordon, George Lees and Colin MacFadyen (all from Scottish Natural Heritage) in the World Heritage submission (2003). It is from these sources that the following brief description is constructed.

As the early geologists had surmised, the oldest rocks exposed on St Kilda today are the western gabbros of the Cambir on Hirta, and on Dun – coarse, granular and rich in iron to give them their particular durability. Molten basalt and dolerite lava then intruded through any lines of weakness, cooling quickly into a fine-grained complex of dykes that are evident on the cliff faces as black streaks. The islands of Soay, Boreray, Levenish and parts of the main island of Hirta (e.g. around Glen Bay) are, in fact, made up of a crushed and reconstituted mix of the western gabbros and dolerites, known as breccias.

The next phase of geological activity – a few million years later perhaps – injected into the dark gabbro a different magma called granophyre or granite. Cooling more slowly, these rocks are medium- to fine-grained and, rich in silica, assume distinctive cream, grey or pink colours, with occasional larger pink or white crystals of feldspar and quartz. One pale slab forms a conspicuous feature against the dark gabbro shores of Glen Bay in Hirta. It exhibits a characteristic glassy consistency along its eastern margin where it makes contact with the darker breccias, indicating very rapid cooling. This can be up to 45 m in places; no other such feature in the Tertiary rocks of Scotland is as wide.

The centre of Hirta consists of breccias formed from fragments of earlier gabbros trapped within molten magma and is known as 'the Mullach Sgar Complex'. In places, dark melts low in silica have intruded into pale silica-rich patterns – a relatively rare occurrence in Tertiary rocks – to form dramatic and distinctive light and dark patterns. At least four major phases of igneous activity occurred in quick succession, leaving the St Kilda Complex one of the best such examples in Scotland.

The granite of Conachair represents the final major igneous event on St Kilda, about 55 million years ago, and makes up much of the north-east part of Hirta, including Oiseval and Conachair itself. These granophyre rocks are less resistant to erosion than the gabbros so the hills are smooth and rounded in appearance, contrasting with the ragged north and west coast. All volcanic activity came to an end about 35 million years ago, with the intrusion of a new and extensive suite of dykes and sills of black, fine-grained basalt and dolerite, especially visible in the high sea cliffs north of Conachair, and sketched by Geikie in 1897.

Hirta is by far the most varied and complex island in the archipelago. Soay, Boreray and Levenish consist largely of breccias, a crushed and consolidated mix of gabbros and dolerite. Nonetheless, they are no less awe-inspiring in aspect.

Back on Surtsey the birth of Iceland's newest island is re-enacting a battle between earth and ocean, as described in the ancient sagas:

> the sea will lash against the land
> because the Midgard Serpent is writhing in giant fury
> trying to come ashore.

'Voluspa', 10th-century Icelandic poem

From the outset of the Surtsey eruption, the soft ash and tuff of the embryonic island was subject to erosion by the sea around it. Wave action undercut the south-west coast by about 30 m annually to produce soft temporary cliffs 5–12 m high, while a boulder spit and black sandy beaches formed on the sheltered northern side. The rate of accretion has slowed, but Surtsey's 270 ha have now been reduced to 130 ha. Eventually, hundreds of years from now, its hard inner core will be exposed as little more than a group of steep isolated stacs. Two other islands nearby, formed by the early eruptions, have already disappeared under the sea.

Millions of years earlier, St Kilda had offered a bigger and more resilient target against the might of the ocean. Even today variations in hardness and structure of its different rock types are being differentially exploited by severe Atlantic storms to sculpt 35 km of exceptionally varied, convoluted and dramatic coastline. Geomorphologists refer to it as 'a high-energy environment'. As a result, the archipelago boasts a superb array of geos, sea caves, arches, tunnels, blowholes and stacs – above and below the waves.

Describing Conachair, Sir Archibald Geikie had written:

> Nowhere among the Inner Hebrides, not even on the south-western side of Rum, is there any such display of the capacity of the youngest granite to assume the most rugged and picturesque forms. It is hardly possible to exaggerate the variety of outline assumed by the rock. To one who boats underneath these cliffs, the scene of ceaseless destruction which they represent is vividly impressive. Boreray and Soay are no less impressive with their cliff-girt green turf pasture, and Dun has a highly crenellated profile.

The sheer wall of Conachair forms the highest sea cliff in the British Isles. Its actual height long proved elusive. Martin Martin was not far off the mark when he judged 200 fathoms, but, somehow, the Reverend Kenneth MacAulay resolved 'to take the height with some degree of exactness, and found it to be no less than 900 fathoms' (5,400 feet)! He then added:

> Had I never seen the immense mass, I should very probably dispute the credibility of the account now given, just as much as any one else may do after perusing this account.

John MacCulloch's mountain barometer gave 1,380 feet, 'a dizzy height to the spectator who looks down upon the almost inaudible waves dashing below'.

MacCulloch was first to judge it against the equally impressive precipice on the Isle of Foula in Shetland. Although almost exactly the same height above the sea, the Kame of Foula is interrupted some way down by a wide grassy ledge so perhaps cannot be considered totally 'sheer'.

Back on St Kilda in 1860, a naval surveyor Captain Henry Otter made Conachair's summit 1,262 ft. Three decades later, with his aneroid, Professor Heddle came up with 1,462 ft, the actual clifftop being 93 ft lower. Nowadays Conachair is judged to be 1,407 ft/430 m high (though Mathieson's 1928 map still opts for 1,396 ft (he actually measured 1,396.8 ft so other maps sometimes round it up to 1,397 ft). The actual cliff face is usually claimed to be 1,297 ft, 100 ft or so lower than Conachair itself (but some writers still persist in claiming it to be the full height of the summit).

Being over a quarter of a mile high, it is hard to gain a perspective on Conachair's astonishing vista. Looking down, Julian Huxley, one of James Fisher's 1939 expedition and the first Director General of UNESCO, noted:

... the entire slope is dotted with white specks. The impression is of strange cliff flowers; but they are in reality fulmars.

In actual fact, from the sea, both Soay and Boreray look even more dramatic than Hirta, being almost as high (1,239 ft/378 m and 1,259 ft/384 m respectively) but much smaller in area (only 237 acres/99 ha and 217 acres/77 ha, set against the 1,567 acres/639 ha of Hirta).

At 644 ft (196 m) – again the actual height quoted may vary – Stac an Armin, off the northern tip of Boreray, is the highest sea stack in Britain. Its distinctive triangular shape derives from a fault line cutting across its east face. It was described by Sir Julian Huxley (1939), as 'the most majestic sea rock in existence'. The sharp-crowned tooth of Stac Lee looks more awe-inspiring, however, towering vertically 564 ft (172 m). It looks unclimbable, yet the St Kildans regularly harvested gannets from it and Martin first described the bothy they had built halfway up. Norman Heathcote in fact may have been the first outsider to achieve the climb in July 1898.

Heathcote judged the landing at Stac Lee was more difficult than the ascent. He even went back a second time with his sister Evelyn, still the only woman ever to have reached the summit of Stac Lee – and whilst wearing a long tweed skirt! The party went on to land on Boreray, but then had to seek shelter in a cave where they stayed overnight in the boat. Once inside, the islanders had a Gaelic service and next morning rowed home for all their worth, with Evelyn

Fig. 3. Evelyn Heathcote climbing (N. Heathcote).

at the tiller. According to his St Kildan companions, Heathcote was the first outsider to land on and climb Levenish.

Lines of weakness in rocks, such as fault lines, are quickly exploited by the sea, often firstly creating a natural arch and ultimately collapsing to leave an isolated stack or island. Dun has one remaining natural arch; a second has long since collapsed to leave it isolated from Hirta by what is known as *Caolas an Dùin* – the Dun Narrows. MacAulay described Dun merely cut off from Hirta at high water, whilst, a century later, Heathcote noted that it could only be reached by jumping from stone to stone at low spring tides. Nowadays even this is hardly possible and certainly not to be recommended.

Lazy beds or cultivation rigs are visible on Dun's nearer slopes which leads us to wonder whether it only became an island after people came to inhabit and cultivate Hirta. Certainly one edge of this field system is truncated by erosion, but this could have been a fairly recent development. However, we know mice are to be found on Dun. Did they, at some time, walk over a land bridge from Hirta? We will see in Chapter 11 that the St Kildans took pains

Fig. 4. A St Kildan boat sailing through a natural arch (N. Heathcote).

to avoid taking mice to Boreray, so we might surmise they might have felt the same about Dun. So perhaps the mice had got there under their own steam. We do not know when the St Kildans finally abandoned cultivation on Dun, but certainly tending crops there would have become difficult in recent times without a boat.

Much further back in the past, Soay would similarly have been attached to Hirta at the Cambir. Successive stages in coastal erosion would have created tunnels and natural arches which have long since collapsed into the sea. Only the isolated rock pillars of Soay Stac (61 m, 200 ft), Stac Biorach (73 m, 240 ft) and Stac Dona (27 m, 87 ft) remain within the Sound of Soay. At some stage in the future the narrow neck of the Cambir itself will be totally undercut to create a new small island or stac, separate from Hirta.

Such processes have occurred in recent centuries, albeit on a lesser scale. It seems from Martin Martin's map that Mina Stack was joined to Hirta by a natural arch. Now it is an island some 50 m offshore. Alastair Alpin Macgregor (1931) had a story (presumably gleaned from the islanders) that some four centuries earlier, one of the ships of the Spanish Armada was driven ashore there in a storm. The tip of her mast struck the arch which immediately collapsed on the unfortunate vessel below.

While it could well be true, few other authors recorded this remarkable tale, so perhaps the journalist in Macgregor was indulging in a touch of melodrama, or it may be that the St Kildans were just pulling his leg! So far divers have failed to find any evidence of a wreck below Mina Stack, but the area has long been well scoured by the Atlantic swell. On the other hand, divers did find a cannon in Geo Cambir on 12 July 1977. It was lying within a narrow gully in 15 m of water, apparently sticking out from rocks that the divers thought might have fallen on top of it. There was also a lot of iron ballast, some anchor chain and some wooden wreckage. The cannon, about a metre in length, was recovered illicitly the following year and disappeared for a time.

So it is also possible that the islanders had confused the incident at Mina Stack with the demise of a later galleon in Geo Cambir.

As a footnote, however, Stuart Murray, ornithologist and former warden, recalled that the cannon was cast iron rather than the bronze one that the Armada would have carried. In August 2003, another team of divers on the *Poplar Diver* raised a second cannon from Soay. Since access to this dive site is a rare event due to the swell, it was decided to raise the cannon using air bags. A metre long and 15 cm wide at the butt, the cannon was despatched for conservation to the Western Isles Museum in Benbecula, where it still remains.

Rock falls still occur with some degree of regularity. In 1928, the geologist Alexander Cockburn was disturbed to find that a huge slab of clifftop, many

Fig. 5. Stac Biorach (Scottish Natural Heritage).

thousands of tons in weight, over which he had scrambled the year before, was now lying on a beach called Mol Ghiasgar between Conachair and Oiseval. In 1987, Pete Moore the island warden was on Boreray when panic-stricken gannets took off from near the summit of Stac Lee. A few seconds later he heard the sound of a rock fall hitting the water below. Stuart Murray witnessed a rock tumble at Sunadal on Boreray on 10 July 1998:

> Laughton Johnston and I were landed at Sunadal by *Harmony* and spent all day ashore ... I had just finished the [sheep] count when I saw a large chunk of rock split away from the top of the face, just a few yards to my left. It hit a wide terrace dense with gannet nests, killing one adult, before spinning out into Sunadal. The route to the landing we were using passed close under the length of this cliff, and deep gouges showed in the soft ground where the rock had landed, still with enough momentum to carry it into the sea just yards from our intended departure point ...

No wonder St Kilda is still considered 'a high-energy environment.' The greatest rock fall to have occurred in recent times took place in 2002 on Soay, immediately below the bothy; unfortunately, it was not witnessed. It completely filled Mol Shoay with rubble, and has made the bothy itself more vulnerable to further slippage (Stuart Murray and Sarah Money, personal comment). The roof inside the tunnel cave in Glen Bay collapsed some time in 2005 making it dangerous to enter now.

Waves driven by wind against rock types of varying hardness and lines of weakness are the principal forces sculpting St Kilda's dramatic coastline. The current tidal range is 2.9 m at springs but wave heights of up to 2 m occur for 75 per cent of the year, over 5 m for 10 per cent. Over a period of 50 years the predicted wave height (i.e. the average height of the highest one-third of the waves) in the Outer Hebrides has been estimated at 35 m, significantly higher than the rest of the United Kingdom. Forty-five miles further west, St Kilda will undoubtedly endure even higher surges. Its coastline is prone to attack from any direction, but most storms will be driven by the prevailing south/south-westerly winds. St Kilda is probably the windiest place in Britain, gales occurring on some 75 days a year, with hurricane force not uncommon.

Henry Evans, tenant of Jura deer forest, sportsman and naturalist, had visited St Kilda at least nine times towards the end of the 19th century in his yacht *Erne*. Thus, as Harvie-Brown and Buckley (1888) maintained, he was in a privileged position to explore every cliff, cave and geo along St Kilda's formidable coastline. Who better to describe for us the sheer spectacle of the place?

There are several sea caves in the cliffs of St Kilda [Hirta], and perhaps two or three in Boreray. Some of these contain perpetually rolling boulders, whilst others are clear of them. The caves with boulders have usually the characteristic rounded edges to their rock fractures, the others are sharp-edged and unabraided. The sound, even in the calmest days, of the everlasting thunder in these caves is magnificent, and no doubt the perpetual motion of the boulders is wearing and boring the caves deeper.

There are also several curious little blow-holes in St Kilda and Boreray, the steam issuing from which might be fancifully compared to the breath of the mythical St Kilda giants. None of these caves are very extensive, but some are very beautiful, partly owing to the clearness and colour of the water.

There are only two easy landing places in St Kilda. The village has one, and the other is in the west bay, where a large corrie slopes gradually down to the water. Here is the ledge of rock named after the Garefowl ...

The cliff scenery, if you row round the islands, is grand; many detached rocks have fallen into the sea, and the stack-rocks are magnificent. Stack Lii, Boreray must be 400 feet high [sic] and affords nesting-room for thousands of Gannets, and Stack-an-Armine is scarcely inferior [sic]: a vast number of Gannets nest on the cliffs of Boreray itself ... Boreray has far the grandest scenery of the three chief islands. I have been round the islands and stack-rocks of St Kilda, and Boreray at my leisure, and into every cave in a rowing boat. There is no easy landing-place on any of the islands besides those I have mentioned. Even in the finest weather there is a surge, but by choosing one's time when the sea is settled one can go anywhere in a row-boat. In the narrow passage between St Kilda and Soay is a handsome stack-rock, called the Stack of Difficulty [Stac Dona], and also some extremely picturesque rocks which form a beautiful natural archway, through which one may pass in a boat amid the croaks and cries of the Guillemots. The Rock of Levenish, about a mile from the entrance of the bay of the landing-place, does not compare in beauty with the chief stack-rocks of the islands, and few, if any, birds nest on it.

While wind and wave shape its coast, the landforms and landscape of St Kilda – as Cockburn had surmised but failed to confirm – owed a great deal to the effects of the last Ice Age. Hard rocks such as the gabbros are more resistant to erosion than the softer granophyre. Thus the west side of Hirta and Dun exhibit an irregular, jagged outline, much like the Black Cuillin of Skye. The granites of Conachair and Oiseval in contrast present a smoother, more rounded appearance, like Skye's Red Cuillin.

Over the last two and a half million years our climate has fluctuated from being somewhat warmer than today to intense cold, resulting in vast polar ice sheets periodically extending southwards across Europe, North America and Siberia. At the last glacial maximum some 22,000 years ago the ice sheet could have stretched out across the continental shelf beyond St Kilda. There is some debate as to whether ice ever reached St Kilda, but fragments of sandstone around Village Bay – obviously from the mainland – indicate that it may well have done at some stage. Whatever happened, during that last glacial maximum – one of the most extreme – Village Glen and Glen Bay in Hirta would have spawned their own glaciers. Both major streams (in Glen Bay and in Village Bay) are misfits, indicating their U-shaped valleys have been enlarged by glacial action rather than by the water in the streams.

Erosion produces debris that will be washed downhill by water, carried by glaciers or just by gravity. Weathered debris from the slopes above have been deposited as boulder clay or till on the floor of the glens. Most of the higher slopes of Hirta are mantled by rocks which have through time been shattered by frost. This has generated some fine scree slopes around Village Bay, below Conachair and below Mullach Sgar. Carn Mor – now much favoured as a nesting area by petrels and puffins – is an extreme example, where boulders span up to 7 m across. Similar block fields are strewn over Soay, Boreray and – albeit on a much reduced scale – even on the summit of Stac an Armin. About 12,000 years ago a later cold snap, termed the Loch Lomond Readvance, would have generated permanent snow patches if not small glaciers, adding more frost-debris to these scree slopes.

With so much water locked into ice during the peak of the Ice Age 22,000 years ago, sea levels would have dropped considerably. The sea would then have been crashing on to rocks 120 m below the present tideline. In time it carved a wave-cut platform around what then would have been one large island consisting of Hirta, Soay and Boreray combined. A second such feature – probably dating from the Loch Lomond Readvance – is also visible 40 m below the surface. At the time of the Readvance too, the three islands would still have been connected. This submerged horizon is full of spectacular crevices, tunnels and caves that so delight divers today.

In his *Submarine Guide* (1983), which has some superb perspective drawings by Maurice Davidson, the diver Gordon Ridley concluded:

> The dive sites at St Kilda represent some of the best and most exciting diving in British waters, due mainly to the rock structures, the clear waters and the rich marine life ... The caves in Dun and Soay are rather challenging; the fantastic tunnels are numerous – through Sgarbhstac, Levenish, Am Plaisair, Soay Stac, Stac Biorach, Rubha Bhrengadal and Stac an Armin; the dreamlike submarine shoals are all infinitely memorable; the vertical and overhanging walls of Soay, Boreray, Stac an Armin and Stac Lee are mindblowing. If I had to pick my favourites these would be Sgarbhstac Arch, the 'volcano rim' shoal, and the overhanging wall at the east corner of Stac Lee ...

The 40 m wave-cut platform is backed by cliffs that thrust still further above the present sea surface. Thus 12,000 years ago, the precipice of Conachair would have been even higher, towering 470 m above the sea, while Stac an Armin would have been 231 m high. There has not been sufficient time to create an equivalent wave-cut platform at today's sea level. So most of St Kilda remains cliff-bound, albeit less dramatic than it once may have been.

If any of St Kilda remained free from ice, it would have been subject to extreme Arctic conditions in which little or no life survived. The Ice Ages would largely have wiped the slate clean, ready for a completely new wave of colonists.

.3.

Vegetation

In the beginning, not anything existed.
There was no sand nor sea, nor cooling waves.
'Voluspa', 10th-century Icelandic poem

WE WILL NEVER KNOW how exactly St Kilda came to be the wildlife haven we know today. Inferences on early colonisation may be drawn from its current flora and fauna but the story was a lot more complex. We know from other oceanic islands such as Galapagos that animals and plants came and went. Similarly, not all that arrived on St Kilda's shores could survive there. Some were alone and never found a partner, or others were replaced by later, more successful colonists. Whatever the volcanic archipelago came to look like after the Age of Dinosaurs, a succession of Ice Ages obliterated all life on St Kilda. This was especially effective during the last glacial maximum some 18,000–22,000 years ago.

After the last Ice Age, the process of colonisation of St Kilda would have had to start all over again. Nowadays we can gain insights into this sequence of vegetation development, from studies on the 50-year-old volcanic island of Surtsey. But first it is necessary to consider the physical conditions on offer since St Kilda's last glaciation – the changing climate, the formation of soils and the succession of the earliest plant cover.

Samples of peat were collected from Hirta in 1948 and again in 1958. Under the microscope, pollen can be seen, different plant species each having grains that are distinctive in shape and appearance. Pollen, however, can be blown considerable distances by the wind or on air currents so perhaps not everything that is identified on St Kilda might have originated there. All that could be deduced from these early profiles, about tree cover for instance, was that birch/hazel scrub may have existed, if not on St Kilda then close to it.

Detailed analyses, including radiocarbon dating of samples taken in 1984, have proved more instructive. From the deepest peat 2 m down it appears that, during a resurgence of glaciers some 12,000 years ago – the Loch Lomond Readvance – an open tundra would have prevailed, with Arctic–Alpine plants such as dwarf willow and purple saxifrage. The climate then improved until, about 6,000 years ago, a greater diversity of species was able to establish. This was principally grassland and heathland but there is no evidence of trees or even scrub cover. Conditions then became cooler, wetter and stormier so that heath retreated while maritime grassland spread, rich in plantains and other salt-tolerant plants. About 2,000 years ago heathland may have been able to recover somewhat as the climate improved before another lapse into more maritime plantain grassland about 400 years ago, in what is often referred to as the Little Ice Age. It is only in the top few centimetres of peat that cereal pollen becomes obvious – evidence of human activity.

In the long term the climate of St Kilda has been highly changeable, while in modern times it is highly fickle. In his 1824 book John MacCulloch mused on the islands' moods:

> Fertile as the other islands of the sea [are] in all the accidents of colour and light that arise from these changes, they fall far short of this one, where the variations of the atmosphere are incessant, where they are accompanied by effects, equally various and changeable, of light and shadow, of rain and mist, and storm, and of clouds in a thousand new and romantic forms, and colours such as neither poet nor painter ever imagined; the whole producing the most splendid and unexpected combination with the land, and the ever restless and changeless sea.

It might be too easy to dismiss the climate of St Kilda today as continuously dull and wet through the greater part of the year. Many visitors will already know this to their cost, but others will appreciate that it is not always the case. We need not be surprised to learn that the Reverend Neil Mackenzie kept records of temperature and wind direction, and his data for January and February 1840 were published by James Wilson in 1842, with some quick observations on summer temperatures. Apparently, at the end of the century, both ministers, John Mackay and Alexander Fiddes, maintained a rain gauge in the Manse garden, Mackay submitting the data to the Scottish Meteorological Society. John Mathieson and Alexander Cockburn kept weather records for the five months they were surveying the islands from April to October 1927, finding that in the same time period Edinburgh had enjoyed 17 hours more sunshine, 2½ inches more rain and average daily temperatures 4 °F higher than St Kilda. The Nature Conservancy encouraged the army medical officers to maintain a weather station in the early years of the National Nature Reserve (1958–65). Not surprisingly, the bird-watching Captains David Boddington and Estlin Waters were the most diligent, but the data is still incomplete.

The meteorologist Frank Green summarised the first six-months data from St Kilda and comparisons are often made with the next nearest met station 45 miles away at Balivanich airport in Benbecula, from where the helicopter transport to St Kilda operates. Between 1950 and 1981 mean temperatures at Balivanich ranged from 16 °C in July and August to 2 °C in January and February. During the period 1976–85 extremes of 25 °C and −8.4 °C were recorded in July 1976 and December 1985 respectively The 30-year average for monthly sunshine totals at Balivanich was 1,361 hours, with May the sunniest and December the most gloomy. Annual rainfall was 1,203 mm (with October to December the wettest months, and April/May the driest) with some 250 days with measurable rain. In 1982, there were 44 days when gales were recorded, though only 11 days in 1985. It seems that St Kilda is slightly milder and drier than Balivanich though windier, with gales persisting for longer periods.

Unfortunately, no longer-term weather data is available for St Kilda so, again, we must look to other oceanic islands nearby. There exists a body of information collected between 1951 and 1971 by the lighthousekeepers living on Sule Skerry for instance, over 150 miles from St Kilda. They noted gales blew at Sule Skerry on 39 days of the year, with ground frost on another 39 days of the year on average; snow fell on 23, but lay for only 6. Comparable figures for Balivanich 1957–84 were 80 days with ground frost, 35 days when snow fell, and 7 days when it lay. The wettest month on Sule Skerry was October with 52.6 mm (4.84 in) and the driest (April) averaging 22.5 mm (2.07 in). The average annual rainfall was 996 mm (39.2 in).

St Kilda certainly suffers from a high rainfall. The naturalist and conservationist Morton Boyd who was camped on Hirta during Operation Hardrock in May 1957 described (Nature Conservancy File Note):

> The rain started about 10pm [*on the 10th*] and by 11 it was pouring down. The steady downfall continued all night, the sullen relentlessness of it reaching a climax about 2.30 when, after some distant murmurs, a sheet of lightning tore open the sky to be succeeded by thunder claps to end all thunder claps which beat back and forth between the encircling hills to fade out finally with a crack, crack, crack from Oiseaval, Conachair and Ruaival, a rolling mutter from Dun and finally a far off shoosh from Levenish. When we rose at 7.30 am the island was awash with water. Pools and seeps were everywhere. Amhuin Mor [*sic*] was in full spate and all its tributaries making white streaks down the face of Mullach More, Mullach Geal, Am Blaid and Mullach Sgar. The 'Dry Burn' was a raging

torrent, with a waterfall at its foot tumbling over the cliff into the sea. The fields were all soaking wet, many of the tents had rivulets running through them and the bulldozed sites for the Nissen huts and the whole beach-head area were seas of mud.

Again, on Sunday 27 July 1969, no less than 1.32 in of rain fell between 3 a.m. and 9 p.m. The Dry Burn overflowed its banks, while, according to the warden, the late Donald Stewart, An Lag looked one big sheet of water with 3 ft of water on the site of new buildings behind the Officers' Mess. This probably did wonders for topping up the storage tanks in the Base and ensuring plenty water for all 104 people present on island at that time (72 of whom were visiting contractors). At the other extreme, in June 1975, there was a water shortage on St Kilda, and none of the 70 residents was allowed a bath! In June 2008, some staff had to be evacuated from the Hirta Base to conserve a fast diminishing water supply. To avoid this happening in the future the natural springs feeding the Base's water tanks are to be supplemented with a desalination plant.

Snow on the other hand is a relatively rare phenomenon on St Kilda, at least nowadays. Diaries of islanders, teachers and ministers alike often refer to heavy snowfalls, even in May, while Brigadier Tony Spackman recalled one in late December 1973. 1979 began with heavy falls of snow, with 5-ft drifts on top of Mullach Mor which stopped Land Rovers, even with chains fitted, getting up to the radars. Snow rarely lingers longer than a few days however, due to the warming influence of the sea.

Once the lighthouse on Sule Skerry went automatic, the Meteorological Office established an automatic weather station on the rock. But in 1990 they also installed another on North Rona, which, being 120 miles away, is much nearer to St Kilda than Sule Skerry. It was intended to operate as a marine buoy – hence its curious appearance – but, unfortunately, it leaked so came to be bolted on to the lesser rock summit of Rona. The highest point Toa Rona (355 ft) is occupied by an automatic lighthouse built a year or two before. Rona's automatic weather station, above the old village and about 100 m above sea level, does not measure precipitation, but takes hourly readings each day of wind speed and direction, air temperature and humidity, all of which are immediately transmitted back to the Met Office in the south of England. They kindly provided me with the raw data (for the years 1991 to 2004 inclusive), which was subjected to a rough unofficial analysis by a colleague for inclusion in the Rona Nature Reserve Management Plan and which will prove relevant to our purposes here.

The range of temperature experienced on Rona is small and extremes are rare. Temperatures ranged from −3.2 °C (in April 1998) to 21.6 °C (in August

1997). The average monthly temperature in February (the coldest month) was 5.3 °C, and in the warmest (August) 12.2 °C.

Wind is of course the most significant feature of St Kildan weather. David Boddington registered some 40 days with gales over the three winter months December to February. He recalled:

> The worst storm we had occurred on the 27th December 1958. Force 12 it was, a full-blown rip-roaring hurricane. It lashed us for fully three hours. What a sight that was! ... the end of Dun 320 feet high was completely enveloped in spray. You have to live in a place like this to appreciate the fury and violence of nature at her worst.

Winds of up to 130 miles per hour were recorded at the summit of Mullach Sgar on Sunday 21 January 1962 when Estlin Waters recorded how:

> There was widespread damage to the camp here – not only were slates blown off the roof and windows blown out but sections of precast concrete roofing were blown off and human bodies were blown around uncontrollably in the most severe gusts. During one gust I had a feeling that I was just going to be blown away although I was lying face down on the ground pressing myself to it to remain in the same position.

Another serviceman, James Mackay (2002), remembered a year later when waves hit the 200-ft cliffs on Dun's Atlantic face, broke right over the top and cascaded down the rock slopes into Village Bay. Brigadier Spackman noted gusts of reputedly 180 knots on New Year's Eve 1980/81 before the anemometer was ripped out. A Land Rover was lifted bodily off the road and wrecked beyond repair. The two occupants were badly shaken but otherwise unhurt. A 50-ft mast was blown down, and radar domes badly damaged, as were numerous walls, roofs, doors and windows.

In January 2000, the island of Rona experienced winds of up to 94 knots; and then again just before midnight on 11 January 2005, when they persisted above hurricane force 12 for no less than six hours! The terrible storm caused five fatalities on South Uist – and much damage on both Uist and St Kilda too. Rona was nearer the eye of the storm so the tightest isobars, and hence the strongest winds, actually hit Benbecula. The airport claimed 140 mph winds so St Kilda must have been even worse.

The Rona data revealed that mean monthly wind speeds ranged from 15.4 knots in July to 28.3 knots in February. Gales can occur in any month and all that can be concluded is that May to August tend to be the least windy. Out on St Kilda, Dr Jeff Stone (1988) noted how, for example, in January 1962, 17 consecutive days of almost continuously gale-force winds were recorded. No one can doubt the damage wrought every winter to structures around the

Base. Winds predominate from a direction just west of south. Visitors should never underestimate the power of the elements, even in summer.

While wind and wave batter away at Britain's shores, the ocean has been more forgiving to its inland surfaces. Tempered by the Atlantic, the British Isles currently experiences a mild, oceanic climate. Despite its extreme exposure, St Kilda is no exception. Six months of sea temperatures in Village Bay in 1957/58 decreased from an average of 51.9 °F in October to 46.2 °F in March. The archipelago's winters are mild, but the summers cool; frost and snow are rare. Its daily range of temperatures – in the region of 6 °C in summer and 3 °C in winter – is probably the narrowest anywhere in Britain, with the exception of the Scillies. Not surprisingly, the lofty cliffs and hills of St Kilda attract cloud, so humidity is high. However, at about 1,200 mm, the annual rainfall is barely twice that of Edinburgh, and is fairly evenly spread through the year. There is only one small brackish pool – in Glen Bay on Hirta – while freshwater streams are few. In hot summers they may even run dry. As the St Kildans were aware, however, some of the wells prove pretty reliable.

Undoubtedly – as Mathieson and Cockburn had experienced to their cost in 1927 – St Kilda is the windiest place in Britain. Wind speed and direction will affect the ability of plants and animals able to reach St Kilda. On the other hand, strong winds result in salt spray being deposited all over the island, from sea to summit, which is a major influence on the vegetation that is able to survive there. The same is true for other oceanic islands in the Atlantic, Surtsey included.

Where salinity affects survival, a major factor influencing initial colonisation by plants or animals is the degree of isolation. The nearest island to Surtsey is Geirfuglasker, 5.5 km away – a rock stack which, like St Kilda, was once a breeding haunt for the now extinct great auk (or geirfugle) and from which the rock derives its name. This, together with the other Westmann Islands, has been the nearest source of animal and plant colonists. Iceland itself offers a much bigger and more biologically rich catchment, first to serve the Westmann Islands and finally Surtsey itself. A few species even reach Surtsey from Europe and North America.

As expected though, marine plants and animals were among the first life forms to drift to the inshore waters and rocky shores of Surtsey. On land, mosses and lichens might be anticipated as the earliest colonists. But bacteria, moulds, algae and even some vascular plants were to be discovered on Surtsey first, it being another three years before the first moss established, and eight years before the first lichen. Bare lava offers the most sterile of substrates. Lichens are a coalition of algae and fungi that form crusts on bare rock surfaces. They corrode the rock, while mosses accumulate dust and minerals and retain enough moisture for the first useful soils to form. There are now over 70 species of moss on Surtsey and bryophytes form the dominant plant cover inland. Perhaps eventually some heath vegetation will establish, but salt spray is always likely to limit plant growth and diversity.

Beaches offer ideal opportunities for new arrivals. The first bacteria and moulds established on dried seaweed, driftwood or carcases washed up on the shores of Surtsey. They also grew on excrement from seabirds that early came to roost on the island. Scientists collected a number of seeds of higher plants along the strandline as early as 1964, and the following summer several small sea rocket shoots were found growing on a seaweed/tephra mix; the nearest colony is 20 km away on the Westmann Islands. Sea sandwort, scurvy grass, oysterplant, chickweed, sea sedge and lyme grass were other early pioneers, all of them typical coastal plants. Sandwort and scurvy grass are now especially widespread.

But beaches can also present a fickle existence. The first sea rocket seedlings on Surtsey were killed under a fresh fall of ash from the volcano, while many other coastal plants were washed away in storms. Establishment can be slow and erratic, as the 10th-century Icelandic poem 'Voluspa', had anticipated:

> At that time earth will rise out of the sea,
> And be green and fair,
> And fields of corn will grow
> That were never sown . . .
> So neither sea nor Surt's fire
> Will have done them injury.

Beaches are almost non-existent in a cliff-girt archipelago like St Kilda. Hirta possesses the only one at Village Bay. It is a small bay of huge boulders, but nearer the sea a sandy beach forms every summer, only to be washed away again each winter. Not only has this feature been important in the colonisation of Hirta by plants and animals, but it has proved crucial to the survival of the people. As soon as the island was discovered, the beach allowed them to step ashore, unload supplies, draw up and launch their boats. The only small pier came to be built at one end in modern times, while, from 1957, landing craft could draw up on the sands and unload materials for the radar base. This was, of course, weather and tides permitting, and is still only possible between the months of April to October while the sandy shoreline exists. Resupply by such landing craft remains essential to the maintenance of humans to this day.

Thus coastal lifeforms could gain access to Hirta, but the chance of strays arriving to occupy inland habitats and managing to survive the rigorous conditions is very much smaller. On Surtsey the breeding activities of gulls in summer, generating food remains and guano, have contributed to the rapid development of soil, but they have also been responsible for the arrival of seeds

Fig. 6 Cleits in the village meadows from a house window (J. Love).

of higher plants. This is a topic to which we will return. Plant cover inland on Surtsey has been most vigorous around the gull colonies. Fifty species of flowering plants have now been recorded in Surtsey as a whole, although at least five of these have failed to establish. So far, 40 years on, plant cover amounts to little more than 4 per cent of the island area.

Nowhere on Surtsey, nor on St Kilda, is free from the influence of salt spray. On the other hand, the greater expanse of Hirta, and its more varied topography, offers more opportunities for non-coastal species to survive, and to find some refuge from salt-laden winds. Where salt immersion is highest, on the most exposed clifftops and shores, relatively few species persist, all of them very salt-tolerant – sea plantains, sea pink, sea campion and fescue grass. Although heavily grazed by sheep in summer, the exposure in winter tends to prevent much dung enrichment. On the steepest cliffs, the absence of grazing together with fertilisation by seabirds such as fulmars are important factors. The most extreme form of bird-dominated vegetation is to be found on the ungrazed island of Dun.

A cool, wet climate not only conspires to reduce plant growth but also increases the leaching of nutrients. Furthermore, plant material is slow to decay in waterlogged conditions, all of which favours the development of acid, peaty soils. The steepness of St Kilda's slopes has limited the actual amount of peat deposited, so it is found only under cotton-grass bog, such as at the top of Mullach Mor. Good burning peats might have been obtained from here in the past, but the islanders preferred to cut moorland turf nearer to the village – to the detriment of their pastures. Here the soil is liable to wash away, leaving a stony area where only stragglers from a moorland flora struggle to survive between the rocks.

Soil formation is also influenced by the underlying rock. The basic and ultra-basic rocks of much of Hirta, and the Mullach Bi Ridge in particular, have a much higher calcium and magnesium content than the more acid granophyre of Conachair and Oiseval. But the availability of such minerals would be reduced as thicker soil cover developed.

To some extent these negative effects are countered by the manure of seabirds and sheep, which adds nitrogen, phosphate and calcium. Considerable quantities of magnesium, sodium and potassium are continually being applied from sea spray. Salt content in the soils of St Kilda is unusually high, 30–320 mg/100 g compared with only 2 mg/100 g in an Edinburgh garden.

This was highlighted by summer warden Andy Robinson who noted in his 2000 report:

> Unseasonal storms of the 13–14th June caused major wind/salt damage to vegetation all over the island. Nettle patches, iris, thistles and bracken were all badly blackened and withered. Hardest hit were those in flower, especially sea campion and thrift which came out of the gale with dead flowers.

In April 2002, he reported large numbers of dead earthworms following the winter storms, especially in front of the Base where they were being fed upon by gulls.

Professor Andy Meharg and a team from Aberdeen University have been studying samples of soil from different parts of Hirta, the main island of the St Kilda archipelago. Samples were collected from grazing lands, from fields, and from midden pits where in the past waste was collected for manuring. Analysis showed that levels of toxic chemicals from some of the fields and from the pits even now remain at high levels – which may have affected the fertility of the land. The pollutants, including lead, zinc, cadmium and arsenic, were mainly attributed to the use of seabird carcases in the manure that was spread across the village fields. Tens of thousands of birds were captured each year, so a considerable amount of waste was generated. Seabirds tend to have elevated levels of a range of potentially toxic metals in their organs. When traveller Martin Martin visited in 1697, he commented on the island's fertility. A deterioration in the crops is recorded by the mid-18th century. The implication is made in Meharg's study that this pollution caused the reduction in crop quality, but in fact it must also be borne in mind that there was a general deterioration in climate (often referred to as the Little Ice Age) throughout Britain at this time, with many poor harvests recorded in the Hebrides during the 18th century. Furthermore, heavy metals might be being added to the soil from modern marine pollutants in salt spray, something that could have been enhanced during modern industrial times.

Limited, harsh and challenging though the physical environment of St Kilda may be, it can nonetheless offer a variety of opportunities for an albeit limited flora. But just how did plants reach the island in the first place? Back from his round-the-world cruise in the *Beagle*, when in 1835 he had famously stopped off in Galapagos, no less a scientific authority than Charles Darwin (1809–82) applied himself to the problem in 1866:

> Remember how recently you and others thought that salt water would soon kill seeds? Remember that no one knew that seeds would remain for many hours in the crops of birds and retain their viability ... Remember that every year many birds are blown to Madeira and to the Bermudas. Remember that dust is blown 1000 miles over the Atlantic. Now, bearing all that in mind, would it not be a prodigy if an unstocked island did not in the course of ages receive colonists from coasts whence the currents flow, trees are drifted, and birds are driven by gales?

Since it is extremely unlikely that the islands of St Kilda were ever connected to the Hebrides by a land bridge, plants (and animals) could not have arrived overland. Thus, as Darwin had surmised, they must have arrived by air or by sea. A third option is that they arrived on board or inside something else (be it a raft of vegetation or a boat, on driftwood, even inside or attached to other animals such birds, bats or domestic stock). The St Kildan archipelago is 64 km from the nearest land and lies against the prevailing winds and currents. Furthermore, it presents a small target for potential colonists. All these factors conspire to any island having a rather impoverished flora and fauna.

Plants such as mosses, lichens, fungi and ferns that produce light airborne spores are obvious pioneers. For all its limited resources and isolation, St Kilda, as we will see, is surprisingly well-endowed in some of these departments. Fungal spores have been recorded at altitudes of 3,000 m in the jet stream. Scientists have also shown how moss spores carried 1,250 miles on air currents from Siberia have successfully developed when they came to ground near the Baltic. Clouds gather over islands, especially high ones such as St Kilda, and rain will encourage them to dispense with their cargo of spores, even insects. Nearly 200 species of larger fungi have been recorded on St Kilda, including a couple of British alpines and some typically woodland species, for example under the woodrush on the top of Conachair.

Many plants, such as grasses, produce tiny airborne seeds, while others, such as the daisy/dandelion family Compositae, have developed parachute mechanisms to facilitate dispersal. For some reason though, composites are poorly represented on St Kilda, perhaps because the moisture-laden prevailing winds are not in their favour.

Other plants, especially coastal ones, have air spaces in their seeds to enhance buoyancy. Many, such as those that first colonised Surtsey, are well able to withstand immersion in salt water. Charles Darwin looked in detail at this problem. He successfully germinated 64 of the 87 plant species that had their seeds immersed in seawater for up to 28 days. Scientists on Surtsey have demonstrated another novel mode of transport. One hundred and thirty-one seeds of five grass or sedge species (some of them hairy) were found attached to the rough surface of mermaid's purses, the egg cases of skate and dogfish, presumably having accumulated their cargo from another strandline along a distant beach.

Since bats are rare in the Hebrides and have yet to be recorded in St Kilda, it is only birds that can provide aerial transport for plants and animals. Some plants have sticky secretions or hooks on their seeds, specially to hitch a lift on birds. Others are still viable after passing through a bird's gut. Thus some plants have been found growing out of bird droppings, or on carcases on the ground or along the shore. Investigation of 13 species of migrant birds on Surtsey revealed them to be carrying diatoms, spores of moulds and mosses and even fragments of higher plants. Ten snow buntings, on migration between Greenland and the United Kingdom, were trapped on Surtsey and found to have seeds in their gizzards, the majority of which proved viable. Again, Darwin looked into this by scraping a small quantity of dried mud from the leg of a partridge from which he successfully germinated 82 seedlings of five plant species.

Many other plant forms, however, have poor dispersal abilities so are totally unsuited to such modes of transport. Darwin found that the seeds of peas and vetches, for example, cannot withstand more than a day or two immersed in seawater. Such species are likely to be entirely absent from remote offshore islands. Even if some species do manage to complete the journey, they may fail to find conditions suitable for survival. Plants arriving by sea find themselves on a hostile, intertidal beach, unless of course they were adapted to that habitat in the first place.

Plants (or animals) may either fail to reach an island or may fail to establish once there. Thus the diversity of species on islands will always be impoverished compared with the nearest land mass. For instance, St Kilda has only 184 species of flowering plants, grasses and ferns, compared with some 700 on the Outer Hebrides. St Kilda lacks proper trees or shrubs, such as holly, ivy, hawthorn or rose. Whole families, such as labiates and composites, are poorly represented there. Many flowers typical of similar plant communities on the mainland are absent, while the lack of habitats such as standing freshwater precludes the existence of species so typical elsewhere in the Highlands and Islands. As one biologist so aptly concluded, 'a community reflects both its applicant pool as well as its admission policies'. But yet another factor can be involved – pure chance, simple luck. All this results in islands displaying what is referred to as a 'disharmonic' or unbalanced flora.

The flora of St Kilda also demonstrates another phenomenon, called 'niche expansion'. With limited competitors those plants that thrive often expand their ecological niche to include that of related plants that are absent. St Kildan examples have been cited by Professor Mick Crawley in a recent unpublished *Flora of St Kilda* (1993). The meadow buttercup *Ranunculus acris* not surprisingly occurs in meadows, but on St Kilda it is also to be found in drier places typical of bulbous buttercup *R. bulbosus*, and also in wetter places typical of creeping buttercup *R. repens* – neither of which is to be found on St Kilda. Similarly, only one species belonging to the Compositae has made it to St Kilda – autumn hawkbit *Leontodon autumnalis*. However, here it appears to be doing the jobs of others that are missing, such as smooth hawksbeard *Crepis capillaris*, cat's ear *Hypochaeris radicata* and the common dandelion *Taraxacum officinale*.

There are no woody plants, no lime-rich rocks nor is there much fresh water, leaving St Kilda deficient in what would otherwise prove rich habitats for lower plants. Nonetheless, the archipelago is surprisingly rich in these departments, with 194 lichens, 56 liverworts and 104 mosses. The lichens of Hirta were surveyed in detail in 1978 by Dr Oliver Gilbert (1936–2005) of Sheffield University, whom I first had the pleasure of meeting on an expedition to North Rona, and later on the isles of Rum and Eigg. Oliver found that the tops of St Kilda's volcanic cliffs support a number of large, showy lichens that are normally found growing on trees. They probably survive there because of the high humidity.

The tiny sheltered gorge of Abhainne Mhor also contains a number of extreme Atlantic species surviving on damp, vertical rock faces. One of these, *Verrucaria laetebrosa*, had only previously been recorded from Lentrim in Ireland. Oliver found lichens to achieve their maximum development on large, guano-spattered boulders in seabird colonies such as on Dun and Carn Mor (with up to 25 species on a single, well-manured boulder). Spectacular creamy rosettes of the rare Arctic-maritime *Lecanora straminea* have even colonised the guano-smeared aluminium body of the Wellington bomber which crashed on Soay in World War II. Oliver described this in his memoir *The Lichen Hunters* (2004):

> Wally [Wright] the Nature Conservancy warden called in for coffee, very pleased with himself, having just made only the third recorded visit to Soay since the

St Kildans left. He had gone with a yachtsman who was interested in crashed planes to get the serial number of a Wellington bomber that had ditched there in the war. He brought a piece of aluminium, bearing *Lecanora straminea* that is now in the herbarium of the Royal Botanic Garden, Edinburgh.

Between the 30- and 40-m contours, the slopes of Hirta are especially rich in lichens, a close-cropped sward maintaining as many as 12 lichen species per square metre. Here the lichen *Solenopsora vulturiensis* is at its northernmost limit in Britain. The mass of dead vegetation, decaying so slowly in the salty conditions, together with the long history of sheep grazing, help maintain the open sward so favoured by the lichens. Salt-tolerant mosses and liverworts are amazingly lush on St Kilda, even at the summit of Conachair where in sheltered cliff crevices ferns can also thrive in the humid atmosphere.

In Martin Martin's time botany tended to be principally the investigation of the medicinal properties of plants. Going on to study medicine, it was not surprising that he should often refer to herbal remedies in both his books. Martin commented:

> The inhabitants are ignorant of the virtues of these herbs; they never had a potion of Physic given them in their lives, nor know any thing of Phlebotomy; so that a physician could not expect his bread in this Commonwealth. They have generally good voices, and sound lungs; to this the Solan Goose egg supped raw doth not a little contribute . . .
>
> [To ward against a cough when the Steward lands, they take] their great and beloved Catholicon, the Giben, ie the fat of their fowls, with which they stuff the stomach of a Solan Goose, in fashion of a pudding; this they put in the infusion of oatmeal, which in their language they call Brochan . . . They love to have it frequently in their meat as well as drink.

Martin later continued his account of the islanders' habits:

> Their ordinary food is barley and some oat-bread baked with water; they eat all the fowl, already described, being dried in their stone-houses, without any salt or spice to preserve them; and all their beef and mutton is eat fresh . . . They boil the sea-plants, dulse, and Slake, melting the roots of Silver-weed and Dock boiled, and also with their Scurvy-grass stoved, which is very purgative, and is here of an extraordinary breadth . . . They are undone for want of salt, of which as yet they are but little sensible; they use no set times for their meals, but are determined purely by their appetites.
>
> They use only the ashes of Sea-ware for salting their cheese, and the shortest only, which grows in the rocks, is used by them, that being reckoned the mildest.

In 1758, the Reverend Kenneth MacAulay made a few interesting observations from his brief visit to the islands, but added little new:

Their arable land hardly exceed eighty acres ...

All the grass in Boreray is excessively fine and very thick, though too short. There is a plot of it which consists entirely of sorrel, like that in the Campar or Hirta.

According to the Reverend James Wilson, the Reverend Neil Mackenzie sought to improve the agriculture of the islanders and introduced better drainage and a new strip system of cultivation, using the English spade rather than the *cas chrom* – and, it has to be said, demolishing numerous archaeo-logical sites in the process! Mackenzie noted:

Each family possesses from three to four acres of arable land ... The barley, which is the principal crop, gets most of the manure ... they also grow some oats, chiefly the black variety, but it does not get much attention. Their only other crop is a small quantity of potatoes, which does not receive much attention either.

The barley and oats however were barely sufficient for the islanders. So Wilson reported that Mackenzie also tried carrots and onions with some success:

Turnips seem to thrive well for a time, but are speedily cut off by some kind of destructive insect, and peas and beans blossom, but produce no pods. A little mustard was growing merrily near the manse.

It was around this same time that botany became more of a science. Early interest seems to have been directed towards finding and listing plants and to discovering new species. A strange, isolated place like St Kilda attracted a fair degree of interest, a point anticipated by the geologist John MacCulloch in 1815:

The peculiarly unconnected situation of St Kilda would have rendered it desirable to know the number and names of all the plants which grow on it: but my time unfortunately did not permit a full examination. No rare plants were observed. The *Leontodon autumnale* [a dandelion called autumn hawkbit] is the only one which can lay the slightest claim to this character; and the botanical catalogue appeared indeed to be extremely meagre. *Juncus sylvaticus* [a sedge] is among the most conspicuous, covering the cliffs with its bright green leaves; but this plant is common in the exposed Highland mountains. *Cochlearia vulgaris* [scurvy grass] and *Matricaria maritima* [mayweed], both of an enormous size, also abound among the rocks wherever they can find lodgement.

The earliest plant list seems to be that of Robert Campbell of Shawfield or 'The Laird of Islay' (1775–1814) who was one of the party accompanying

Lord Henry Brougham, and who benefited from the Reverend Mackenzie's guidance.

As an aside, it must have been the previous year – on a visit in his yacht – that Campbell had fallen in love with a local beauty, Marion Morrison or Gillies. She had composed a Gaelic lament when he left. He returned the following year, as promised, to marry her. She sang the song for him:

Oh, handsome Donald Gillies,	*Dhòmhnaill uallaich MhicGillÌosa,*
There was a time when you courted me	*Bha uair a bhathu a'strì rium,*
But since the Islay lord arrived	*Ach on thàinig an tighearn' Ìleach,*
I ignored your flirting.	*Sguir(idh) mi dhed bhrìodal beòil.*
My young brown-haired sweetheart,	*Mo ghaol òigear a'chùil duinn,*
For whom I feel so passionately.	*Dhan tug mi mo loinn cho mòr.*

But he departed a disappointed bachelor! Donald Gillies must have won the day. (Calum Ferguson in his book *St Kilda Heritage* gave the date as the 1820s.)

Prominent in Campbell's party was the Edinburgh-born Henry, later Lord, Brougham (1778–1868), who became an eminent barrister and parliamentarian – despite his arrogance, self-confidence and numerous eccentricities. His visit to St Kilda was described in a letter to a friend dated Stornoway, 14 August 1799. They called at Hirta on 10–11 August 1799 when Brougham reported how, at first, the islanders were suspicious of the boat in the bay, fearing it might be a French privateer.

Despite romantic distractions, the love-struck Campbell's botanical list contained a credible 53 species, though not all may have been identified correctly. St Kilda's flora was not quite as 'meagre' as MacCulloch had prophesied.

One of the first all-round naturalists to reach St Kilda was John MacGillivray (see Chapter 4), the son of the famous zoology professor William MacGillivray. After a short excursion with the Reverend Mackenzie, 'the worthy minister of the island', John MacGillivray recorded a similar 50 higher plants over four days in early July 1840 (although he named only 29 in his published account). These included the dwarf willow *Salix herbacea* 'on the summit of one of the hills'. MacGillivray was surprised to find this montane willow growing at such low altitude, 'shewing the influence of the sea-coast upon Alpine vegetation'.

The 34-year-old Irish-born Richard Manliffe Barrington (1849–1915) was critical of MacGillivray's 'meagre' list, 11 species of which he could not find himself. Barrington brought his own Gaelic interpreter from Glasgow, but, since the poor fellow could not understand the St Kilda dialect and was afraid of heights, all he proved good for was minding the Crimean tent which the pair had pitched near the landing place. Barrington's Alpine ropes – that the

St Kildans refused to use – helped weigh the tent down against the wind. It was in June 1883 that Barrington made his historic climb of Stac Biorach with two St Kildans. During his three-week stay Barrington recorded 120 species of plants. This included the dwarf willow on Conachair (down to 500 ft) and a second dwarf 'tree'- the creeping willow *Salix repens*. The observations of botanist Alexander Gibson in August 1889 brought St Kilda's plant list to 140 species, but he too failed to find ten of MacGillivray's plants.

Barrington had studied law but chose the outdoor life of a land valuer. Later he was to turn more to ornithology than botany, and organised Irish lightkeepers into submitting bird records and specimens. His book on bird migration was published in 1900. Barrington's last visit to St Kilda was in June 1896 aboard the Irish Congested Districts Board steamer *Granuaile*, the intention being to land on Rockall – 170 miles west of St Kilda. Accompanying him were the eminent Irish botanist Robert Lloyd Praeger (1865–1953) and the redoubtable Scots naturalist J. A. Harvie-Brown (1844–1916) who had paid the first of several visits to St Kilda in 1877. Although the party failed to get ashore on Rockall in 1896, they did call in at St Kilda on the way home where, according to Praeger:

> We explored the cliffs and great bird colonies in mist and pouring rain in the company of the Kearton brothers.

Praeger added three new species to the plant list of 140.

The next contribution towards the botany of St Kilda came in 1927 from John Gladstone (1908–1977). Although a young history student from Cambridge, Gladstone volunteered his passion for botany to the surveyor John Mathieson and geologist Alexander Cockburn. David Quine included extracts from their diaries in his book *St Kilda Portraits* (1988). Gladstone produced three volumes of diaries, letters and press cuttings. In 1931, Professor James Ritchie of Aberdeen University commented, 'It is a most interesting record and I thoroughly enjoyed the reading of it. Its records, gathered from so many sources, will become more and more valuable as the years pass.'

Gladstone arrived off the *Dunara Castle* on Sunday 3 July 1927, accompanied by two friends. All three were boarded in the Manse with Mrs Macleod, the wife of the missionary, who happened to be away on holiday. Gladstone immediately began botanising, and four days later was able to reach Boreray on a visiting trawler.

Here, he finally met up with Mathieson and Cockburn who had been there for several days. All three returned to Hirta later that day. The following Monday they were all able to spend the day on Dun. Gladstone's two friends departed on 14 July aboard a whaler. Mr Macleod, the missionary, had failed to catch the *Hebrides* on 18 July, which seemed to upset his wife. There then unfolded a rather strange state of affairs. Whatever gossip Gladstone had recorded in his diary for 20 and 21 July, Mrs Macleod not only read it but apparently tore out the pages! By the next entry Gladstone had resolved to leave the island early, on the *Dunara Castle* on 25 July. Notwithstanding, he and his kind host departed on good terms and he later sent her a box of onions – which took two months to arrive! Her letter of thanks took nearly a month to reach him.

Gladstone did his job thoroughly. His particular friend Donald Gillies – one of the islanders – brought him specimens, as did his colleague Alexander Cockburn 'who collected all that he could lay his hands on'. It was the geologist who first located some honeysuckle *Lonicera periclymenum* growing wild (though first recorded by Barrington in 1883). This seemed a surprising plant to find on treeless Hirta, where it occurred on both Oiseval and Mullach Bi. Gladstone considered that it had been introduced by birds, a perfectly logical explanation. He even collected some to give to Mrs Macleod! Where previous authors had concluded that only Hirta, Boreray, Soay and Dun were vegetated, Cockburn was able to report at least four species of maritime plants on Levenish.

One of the most striking features about St Kilda was the abundance of grasses, sedges and rushes, representing no fewer than a third of the species found in Britain; indeed, only two of the more common grasses were missing. Like MacGillivray, Gladstone also commented on the Alpine species growing at such low levels, purple saxifrage *Saxifraga oppositifolia* and the rare moss campion *Silene acaulis* at the 300-ft contour, for example, with roseroot *Sedum rosea* plentiful on the sea cliffs. Gladstone realised that St Kilda offered few sheltered spots for ferns and only recorded 11 species. In just three weeks he had made a thorough search of Hirta as well as having collected on Boreray and Dun, but he had a few disappointments:

> I am afraid I have failed to find one or two rarities and, of course, I now wish I had a week more on the island.

Nonetheless, David Lack, who had taken part in the 1931 expedition from Oxbridge (see Chapter 4), was impressed and wrote to Gladstone:

> Our botanist [C. P. Petch] was very annoyed that you had done your work so thoroughly!

Gladstone sent his collection of 120 species to William Bertram Turrill (1890–1961) at Kew Gardens who compiled *The Flora of St Kilda* from this and previous written accounts. St Kilda's higher plant list now stood at 148 species. From Gladstone's careful notes Turrill was able to give an indication of abundance and distribution. He also ventured some comments on the unexpected occurrence of five woodland species (such as honeysuckle), but did not consider them to overturn the accepted wisdom that St Kilda had never been wooded. Gladstone had also found two thick patches of daisies *Bellis perennis* where there were none in 1897. (The Heathcotes had been surprised at this lack of daisies, lamenting how the St Kildan children could never make daisy chains!) Gladstone was impressed at such a complete spectrum of heathland plants and postulated a view that is not necessarily held today:

> I have been unable to obtain evidence that St Kilda was glaciated during the Quaternary Ice Age or Ages. It might well be that its flora, as represented by the dominant heath-moor types, survived the Ice Age in the islands ... It is not denied that wind or birds could introduce new plants but it seems unlikely that such a selection would have been made by these agencies. As the list proves, the flora is a typical piece of Scottish 'moor' ecologically ... and suggests that St Kilda is merely a detached portion of Scotland.

For centuries, the islanders had added organic fertiliser to their fields, in the form of domestic and animal waste, offal, bird carcases and old thatch. The improved nutrient status of the soils around Village Bay is reflected in the fact that no fewer than nine species of earthworm are to be found there, two of them also occurring on Boreray. Martin, MacAulay and MacCulloch all considered the barley on St Kilda to be the best in the Hebrides. The islanders also grew oats. Towards the end of the 19th century, however, the yield was poor, so the St Kildans used it as animal fodder and imported meal for domestic use. Since at least 1758 they had also been growing a few potatoes, but in the end their efforts were largely directed towards grass production for hay.

The botanist on David Lack's 1931 expedition was Charles Plowright Petch (1909–1987). He went on to become a teacher and then a physician, but botany remained his passion; he compiled a comprehensive *Flora of Norfolk*. As the botanist on the St Kilda expedition he also extended his interest to include mosses, lichens and seaweeds. He did his work thoroughly, finding two bog orchids *Hammarbya paludosa*, one of which he collected for verification back in Cambridge – a new species for the island. In the end he could only add 14 species to Gladstone and Turrill's flora.

Despite careful searching, he failed to find 22 on the list. Some were perhaps misidentifications in the past, but several – mostly agricultural 'weeds' – very likely had become extinct. These included corn marigold *Chrysanthemum segetum*, shepherd's purse *Capsella bursa-pastoris*, corn spurrey *Spergula arvensis*, hairy bittercress *Cardamine hirsuta* and groundsel *Senecio vulgaris*. These all disappeared when cultivation ceased altogether in 1930, and the island was finally abandoned by both the St Kildans and their stock. Petch was quick to realise an opportunity:

After being under the hand of man for many centuries the island thus lapses into an almost natural state ... Owing to the removal of the biotic factors of grazing and cultivation, the future development of the vegetation may be regarded as a large-scale experiment in plant ecology.

By now scientific interest was turning away from plant lists and more to plant communities – perhaps Gladstone had left Petch with little else to do! So Petch set up some permanent quadrats and a system of random sample plots. Another companion John Buchan described him 'pegging out a square yard of ground to analyse every blade and stem that sprouted from it'.

It was not until July 1948 that a party of eight biologists from Edinburgh University, led by Dr Frank Fraser Darling (1903–79), spent a fortnight on St Kilda to record any changes in the vegetation since Petch's survey from 17 years before. Unfortunately, Darling's team failed to relocate Petch's permanent quadrats. They did find, even in the absence of cultivation, that changes had already taken place and a new equilibrium had been reached through trampling and manuring by sheep and seabirds (Poore and Robertson 1949). A few arable weeds had managed to survive in disturbed ground. In fact, Hirta had only lain ungrazed for two years for, by 1932, a flock of 107 Soay sheep from the island of Soay were released to replace the islanders' 1,300 or so blackface which they had taken with them to help pay for the evacuation.

It had been two years earlier, suffering from air sickness, that Frank Fraser Darling had first glimpsed St Kilda from a Sunderland flying boat while engaged in an aerial survey of grey seal colonies with James Fisher. A veteran island-goer, Darling had previously farmed on the Summer Isles and had spent weeks studying seals on Treshnish and North Rona. It is surprising then – and disappointing – that the diary about his visit to St Kilda (quoted in Morton Boyd's *Fraser Darling's Islands* 1986) should be so brief. In Scottish Natural Heritage files there is a photograph of him, holding a Soay lamb, in front of the Factor's House.

As a member of the government's Scottish Wildlife Conservation Committee and Director of the West Highland Survey, Frank was able to enlist the services of the Fishery cruiser *Vaila* to reach St Kilda. On arrival, the party cleaned out the Manse as their base. Duncan Poore and Vernon C. Robertson were the expedition botanists, surveying and mapping the vegetation, though not in as much detail as they would have liked. They also collected peat samples from the neck of the Cambir which were later examined by W. H. Gibson of Cambridge. Some of the other expedition members were taken round Boreray and the stacs by a visiting yacht *Lady Elspeth*, enabling James Fisher to undertake bird counts. Although Lord Bute had given the necessary permissions for landing, he forbade any collecting. Yet he later asked if the expedition could take some live gannets and gulls for Glasgow Zoo! Darling flatly refused to oblige since it was not only against his own principles but contrary to the ethos of his Wildlife Conservation Committee.

In a radio broadcast for James Fisher in November 1951 Duncan Poore recalled his survey:

> The number of species is rather small and there is none among them that a botanist on the mainland would go out of his way to see. The plants apparently have no special St Kilda forms [like the animals], and what there are, are not even very beautiful. Of course thrift and sea-campion make a brilliant display of pink and white in the early summer; the sea chamomile makes a gay show on the cliffs and on the rocks by the sea; primroses were still in flower by the burn sides. And two of our prettiest alpine flowers, the moss campion and the purple saxifrage can be found, if you know where to look. But we weren't mainly interested in the kinds of plants we should find. St Kilda has drawn other botanists than ourselves and there was little possibility that anything remained unfound. We wanted instead to study the vegetation as a whole. Freedom of interference makes these islands a wonderful field of study ... almost free from disturbance by men, where a natural balance of plants may be attained without let or hindrance. It has an other advantage; it is one of the few places in Scotland where good sense has prevailed and no one has introduced that universal pest the rabbit.

By 1957 the fifth Marquis of Bute had died and passed the ownership of St Kilda to the National Trust for Scotland. The Trust then leased the property to the Nature Conservancy who, that same year, declared it a National Nature Reserve. Dr Donald McVean was able to take advantage of the army transport to embark on a botanical survey in July 1958. Behind the village, despite the presence of the Soay sheep, heather *Calluna vulgaris* had spread amongst the abundant purple moor grass *Molinia caerulea*. McVean was unable to locate the single, sickly specimen of cross-leaved heath *Erica tetralix* found in the two previous surveys.

Much of the rest of Hirta was covered with a mixed and varied boggy grassland, including profuse woodrush *Luzula sylvatica* near the summits of Conachair and Mullach Bi. The maritime grasslands on Ruaival and the Cambir were a lot more diverse in species than Poore and Robertson had realised, with patches intensely manured by sheep and seabirds. The grassland around the old village fields had altered less in the last 10 years than it had in the first 17 years following the evacuation in 1930. Few of the arable weeds had been able to re-establish and were now extinct. The following summer of 1959, Dr Derek Ratcliffe (1929–2005), also of the Nature Conservancy, was able to supply botanical notes from the other islands. He found the heavily grazed swards on Soay and Boreray to be like those in the old village fields. Soay's south-eastern slope in particular is much influenced by burrowing puffins, having a fringe of plantains near the sea. Dun – with no sheep – has thickest cover, which is especially species-rich over the old lazy beds. Ratcliffe found the vegetation at the summit of Stac an Armin to be similar to the ridge on Dun.

David Gwynne of the West of Scotland College of Agriculture in Auchen-cruive, with botanist Cedric Milner and soil scientist M. Hornung, both of the Nature Conservancy, usefully summarised the vegetation and soils of Hirta in 1971 for *Island Survivors*, a book about Soay sheep. Hornung noted:

> Soil biological activity is low, leaching is intense and the rate of chemical weathering slow; as a result acid, peaty soils and peats predominate and blanket peat is the natural climax soil.

Deep peat has been limited by the instability of Hirta's steep slopes. Soil formation has also been influenced by the underlying rock, while soil chemistry has been influenced by the heavy application of guano, sheep dung and sea spray; the guano and dung add nitrogen, phosphate and calcium to offset leaching, while sea spray adds magnesium, sodium and potassium to counteract soil acidity.

Vegetation in turn is influenced by the soil of course, but also by the altitude above the sea, the aspect, the slope, the ultimate exposure to salt spray and even by the grazing pressure and seabird activity. All these effects were described by Gwynne, Milner and Hornung:

> There is no doubt that the vegetation of Hirta provides a valuable study of the dynamics of vegetation and soil on a sub-oceanic island.

Ultimately, in 1995, Alan Booth was contracted by Scottish Natural Heritage to fit the unusual flora of St Kilda into the communities described by the National Vegetation Classification. He added only one new species to the list – bird's foot trefoil *Lotus corniculatus*, which was found, like many other recent introductions, close to the verge of the army road. Another such example was strawberry clover *Trifolium fragiferum*, found in a similar location in 1980 by Patsy Castro (McShane) and Joe Keppie. They noted some evidence of reseeding disturbed ground and it is likely that this plant, often used in commercial seed mix, was introduced artificially. That year Joe and Patsy also added sneezewort *Achillea ptarmica* to the island list and found self-heal *Prunella vulgaris* to be much more abundant around the village than previously noted.

The lower sward around Village Bay is tussocky with bent grass and Yorkshire fog, the close-cropped gaps being dominated by clover, creeping bent grass, meadow grass, fescue, sweet vernal grass, mosses and liverworts. The sheep graze these gaps more intensely than the tussocks. A more extreme grass community, called 'lair flora', occurs behind walls and around the entrance of cleits, wherever sheep persistently seek shelter and leave copious dung and urine. A dense and vigorous growth of Yorkshire fog and meadow grass results, with the herbs mouse ear, celandine and clover. Where fulmar guano is added, such as on Oiseval, on the north-west face of the Cambir and the north-west face of Ard Uachdarachd, sorrel becomes particularly abundant.

The damper, marshy areas support poor-quality grasses and a variety of heath plants such as sphagnum and other mosses, asphodel, sundew, sedges and rushes. One such area between the summits of Mullach Mor and Conachair is a mix of peat hags and cotton grass where great skuas nest. Woodrush thrives on or near the drier summits, while the most windswept tops contain several interesting species including St Kilda's only 'trees' – the dwarf willow and the creeping willow, each only a few centimetres high.

The dominant vegetation on Boreray is similar to the rich grasslands of Village Bay in Hirta but supports fewer species, perhaps because of its simpler topography and geology. Although Soay is grazed, it is, on the other hand, more varied, with more grasses but less heather and crowberry than equivalent communities in Hirta.

.4.

Invertebrates

ONE OF THE defining scientific expeditions to St Kilda took place in July 1931, barely a year after the evacuation. Several of the islanders were still able to return to their homes for several weeks each summer. Six students from Oxford and Cambridge came to live amongst them for a month to investigate the geology, flora and fauna. Previously, only individual specialists chose to visit St Kilda, assembling an inventory of its natural history in a piecemeal fashion.

The Oxbridge graduates brought together an impressive range of expertise. We have already encountered the botanist Charles Petch. Zoologist and leader of the expedition was David Lack who would become one of the foremost scientists of his generation – albeit as an ornithologist more than an entomologist.

One day Petch was working on the slopes of Conachair while Lack was looking for beetles along the clifftop high above him. When Lack moved the stone, it crashed over the edge and eventually lodged itself beside a cleit 600 ft below, narrowly missing Petch who was preoccupied with his fifth new plant for St Kilda!

Later, on Dun, Lack discovered a curious little weevil *Ceutorhynchus*, a species that even today has only ever been recorded in two other localities – in southern Iceland, on the recently created island of Surtsey, and on Suderey in the nearby Westmann Islands. We will return to this little creature later in the chapter. We still do not understand what has caused its strange disjunct distribution, but we do know a bit more about how plants and animals come to establish in remote situations.

It is a characteristic of oceanic islands like St Kilda that they are separated from other reservoirs of living organisms by a barrier that is inhospitable to terrestrial life – the sea. The further these islands are situated offshore the fewer the plants and animals that will survive the journey, while the smaller the island, the smaller the target it presents. Thus small islands and those farthest offshore support the fewest species. It is not every plant and animal that is equipped to travel great distances in the first place, so islands will never boast as many species as the nearby mainland.

Larger islands not only accumulate more pioneers but are likely to offer a diversity of habitats which in turn will sustain a greater variety of species. Ultimately, there will be a limit to the resources they offer so that once an ecological equilibrium is reached, new colonists may find it difficult to establish. However, if one new arrival is particularly well adapted to the new conditions, with a wide ecological tolerance, it may well outcompete some of the original inhabitants. So extinction is a constant risk, especially since the population size on small islands is so restricted. These are the fundamental principles in the theory of island biogeography.

Colonists have three means of transport to an island – by sea (swimming, drifting or rafting), by air (flying, gliding or ballooning), or as passengers (on other animals or on boats). St Kilda is outwith the swimming capabilities of most creatures. The prevailing winds blow in the opposite direction and only Hirta possesses a small beach where arrivals might pitch up. So rafts are unlikely to have made much of a contribution to the archipelago's fauna, as they might have done in more tropical latitudes.

It is just possible though that bark-living or wood-boring invertebrates may have reached St Kilda on driftwood. Despite only one effective beach, the archipelago has a surprising array of ground-dwelling invertebrates such as mites, collembolans and other arthropods. There are 140 or so species of beetle, including a small rare weevil (*Ceutorhynchus insularis*) found on scurvy grass on Hirta and Dun. However, many species that one might expect to occur on St Kilda are missing, either because they were unable to reach St Kilda in the first place, or if they did, they proved unable to survive the limited opportunities and the harsh environment.

Going back to the genesis of Surtsey's story, it is not surprising that the first creatures that scientists recorded on the island had flown there. Birds, and seabirds in particular, were immediate contenders as we will see. Flies are the equivalent amongst invertebrates. The first fly *Diamesia zernyi* arrived on Surtsey within six months of the island's formation. Five more types of fly turned up the following summer along with a mite and two silver Y moths *Autographa gamma*, active fliers and migrants all the way from Europe.

By 1973 some 3,000 flies of 104 species had been recorded, many more than all the other insects and arthropods put together. But, in order to become established, animals ultimately depend on the presence of plants, or upon other animals that do. Many of the first insects to establish on Surtsey did so around the beach, where there was a supply of carcases and other debris washed ashore; it would be a long time before any invertebrate managed to colonise any further inland.

We will never know what was the first creature to set foot on St Kilda. All we can say is that – given the Surtsey experience – it is likely to have flown there. However, St Kilda is lacking in many animals that would seem to have been capable of flying there. Amongst winged insects, mayflies, dragonflies, stoneflies and lacewings never made it, but it is perhaps less surprising that there are no grasshoppers. Only one species of scorpion fly has been recorded (though this old record is suspect) and one earwig (abundant even on Levenish), but 10 caddisflies and about a score of bug species. Three bark lice are found on St Kilda, but are not at all common. Two of them are wingless, while the third is normally found in tree bark on the mainland. A few parasitic lice are recorded from sheep and birds, while one tick *Ixodes uriae* is common in seabird nests. Seven species of flea have been found in wren nests, three of them on field mice. The single silverfish and five species of Collembolan are primitive wingless insects that live in soil and, along with the 19 species of earthworm, must have originated as stowaways.

We need not be surprised that by far the most successful insect colonists on St Kilda have been the flies (Diptera), with nearly 200 species now recorded. Since there are no bees (Hymenoptera) and few butterflies and moths (Lepidoptera), flies may well act as important pollinators of flowers. Amongst the other Hymenopterans are 19 types of parasitic ichneumons (which are obviously successful colonists), but only one ant, the red ant *Myrmica ruginodis*, occurs.

Butterflies and moths (Lepidoptera) are often large and conspicuous and usually immediately recognisable. As a result, they attract more interest than almost any other invertebrate group. At least 367 Lepidoptera species are to be found in the Outer Hebrides – representing only about 14 per cent of those on the British list. On the other hand, fewer than a hundred of these have made it out to St Kilda. Being robust and widespread, migrant species such as the silver Y moth, red admiral and painted lady butterflies *Vanessa atalanta* and *Cynthia cardui* feature prominently on the island list. Antler moth *Cerapteryx grammis* and dark arches *Apamea monoglypha* are the most common moths, being seen every summer.

After Geoff Hancock's recent visits, nine centipedes and millipedes have been added to St Kilda's list. Curiously, the first spider to reach Surtsey (in 1966) was a forest species from Europe which was hitherto unknown in Iceland. Over 60 species of spider have been recorded on St Kilda, however, two-thirds of them belonging to the family Linyphiidae or 'money spiders' which are accomplished balloonists. Their young spin threads of gossamer to aid dispersal by wind and thus have a unique ability to reach offshore islands. On the other hand, only six species of harvestmen have been found in St Kilda. Harvestmen lack the waterproof cuticle of spiders, but one widespread British species *Mitopus morio* reaches astonishing densities at the damp, misty summit of Conachair, where the lush woodrush offers shelter from desiccating winds; here it lives alongside one particular spider *Pirata piraticus* whose thin cuticle confines it to marshy environments.

Being a remote and enticing place, small in size, St Kilda – or at least Hirta – has long attracted the attention of scientists. As a result, Hirta boasts quite respectable species lists for most plant and animal varieties. The following table includes the invertebrates which are the subject of this chapter, alongside vertebrates and plants referred to elsewhere.

Table 1. Some species lists for St Kilda

Plants			
Fungi	200	Mosses	104
Lichens	194	Ferns	19
Liverworts	56	Flowering plants/grasses	165
Animals			
Molluscs	26		
Earthworms	19	Moths	82
Collembolans	5	Beetles	140
Centipedes/millipedes	9	Flies	200
Spiders	60		
Harvestmen	6	Fish: incomplete list	41+
Fleas	7	Reptiles: leathery turtle	1
Lice	4	Birds: breeding seabirds	17
Earwigs	1	breeding landbirds	10
Bees/wasps	0	All species incl vagrants	230
Dragonflies	0	Mammals: mice	2
Ants	1	seals	1
Caddisflies	10	whales/dolphins	10
Bugs	12	feral Soay sheep	1
Butterflies	7	domestic spp.*	6*

*cattle, sheep, ponies, dog, cat, hen – all now extinct

*Fig. 7. John MacGillivray
(Harvie-Brown and Buckley,*
A Vertebrate Fauna of the
Outer Hebrides).

Probably the first visitor to describe any of the insects of St Kilda was John MacGillivray (1821–67). He was the eldest son of William MacGillivray (1796–1852), a Professor of Natural History at Aberdeen University who had been brought up in Harris. William doubtless knew much about the St Kildans from Macleod's Factor or tacksman, who made annual visits from Harris. As a student, he would walk home from Aberdeen for the holidays, and once walked to London to visit the British Museum. Given his intrepid nature, it is perhaps surprising that he never got to St Kilda.

But his son did. John was only 18 years old when he visited St Kilda in 1840. In the next issue of the prestigious *Edinburgh New Philosophical Journal,* he wrote:

> Believing that some account of a place so seldom visited, yet so interesting in every respect to the naturalist, may prove acceptable to the readers of this Journal, I have been induced to complete a series of hasty notes which were written during a few days spent in the principal island of the group.

Having been delayed by bad weather for several weeks, John MacGillivray finally procured a suitable boat and crew in Pabay, in the Sound of Harris. Although they departed at daybreak on 29 June 1840 with a strong easterly breeze in their favour, they quickly encountered fog and rain:

> As we had still 40 miles to go, without a compass, our situation became rather

unpleasant, the more so as it was judged a still greater hazard to turn back. Having proceeded another 20 miles further, we fell in with a large yacht belonging to the tacksman of St Kilda, who was on board, and like us, on his way to St Kilda. After following in the vessel's wake for some time, we eventually lost sight of her in the fog ... By this time the wind had judged to have shifted, and no landmark of course being visible, our only chance of ever making St Kilda lay in following in the course of the long strings of puffins, auks, and guillemots, and the small parties of gannets, which passed overhead almost incessantly, all flying in the same direction, or towards their home. Several fulmars were now seen for the first time, and land was judged to be not very far distant. Evening was approaching fast, and yet nothing could be seen but the monotonous expanse of waters, and the dreary fog which covered it as with a mantle. The boatmen had begun to lose all hope, and told dismal stories of boats leaving for St Kilda that had never since been heard of, and of others that had been several nights at sea, or glad to take shelter under a rock for a fortnight, as happened once to Mr MacNeil, a former tacksman. When matters were in this state, the fog partially cleared up for a few moments, and to our great joy disclosed a black-looking rock of vast height, two or three miles to windward.

Rowing with all their might, MacGillivray's crew finally entered Village Bay at midnight. A tender from a gun-brig *Prince of Wales* that had arrived with the Factor's yacht a short time earlier was despatched to ferry him ashore. MacGillivray gratefully spent the night in one of the 'huts' and began his explorations next morning. He remained only four days but recorded nearly 50 plant species (as described in Chapter 3). He noted:

> The vegetation of St Kilda, though profuse among some of the cliffs, is in general extremely stunted. It is truly surprising how so many horses, cattle, and sheep, contrive to subsist on the scanty herbage of the hill pastures, which are, moreover, in many places, nearly ruined by the quantities of turf taken away for fuel, leaving exposed the subjacent rock ... the fields of barley and oats were much farther advanced than any of those I had just left in the Long Island. It is curious, that throughout the greater part of the Outer Hebrides the small dark, barley termed *black oats* alone seems to thrive. The inhabitants of St Kilda are about 120 in number, divided into 23 families ...

After a brief description of the islanders and their way of life, MacGillivray then described the birds and the seabird harvest in some detail, more of which in Chapter 8. He then went on to describe the insect life:

> Of the entomology of St Kilda I can give but a very meagre account. Among the few Coleoptera picked up during my rambles, by far the most interesting

are *Elaphrus lapponicus* [a rare ground beetle] and *Byrrhus aeneus*, both recent acquisitions to the British Fauna. The latter occurred beneath stones in several places, the former only in some wet ground in a valley on the west side of the principal island. *Carabus catenulatus* and *granulatus* (*cancellatus* of most authors), *Elaphrus cupreus*, *Atopa cervina*, *Sclatosomus oineus*, *Ctenicerus cupreus* and *tesselatus*, and *Geotrupes sylvaticus* complete the list of coleoptera of which I preserved specimens.

Hipparchia pamphilus [small heath butterfly], *Chaoeas graminis* [antler moth] and *Plusia gamma* [silver-Y moth] were the sole representatives of the Lepidoptera that I remember having observed.

Haematopoda pluvialis [common cleg], *Chrysops caecutiens*, and an undetermined species of *Tabanus* include the principal Diptera; with the exception of *Gasterophilus equinus*, a pair of which I captured.

With the common *Panorpa communis* I may conclude this brief list of insects, some of which are, however, of considerable rarity. A diligent search would no doubt produce many more.

Having now brought to a close these cursory remarks upon St Kilda, I may mention, that after a residence of only four days I was unexpectedly forced to hurry my departure, in order to take advantage of a favourable breeze that had just sprung up. Accordingly, at noon, on Saturday the 4th July, I bade farewell to this rugged isle and its hospitable inhabitants.

MacGillivray's return voyage proved even more harrowing. The weather deteriorated again and the leaky boat had to be rowed through the night. By dawn the party had reached the Sound of Harris where they were forced to land and wait out the storm. They were unable to light a fire so MacGillivray breakfasted on brackish water and raw limpets until they could proceed onwards to Pabay, their home port.

Undaunted by his St Kilda experience, MacGillivray went on to pursue a career in natural history. From 1842 to 1846 he served as naturalist on HMS *Fly* in the South Pacific, then on HMS *Rattlesnake* for four years in the company of another eminent scientist, friend and ally of Charles Darwin, none other than Thomas Henry Huxley (1825–1895). Together they sent many Australian specimens to the British Museum and Edinburgh University Museum, continuing the work on the *Herald* between 1852 and 1863.

Whilst on St Kilda, MacGillivray had drunk from *Tobar na h'oige* – the Well of Youth – which apparently lay in a rather precipitous and dangerous situation near the landing place:

> Having tasted of the waters ... I can answer for their goodness; but, with respect to the probable longevity to be expected through their means, I can as yet say nothing.

Alas, the well on St Kilda was to prove ineffectual. In 1867, John MacGillivray died in Sydney of a lung infection at the early age of 46.

But perhaps it was not from the 'Well of Youth' that MacGillivray had supped after all, for John Sands related a St Kildan folktale about an old man struggling up Conachair with a sheep on his back. He stumbled upon a well that had never been seen or heard of before:

> The water looked like cream, and was so tempting, that he knelt down and took a hearty drink. To his surprise all the infirmities of age immediately left him, and all the vigour and activity of youth returned. He laid down the sheep to mark the spot, and ran down the hill to tell his neighbours. But when he came up again neither sheep nor well were to be found, nor has anyone been able to find the [Tobar na h-oìge] to this day. Some say that if he had left a small bit of iron at the well ... the fairies would have been unable to take back their gift.

It sounds as if this magical event could well have taken place long before MacGillivray's visit. In 1752, the Reverend Buchan mentioned how the Well of Youth was inaccessible to all but a St Kildan. Perhaps MacGillivray was confusing it with *Tobar nam Buaidh* – the Well of Virtues – in Glen Bay.

Amongst MacGillivray's four flies, only clegs *Haematopoda* have been recorded since. His horse bot fly *Gasterophilus equinus* presumably disappeared from St Kilda at the same time as horses. MacGillivray may have misidentified the other two. Of his ten most conspicuous beetles, two have not been recorded since from anywhere in the Outer Hebrides, sadly including his rare *Elaphrus lapponicus*. The names of some others have now been revised. His small heath butterfly remained the only record until another was seen in July 1991 (in the wardens' reports there is also a recent record of large heath); his other two moths are still recorded regularly.

It has been worth dwelling on MacGillivray because he was probably the first serious naturalist to visit and to describe St Kilda's flora and fauna. Indeed, his St Kilda collection constituted the first insect list for anywhere in the Outer Hebrides. In four days he also managed to list 18 species of insect. Just as with some of his plants, MacGillivray had encountered a rare ground beetle typical of mountain tops on the mainland, occurring at low levels on St Kilda.

The following year, in August 1841, the Paisley-born naturalist Reverend James Wilson (1795–1856) added to the island list. Although a member of the SSPCK, he was visiting St Kilda on behalf of the White Herring Fishery Board. Seton regarded Wilson's *Voyage Round the Coasts of Scotland and the Isles*, published in 1842, as the best account of St Kilda. Even as he arrived in the government cutter *Princess Royal*, Wilson made an interesting observation:

While entering the Eastern Bay, the very first insect which met our eyes was a small vagrant bee, which flew at a great rate across our bows, and from the slanting course which he pursued was evidently making his way from the adjacent Borrera to the main island. What was his aim or object, his hope or expectation from the flight? What 'odorous bushy shrub' had tempted him across those briny waves? ... Alas! We fear that the floral treasures of St Kilda are few and feeble, but soon after landing we fortunately found that the insect in question was not a honey-bee, but a sand one ...

Little of course is known of the entomology of St Kilda, and our own short sojourn, with so many other sights to see during its continuance, scarcely admitted of any personal observation of that department. We understand, however, from the minister, that although there were several kinds of moth, yet not a single species of diurnal lepidopterous insect, or butterfly, had ever been seen upon the island [though Wilson acknowledged MacGillivray's butterflies] ... House flies and other diptera were common. It is probable that many kinds of carcass-eating coleoptera exist in considerable quantities ... Mr Mackenzie had never seen or heard of any thing resembling either grasshopper, cockroach or cricket ... Spiders of various sorts exist, and their out of door manipulations [webs?] are found to afford a pretty sure index of the weather ...

Wilson could add little to John MacGillivray's faunal account which, in addition, had made it abundantly clear just what an adventure it was reaching St Kilda in those days. Perhaps his experiences put off many future naturalists! It was not really until the end of the 19th century and into the 20th century, when a steamer service operated to St Kilda during the summer months, that naturalists could easily venture out again. Some could stay only a few hours, others somewhat longer, while a few still preferred to let others do their collecting for them!

During an entomological tour of the Outer Hebrides in the summer of 1883, C. W. Dale landed for a few hours at St Kilda on 23 July. He collected only ten species of insects. At a meeting of the Entomological Society of London on 5 September 1888 a Dr Sharp exhibited his collection of 144 specimens of nine species of beetles (Coleoptera) from St Kilda. The Canadian-born biologist John (later Sir John) Murray (1841–1914) had been a young scientist on the *Challenger* expedition round the world's oceans from 1873 to 1876. Later, between 1897 and 1909, he engaged in a privately-funded bathymetrical survey of 562 Scottish lochs. It was while on North Uist and Benbecula that he managed three hours ashore on St Kilda early in the summer of 1904. All he could manage was to grab handfuls of wet moss from which, on his return to Lochmaddy later that day, he was able to identify 20 kinds of microscopic rotifers, tardigrades, rhizopods, nematodes and tiny algae called desmids.

But it was not until a lengthy visit by James Waterston in July 1905 that science really began to get to grips with the invertebrates of St Kilda. The Reverend James Waterston (1879–1930) was born in Paisley and had been a Free Church minister in Shetland before moving to London to take up an appointment at the Natural History Museum. He would then refer to himself as Dr Waterston. We shall encounter his younger son Rodger shortly, who also became an eminent zoologist.

On St Kilda, in 1905, James Waterston collected 17 ichneumons of nine species, three mites, 21 land and freshwater slugs and snails, three slaters, two aquatic amphipods, a hemipteran, two cestode parasites from mouse livers, three myriapods, three springtails, and so on. Earwigs and one type of ant *Myrmica ruginodis* var. *rubra* were common. Many of these mixed specimens were identified and written up by the eminent Edinburgh entomologist, botanist and ornithologist William Evans (1850–1922). None proved unusual and Evans only enthused over several large reddish-brown ticks *Ixodes borealis* from puffins and fulmars that Waterston had caught himself over the cliffs. They were also to be found under stones in the seabird colonies; the St Kildans greatly dreaded their bite. At that time, this species had never before been recorded in Scotland, and only once from England. This species has now reverted to the name *Ixodes uriae*, given when it was first described from specimens collected from guillemots at Baffin Bay in 1852.

Evans tells us that a similar species, *Ixodes puta*, had been identified from a penguin in Kerguelen Island in the Sub-Antarctic by the Reverend O. Pickard-Cambridge. It was this vicar who later examined Waterston's spiders, but again he sounded slightly disappointed to find only 29 species, none of which were new to science, and all of which were typical of mainland Britain. In fact, as we have seen, the arachnid community of St Kilda is rather interesting in its island context.

The following July (1906) C. Gordon Hewitt (1885–1920) reached St Kilda to collect insects. Hewitt had graduated and was to lecture in zoology at Manchester University, where he specialised in medical and economic entomology. He emigrated to Canada in 1909 for an illustrious career as Dominion Entomologist and Consulting Zoologist, drafting the Destructive Insect and Pest Act, instigating the Migratory Birds Treaty in 1916, and receiving the RSPB Gold Medal two years later, only to die of influenza and pneumonia at the early age of 35. His monumental *The Conservation of the Wildlife of Canada* was published posthumously in 1921. His contribution to the fauna of St Kilda seems modest when compared with his later, albeit short, career.

Hewitt admitted how:

Owing to the very bad state of the weather during the whole of my visit, it was impossible to do much collecting of insects of this order. About 40 species were obtained ...

Nor had Waterston been able to devote much attention to collecting butterflies and moths. Indeed, on such a windy island, all too often it could prove a rather fruitless exercise. One little geometrid moth, the least carpet *Eois rusticata*, proved one of Hewitt's more remarkable captures. He claimed it was by far the most common moth he encountered, although none of his specimens survive. It is now known as *Idaea vulpinaria* and has never again been recorded from St Kilda; it only occurs on the south coast of England so it is evident that Hewitt had misidentified it (Geoff Hancock, personal comment).

Despite enjoying better weather, Waterston collected only six species of moth. Small tortoise *Aglais urtica* and painted lady *Cynthia cardui* were the only butterflies he saw, forcing him to conclude:

> Any butterflies on St Kilda must, I think, be stragglers; occasionally one or more of our three common Pierids must visit or breed on the island, for a native has seen white butterflies [only one has been seen since – a green-veined white in May 1992] ... The Diptera formed by far the largest part of the insect fauna noted, In one little patch – the Marsh – they rose in swarms in hot days.

Waterston had carefully pinned over a thousand flies of 119 species which were verified for him by Percy Grimshaw (1869–1939), Keeper of Natural History at the Royal Scottish Museum in Edinburgh. Grimshaw was a colleague of Eagle Clarke's at the museum, and his obituary was written by his friend Professor James Ritchie. Amongst Waterston's dipterans Grimshaw found one specimen that had not been seen since it was first named 50 years previously; three others were new to Britain. Several could not be named, however, and may have been new species. Grimshaw noted how Waterston found conditions unusually conducive for insect life, particularly Dipterans. Flies rose in swarms on hot days, and 2,000 specimens were gathered by sweeping in quarter of an hour on one evening. Grimshaw concluded:

> All the specimens are in beautiful condition, and it is a pleasure to add that with characteristic generosity Mr Waterston is presenting a selection of them to the Royal Scottish Museum.

Together Waterston and then Hewitt had collected 66 species of beetle. Hewitt enlisted J. R. Hardy in helping with his identification. Waterston's beetles were identified by T. Hudson Beare who added Hewitt's list to his own summary published in 1908. Despite not having set foot on the islands,

Beare revisited the St Kilda beetle list in 1916 and was able to include 35 species that island children had collected for Eagle Clarke during his autumn visits in 1910 and 1911.

In 1907 and 1908, Dr Norman Joy came up with the idea of asking a visitor to St Kilda (possibly Edward Peake?) to pull up some grass and moss for him, in the hope of collecting some novel species of beetles. He was sent a very weighty sack filled with large pieces of turf, with much earth, from which he added eight beetles to St Kilda's list. He had also asked for some haystack refuse, sheep's dung and birds' nests which he described:

> It was extremely interesting examining this mass of rubbish, although some of it – the Cormorant's [sic] nest, for instance – was by no means pleasant to the olfactory nerves.

Joy's bizarre efforts proved worthwhile, however, for he identified another 49 species, some of them new to Scotland. When added to Beare's list, St Kilda could now boast 126 beetle species. It would be another 25 years before Waterston and Hewitt's surveys were matched.

In 1931, the year after the islanders' evacuation, the illustrious party of biologists from Oxford and Cambridge Universities mounted their expedition to St Kilda. It was led by David Lack (1910–1973) as ornithologist and entomologist.

Lack's lifelong passion for birds began at an early age in the marshes of rural Norfolk. In 1929, he went up to Cambridge to read zoology, but apparently did not enjoy formal academic training which contained 'nothing about evolution, ecology, behaviour or genetics, and of course nothing about birds!' However, he enlivened his dry undergraduate programme by running the Cambridge Bird Club and going on expeditions to places like Greenland and St Kilda. At the end of his fourth year, he accepted a post as biology master at Dartington Hall in Devon where he was able to indulge his love for field work, completing the classic book *The Life of the Robin*. Julian Huxley sponsored Lack to study Darwin's finches on the Galapagos archipelago over five months in 1938–9. He worked with radar during the war and was able to investigate bird migration at the same time. Ultimately, he spearheaded the famous Edward Grey Institute for Ornithology at Oxford University, where he undertook ground-breaking studies on swifts, great tits, the regulation of animal populations, island birds and much more.

His 1931 St Kilda expedition included the botanist Charles Petch (see Chapter 3), and a geologist Malcolm Stewart (1910–1989) who later wrote a useful little book about the island of North Rona, and latterly bought himself an estate on Hoy where, ultimately, he was buried. Tom Harrisson (1911–1976) and James Allan Moy-Thomas (1908–1944) were the zoologists on the expedition, specialising in mammals. Harrisson was to quit university soon after returning from St Kilda, but went on to lead a colourful and swashbuckling career in the war, while Moy-Thomas went on to become a fish paleontologist. The final member of the party was none other than John Norman Stuart Buchan, ornithologist and son of the famous novelist of the same name. As holiday reading on St Kilda he had brought with him *Silas Marner* but did not enjoy it. So he turned over every house on St Kilda, to find only one other book – written by his father! He was still not impressed and, before he left, he blew *Silas Marner* to pieces with the expedition gun! He went on to visit the Faroes with his father, served as District Commissioner in Africa, and had a year fur-trapping in the Arctic before joining the Canadian army. He succeeded to his father's title as the second Baron Tweedsmuir and in 1953 wrote a book *Always a Countryman* in which he recounted his adventures on St Kilda and elsewhere.

The Oxbridge party travelled north, to board the SS *Hebrides* at Glasgow on 16 July 1931, and reached Harris in bad weather five days later. It was little better when they set off for St Kilda early next morning, for the 7-hour sail to Village Bay. In his diary Lack wrote:

> The next hour was all confusion. There were three St Kildans in the boat, and when we landed at the pier there was a gabble of voices in Gaelic and English. The heavy food crates proved an arduous task.
>
> The boat loads of trippers now came ashore, the St Kildans duly exacting from the first boat load one shilling per person. Finding this easily paid they exacted two shillings per person from the second boat. They presented us with a bill for one pound five shillings for landing, but after much subsequent arguing we made this pay for our return journey as well. We were thus early introduced to the craving of the inhabitants for money. Of the thirty or so trippers who came ashore and saw us struggling up with vast piles of luggage, only one boy and one girl lent us a hand.

Once the bird count was completed Lack could turn to collecting insects. The party used a wooden hut behind the Factor's House as a laboratory – which apparently had been fitted up by Cockburn the geologist a few years earlier.

The three St Kildans were the legendary cragsman Finlay MacQueen (1862–1941), Lord Dumfries's bird warden Neill Gillies (1896–1989) and his mother, Anne Ferguson or Mrs John Gillies (1865–1952). Neither she nor old Finlay knew much English. Another St Kildan was Alex Ferguson (1872–1960) who was by then a successful tweed merchant in Glasgow. Ferguson was accompanied by his two sons. Yet another elderly St Kildan, Finlay Gillies (1856–1940), had just left in the *Hebrides*. For several years a few islanders would return to their old home for the summer months. The houses were dilapidated, however, and several had been broken into. Indeed, crew from a Fleetwood trawler in Village Bay had tried to make off with an old spinning wheel while Lack and his friends were on Hirta.

Once the Factor's House had been put in order, the expedition began their bird counts and Petch his botanical survey. Traps were set to catch mice.

On Sundays the party joined the St Kildans for a service in the church. Lack, a spiritual man himself, was impressed by Finlay MacQueen's Gaelic prayers. He even wrote an article about the St Kildan Sabbath for the Magdalene College magazine the following year.

On 30 July 1931 the St Kildans landed the biologists on Dun, but, due to deteriorating weather, they could remain only an hour and a half. Harrisson judged that Lundy – the Isle of Puffins – which he knew quite well, was nothing compared to St Kilda. The islanders showed the biologists how to snare fulmars and before long they were all tucking into them on a regular basis. Harrisson thought them tastier than puffins and was to comment:

Can you imagine what spring chicken injected with anchovy paste tastes like?

That night a Fleetwood trawler came into the bay.

When we were in Oban the newspapers placarded that St Kilda had been sold to an unknown ornithologist. The crew of the 'Richard Crofts' told us that the newspapers now stated Lord Durham [*sic*] had bought the island ...

A later boat verified that it was in fact Lord Dumfries who had purchased St Kilda.

On the last day of July the islanders went over to Boreray for some sheep and took Stewart and Harrisson with them. They returned with wonderful accounts of the gannetry, the largest in the world, and stated that the puffins were commoner there than on Dun.

By the next Sabbath the party had caught nine house mice and two field mice. On 7 August the party were rowed round to Soay for the day and old Finlay MacQueen led them ashore. Before they departed St Kilda on the *Dunara Castle* on 13 August, they all got a chance to return to Dun where Finlay showed Lack three Leach's petrel nests. The old man was surprised when Lack said the petrels were protected so must not be killed. Nor could the St Kildan comprehend, however, how Lack could collect flies and beetles in glass bottles.

Although Lack had not preserved quite as many flies as had Waterston, he found 40 that were new to St Kilda's list – which now totalled 153 species. He also added 11 new moths, noting painted ladies everywhere; Harrisson had also seen a red admiral.

Lack collected 63 beetles, just under half of those on the island list. The ones he missed tended to be the carrion-feeders, which he put down to a lack of livestock and dung on the island. He thought it unlikely that he would have missed some of the more colourful dung beetles and so considered they had actually become extinct. Some of his new species he thought were recent colonists. His list was also deficient in beetles that normally occurred in birds' nests, none of which he could reach. All the species he had found on Hirta and Dun were typical of the nearby mainland, except for one which he identified as the common and widespread cabbage weevil *Ceutorhynchus contractus* var. *pallipes*, a variety previously recorded from Lundy Island where it fed on wild cabbage. Both his St Kilda specimens had been collected on Dun by sweeping his net over a cliff where scurvy grass, a related brassica, was abundant.

In 1981, as part of the Royal Society of Edinburgh's Symposium on the *Natural Environment of the Outer Hebrides* (held in 1977), a major paper was published summarising the current state of knowledge about each of the islands, including St Kilda. Its author, Andrew Rodger Waterston (1912–96), had been born in Shetland, two years before his father James gave up his ministry to join the British Museum of Natural History. In 1934, Rodger gained a first-class Honours degree from Edinburgh and the following year he joined a university expedition to Barra. He then worked abroad for a time before returning to Edinburgh's Royal Scottish Museum. He became Keeper of Natural History there until he retired 15 years later. Meantime he often returned to Barra and knew the rest of the Outer Hebrides well. Waterston died in 1996, aged 84.

Rodger Waterston's monograph has indicated how certain invertebrate groups on St Kilda are now well-known, but other more obscure groups still require specialist attention. There is also a need to investigate the ectoparasites on St Kilda's resident birds and mammals. The louse *Damalinia ovis* has been recorded in the fleece of Soay sheep and recent detailed studies of the internal parasites suggest they may be implicated in the sheep's dramatic population cycles (see later Chapter 12).

In recent decades occasional summer wardens on St Kilda have taken an interest in invertebrates, but they usually choose the more familiar ones such as butterflies or the larger moths. A few have taken the time to set pitfall traps for beetles and other ground insects, or have made collections of micro-moths or spiders for instance, later to be sent to specialists for identification.

The very first Nature Conservancy warden on St Kilda was Ken Williamson (1914–1977). In 1957, he sent some St Kilda wren nests to the Hon. Miriam Rothschild who specialised in fleas. She identified seven species, three of which were amongst the five previously recorded; four more were new to the island. Three of them were rodent fleas, all from the same wren's nest, indicating that

St Kilda field mice might be in the habit of occupying disused wren's nests. Ken had also collected fleas from 207 field mice he had trapped. Half of the mice he examined yielded a total of 384 fleas – an average of two per mouse, or four per infested mouse! For some reason adult males tended to be most flea-ridden. Of the three species noted on mice, one was twice as common as the others and widespread throughout Britain. One of the other two less common species usually has a more southern distribution, being found on a few other Scottish islands from Shetland to Arran but not on the Scottish mainland.

These were not the first fleas to be noted in St Kilda. In 1930, Alasdair Alpin Macgregor wrote:

> The common or garden flea is familiar with the flesh of the St Kildans. But during my stay I arrested only a couple of these marauders. This is a poor record for me, since I accredit myself with being one of the most proficient flea-catchers in the land. Fleas make for me immediately I enter the house in which they reside. I have been known to rob a respectable dwelling of its only flea. Fleas seem to love me. Even in the cleanest church they find their way to me before the service terminates.
>
> The comparative scarcity of fleas on St Kilda, I should think, may be due more to the lasting influences of fulmar oil than to over-cleanliness on the part of the natives. Fulmar oil is more efficient than Keating's powder.

Amongst those who have collected invertebrate records on St Kilda are J. D. Hamilton (freshwater fauna – June/July 1956), Eric Duffey (spiders – June 1959), E. C. Pelham-Clinton (July 1959), D. R. Gifford (July 1960), H. A. Russell (Diptera – June 1961), Malcolm Smith (1961–3), Sandy Tewnion (arachnids – July/August 1962), D. I. Chapman (ants, woodlice – August 1963), Lewis Davies and John Richardson (July 1970), Mike Brooke (bristletails – July 1971), Iain MacGowan (July 1980), Andrew Buckham (June 1981), Nigel Buxton (July–September 1993), Dick Hendry (May 1994), Jim Vaughan (pitfall trapping – summer 1994), Geoff Hancock (June 2004), Hellen Dyer (July 2004), Geoff Hancock and Jeanne Robinson (June 2005) and Peter Brotherton (August 2005). Wardens Peter Duncan, Jim Vaughan, Stuart Murray and Andy Robinson have all been especially diligent in recording Lepidoptera in particular. Neil Duncan, Dave Bullock and Kenny Taylor were able to make a unique collection on Boreray between 8 and 15 July 1980.

Undoubtedly, naturalists will continue to add further species to the lists presented here in Table 1, a goal that adds to the attraction of visiting St Kilda. In March 1994, the Inverness entomologist Stephen Moran submitted a detailed report to Scottish Natural Heritage analysing pitfall results from the

PLATE 1. Hirta and Dun, St Kilda, from the air. (Scottish Natural Heritage)

LATE 2. A bathymetric diagram of the sea floor around St Kilda in July 2000 – yellow, red and urple lie above the surface indicating the positions of Dun, Hirta and Soay at the top right, Boreray to the left. The circular outline of the submarine volcanic caldera can be made out in light rey linking the islands together, with shallower water in the collapsed centre of the volcano. Scottish Natural Heritage)

PLATE 3. An SNH marine survey boat braves a storm on the way to Boreray. (Scottish Natural Heritage)

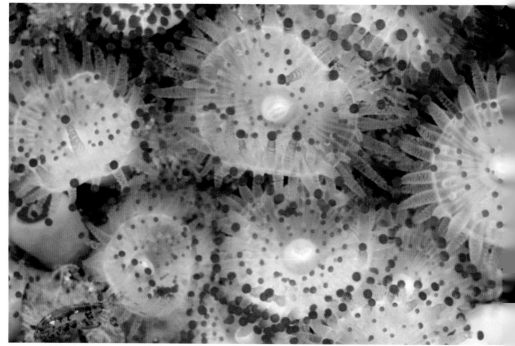

PLATE 4. Jewel anemones underwater. (Scottish Natural Heritage)

PLATE 5. A mosaic of marine creatures on an underwater rock face off St Kilda. (Scottish Natural Heritage)

LATE 6. An orca family in waters off St Kilda in June 2008. (J. Love)

PLATE 7. Looking across Village Bay, Hirta, in 1956, before the Army Base was built. (J Morton Boyd/Scottish Natural Heritage)

PLATE 8. The smoky village street on Hirta. (J. Love)

PLATE 9. Tan-coloured ewe with dark twins on Hirta. (J. Love)

PLATE 10. A young Soay lamb. (J. Love)

PLATE 11. The extinct St Kilda house mouse as painted by Archibald Thorburn.

PLATE 12. St Kilda field mouse. (J. Love)

PLATE 13. A yellow morph of the rare weevil *Ceutorhynchus insularis*. (Geoff Hancock)

PLATE 14. A St Kilda wren on Hirta. (J. Love)

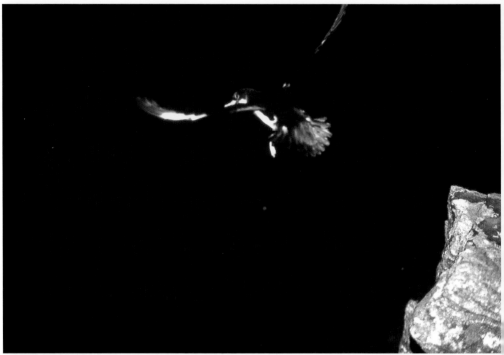

PLATE 15. A Manx shearwater taking off at night. (J. Love)

PLATE 16. A Leach's petrel caught under licence for ringing. (J. Love)

collection made by Nigel Buxton and other Scottish Natural Heritage staff the previous summer. Stephen's report included a useful annotated bibliography of the non-marine invertebrates of St Kilda. At the time, he considered that St Kilda had had a fairly balanced coverage of its invertebrate groups, making it one of the best known faunas in the Western Isles. While Hirta probably boasts a respectable invertebrate list, more work is required on its other, less accessible islands and stacs.

Geoff Hancock of the Hunterian Museum in Glasgow is currently compiling a more complete invertebrate list for St Kilda. He took an early interest in Lack's two tiny weevils from Dun. Lack had considered them a rare form of an otherwise widespread species of cabbage weevil. A species first discovered at Surtsey in 1968, five years after the volcano had erupted from the sea, was described as new to science in 1971 by Dieckmann, who named it *Ceutorhynchus insularis*. Lack's two examples were then re-examined and judged to be the same new species.

In June 2004, Geoff Hancock found *C. insularis* in Glen Bay on Hirta (Plate 13), where, as anticipated, the grubs were mining into the fleshy leaves of scurvy grass. This plant, of course, is not a grass but related to the cabbage, and was relished by sailors as a rich source of vitamin C. And, indeed, Geoff could confirm that none of his weevil grubs suffered from scurvy! Later the same year Hellen Dyer found more specimens on Dun where Lack had originally recorded it. Two more St Kilda specimens found in the National Museum of Scotland, Edinburgh, were collected on Dun by the Nature Conservancy warden Malcolm Smith in 1963. Geoff Hancock returned in June 2005 and August 2006 with Jeanne Robinson from the Kelvingrove Museum in Glasgow. They collected mined leaves from Glen Bay on Hirta from which some 150 adults would later hatch in the laboratory.

The St Kilda and Surtsey beetles are closely related to the species common on the mainland, *Ceutorhynchus contractus*, and to another population var. *pallipes* on Lundy in the Bristol Channel – all being about 2 mm in length. About half of Robinson and Hancock's sample were black in colour, typical of the mainland form, the rest varying from brown with yellowish legs (similar to the Lundy form) to entirely yellow. The St Kilda specimens, however, have shorter wings than *C. contractus*, fitting beneath the wing cases or elytra without folding and they are thus incapable of flight. Such an adaptation, termed brachyptery, reduces the risk of the *C. insularis* weevils being blown away and may also reduce water loss in the desiccating winds. There is also evidence from other beetles that brachypterous individuals breed better and earlier.

Although sample sizes are yet small, it may be that the St Kilda weevil is adapting to its isolation in such an extreme environment, just as the mice and wrens have done. Brachyptery and colour variability, however, may not be features robust enough to warrant specific status. Genetic studies have not revealed any difference at the molecular level between the mainland, St Kildan and Icelandic weevils. Recent research at Leeds University, however, has revealed genetic differences in those found on Lundy. Since cabbages were once cultivated on Hirta, there is the possibility that this rare little weevil was introduced by humans, but its appearance on Surtsey would seem to confirm that it may have arrived naturally.

Compared with its bird fauna, however, there are still clear gaps and much yet remains to be discovered about the entomology of this fascinating archipelago. While new species are continually being added, the changes in the invertebrate fauna since the evacuation is lagging behind what we know of the vegetation. In contrast, we do know a lot about the birds of St Kilda, but as to how the avian community came to colonise the archipelago in the first place we can only draw inferences from elsewhere. Once again Surtsey provides a unique, and a convenient, opportunity, as the old Icelandic poem seems to be suggesting:

> In the dim, the sky will be rent asunder,
> and the sons of Muspell ride forth from it.
> Surtur will ride first and with him fire.
>
> 'Voluspa', 10th-century Icelandic poem

Not surprisingly, gulls were the first living creatures to set foot on the volcanic island of Surtsey and they have continued to frequent its shores ever since. Kittiwakes may even have ventured ashore to roost whilst the eruptions were still occurring. The gulls caught prey at sea and brought it to land to be consumed or else fed on carcases washed up on the beach. Such food remains have added to the island's organic food sources and to its nutrient status. In addition, bird guano provided fertiliser, especially along the cliffs and beaches, or on the summit of prominences further inland.

Birds, not just gulls but other migrant birds, have also played a part in bringing plant seed and tiny animals to the island. Nearly half of all the 250 or so bird species so far recorded in Iceland have turned up on Surtsey at some time or another. Following the first gull flocks, a group of migratory redwing was seen early in the spring of 1964, and a snow bunting appeared soon afterwards. In October 1964, a single turtle dove arrived and could perhaps have made a useful contribution to the island's flora if it had come all the way from Europe with a full crop.

But the greatest ornithological event occurred in the summer of 1970 when a pair of fulmars built a nest on a small cliff and some black guillemots nested in a lava crevice. Their breeding numbers have continued to increase ever since.

It was not until 1996 that gulls and kittiwakes began to nest. That same year a snow bunting was also seen feeding young, the first land bird to establish.

Birds are undoubtedly the most accomplished aeronauts of all. All those millions of years ago, when St Kilda first erupted, no birds had yet evolved on earth. Flying reptiles, such as pterodactyls, might well have dominated its skies instead! Ten or fifteen thousand years ago, however, after the Ice Age ended, birds were abundant and it is highly likely that they would have been the first creatures to set foot on St Kilda. Indeed, more than likely – as on Surtsey – these would have been seabirds.

.5.

Seabirds 1

In this respect nature has been as bountiful to St Kilda as to any spot on the globe. The countless millions which perpetually swarm around the principal island and the smaller adjacent isles, literally darken the air.

J. MacDonald 1811.

ANYONE VOYAGING to St Kilda is conscious of a constant passage of seabirds flying to and from the island – that is, if one is not unconscious with seasickness! Martin Martin was no exception:

By this time we were so far advanced in the Ocean ... this obliged us to make the best of our way for St Kilda, though labouring under the disadvantages of wind and tide. Our crew extremely fatigued and discouraged without sight of land for sixteen hours; at length one of them discovered several tribes of the fowls of St Kilda, flying, holding their course ...

They followed the birds and at last found St Kilda. In fact, Martin Martin's party was to be unusual amongst most subsequent visitors in finding Boreray first. They had to take shelter under its massive cliffs, constantly splattered by the multitude of seabirds circling overhead. Most voyagers enter directly into Village Bay – always with a sense of relief, sick or not – where vast seabird cliffs are not immediately obvious. In the summer of 1884, for example, the London naturalist Charles Dixon (1858–1926) was quite disappointed:

When I landed scarcely a sea-bird was to be seen, save a few Puffins and Gulls in the bay; the great bird-nurseries are away behind the frowning hills, where the cliffs fall almost sheer down to the water, and on the adjoining islands and 'stack'.

In 1896, the naturalist/photographer Richard Kearton (1862–1928) had a similar reaction:

> The first two things which struck me upon landing at St Kilda were the apparent dearth of seabird life and the joyous songs of the Wrens.

Again, in 1914, Mary, Duchess of Bedford (1865–1937) seemed unimpressed as she sailed into St Kilda on her steam yacht *Sapphire*:

> Having read of St Kilda as the resort of myriads of sea-fowl – ie kittiwakes, razorbills, guillemots and puffins – I was somewhat surprised to find that, with the exception of the last, they were by no means so plentiful as I had expected ... On the whole, the cliffs do not seem to have the type of ledges they require for nesting. The greater part of them consists of small grass slopes and short precipitous rock faces, far better adapted to fulmars and puffins than to guillemots and razorbills. I have seen kittiwakes nesting on similar cliffs, but possibly the atmosphere of fulmar is too strong for them at St Kilda.
>
> There are more of the cliff-breeding birds on the south side of Dun than any other part of the islands that I visited, but I did not go round Soay.

Soon after this the *Sapphire* was commandeered for use during the war, while the Duchess ran her own private hospital near her home. In her sixties this remarkable woman took up flying. She died on a solo flight over East Anglia in March 1937.

From Village Bay one needs to scan Dun carefully to realise just how many puffins are in fact wheeling around, or sitting in rafts just offshore. Hirta's main fulmar colonies lie largely out of sight, on the far side of the island. Furthermore, even the hidden bird cliffs of Hirta do not offer the same spectacle as Soay, or Boreray and its Stacs. So it is not surprising that, on arrival, few visitors have registered awe at St Kilda's seabird cliffs. The Duchess's suggestion that the smell of fulmar put off the kittiwakes is a novel one! Fulmars have since spread all around the coast of Britain but have not deterred other cliff-nesters.

It is the sheer scale of St Kilda's cliffs that dwarf any living thing upon them. George Clayton Atkinson (1808–1877) put it so well when he visited in 1831:

> With regard to the scenery of this group of islands, it is so decidedly unlike anything else I have seen, that I scarcely know how to venture on the description ... To convey in writing any idea of size requires some similar object to refer and compare with ... I have seen much very fine scenery, but never anything so vast and imposing ... I know no rocks which it would not be absolutely ridiculous to select for the purpose of comparison.

Fig. 8. James Fisher
(J. MacGeoch).

I have said the Islands St Kilda and Boreray rise from the sea perpendicularly, nearly on every side, and they each in some places present to the eye an unbroken precipice of nearly 1400 feet in height. If it be remembered that Arthur's Seat near Edinburgh ... is far from being an insignificant object, yet is only about 800 feet in elevation: let it be conceived how imposing a mass must be presented by an island in the open sea, rising almost perpendicularly in gigantic grandeur to a height so much greater ... when human beings are suspended and crawling among these cliffs, our faculties are scarcely able to distinguish their diminished forms in the chaos of rocks which surround them.

A keen naturalist since boyhood, Atkinson was a founder member of his local society in Northumberland, and was a friend of the accomplished engraver Thomas Bewick (1753–1828). His travels resulted in meetings with the eminent zoologist Professor William MacGillivray and the botanist Dr William Hooker. Atkinson went on to become the first Curator of Birds at the Hancock Museum in Newcastle. His large leather-bound journals, richly embellished with watercolours and drawings, remained with his family until a great-grandson, Dennis, lent them to his friend, the ornithologist James Fisher.

Fisher, with his passion for St Kilda, carefully typed out the handwritten account, but died in a car accident before he could do much with it. Edited by David Quine, it was finally published in 2001 in a handsome volume entitled *Expeditions to the Hebrides*. This book appends a lecture about St Kilda that Atkinson had delivered to his Natural History Society in January 1832. Preceding the scientist John MacGillivray by nine years, Atkinson might be considered the first serious naturalist to visit St Kilda, the first of a long distinguished line.

George Clayton Atkinson was only 23 when he set off to explore the Hebrides and St Kilda, accompanied by his brother Dick and the artist William Train. They hired an 18-ft boat in Harris for £5 and set out with three crew on the evening of 30 May 1831. Atkinson commented:

> I will not say that the voyage is entirely without danger, for St Kilda is so exposed to the Atlantic, that only vessels capable of riding at anchor in safety on its heavy swell, or small enough to be hauled up on the beach on arrival, are safe to go in.

Passenger 'facilities' were bundles of straw to sleep on, a sack of oatmeal, a peat fire in an iron pot and five or six bottles of whisky. Luckily it proved a beautiful moonless night and they arrived an hour before noon the next morning. The Reverend Neil Mackenzie met them and offered them both hospitality and guidance.

Two islanders took the party to the summit of Conachair and descended the cliff to collect some fulmar and puffin eggs for them. A dozen others rowed them to Boreray next day and made the landing look so easy. From the summit Atkinson looked down on the gannet colony:

> ... which is a most extraordinary sight; but one of the chasms of the precipice they frequent forms what I conceive to be the most striking object on the island. It is in a part where the elevation is greatest, and though the size of the square gap it forms is immense, it here looks like a large chimney, and is unexceptionally one of the most sublime things I ever saw.

Before the party set off for home, two St Kildan youths procured for Atkinson two young peregrines from a cliff eyrie of four chicks. They paused under Conachair to collect the carcases of seabirds thrown into the sea by a party of young islanders who had been fowling there all day:

> Here we had the opportunity of seeing in perfection their feats of climbing, on the loftiest precipice in Great Britain.

The awesome scene is captured in a wonderful painting by William Train, which is included in the 2001 book (page 65). But as if this was not enough, the islanders demonstrated their true skill next day on Stac Biorach, only 240 ft high, but the ultimate climbing challenge even for St Kildans – all for the price of some tobacco and a glass of whisky each. As they drew near, some of the crew appeared to change their minds until a lad of 18 jumped and exclaimed how:

> It should never be said by the strangers that they were inferior to their fathers in skill and courage, and that if anyone would accompany him, he would lead the way. He was immediately joined by another lad of the same age, and the boat was again brought to the foot of the rock.

It was Roderick MacDonald who tied a rope around his waist and leapt ashore. He skilfully gained a footing and, once past the most dangerous point, hoisted up his companion John Macdonald. While the intrepid pair ascended to harvest guillemots, the boat went over to land on Soay. Atkinson was keen to acquire some Manx shearwater eggs. After a quick lunch of cold lamb, the party returned to pick up the young fowlers on Stac Biorach and the considerable fruits of their heroic efforts. Atkinson and his companions, including the minister and John Macdonald, opted to be landed in Glen Bay and walk home, while the weary islanders rowed back round the island.

Atkinson's own boatmen then had to row his party back to Harris overnight since the weather threatened to deteriorate. It held off however, so Atkinson could relieve the tedium of an uneventful journey by blowing his egg collection, feeding the two peregrine chicks and relieving his exhausted crew at the oars. Dining on oatcakes and St Kilda cheese, they had another night in the boat before reaching Harris.

Atkinson had undoubtedly made the most of his brief visit – facilitated no doubt by his own likeable personality and by his willing guide, the Reverend Neil Mackenzie. At various times and on all sorts of scraps of paper, the good reverend noted down lengthy and informative observations on the birds, as well as, of course, about their exploitation by the islanders. We will refer to these further, suffice it here to quote a few sentences on the puffin, which:

> ... is by far the most numerous of all the birds which frequent these islands. There is not a suitable spot anywhere which does not swarm with them. Everywhere you see them in thousands, while at the same time the air is full of them coming and going.

Atkinson added:

> Puffins do not, generally speaking, affect such inaccessible places, the sloping side of any of the islands, or the mixture of rock and grass at the top of the precipices

affording them either natural holes or crannies to deposit their eggs in, or a loose soft soil fit for their excavations ...

The well-vegetated coastal cliffs of St Kilda do indeed offer abundant nesting opportunities for burrow-nesting puffins, as well as shearwaters and Leach's storm petrels. Storm petrels seem to prefer rock crevices, even in walls and drystone structures. The extensive rocky cliffs provide ideal ledges for breeding guillemots and razorbills, broad ledges for the former and usually nooks and crannies for the latter. Kittiwakes utilise more precipitous sites by building cup-shaped nests of mud, seaweed and guano. Shags and black guillemots prefer boulder fields and scree slopes, or in caves near the foot of cliffs. It is this variety and profusion of suitable nest sites, as well as its proximity to rich feeding grounds, that contribute to St Kilda's being Britain's premier seabird station.

Indeed, St Kilda is one of the largest and most important seabird stations in the North Atlantic. In summer it is frequented by a million seabirds, both breeders and non-breeders – not quite the 'countless millions' that MacDonald surmised in 1811. Modern surveys state this to be some 330,000 breeding pairs of 17 species.

Five of these 17 seabirds are abundant enough to be important in British context. A third of Britain's gannets nest on St Kilda and a quarter of our puffins, although Icelandic and Norwegian totals are larger. The archipelago also has 13 per cent of our fulmars, our oldest and largest single colony. Most of the Leach's petrels in the eastern Atlantic breed in St Kilda, many more than in Norway, Faroe or Iceland, although fewer than the North American total. European storm petrels are scarcer on St Kilda than we might expect, but, nonetheless, are still important in a British context.

The whole assemblage of breeding birds that is St Kilda is of course now acknowledged worldwide. Amongst their multitude three species were especially important to the very survival of the St Kildans, as Charles Dixon testified in 1885:

> Sea-birds form the staple food of the people of this remote island; the Puffin, the Fulmar, and the Gannet are the favourites. These birds are caught in enormous numbers and salted down for future use, the feathers and oil being exported.

The eggs of guillemots and razorbills were also important, but we will devote this chapter to fulmar, gannet and puffin. Chapter 6 will deal with the remaining seabirds. The now extinct great auk merits a chapter to itself, as does the seabird harvest of the islanders.

One of the first modern ornithologists to recognise the ornithological importance of St Kilda was James Fisher (1912–70) who long nurtured a consuming interest in St Kilda, its seabirds and in the fulmar and gannet particularly. His father had encouraged his early interest in natural history and after an Oxford University expedition to Spitzbergen in 1933, James switched from the study of medicine to zoology.

He became the first secretary of the embryonic British Trust for Ornithology, where he encouraged the first national censuses of rooks and fulmars. He went on to participate in over a thousand broadcasts about various aspects of natural history, birds and islands in particular. In addition, he wrote or co-authored about 40 books, including a biography of the Antarctic explorer Ernest Shackleton (1958) with his wife Margery. One of his first books, *Watching Birds* (1939), sold over three million copies. Fisher was one of the party of three who took official possession of Rockall for Britain in 1955, an event that is described in his book of the same name published the following year.

Fisher was a founding editor of the acclaimed, long-running series of *New Naturalist* volumes in which his 500-page monograph *The Fulmar* remains a classic to this day. This was followed by another in the series, *Seabirds*, with Ronald Lockley (1954). He was working on yet another monograph on the gannet and a book titled *Birds of St Kilda* when he was killed in a car crash in 1970, aged 58.

Fisher had paid a first brief visit to St Kilda on 1 June 1939 aboard the ocean-going ketch *Escape* with fellow naturalists Julian Huxley (1887–1975) and Max Nicholson (1904–2003). Huxley went on to an eminent career in science, while Nicholson became Director-General of the Nature Conservancy. Fisher returned in mid-June 1947 in Robert Atkinson's boat *Heather*, departing the Sound of Harris exactly 250 years to the day from Martin Martin's pioneering voyage. He was back the following year as co-leader, with Fraser Darling, of Edinburgh University's expedition. He called in yet again in 1949, having failed to land on Rockall with the *Petula*. After finally stepping ashore on Rockall in 1955 with the Royal Navy (to ensure new territorial limits for Britain and its impending rocket range on South Uist), he became involved in the establishment of St Kilda as a National Nature Reserve in 1957. Thus, along with his extensive researches into the history of the islands, he was well qualified as a guide on the *Devonia* when the cruise ship called at St Kilda in 1966 with delegates from the 14th International Ornithological Congress.

As Fisher confessed in the foreword to *The Fulmar* in 1952:

> This book is the result of an obsession. I have been haunted by the fulmar for half my life; and have needed no spur to explore its history, and uncover its mysteries, save the ghost-grey bird itself, and green islands in grey seas ... Since 1933 I have lived no summer season without sight of at least some of the great cliffs and fulmar colonies of Spitzbergen, Iceland, Shetland, Orkney, St Kilda ...

One whole chapter in his monograph is devoted to the fulmar on St Kilda, acknowledging its supreme importance to the islanders. He then follows with a detailed history of its subsequent spread across the North Atlantic. St Kilda is the oldest known colony of fulmars in the eastern Atlantic, the birds apparently being present on St Kilda since the 9th century. Indeed, Fisher mentioned archaeological evidence suggesting a much older presence. Although the species began its rapid occupation of the rest of the British coastline in 1878, the unique provenance of the St Kilda fulmar continued to be recognised by Hebrideans into the 21st century. In the west of Lewis the species was known as *calman Hirteach* – the St Kilda pigeon – while fishermen in Grimsay, North Uist, knew it as *guga Hirteach* – the St Kilda fatling, implying a taste for its flesh.

In 1831, George Clayton Atkinson had recorded how the fulmar:

… is almost peculiar to the island; with the exception of a few among the precipices of the south isles of Barra, and some of the Shetland Isles, they are almost unknown as birds which breed in Great Britain: here [viz. St Kilda] fulmars are in vast numbers.

However, in his book *The Birds of the West of Scotland* (1871) Robert Gray (1825–87) commented that fulmars had not been known to breed on the Barra Isles (Mingulay and Berneray) since 1844. While acknowledging the contribution of Robert Gray to Scottish ornithology, Harvie-Brown and Buckley in their own encyclopaedic *A Vertebrate Fauna of the Outer Hebrides* (1888) were quick to point out:

[Gray's] personal experience of the Outer Hebrides was confined to two or three short visits made in his business capacity as bank inspector, and a fortnight's detention in North Uist, and that, therefore, his book must be looked upon, as regards the area with which we are now dealing, as almost entirely a compilation, unverified by personal experience.

Robert Gray never visited St Kilda and Fisher preferred to treat Atkinson's unsubstantiated reference to fulmars in the Barra Isles with caution. No fulmars would be found breeding there until 1899. Fisher recognised how, between 1816 and 1839, fulmars had arrived in the Faroe Islands from Iceland 430 miles away. Here they quickly multiplied. He took their first appearance in Britain, outside St Kilda, to be 1878. However, he did acknowledge this date as the first year in which fulmars were *proved* to breed – in Foula in Shetland – although some must have been prospecting around the cliffs some years earlier.

It is appropriate that these twelve initial pairs on Foula chose to nest on The Kame, which vies with Conachair on St Kilda as the highest sea cliff in Britain.

Of course, that does not mean that these first pioneers were attracted there from a similar precipice on St Kilda. There are plenty of equally spectacular cliffs, some much higher, in the Faroes. Here the fulmars were still increasing in number at a time when Fisher considered the fulmar population on St Kilda to be relatively stable. So the new arrivals on Foula probably had indeed derived from Faroe 180 miles (288 km) away. Within a couple of decades there were said to be 'multitudes' of fulmars on the cliffs of Foula. Since fulmars take at least five or six years to breed and only produce a single egg each year, such an increase could not have come from local recruits alone but from further new arrivals from Faroe.

In 1886, Richard Barrington saw a fulmar flying around the cliffs of North Rona, 160 miles (256 km) from Faroe and 150 miles (240 km) from Foula. The following year his friend J. A. Harvie-Brown saw several more, one of which was sitting on a ledge but it did not have an egg. By 1894, fulmars still did not appear to be that plentiful on Rona, but at least one pair was incubating. Thereafter the numbers increased.

John Alexander Harvie-Brown (1844–1916) had inherited the family estate at Dunipace in Stirlingshire where he was a popular and genial host, active in public life. Having private means he was able to indulge in his passions for fishing, shooting and natural history. He was an obsessive collector, though sadly his private museum was destroyed in a fire in 1897. With his private yacht *Shiantelle* he was able to visit the more remote Hebrides, though his first of several visits to St Kilda in 1877 was in an Irish government cutter. He died aged 72, having published some 250 titles, not least his monumental series of *Vertebrate Faunas* of Scotland (Love 1982).

It was Harvie-Brown who in 1912 first documented the spread of fulmars in Britain, from a study of the literature as well as through prodigious correspondence with islanders, lighthouse keepers, ornithologists, etc. – a technique he was always to utilise to maximum effect. James Fisher initiated a similar but more ambitious survey in 1934, putting a young Edinburgh ornithologist George Waterston (1911–80) in charge. Together, they collated the results, incorporating information from some 172 correspondents. Fisher commented:

> I came into the partnership with great enthusiasm for the subject, an enthusiasm which has now become a (mild – I hope) mania.

Their joint paper was published in the *Journal of Animal Ecology* in 1941, by which time Waterston was in a German prisoner-of-war camp. When repatriated due to ill health, the first place Waterston sighted from the hospital ship was Fair Isle in Shetland, which he went on to purchase and where he established the famous bird observatory. George never enjoyed the best of

Fig. 9.
John Alexander
Harvie-Brown
(National Museum
of Scotland).

health, but went on to a hugely influential career as Scottish Director of the Royal Society for the Protection of Birds.

Fulmars first bred on Fair Isle in 1903. Although Foula is only 100 km away, fulmars first colonised the west and north coasts and islands of Shetland before reaching Fair Isle further to the south. Now, of course, the species nests all round the coast of the British Isles, increasing at about 4 per cent per annum during the last century. St Kilda remains the largest colony. With nearly 47,000 pairs in 1988, Foula was, until recent declines throughout Shetland, the second largest colony of fulmars in Britain.

Concluding his careful study of the spread of fulmars, Harvie-Brown then offered a theory as to why the species underwent such a population explosion:

Of their decided and very marked increase at St Kilda, however, we wish just to say, that the fact seems perfectly established by the evidence of eye-witnesses, amongst whom particularly may be mentioned Mr. Mackenzie of Dunvegan, Skye, who, in his capacity of factor to The Macleod, has long been an annual visitor to the group. He speaks to the evident and considerable increase of the birds since the natives have in great measure ceased to utilise such large numbers for food, i.e. since the place has been more regularly visited by the SS. 'Dunara Castle' and other vessels of the west coast service, and by the trawlers and Norwegian whalers that use St Kilda as a harbour of refuge, etc. The visits of the 'Dunara Castle' date back to the year 1877.

The biologist Professor James Ritchie was an Aberdeen graduate working in the Royal Scottish Museum, who in 1930 was appointed to the Chair of Zoology at Aberdeen and then six years later at Edinburgh. He took up Harvie-Brown's idea and, carelessly, once happened to mention in conversation how he thought that:

> ... the cause of the extraordinary spread of the Fulmar Petrel ... was due in the first place to the importation of tinned food to St Kilda!

In an article entitled 'Some Considerations on Bird Fluctuation' published in the *Scottish Naturalist* in 1929, Father J. M. McWilliam of Govan denounced this 'ingenious suggestion' as trivial, more deserving a medal for the most futile of speculations.

The following year, in the same journal, Dr Ritchie went on to defend his statement. He noted how Martin estimated 20,000 gannets being killed annually, while the Reverend Kenneth MacAulay considered the fulmar to be the mainstay of the islanders' seabird harvest instead. Since the fulmar was a smaller bird than the gannet, the islanders must have killed more of them to sustain themselves. Then, as the human population diminished and was obtaining supplementary food supplies from visiting ships after 1877, the pressure of hunting on the fulmar would have been reduced considerably:

> There appears to be more than coincidence in the dates. The final impetus which drove the Fulmar to seek new breeding sites was the lack of nesting accommodation on St Kilda and its sister isles, due to the cumulative increase of the birds themselves, and that followed in the last instance from the sparing of thousands of birds annually because the St Kildans turned from their old food to the new food brought within their knowledge and their reach ...
>
> When I said that tinned food drove the Fulmar on its exodus from St Kilda round our coasts, I did not mean that the sight of the tins or the smell of their contents scared the birds from their ancient home. I used 'tinned food' as a shorthand and picturesque symbol of the food-stuffs of modern civilisation.

To be fair, it is hard to believe that Father McWilliam would not have been aware of that. In his monograph James Fisher chose to express utter disdain for Harvie-Brown and Ritchie's theory:

> This statement has done a great deal of damage. Most of it is untrue, and the rest special pleading. It has deceived a generation of writers, among them Ritchie (1930). It was resisted by few, notably Wiglesworth and McWilliam. The remarks

of Mr. Mackenzie of Dunvegan appear to be completely without foundation. The natives did not cease to use fulmars as food; their own population remained stable; the number killed per head remained stable. And there is no indication that the fulmar numbers changed on St Kilda while the fowlers were in full activity, or after the marked reduction of the human population (in 1921) or immediately after the evacuation (1930). (It was not until 17 years after the evacuation that there was evidence of significant change) ... If the *Dunara Castle* ever brought any 'tinned food', the St Kildans certainly could not afford to buy it.

Instead Fisher offered a plausible alternative for this dramatic increase in numbers in the North Atlantic, ultimately to colonise virtually the entire British coastline. He considered their habit of scavenging behind whaling and fishing boats offered a whole new food supply. The St Kildan fulmars may never have been as dependent upon marine discards which may be why their numbers have long remained so static. Others now dispute this, one camp suggesting some genetic factor in the fulmar population may have been involved, with another considering that change in sea temperatures has increased food supplies.

In 1697, Martin Martin was astounded how St Kilda:

... abounds with an infinite number of fowl, such as Fulmar, Lavy [guillemot], Falk [razorbill], Bowger [puffin], etc.

He made no attempt to count them although he offered extensive notes on their biology and behaviour. His use of the word 'fulmar' seems to be a first for the English language. Captain Henry Elwes, visiting St Kilda on 22 May 1868, offered this interesting appendum to the name:

... which is pronounced here as a word of three syllables, 'Ful-a-mair' is the only case I know of, beside the ptarmigan and capercally, in which our common English name is taken from the Gaelic.

But back to Martin's observations on the fulmar:

It lays its egg commonly the first, second, or third day of May, which is larger than that of a Solan goose [gannet] egg, of a white colour, and very thin, the shell so very tender that it breaks in pieces if the season proves rainy, when the egg is once taken away it lays no more that year like other fowl; the young ones are hatched in the middle of June, and are ready to take wing before the twentieth of July ... and is the only sea –fowl that stays here all year, except for the month of September, and part of October.

At first Fisher was puzzled by Martin's dates until he remembered that the Julian calendar had been corrected to the Gregorian in 1752 by adding 11 days.

But Fisher was wrong in persisting with only 11 days when he wrote his book; things have moved on from 1752, so nowadays 13 days have to be added. A 14th will be added in the year 2100.

The Reverend Neil MacKenzie's breeding dates followed Martin:

> It begins to lay early in May, and does not select for its nest the more inaccessible rocks, but prefers those places where there are steep grassy slopes with tufts of earth or sorrel. It frequents every slope of this description, numerously in the island of Soay and St Kilda [Hirta], and sparingly in the Boreray group, which are frequented by the Gannet.

Astutely, he came to this very interesting first estimate of fulmar numbers:

> In a season when the circumstances are favourable a large number of these young birds are killed [by the islanders]. On an average twelve thousand will be killed as they are about ready to leave the nest. I estimate that the average number of young fulmars hatched will be about twenty thousand. These represent forty thousand parents. There are also a large number of birds which either do not find suitable partners or are confirmed celibates, bringing up the total to about fifty thousand. These will take with them about eight thousand young birds when they leave, which seems to be sufficient to keep up their numbers and no more.

Presumably Mackenzie's figure referred to the whole archipelago and seems remarkably coincident with first estimates by later ornithologists. Furthermore, he is implying that the St Kildans' fulmar harvest might well have been self-sustaining. All this information was especially valuable since St Kilda was still the only place in Britain where one could study fulmars, as John MacGillivray appreciated in 1840:

> On the 30th June, having partially descended a nearly perpendicular precipice 600 feet in height ... the whole face of which was covered with the nests of the fulmar, I enjoyed an opportunity of observing the habits of this birds, which has fallen to the lot of few of those who have described them, as if from personal observation.

Now the challenge was to find out exactly how many fulmars did live on St Kilda. Given the scale of the island and its hazards, this was not to be achieved lightly. Apart from the Reverend Neil Mackenzie's educated estimate of 20,000 pairs, apparently the first census of fulmars on St Kilda was not attempted until a century later by David Lack's party in 1931. In their paper 'The Breeding Birds of St Kilda' (1934) Harrisson and Lack – strangely – did not actually quote any figure at all. But it was Tom Harrisson who later wrote to James Fisher for his monograph:

By a series of cliff counts and section transects I estimated that there were about 25,500 pairs.

Harrisson had only a few hours ashore on Boreray and Soay. Similarly, in 1939, Fisher, Huxley and Nicholson had only a few days on St Kilda, but they employed their ketch *Escape* to view parts of the archipelago they were not able to see from clifftop vantage points. Acknowledging any dead ground they could not see, they estimated a minimum of 20,780 pairs. In 1947, as one of Darling's party, Fisher revised this to 30,000 or more. The next census by James Fisher was while his monograph was in press. In May 1949, from a boat, he could manage to count only Hirta; he totalled 19,943 pairs.

Sandy Anderson managed to spend a week on St Kilda in mid-July 1956. Involved with Dr George Dunnet (1928–95) of Aberdeen University in setting up a long-term scientific study of breeding fulmars on Eynhallow in Orkney, Sandy was already familiar with fulmars, and how to count them. He meticulously divided the coastline of Hirta into sections to facilitate counting from the cliff top and these divisions are still being employed to this day. He estimated 37,000 pairs in the whole archipelago, with 19,415 or 52 per cent of them on Hirta. Sandy was able to repeat his count in 1961, again in mid-July, but only on Hirta: his total came to 19,716 pairs.

In early July 1977, Dr Mike Harris and Stuart Murray counted 24,809 pairs on Hirta for their *Birds of St Kilda* (1978). Stuart went on to update this in 2002, quoting Seabird 2000's preliminary figures for Apparently Occupied Sites or AOS – and comparing them to the earlier Seabird Colony Register. In June 1987, the total for Hirta was 35,349 sites and, in June 1999, some 41,562.

Regarding St Kilda as a whole, Harris and Murray's total in 1977 had been 43,977 AOS. In 1987, there were 62,786 and by 1999 – according to Mitchell *et al.* (2004) and slightly more than quoted in Murray (2002) – 68,448, nearly 14 per cent of the British and Irish fulmar population. The increase at St Kilda from 1977 to 1987 was 43 per cent (or 3.62 per cent per annum) but has since slowed to only 0.7 per cent per annum.

A breakdown of the 1999 figures showed how, besides the 41,562 AOS on Hirta, there were another 11,206 nesting on Dun, 9,137 on Soay, 2,637 on Boreray, 2,107 on Stac an Armin, 222 on the Stacs in Soay Sound, 63 on Levenish and 8 on Stac Lee. The Levenish fulmars have increased from 12 AOS in 1977, while Stac Lee has declined from 50 AOS in 1977. Since 1987 there has been an overall decline of some 4,165 fulmar sites on Boreray, whilst they have increased in Soay by 3,458 and in Hirta by 6,213. At some 11,000 to 12,000 AOS, Dun has remained stable, as has Stac an Armin at around 2000.

The ever-observant Reverend MacAulay offered an early glimpse of what was then a novel habit of the fulmar – nesting inland:

> Some different tribes of the Hirta birds, particularly the Tulmer [fulmar], the large Sea-Gull and smaller Maws, quit their native element upon certain occasions, and retire to the land. Here they flutter about the fields, or hover above the houses; and as if highly dissatisfied with their condition, shift every moment from place to place, now rising up and immediately lighting upon the ground, or threatening to do so. This phenomenon is by the St Kildians, and all the other islanders reckoned an infallible prognostic of an approaching tempest.

This is now more commonplace throughout its range. In his updated *Birds of St Kilda* (2002) Stuart Murray noted how Hirta fulmars have nested inland in Gleann Mor since the early 1950s, with the first nest in the quarry in Village Glen in 1979. Fulmars now nest on several rock outcrops in Hirta and inside many village structures (where 23 young fledged in 1998).

We now come to the second of the seabirds so vital to the St Kildans' existence – the gannet. In his *Scotia Illustrata* (1684) Sir Robert Sibbald (1641–1722) was probably referring to gannets in St Kilda when he mentioned them nesting in the Hebrides. In a later book (1710) Sibbald confirmed there were gannets 'in the desert Isles, adjacent to Hirta, called St Kilda's Isle', but by then he would have had the benefit of a careful correspondent, namely Martin Martin. As ever, in 1697, Martin offered a pretty definitive account of the habits of the solan goose (gannet), which later writers were happy to plagiarise:

> The Solan Goose, as some imagine from the Irish word Sou'ler, corrupted and adapted to the Scottish language [which Rev. Mackenzie later explained means 'sharp-eyed'] ... equals a common goose in bigness ... the wings extend very far ... its egg somewhat less than that of a Land-Goose ... the inhabitants are accustomed to drink it raw, having from experience found it very pectoral, and cepahlic. The Solan Geese hatch [incubate] by turns. When it returns from fishing, it carries five or six herrings in its gorget, all entire and undigested: Upon its arrival at the nest, the hatching fowl puts its head in the fisher's throat, and pulls out the fish with its bill as with a pincer, and that with very great noise, which I had occasion frequently to observe. They continue to pluck grass for their nests from their coming in March till the young fowl is ready to fly in August or September, according as the inhabitants take or leave the first or second eggs ... Their food is herring, mackerel, and syes. Hooks are often found in the stomachs both of young and old Solan Geese, though none of this kind are used nearer than the Isles Twenty leagues distant; this must happen either from the fish pulling away the hooks in

those Isles and then going to St Kilda, or by their being carried thither; by the old geese.

The Solan Geese are always the surest sign of herrings, for where-ever the one is seen, the other is never far off. There is a tribe of barren Solan Geese which have no nests, and sit upon the bare rock; they are not the young fowls of a year old, whose dark colour would soon distinguish them, but old ones, in all things like the rest ...; neither do they meddle with, or approach to those hatching, or any other fowl; they sympathize and fish together; this was told me by the inhabitants, and afterwards confirmed several times by my own observations.

Sixty years later, the Reverend MacAulay added yet more:

The nest of the Solan-Goose is a large collection made up of very different materials; he carries any thing that is fit for his purpose, whether at land or floating on the waters, to the place where he builds, grass, sea-ware, shavings of timber, pieces of cloth, and very often other implements which he must have got in some foreign land ... If a Solan-Goose finds his neighbours nest at any time without the fowl, he takes advantage of his absence, steals as much of the materials of it as he can conveniently carry, and sensible of the injustice he hath done, takes his flight directly towards the ocean; if the lawful owner does not discover the injury he has suffered, before the thief is out of sight, he escapes with impunity, and returns soon with his burden, as if he had made a foreign purchase.

Before the young Solan-Geese, which they call Goug, fly off, they are larger than the mothers, and excessively fat. The fat on their breasts is sometimes three inches deep.

Martin noted that gannets arrived at St Kilda in March and remained until the beginning of November, after which time no seabirds were to be seen on the cliffs until the middle of February. Presumably he learned all this from the islanders, but went on to surmise how it might be poor weather, abundance of fish, or a combination of both which drove the seabirds away. He then described how they caught their favourite food – herring:

He observes his prey from a considerable height, and darts down upon it with incredible force ... From the account given above of the vast multitudes of sea fowls that seek their food on this coast, we may justly conclude, that there must be inexhaustible stores of fish there ...

We now know that gannets achieve speeds of up to 100 km/h in their dramatic plunge-dives, hitting the water like javelins, with wings folded neatly behind. Thus they can reach depths of 20 m or so to catch medium-sized fish such as mackerel and herring. Recent satellite tracking at the Bass Rock has revealed that a gannet feeding its chick may travel up to 540 km from its colony (Mitchell *et al.* 2004).

The Duchess of Bedford (1914) made an interesting reference which indicated an early concern from trawlermen about gannet depredations upon fish stocks:

> A propos of the destruction of fish by these birds, which is now being investigated by a committee appointed by the Fishery Board, it may be worth mentioning that a trawler which had been fishing round Stac Lii and Boreray had made such a big haul of fish that they took a rest in St Kilda Bay from early Saturday afternoon to Monday morning before returning home. The mate supplied the information to my captain, and those who know anything of life on board these trawlers will be aware that only when the fishing has been exceptionally good can they afford themselves the luxury of a voluntary rest both night and day.

The Reverend Neil Mackenzie capably summarised earlier accounts of gannet behaviour and added some interesting observations of his own:

> A few birds will sometimes come as early as the 13th of January, and from that time more and more gradually arrive. By the end of February only about a third of the birds will have come, and it is not till the end of March that they are caught in any numbers and then only if the weather is suitable when they arrive they are fat and very good eating ... They begin to lay about the 10th of May and it is very probable that they all return to their old nests ... It lays only one egg, which the parents hatch [incubate] by turns for about six weeks, and then feed the chick for at least as long ... If the first egg is taken away it will lay a second, and if it is again robbed it will lay a third time. All of them will not lay again. You may get on a ledge the first time say twenty eggs, the second time fifteen, and the third time about twelve ... When it is about a month old it is called a 'guga' ... A little before it is ready to leave the nest it is very fat, but by the time it is fully fledged it is leaner ... When it returns in spring it is distinctly speckled, and is then called by the same name as the young shearwater – 'fathach'.

In his *Ornithology of St Kilda* (1885) Charles Dixon contributed his own account:

> The Gannet breeds in tens of thousands on the island of Boreray and the adjacent 'stacks'. Stac Lii is the great breeding station, and from a distance looks as if it was covered with a gigantic tablecloth, the masses of birds that crowd upon its sloping summit make this rock a very conspicuous object, and it may be distinctly seen from the Long Island, forty miles away, like a large ship under full sail bending to windward ... Many of the St Kildan Gannets obtain their food in the Minch, fifty miles away.

Fig. 10. Charles Dixon.

There are currently some 390,000 pairs of northern gannets in the world, scattered in only 41 colonies, six of them in Canada. The remainder are in the East Atlantic totalling some 263,000 pairs, though a second table in Mitchell *et al.* (2004) claimed only 231,565 pairs. Twenty-one of these colonies are in Britain and Ireland, three-quarters of them in Scotland.

St Kilda holds the largest known colony of northern gannets, currently 14.4 per cent of the world population. The status has changed over time. Indeed, Henry Evans of Jura who sailed to St Kilda a dozen times – once in 1887 in the company of the eminent Cambridge ornithologist Professor Alfred Newton (1829–1907) – went as far as to claim:

> I am prepared to believe that there may be more Gannets there than in all the rest of the world beside.

On his visit in 1894 the ornithologist J. Steele Elliott (1895) gave a first assessment of gannet numbers on St Kilda, though he does not really indicate how he came about this figure:

> Its numbers are estimated at about 25,000 pairs, this being the second largest gannet nursery in our islands.

In 1913, an important book was published – *The Gannet, a Bird with a History* – written by a Norfolk ornithologist and antiquarian John Henry Gurney (1848–1922). This was one of the first authoritative monographs on any species and James Fisher's favourite bird book. Gurney had been fascinated by the gannet ever since he had first visited Ailsa Craig as a boy 46 years earlier. He never got to St Kilda, but in 1876 he did visit the Bass Rock. He was later helped in his researches by a friend of his father's, the now ageing Professor Newton. Gurney unearthed many accounts about gannets and gannetries but considered Martin's book *A Late Voyage to St Kilda* the 'best told story of all – save for some exaggeration in numbers'.

Gurney ended the Preface of his 1913 monograph with a puzzling apology:

> My conscience pricks me with having occupied five hundred and sixty pages with the history of one bird, but I console myself with the reflection that had the bird been the Cuckoo or the Raven, the book would have been much longer.

The first, albeit crude, census of St Kilda's gannets was undertaken by Dr Joseph Wiglesworth between 5 and 26 June 1902; his modest 68-page pamphlet was delivered as a lecture at Liverpool the following year. Gurney quoted a letter from Wiglesworth which explained how he had reached his conclusions:

> Almost every nest contained a single egg ... I endeavoured to form some sort of estimate as to the number of Gannets resident in St Kilda during the summer by ascertaining the number of eggs taken ... On May 14th there were taken from the top of Stack Lii (from the summit only) 1,400 fresh eggs ... but the men say that on the whole of the rest of this Stack there are more nests than on the summit, and if this be so, the total number of nests of Stack Lii may perhaps be put at 3,500 to 4,000. On Stack an Armin, though the birds are very numerous, they are appreciably less so than on Stack Lii, and the number of nests may perhaps be put at about 3,000. On the cliffs of Boreray the natives consider that there are more nests than on the two Stacks put together, and the number may therefore be approximately reckoned at about 8,000. Doubling the number of nests to get the number of birds and allowing for a fair sprinkling of non-breeding birds, of which the natives say there are a good many, we get a total of some 30,000 birds. This estimate is much less than that given by some writers, and it of course does not pretend to be more than a rough calculation.

As with fulmar numbers, nobody seemed prepared to tackle the daunting task of physically counting nests. Even Tom Harrisson in July 1931, with David Lack, only managed crude counts from a boat – 4,300 gannets on Boreray, 10,000 on Stac Lee and 7,000 on Stac an Armin, making a total of 21,000 adults. Harrisson appreciated the deficiencies of his approach but considered Wiglesworth's estimate too great. Five years later Professor V. C. Wynne Edwards *et al.* (1936) reassessed Harrisson's counts to suggest upwards of 16,500 pairs.

On 31 May 1939, Max Nicholson, Julian Huxley and James Fisher counted St Kilda's gannetry from a boat and from vantage points ashore. (Huxley actually went on to win a Hollywood oscar for a documentary he made about gannets – though this was not filmed on St Kilda!) The party estimated between 15,500 and 20,000 pairs:

> 16,900 pairs is the figure we consider to have the greatest chance of approaching the reality.

On 30 July 1947, through a courtesy from the RAF, James Fisher (1948) was able to photograph the stacs from the air, enabling him to make some estimates. In 1949, with a few photographs from a boat as checks, Fisher reckoned 17,035 pairs, conveniently close to his and Nicholson's earlier 1939 estimate. The matter was not satisfactorily resolved until Morton Boyd of the Nature Conservancy seized another aerial opportunity. He was on St Kilda in 1959 while the RAF were flying over Boreray as part of a training exercise. At the same time Boyd photographed the cliffs himself, both from land and sea. Then, armed with the RAF's aerial photographs, he was able to reach a total of 44,526 pairs – 24,133 of them sited in Boreray, 10,775 in Stac Lee, and 9,618 on Stac an Armin. He concluded:

> The difference between my figures and those of Harrisson and Fisher are not so much those of numbers present, as of the methods used to obtain them.

His figures are considered to be as accurate as could be attained. It seemed likely that the considerable increase in gannets on St Kilda was an artefact of the counting approach. Boyd's methodical delineation of the cliffs into 116 recognisable sections has had to be modified only slightly, and has formed the basis for all later surveys, including the estimates made from partial counts in 1969 and 1973.

Since then, Stuart Murray, with Professor Sarah Wanless, has been involved in all further aerial surveys. The aircraft first flies carefully over the colony to scare off the non-breeding birds, leaving only the incubating adults tight on their nests. The next fly-past enables numerous, overlapping photographs of the colony to be taken. These are then sorted and counted methodically, back at base.

The 1985 census gave a total of 24,673 pairs on Boreray (which is now suspected to be on the low side), with 13,521 on Stac Lee, 11,853 on Stac an Armin – a total for St Kilda of 50,050 AOS. The next aerial survey in 1994 found 32,818 AOS on Boreray, 14,660 on Stac Lee, and 12,950 on Stac an Armin, giving a slightly increased total of 60,428 AOS in St Kilda as a whole. This increase represents 0.8–0.9 per cent per annum on each island. Finally, June 2004 revealed little change with 59,622 AOS on Boreray and its stacs

– a very slight decrease on Stac Lee compensated by a slight increase on Stac an Armin (see Table 2).

While St Kilda has remained relatively stable in the last three decades, the ancient gannetry on the Bass Rock appears to have increased from 8,000 to 48,000 pairs in that time. Since there is little room on the Bass for many more, there may be little danger in its overtaking St Kilda as the largest colony in the world. However, Bonaventure Island in the Gulf of St Lawrence could soon take over St Kilda's mantle; the most recent count was 53,635 nests and if the current rate of increase is maintained the total will exceed that of St Kilda in 2009 (Professor Mike Harris, personal comment)

For about a century the gannet has been increasing in the North Atlantic by about 2–3 per cent per annum. In Britain about eight new colonies have been founded in the last century, with nesting in Brittany, France, occurring in 1939, in Norway from 1946, in Germany in 1991 and even in Kola in Russia four years later. This increase in numbers is not as large as other long-lived, slow-breeding seabirds like the fulmar. But the gannet is still doing well, and it is not quite clear why this should be so.

It seems that gannets are able to switch prey when herring, for instance, and then mackerel, have declined. Seabirds in Shetland and the Outer Hebrides have reduced significantly in recent years which may be partly due to overfishing for sandeels, but changes in sea temperatures might also be involved. It remains to be seen how such factors might impact upon gannets. At intervals, gannet eggs have been collected under licence on St Kilda and elsewhere in order to look for chemical pollutants, but levels do not appear to be sufficient to cause infertility. About a third of gannets found dead are caught on baited hooks or in nets, with another 20 per cent suffering from the effects of oil. Another 25 per cent are shot or deliberately caught for food.

The only other Scottish gannetry that is not experiencing an increase is on Sulaisgeir where it is still permitted by law to harvest gannets. It does seem that, as soon as fowling ceased on St Kilda and the island was evacuated, the gannet population began to increase, only to level out again 40 years later. We shall return to the exploitation of gannets on St Kilda in Chapter 8.

The Atlantic puffin is by far the most abundant auk in St Kilda and the seabird that the St Kildans exploited most. It is universally popular nowadays for its clown-like looks and behaviour, and Steele Elliott (1895) seemed rather uncharitable when he commented:

> That odd little piece of grotesque animation, the Puffin, is the gold mine of the St Kildan natives; greater numbers of this bird are taken than of all the rest together.

The Reverend MacAulay was more gracious:

The Bougir of Hirta, is by some called the Coulterneb, and by others the Puffin. This is a very sprightly bird, in size much like a pigeon: It seems to be conscious of its own beauty, cocking its head very smartly, and assuming great airs of majesty: Its colour is black on the outer parts, and about the breast, red and white: The legs are red, and the beak fashioned like a coulter, edged above, and most charmingly painted with red and yellow below.

Incredible flights of these Puffins flutter, during the whole summer season, round about St Kilda and the two isles pertaining to it: sometimes they cover whole plots of ground, and sometimes while on the wing, involve every thing below them in darkness, like a small cloud of locusts in another country.

Years before, Martin Martin had observed:

They breed in holes under ground, and come with a S.W. wind about the twenty-second of March [i.e. 4 April by the new calendar], lay their egg the twenty-second of April [i.e. 5 May].

Most puffins nest on Dun, Soay and Boreray, with a small population in Hirta scattered amongst boulder fields; until the 1950s they also bred on the north slopes of Conachair. A decline is known to have taken place in Hirta during the 20th century, mostly between 1947 and 1957, notably from Conachair's north slopes. But elsewhere in Hirta the numbers appear to have remained stable, with the main concentrations being at Carn Mor and the Cambir. There are only two estimates for Hirta. Over two consecutive seasons, 1975 and 1976, some 8,100 to 13,500 pairs were estimated. The 1999 attempt is more difficult to evaluate – 1,819 Apparently Occupied Burrows plus 6,062 individuals.

There have been five attempts to census Boreray, giving about 100,000 Apparently Occupied Burrows in 1977, about 79,000 in 1980, 63,000 in 1987 and 51,000 in 2000. Soay is even more difficult for scientists to land upon. It is thought to have the largest colony, although spread out, and estimated in 1971 at 77,000 Apparently Occupied Burrows. Puffins have since declined there, to 39,500 in 1989, and to only 27,500 in the year 2000. Small numbers occur on Stac an Armin, but puffins no longer breed in Levenish.

Dun, being the most accessible of St Kilda's other islands, can be monitored more regularly. Between 1974 and 1976 it was estimated to hold 40–60,000 pairs. With the fixing of permanent sampling quadrats, estimates could be refined and by 1987 the number of burrows had apparently increased and was estimated at 42,000. A count in 1990 indicated 27,500 more and 55,400 in 1999.

The Atlantic puffin colony on Dun is one of the largest breeding concentrations in Britain and invites detailed study. Access to the island can be difficult with a boat, so in 1975 a breeches buoy was put in place across the

Fig. 11. Flying puffins over Dun in 1979 (J. Love).

gap, permitting Dr Mike Harris, Stuart Murray and other researchers regular access every summer. This functioned well until July 1978, as the lichenologist Oliver Gilbert remembered in his memoir, though not strictly accurately according to Stuart Murray:

> When Bob was crossing to Dun the cable of the breeches buoy had snapped and he fell fifty feet onto inaccessible rocks at the water's edge, knocking himself unconscious. Stuart ran back to the army camp and an inflatable with the medical officer was launched to recover him. The doctor summoned a Sea King helicopter from Prestwick and Bob was soon in hospital in Benbecula [actually Daliburgh in South Uist]. He appeared to be not too bad except for his back. We all felt rather shocked and had mixed feelings, because it could have happened to any one of four of us.

One aspect of the study – the fledging success of Dun's puffins – was facilitated by a curious happenstance. It began with a problem. Back in August 1961, Nature Conservancy files reveal how the army surgeon cum ornithologist Dr W. Estlin Waters, with the warden Malcolm Smith, were:

> ... mystified by the influx of young puffins into the camp area ... at peak that August as many as 15 were being found nightly in the generator sheds ... Some oil was lying on the floor of the generator shed and one or two birds required cleaning. By the end of the season the generator operators on night duty were

collecting the birds as soon as they arrived and boxing them safely for the warden next morning. In 1962 [there occurred the] same frequency of birds but, owing to less interest from the soldiers there, incidents of oiling greatly increased – a few had to be destroyed. Conditions became even worse in 1963 when leakage and spillage (and deliberate dumping) left the generator bays swimming in oil. Although there were a few birds arriving by the 13–14th of August, things didn't really get out of hand until the 20th when 11 birds out of 25 caught in the bays had to be destroyed – a melancholy business … We had realised by this time that the increase in birds was due to the new fluorescent lighting fitted in the bays and joiner's shop in October 1962. In consultation with the generator operators and with agreement of Captain Molesworth we hit on the plan of running the seaward generators at night (four run by day, four by night) so that the doors of the upper bays (the left of which are the worst offenders) could be lowered (the doors cannot be lowered whilst the generators are running because of overheating). From the 21st on [Waters] went out after dusk and pulled the bay doors closed, then walked round the camp extinguishing all unnecessary light. After this I waited for the birds arrival with a net for capturing. On the 21st we had only 8 birds, then 9 on the 22nd. From then on they came in two and three a night, with the last bird on the 29th. Single birds however, over this period were found in other places, but all places with strong lighting which for safety's sake could not be extinguished. Only a few birds needed cleaning after the 21st and only two had to be destroyed … Smith suggested mitigating measures but Captain Molesworth intimated that as much as he loved birds and was saddened by the sight of oiled puffins he could not have his men neglect their duty over them.

Soon after, however, the army became very co-operative, the camp was cleaned up and all unnecessary lighting extinguished. Unfortunately, fledging puffins – or 'pufflings' as they came to be known – continued to be attracted to the remaining essential lights. Thus from the end of July into August it became a nightly duty for wardens, soldiers and National Trust volunteers to patrol the Base for disorientated pufflings. Since annual monitoring of the puffin population on Dun has ceased, this unfortunate situation across Village Bay has been turned to good use.

A measure of the annual breeding success of puffins can be gained by comparing the number of unfortunates collected below the lights. The number of birds collected each year can range from 1,409 pufflings in 1978 to only one in 2004. Since 1973, each bird has been weighed, ringed and then released off the end of the pier. The numbers and body weight of the stranded fledglings caught each year tend to be linked to growth rates, fledgling weights and annual breeding success back on Dun. Thus the data are still providing valuable long-term information on the fortunes of St Kilda's Atlantic puffins (Harris, Murray and Wanless 1998). Worryingly, it seems that puffins are now fledging a few weeks later than in the 1970s, and are some 15 per cent lighter in weight, so breeding success is far from healthy. In recent years, hardly any pufflings have turned up in the Base, reflecting some disastrous breeding seasons.

Out of 600,000 pairs of puffins in the British Isles, 82 per cent are to be found in Scotland, and 24 per cent of them in St Kilda. Indeed St Kilda currently holds some 2 per cent of the world population. But in the year 2000 the St Kilda total stood at some 135,752, a serious drop from the estimated 310,000 in 1978 and 230,500 in 1988. It is difficult, however, to maintain consistency in counting so it is uncertain whether this does in fact reflect such a significant decline. Puffins dive for small fish such as sandeels, but only to relatively shallow depths. During a disastrous breeding season in 2005 for instance, puffins had to resort to pipefish, a poor substitute nutritionally. This change, which seems to have persisted, could be the result of changing sea temperatures perhaps, as much as commercial overfishing.

In autumn, pufflings and their parents disappear out to sea to moult and, in the case of the adults, to shed the brightly coloured skin ornamentation on the bill and head.

Fulmars, gannets and puffins were by far the most important seabirds to the islanders. St Kilda is home to other seabirds too, other auks – guillemots and razorbills – proving especially useful to them. In Chapter 6 we will review the status of these other seabird species on St Kilda, before considering the techniques that the islanders employed in fowling.

.6.

Seabirds 2

I have often been entertained with the extraordinary concerts of the sea-fowl in Ailsa, the Shiant Islands and elsewhere; but I never heard any orchestra so numerous so various, and so perfect as this one, which seemed to consist of almost all the birds that frequent the seas and rocks of these wild coasts.

John MacCulloch 1815.

FULMARS, GANNETS AND PUFFINS were vital to the survival of the St Kildans, but they utilised other seabirds too. The guillemot was the most important of these, so it is strange that Martin Martin should have given it so little space:

The Lavy so called by the inhabitants of St Kilda, by the Welch Guillem, is nearly as big as a duck ... Its egg in bigness is near to that of a goose egg, sharp at one end, and blunt at the other; the colour of it prettily mixed with green and black; others of them are of a pale colour, with red and brown streaks; but the latter is very rare; this egg for ordinary food is by the inhabitants, and others, preferred above all the eggs had here. This fowl comes from a S.W. wind, if fair, the twentieth of February [but add thirteen days, of course]; the time of its going away depends upon the inhabitants taking or leaving its first, second, or third egg.

MacAulay added information about the guillemot's habits:

[The Lavie] builds nothing in the way of a nest, but lays her egg on the shelf of a bare rock, where she plants it in so very nice a manner, that if once touched, one will find it impossible to fix it in the same place again. So slender is the hold these eggs have of the rock, that they tumble down into the sea in thick showers, if the fowls are surprised, so as to start away in a hurry.

Common guillemots are present in St Kilda from late February to early August. As MacAulay attested, guillemots do not build nests but lay their single egg on shelves of bare rock. It is often said that the pyramidal shape of their eggs induces them to spin rather than roll if disturbed, but this is probably more myth than reality.

Incubating adults are often joined by off-duty birds. Counting rows of guillemots several deep presents particular difficulties. If possible, it is best to choose the time of day when most off-duty birds are away fishing. All one can then do is count individuals. Early accounts usually overestimated numbers. For example, in 1878, Sands reckoned there to have been three million. Similarly, Mackenzie estimated 50,000 guillemots bred on Stac Biorach alone, but the stac is physically incapable of accommodating such a number. Even the figure of 20,000 pairs on the stac, estimated in 1939, is too high.

The first complete counts of guillemots in St Kilda were undertaken by Morton Boyd in 1959; he reckoned on 14,580 birds, and again in 1969 he found 21,880 birds. Surveys in 1977 (22,085 birds) and 1987 (22,705) are remarkably consistent with the Seabird 2000 count completed in 1999 (23,422 birds). This latest count included 10,903 birds in Hirta, 2,131 in Dun, 2,582 in Soay, 1,822 on the Soay Sound stacs, 487 in Stac Lee, 571 in Stac an Armin, 4,886 in Boreray and 60 in Levenish.

The Hirta colonies seem stable, with slight increases in Boreray and Soay and a decline in Dun. Breeding success is, however, more fickle and very dependent upon food supply. Guillemots fly up to 30 km or more eastwards towards the Hebrides and feed by diving to depths of 180 m for sandeels, herring and sprats. Pairs produce a single chick which departs the nest ledge before it can fly to escape predation by gulls, etc. Out at sea it is still tended by the parents until it fledges.

Table 2. Numbers of seabirds breeding on St Kilda (after Mitchell et al. 2004)

Fulmar	62,786 pairs	Puffin	142,264 pairs
Manx shearwater	4,800 pairs	Shag	50 pairs
Storm petrel	1,000 pairs	Herring gull	35 pairs
Leach's petrel	45,433 pairs	Lesser black-backed gull	35 pairs
Gannet	59,622 pairs	Black guillemot	10 pairs
Great skua	240 pairs	Great black-backed gull	10 pairs
Kittiwake	3,886 pairs	Common gull	5 pairs
Guillemot	23,442 birds	Arctic skua	2 pairs
Razorbill	2,521 birds		

The ringed or bridled guillemot with its conspicuous spectacled appearance was sometimes considered to be a separate species. They are, of course, just a genetic morph. Harrisson and Lack looked at 30 birds and reckoned 10 per cent of them to be bridled. In 1939, Julian Huxley counted 873 birds and found 16.5 per cent of them to be bridled. In 1948, Philip Hugh-Jones examined a total of 1,368 guillemots, of which 143 or 10.5 per cent were bridled. That year, in a sample of only 164, Fisher found 10.3 per cent to be bridled. While Fisher thought that these later counts demonstrated a statistically significant decline in incidence since Huxley, it is known that bridled guillemots can exhibit a rather clumped distribution within colonies. Thus reasonable sample sizes are essential, the larger the better. The incidence of bridled guillemots increases to over 50 per cent further north and west in the guillemots' range, though for some reason this trend is reversed within the Icelandic colonies.

The guillemot's nearest relative is the Brunnich's guillemot, a bird of Iceland and the high Arctic. Milner must have surely been mistaken when in 1847 he maintained that this species was found with eggs in Soay. In his 1898 book Heathcote referred to the common or 'foolish' guillemot as *Uria bruennichi* and perhaps this name caused confusion between the two species, as there had been a century earlier. An undoubted Brunnich's guillemot was seen by Jim Vaughan and Tim Dix off Oiseval at the end of May/early June 1992.

Another close relative is the razorbill, black rather than chocolate brown, less sociable, with a stout blunt beak. Martin had this to say:

> The bird, by the inhabitants called the Falk, the Razor-bill in the west of England, the Awk in the North, the Murre in Cornwall, Alca Hoeri, is a size less than the Lavy; ... It lays its egg in May, its young take wing the middle of July, if the inhabitants do not determine its stay longer, by taking the egg; which in bigness is next to the Lavy, or Guillem egg, and is variously spotted, sharp at one end, and blunt at the other.

MacAulay did not mention razorbills at all, while Martin's dates by the old calendar are of course 13 days early. They are in fact present at colonies in St Kilda from late February to early August. Razorbills may share cliff nest sites with guillemots, but razorbills are less sociable, often choosing secluded nooks and crannies. Most counts are therefore underestimates.

Only three surveys of this retiring auk can be considered useful: about 3,500 individuals counted in 1977, 3,814 in 1987 and 2,521 in 1999. A decrease of over 50 per cent had occurred on Dun, where many breed amongst the boulders near the Fort. The 1999 counts revealed 192 birds on Boreray, with 50 on Stac an Armin, 14 on Stac Lee, 16 on Levenish, 24 on the Soay Sound stacs, 173 on Soay itself, 819 on Dun and 1,233 on Hirta.

Razorbills fly up to 30 km or more eastwards towards the Hebrides to feed, often in the company of guillemots. They can dive to considerable depths for sandeels, herring and sprats. As with guillemots, the single chick departs the nest ledges before it can fly, thus escaping predation by gulls, etc.

Seabirds nesting on St Kilda's cliffs have occasionally been subjected to acute disturbance by passing ships. It seems that the tourist steamers which cruised St Kilda and its stacs at the end of the 19th and in the early 20th centuries regularly subjected the seabird colonies to destructive hooter blasts. In August 1975, for instance, even the National Trust for Scotland cruise ship *Uganda* sounded its hooter several times as it passed between Stac Lee and Boreray, before the skipper was told to stop. Such actions caused mass panic flights, spectacular enough but which caused many eggs to roll off the ledges. Gannets were just as vulnerable as guillemots.

Sadly, tourist ships have not been the only culprits. A warden witnessed some geologists from the Hebridean Margin Seismic Project, Department of Geological Sciences, University of Durham, exploding a depth charge between Hirta and Boreray and killing about 40 auks in the process. This was one of only two charges detonated near St Kilda at the time and doubtless the scientists were horrified by the impact.

None of the other diurnal seabirds on St Kilda are quite as numerous as the auks. The black guillemot or tystie lies at the opposite end of the auk abundance. These neat little characters are present in smart breeding livery from March/April to August. They feed close inshore, on bottom-living fish. The nest is deep in a crack or between boulders near the base of the cliffs and, unusually for auks, they often lay two eggs and not infrequently succeed in rearing twins.

Being the most secretive of all the auks, tysties are also difficult to census. Recently it has been realised that they are best counted just after dawn in the early spring, when they congregate just offshore to mate and display. Only ten pairs were found to frequent Dun and Hirta in 1974–8. There has been little change detected since. There was a maximum of 9 to 12 pairs in 1987 and again in 1994. Another two or three pairs occurred in Soay Sound, with 34 individual birds being counted around Boreray in 1980.

The Reverend Neil Mackenzie (1905) noted that two species of 'cormorant' were breeding when he stayed on Hirta from 1829 to 1844 – obviously shags and cormorants. In 1847, Milner obtained eggs of the great cormorant, and in 1910 a number were also seen by Eagle Clarke. Only single birds have been recorded on St Kilda since that time.

European shags, however, are much more numerous and can be seen throughout the year. Most leave St Kilda after breeding and do not return until January or February. The largest colony, estimated at 600 pairs in

1969, is to be found under boulders at the end of Dun. In 1975 and 1977 about 134–144 nests were found in this colony, but only about 90 pairs were estimated in 1984, with a minimum of 62 nests in 1996. In addition, there may be more than 200 pairs in Hirta, although only 100 or so were counted in 1974–7. There are also some shags nesting in Soay, but in Boreray there is little suitable habitat. Thus St Kilda still holds some 200–300 pairs. Shags feed close inshore, diving for small fish.

After giving brief descriptions of these seabirds, the Reverend MacAulay went on to dismiss the rest of St Kilda's avifauna:

> It will, I apprehend, be thought unnecessary, by this time, to give the minute detail of all the other ignoble or useless tribes of sea and land fowl, that frequent the St Kilda rocks and isles.

He continued:

> There is a great variety of them: one species, numerous enough, is called the Sgrobir, and another the Ashilag ...
>
> The *Sgrobir* is now known as the Manx shearwater. Martin described it:
>
> The Scraber, so called in St Kilda, in the Farn Islands Puffinet, in Holland the Greenland Dove, has a small bill sharp pointed, a little crooked at the end, and prominent; it is as large as a Pigeon, its whole body being black, except a white spot on each wing [?]; its egg grey, sharp at one end, and blunt at the other.
>
> It comes in the month of March, and in the night-time, without regard to any wind; it is never to be seen but in the night, being all the day either abroad at fishing, or upon its nest, which it digs very far under ground, from whence it never comes in day-light; it picks its food out of the living whale, with which, they say, it uses Sorrel, and both are found in its nest. The young Puffin [shearwater] is fat as the young Fulmar, and goes away in August if its first egg be spared.

Manx shearwaters are nocturnal, only coming to their nesting burrows under cover of darkness. They are present ashore in St Kilda from March to September and the distribution of their colonies has changed little in recent decades. There were, however, no counts undertaken until 1999/2000, by which time a census technique had been refined to cope with this difficult species. Playing a tape recording of their call at the mouth of each likely burrow invokes a response from any bird within. Not all occupants answer, so a correction factor has to be applied. Occupied burrows may also show excavated soil, droppings, or down feathers at the mouth. Reaching into the burrows not only may induce the bird to desert its egg but can result in a very painful bite to the hand, or an armful of ticks! In fact, sitting birds tend to be out of reach anyway, many burrows having awkward twists and turns.

Seabird 2000 revealed some 4,581 Apparently Occupied Sites (AOS) of shearwaters in Hirta, concentrated on Carn Mor and the upper slopes of Oiseval. There are fewer than 500 burrows in the Tigh Dugan boulder field on Soay. Dun has an even lower density with fewer than 450 AOS. It would seem there are none in Boreray.

Few shearwaters are seen at sea in the vicinity of the islands, most flying westwards to feed way out to the edge of the continental shelf, where they plunge to modest depths for a variety of small fish, cephalopods such as squid and crustaceans. Like all seabirds, Manx shearwaters are long-lived; one ringed on Bardsey, North Wales, is now 52 years old! There is only ever one chick produced deep underground each year, the parents returning to tend it only during the hours of darkness. On misty nights the fledglings can sometimes be attracted to the lights around the radar base. Manx shearwaters spend the winter out at sea and can penetrate across the equator to the southern coast of South America.

Martin had this to say of the storm petrel:

> The Assilag is as large as a Linnet, black bill, wide nostrils at the upper part, crooked at the point like the Fulmar's bill. It comes about the twenty-second of March, without any regard to winds, lays its egg about the twentieth of May, and produces the Fowl towards the middle of October, then goes away about the end of November.

The Reverend Neil Mackenzie explained how the local Gaelic name *aisleag* means 'the little ferryman', from the bird's habit of flying back and forward from point to point – a very apt description of its feeding habits at sea. He added that it laid its single large egg in a hole like that of a shearwater, but added an erroneous observation that, unlike the shearwater, 'it goes to and fro by day'. Petrels are invariably considered to be nocturnal, except that in colonies in Norway, north of the Arctic Circle, they may visit their burrows in midsummer daylight.

The European storm petrel is a late arrival in St Kilda, present, according to Martin, from early May to early November. Even allowing for his now obsolete calendar, Martin's dates seem unduly extended, but then it seems that the islanders did not distinguish between stormies and the larger Leach's storm petrel which arrives and leaves earlier in the season. As with shearwaters, there had been no counts of these nocturnal little burrow-nesters in St Kilda until 1999/2000, the techniques employed being similar. The Joint Nature Conservancy Committee's Seabirds at Sea Team found 1,121 AOS of storm petrels, 508 of them in Hirta, 84 in Boreray and 529 in Soay. None were found in Dun where they had been recorded in 1987. So it is possible there has been a decline in the European storm petrel in St Kilda, at least since the early 1980s.

The diminutive storm petrels also fly out towards the continental shelf to feed, pattering along the surface (hence the name petrel after St Peter who walked on water). They probably feed mostly at night, taking tiny crustaceans, fish, etc. During the breeding season, storm petrels have turned up between St Kilda and colonies on Rona, Foula and Fair Isle, for example, sometimes within a matter of days. These seem to be wandering non-breeders that have not yet established a breeding site. Again, ringing has shown that after a few years they return to breed in the colony at which they were reared and remain faithful to it thereafter. Ringed birds have been washed up dead along the coast of South Africa so, like shearwaters, petrels often travel far during the winter months.

The Reverend Neil Mackenzie recognised that there were two species of petrel in St Kilda:

> ... the larger having its tail forked like that of a swallow. Otherwise they are similar in appearance and habits. The smaller variety is the more numerous, and frequents all the islands of the group, while the other frequents only Boreray, and the northern part of St Kilda proper [presumably Carn Mor].

In editing his father's notes in 1905, the Reverend J. B. Mackenzie was able to identify this as the Leach's fork-tailed petrel, which had long been recognised by science as a distinct species. Probably his father had been directed to the two distinct species by the islanders themselves. Although they used the same name for both, it is hard to believe that they had not noticed the difference between them.

In Martin's time ornithologists did not recognise the Leach's fork-tailed petrel as distinct. The first British specimen (and only the fourth known) was not acquired until 1818. It had been collected from St Kilda by William Bullock (c 1773–1849). A silversmith, showman and naturalist, Bullock had made several collecting trips in Scotland, participating in an unsuccessful pursuit of a live great auk swimming in the sea off Orkney in 1812 (see Chapter 7). Before embarking upon a mining speculation in Mexico in 1819 and ending his days in obscurity, Bullock sold his famous museum collection, acting as his own auctioneer. His extensive collection of over 3,000 bird specimens included:

> Lot 78 – an undescribed petrel with a forked tail, taken in St Kilda in 1818; the only one known (with egg).

It was bought for £5 15s by an invertebrate biologist at the British Museum called Dr William Elford Leach (1790–1836). He also bought a stuffed great auk (and an egg) for just over £16 – the very bird that Bullock had failed to catch in Orkney and which was killed for him the following year. Later, another collector, a Dutchman C. J. Temminck (1778–1858), spotted the petrel in the British Museum and in 1820 named it *Procellaria Leachii*. A rival collector thought it should be called *Procellaria Bullockii*:

> ... in order to do an act of common justice to the individual who had the energy to undertake a voyage of enquiry, and the sagacity to distinguish the bird in question as an undescribed species.

Later the matter was resolved when three other skins were located in Europe, a French one being the type specimen which had been described in 1817 as *Procellaria leucorhoa* by a French taxonomist Louis Jean Pierre Vieillot (1748–1831). The species is now included in the genus *Oceanodroma*, but in English it has remained Leach's storm petrel. Bullock's original specimen seems to have got lost in the meantime!

Like most seabirds, petrels are long-lived – I ringed an adult Leach's petrel on North Rona in 1972 which was later retrapped there in 2002, 30 years later! Normally they do not return to the breeding colony until at least two or three years old so it must have been at least that when I first ringed it, therefore it is likely to have been even older than its ring indicated.

The Leach's petrel is present at the breeding burrows from late April to early November. Employing an endoscope to probe the contents of some 27 nest burrows on Dun in the summer of 2007 Dr Sarah Money *et al.* (2008) suggested that laying began around mid-May. A single egg was laid in 19 of the burrows. Of these, 60 per cent went on to fledge young, a success rate comparable to that found in north-eastern Canada.

With some 80,000 to 150,000 pairs now reckoned to be breeding on the Westmann Islands in Iceland, St Kilda is the second largest colony in the north-east Atlantic. About 13 islands off Britain and Ireland hold nesting Leach's petrels but St Kilda holds some 94 per cent of the combined population. They are most numerous on Dun with other colonies on Boreray, Soay and Hirta (especially Carn Mor). Breeding birds have been found on Levenish and they are suspected to be present in Stac an Armin. The 1999–2000 survey, using tape calls at burrows, found 45,433 aos, with 27,704 in Dun, 12,093 in Boreray, 3,605 in Hirta and 2,031 in Soay.

Following the national survey Seabird 2000 the response method for burrowing nocturnal species such as Leach's and storm petrels continued to be refined. When the 1999 survey on Dun came to be repeated in sample plots in 2003 it was discovered that the population there had declined by some 48 per cent, to some 14,490 AOS. One likely cause seemed to be predation by great skuas or bonxies, which were seen hunting at night (Votier *et al.* 2005). In 1996–7 Phillips *et al.* (1999) had predicted that the 229 pairs of bonxies by then breeding on St Kilda were consuming approximately 15,000 Leach's storm petrels per year. This, they claimed, could account for the apparent decline in burrow-occupancy on Dun and if correct would obviously be cause for serious concern.

Usually only males are likely to respond to taped calls and they are known to lose interest in responding as incubation of the egg progresses. The lack of a response does not necessarily mean the occupant has been killed, it may only have abandoned the burrow for the season. Instances of non-breeding birds occupying burrows prior to breeding are known, and these birds spend more time at night flying around the colony. Thus one would expect them to be much more vulnerable to predation by bonxies or gulls. Since petrels are such long-lived birds the loss of this youthful age cohort will have less impact on the population than the loss of established breeders. Once incubating, mature petrels tend to fly directly in or out of the burrow thereby reducing the risk of predation. Furthermore I know from my own experience with greater black-backed gulls on North Rona that only those gull pairs nesting near or within the colony were specialising in killing petrels. To assume the habit occurs equally in every pair of bonxies on St Kilda without more evidence will greatly overstate the predation problem. If the bonxies of St Kilda were able to catch petrels at sea it would be a different matter.

Clearly more research was needed so the same tape response method was repeated on Dun in 2006. It revealed another slight drop to 12,770 AOS, but not significantly different from the 2003 results. Furthermore, the most recent count of the predatory bonxies on Hirta, by Will Miles in 2008, revealed a notable decline in numbers (see below) so any impact on the petrels would also have been reduced.

The recent work with Leach's petrel study burrows by Money *et al.* (2006) showed that, in 2007 at least, breeding success appeared good, so food that year did not seem to be particularly scarce. Just like its smaller cousins, Leach's storm petrels fly out towards the Continental shelf to feed in summer, pattering along the surface probably mostly at night to take tiny crustaceans, fish, etc. But just how the two petrels differ in diet and feeding habits is unknown.

The great skua or bonxie was unknown on St Kilda to early visitors such as Martin, MacAulay or Mackenzie. It remained an irregular sight during the 19th century; until in July 1956 a pair were seen in Hirta – although not confirmed breeding. Breeding did not occur until 1963; then there was a 17 per cent increase each year until 1990, then 20 per cent up to 2000 when a peak of 240 AOS were counted. A figure of only 141 AOS in 1999 was too low, and over 200 AOS found in 2000 might have been nearer the true figure. In 2008 Will Miles counted only 140 nests on Hirta. A pair first bred in Soay in 1971 with up to 36 AOS present there by 1997. However, these were counted from the Cambir in Hirta and might have been underestimated. Two pairs of great skuas first bred in Boreray in 1979, fledging one chick but there have never been more than six pairs since. One pair reared a chick in Dun in 1996, and three pairs nested in 2008. Great skuas are present from early April to mid-September (with extreme dates being 27 March to 21 October).

Bonxies specialise in piratical chases on the larger gulls, gannets, etc. to rob their victims of their catch. But they will also kill birds like kittiwakes, and some may have taken to killing small petrels in recent years, perhaps because of changes in fishing practices and the reduced availability of fish. They can be quite aggressive whilst dive-bombing humans and other intruders near their nest, and more than one warden has been concussed on occasion.

Two pairs of Arctic skua defended territories in Hirta in 1999, but they did not actually breed. Then one pair fledged two young in 2000. These nimble skuas indulge in chasing smaller seabirds such as kittiwakes, terns and gulls to rob them of their catch.

Amongst the gulls, Martin noted herring gulls, lesser black-backed gulls and kittiwakes:

> There are three sorts of Sea-Malls here; the first is of a grey colour, like a goose, the second considerably less, and of a grey colour; and the third sort white, and less in size than a tame duck; the Inhabitants call it Reddag; it comes the fifteenth of April with a S.W. wind, lays its egg about the middle of May, and goes away in the month of August.

About 100 herring gulls are resident in Hirta over the winter. There were about 50 pairs breeding in the 1930s, 30 pairs in 1969 and 40 in 1974. Numbers then fell to 14 pairs by 1987, 20–24 pairs during the early 1990s, 17 in 1996 and only one pair in 1999. Herring gulls bred amongst the lazy beds at the west end of Dun where 34 pairs were counted in 1969, but by 1999 there were none. In 1971, 10–15 pairs of herring gulls were found breeding in Boreray and 49 in 1980 and 30–40 pairs in 1987 when nesting success was found to be high (*c.* 1.6 chicks per pair). No more than 30 nests were located in 2000. The only record of breeding in Levenish was three nests found in 1987. Overall, the species has declined in St Kilda from about 120 pairs in the late 1970s to about 35 pairs by 2000.

Lesser black-backed gulls return from their winter quarters in March and April and leave again by early September. Extreme dates are early February and mid-September. The species was known to have bred in Hirta in the 19th century. At least one pair bred in Gleann Mor, Hirta, in 1931, where 15 pairs were counted in 1947 though none in 1952. By 1963 this colony numbered 200 pairs, with a substantial decline thereafter to 46–55 pairs in 1996. The peak count for all of Hirta in 1969 was 263 pairs, 240 in 1976, 86 pairs in 1993 and only 13 pairs in 1999. Breeding peaked at 30 pairs in Dun in 1977, then declined to only 7 pairs in 2000. About 30 pairs bred in Soay in 1971, and about 60 pairs were visible through a telescope from the Cambir two years later. Jim Vaughan found only 15 pairs while ashore in Soay in 1993 and a complete island count in 2000 found only 3 pairs, all in the Tigh Dugan boulder field. The first thorough search of Boreray in 1980 turned up 4 nests, with 12 pairs recorded in 1987, and 7 pairs in 2000. Thus, over all of St Kilda there has been a decline from about 325 pairs during 1974–80 to about 30 pairs in 2000.

Mackenzie went on to describe a third gull:

The kittiwake arrives in great numbers late in the spring. It is here called 'ruideag' ... Early in May it makes its nest in very inaccessible places, and if possible where it has the protection of an overhanging cliff. It lays four eggs, which the parents hatch by turns for four weeks ... It is a very harmless and affectionate bird, and much more social than any of the other gulls. They come to the island together, fish together, and make their nests together.

Black-legged kittiwakes (as they are called nowadays) are present on their cliff colonies from March to August/September. The first complete surveys were made by Boyd in 1959 (7,770 pairs) and in 1969 (11,485 pairs). Seabird 2000 registered the lowest counts on record, only 3,886 AOS, with Boreray down 60 per cent to 1,146, Soay down 70 per cent to 382, Hirta (1,247) and Dun (981) both down 22 per cent. Stac Lee revealed a further 91 AOS and Stac an Armin 39. None have been found breeding on Levenish, while a colony of 150 nests on the stacs in Soay Sound in 1959 has now disappeared. The decline had apparently begun following a peak in 1993 and has continued into this century; a count in 2008 revealed fewer than 1,000 nests in the whole of St Kilda. In contrast to the other more coastal gulls, kittiwakes travel further offshore towards the continental shelf to feed on sandeels and other small fish near the surface.

The Reverend MacAulay was quick to vent his distaste for the largest gull of all, the greater black-backed, a feeling that was obviously shared by the islanders themselves:

At Hirta is too frequently seen, and very severely felt, a large sea-gull, which is detested by every St Kildian. This mischievous bird destroys every egg that falls in its way, very often the young fowls, and sometimes the weakest of the old. It is hardly possible to express the hatred with which this otherwise good natured people pursue these gulls. If one happens to mention them, it throws their whole blood into a ferment: serpents are not at all such detestable objects any where else.

They exert their whole strength of industry and skill to get hold of this cruel enemy, a task very far from being easy, as they are no less vigilant than wicked: If caught, they outvie one another in torturing this imp of hell to death; such is the emphatical language in which they express an action so grateful to their vindictive spirit: They pluck out his eyes, sew his wings together, and send him adrift . . .

This fowl is perfectly white in the breast and downwards, blueish along the back, and black in the wings: It is of the sea-maw kind, and equal in size to a Solan-Goose, or nearly so: They call it Tuliac in St Kilda; but in the other western isles it goes under a different name.

Several hundred great black-backed gulls overwinter in St Kilda. They were fairly common in 1894 and 1910 and probably increased after evacuation in 1930. Hirta peaked at 55 pairs in 1969, but now there are only 4. Dun held up to 40 nests in 1977, but only 2 were found in 2000. Boreray peaked at 27–30 pairs in 1980, but by 2000 there were only 14 pairs. Soay held about 10 pairs in 2000. Ten pairs were found in Levenish in 1987, but only 4 pairs by 1997, when a single pair was also noted on Stac an Armin. Over St Kilda as a whole, there has been a decline from about 150 pairs in the late 1970s to about 40 pairs by 2000. Gulls from St Kilda fly comparatively short distances to forage, but perhaps rely more on natural food sources rather than scavenging like their counterparts elsewhere.

Common or mew gulls first bred in 1963 and possibly may have done so twice in the 1840s. A clutch was trampled by sheep in Village Glen in 1979, but since then a pair has bred most years; young have fledged only four times (1980, 1986, 1991 and 1996). Sometimes a pair also tries to breed in Gleann Mor, while up to five pairs were present on Hirta from 1992 to 1994.

There remains one more seabird to discuss, but one that is so significant that it merits a chapter all to itself. That seabird is the great auk or garefowl.

.7.

The Great Auk

As on the death of an ancient hero, myths gathered around his memory as
quickly as clouds round the setting sun.

Alfred Newton 1896.

In 1863, the children's author Charles Kingsley, a good friend of Alfred
Newton, featured the great auk in his popular story *The Water Babies*. As
it stood on 'the Allalonestone, all alone' the garefowl reflected upon the demise
of his own species and began to cry tears of pure oil:

Soon I shall be gone, my little dear, and nobody will miss me; and then the poor
stone will be left all alone.

In fact, by that time the great auk was already extinct, although ornithologists were reluctant to give up all hope. A somewhat optimistic James Fisher
was to be the last to include the great auk in his standard identification guide
Bird Recognition in 1947.

Perhaps the most celebrated 'allalonestone' is the archipelago of St Kilda. It
is unlikely, however, that its steep cliff-bound coast ever offered many nesting
opportunities for this flightless seabird – the original 'penguin' – but St Kilda
has left for posterity several interesting eye-witness accounts.

One of the earliest accounts was given by Sir George Mackenzie of Tarbat
in the late 17th century. In it he mentioned great auks, though clearly he had
no personal experience of their eggs:

There may be many sorts of these fowls; some of them of strange shapes, among
which there is one which they call the Gare fowl, which is bigger than any goose,
and hath eggs as big almost as those of an ostrich ...

This was quoted by Sir Robert Sibbald (1641–1722) who was Geographer Royal of Scotland in 1682 and who in 1684 published the first volume of a natural history and geography of Scotland. Sibbald collected material from various informants including Martin Martin.

In 1697, Martin was able to give a unique – and fortunately, detailed – account of the great auk, if not from his own personal experience, then from some islanders who had known the bird intimately. His egg size estimate was more accurate for a start!

> The Sea-Fowl are first, Gairfowl, being the stateliest, as well as the largest sort, and above the size of a Solan Goose, of a black colour, red about the eyes, a large white spot under each, a long broad bill; it lays its egg upon the bare rock, which, if taken away, she lays no more for that year; she is whole-footed, and has the hatching spot under her breast, ie a bare spot from which the feathers have fallen off with the heat in hatching; its egg is twice as big as that of a Solan Goose, and is variously spotted, black, green and dark; it comes without regard to any wind, appears the first of May, and goes away about the middle of June.

Remember though, that we need to apply the 13-day correction to Martin's dates. There is still some debate as to what the Skye gentleman meant by 'red about the eyes'. We may never now know. The great auk was soon to become quite an uncommon sight on St Kilda. By 1758 the Reverend Kenneth MacAulay lamented:

> I had not an opportunity of knowing a very curious fowl, sometimes seen upon this coast, and an absolute stranger, I am apt to believe, in every other part of Scotland. The men of Hirta call it the Garefowl, corruptly perhaps instead of Rarefowl, a name probably given it by some one of those foreigners, whom either choice or necessity drew into this secure region. This bird is above four feet in length, from the bill to the extremities of its feet; its wings are in proportion to its size very short, so that they can hardly poise or support the weight of its very large body. His legs, neck, and bill are extremely long; it lays the egg ... close by the sea mark, being incapable on account of its bulk, to soar up to the cliffs. It makes its appearance in the month of July. The St Kildians do not receive an annual visit from this strange bird, as from all the rest in the list, and from many more. It keeps at a distance from them, they know not where, for a couple of years. From what land or ocean it makes its uncertain voyages to their isle, is perhaps a mystery in nature.

Making its appearance in July, it is obvious that the great auk was no longer nesting on St Kilda. Nor is there anything to indicate otherwise in a letter in the National Library of Scotland, probably written by the Reverend Neil Macleod of Mull sometime between 1756 and 1775. Macleod was son and brother of two Factors of St Kilda and his letter recollected a visit he made as a youth in 1746:

> The Gernhell is the most remarkable fowl about St Kilda, for his enormous size and rarity, his wings are so very small in proportion to his bulk that he does not fly: they are taken by surprising them where they sleep, or by intercepting their way to the sea and knocking them on the head with a staff; they lay their eggs a little above the sea mark on rocks of easy access; they carry off their young soon to feed them at sea.

In *Illustrations of Zoology* (1831) the Reverend James Wilson confirmed the bird's difficulties ashore, as quoted by Gray:

> From the total inability of these birds to fly, and their inaptitude at walking, they are seldom observed out of the water. Neither are they often seen beyond soundings. This probably arises from the necessity under which they labour of drying their plumage occasionally by mounting upon a rock or a stone, as their feathers can derive no advantage from the usual effects of flight. This motion of swimming, also, being so much less rapid than that of flying, they are comparatively restricted in their aquatic excursions.

In a letter to a friend in 1885 Professor Newton puzzled over the great auk's inability to fly:

> I can't satisfy myself as to the way in which the Garefowl's flightlessness was produced, and I suppose I never shall, I can only conjecture that he found wings fit for flight articles too expensive for him to indulge in ... On land I take it that the great auk had practically no enemies till man.

Being flightless and cumbersome on land, it is hardly surprising that the great auk had offered an obvious target for the fowlers of St Kilda. In the 17th century, Sir George Mackenzie had added to his brief reference:

> Among the other commodities they export out of the island, this is none of the meanest.

And so, sadly, the St Kildans doubtless played a significant part in the garefowl's demise, at least on their native island. By the 18th century the bird must have been quite scarce but still a fond memory, as a song composed around 1790 may testify. A fowler prepared to go to the bird cliffs with his father:

> *Suas mo lon, nuas mo rioba* – Bring up my rope, bring down my snare –
> *Chuala mis'an gug sa chuan.*   I have heard the gannet in the ocean!

The older man held the rope at the top while his son descended to harvest the seabirds. The edge collapsed and both men plunged to their death. In her grief the young widow composed a lament that in 1865 her daughter, the 76-year-old bard Euphemia MacCrimmon, sang to the folklorist Alexander Carmichael, and which was reproduced by Calum Ferguson (1995, 2006):

> *M'eudail thusa, mo lur 's mo shealgair,*
> > You're my treasure, my hero and my hunter,
> *Thug thu 'n-dè dhomh 'n sùl 's an gearrbhall.*
> > Yesterday you gave me the gannet and the garefowl.
>
> *... Na h-eòin a'tighinn, cluinneam an ceòl!'*
> > The birds are approaching, let me hear their music!

In Lightfoot's *Flora Scotica* (1777) Thomas Pennant gave a description of the great auk that was obviously derived from the Reverend Kenneth MacAulay. But thereafter the bird was rarely mentioned.

In 1900, Norman Heathcote offered a novel explanation of how, nearly a century earlier, Britain's war with Denmark had been implicated in the global extinction of the great auk. In 1807, a British privateer was marauding around Iceland, spending some time killing great auks and destroying their eggs on Geirfuglasker, one of the principal breeding sites. Then, in 1810, when the Faroes were being forbidden by Denmark to trade with Britain,

Fig. 12.
Euphemia MacCrimmon (Captain Thomas).

they despatched a boat to Iceland to stock up on much-needed food supplies. Again the flightless great auk proved an easy target. Warships engaged in the American War of Independence certainly took their toll and once the bird had been hunted to extinction in Newfoundland around 1830, Iceland in the east Atlantic became its last, desperate refuge anywhere in the world.

But first, let us set out on this road to ultimate extinction nearer home in Scotland. According to Orkney-born botanist Professor James W. H. Traill (1851–1919) – a successor to William MacGillivray's Chair of Aberdeen University's Natural History department – a pair of great auks were constantly seen in Papa Westray, Orkney, for several years. In his *Birds of the West of Scotland* Robert Gray said they were christened by the people the King and Queen of the Auks. The private collector and jeweller William Bullock (c 1773–1849) visited Orkney in 1812 (see Chapter 6) and was told by the natives that for many years now only a single male had visited the island of Papa Westray. The female had been stoned to death just before Mr Bullock's arrival. He did see the male though. A witness wrote:

> The male ... Mr Bullock had the pleasure of chasing for several hours in a six-oared boat, but without being able to kill him, for although he frequently got near him, so expert was the bird in its natural element, that it appeared impossible to shoot him. The rapidity with which he pursued his course under water was almost incredible.

In his *General History of Birds* Dr John Latham (1740–1837) added that as soon as Bullock left the island, the native boatmen knocked the bird down with an oar – a 'lucky' (Latham's word!) stroke which secured for the British Museum its finest garefowl. Traill's version was that a fortnight after Bullock's visit one was shot (by local man William Foulis) and sent on to him; the other bird then forsook the place. Professor Traill supposed they had a nest on the island, but on account of its exposed situation the surf must have washed the egg from the rocks.

A modern monument on Papa Westray celebrates the bird as the last in Britain, but this is not in fact correct. Although William Bullock was in St Kilda in 1818, he did not mention the great auk. It was the merchant/amateur naturalist Symington Grieve (1849–1932) who in his 1885 monograph on the species quoted an anonymous note in the *Edinburgh Philosophical Journal* of 1824 which confirmed a capture on St Kilda 'three years ago'. The date August 1821 was confirmed in 1880 from Northern Lighthouse Board records. Grieve went on:

> Two young men and two boys, who were in a boat at the east side of the island, observed it sitting on a low ledge of the cliff. The two young men were landed at opposite points of the ledge, but about equidistant from the bird, which they

gradually approached, whilst meantime the boys had rowed the boat close up to the rock under where it was sitting. At last, becoming frightened by the approach of the men, it leaped down towards the sea, but only to fall into the arms of the youths, who held it fast. Five years ago (1880) one of the boys, Donald McQueen, was still living, aged 73. From these men the bird was obtained by Mr McLellan, the tacksman of Glass or Scalpay [Harris].

At Scalpay, we are told, the bird was presented to Mr Robert Stevenson (1772–1850), grandfather of the writer Robert Louis Stevenson. As engineer to the Board of Commissioners of Northern Lights he was on the annual tour of inspection in the yacht *Regent*. Accompanying Stevenson was a Fife minister, the Reverend Dr John Fleming (1785–1857) who abandoned his calling to become Professor of Natural Philosophy in Aberdeen, and then of Natural Sciences in Edinburgh. Together they intended to keep the great auk alive as long as possible and then present its body to the Edinburgh University Museum. In volume 10 of the *Edinburgh Philosophical Journal*, Fleming (1824) gave this description of his great auk:

> The bird was emaciated, and had the appearance of being sickly, but in the course of a few days became sprightly, having been plentifully supplied with fresh fish, and permitted occasionally to sport in the water with a cord fastened to one of its legs to prevent escape. Even in this state of restraint it performed the motions of diving and swimming under water with a rapidity that set all pursuit from a boat at defiance.

However, after Stevenson and Fleming had left the ship, the great auk made its escape near the entrance to the Firth of Clyde. Robert Gray gave a rather confused account of this incident in 1871 and added that a dead great auk was said to have been washed ashore near Gourock a short time after. Later another dead specimen was found floating in the sea off Lundy.

A further anonymous account in volume 11 of the *Edinburgh Philosophical Journal*, which was probably also contributed by Fleming, gave mention of Stevenson's encounter on Scalpay and then noted yet another specimen from Lewis:

> Of the rare birds which frequent these islands, one is particularly worthy of notice, the great auk *Alca impennis*, a live specimen of which was, three years ago, brought to Harris by Mr Maclellan of Scalpay. This individual afterwards made its escape.
>
> As the great auk is now become a very scarce bird, it may be mentioned, that a specimen came to the hands of Mr Adam, Factor of the Lewis, last year, but being unfortunately in bad condition, the skin was ultimately turned out of doors; it was caught in a fishing net.

By 1831 George Clayton Atkinson could discover little about the species:

The great auk, *'gairfaol'*, is very scarce, coming only once in ten or a dozen years and never breeding there.

Curiously, in his paper read to the Natural History Society of Northumberland and Durham in January 1832, Atkinson listed the great auk as one of the 'birds which we observed in St Kilda', but this is obviously an error.

In the *Edinburgh Journal of Natural and Geographical Science* (1830) Professor William MacGillivray of Aberdeen included amongst 'The Birds of the Outer Hebrides':

Alca impennis, the Great Auk – an Gearbhul – An individual of this very rare species, as I was informed by Mr Adam, was sent to him in Lewis [the second bird mentioned above by Fleming]. The late Mr MacNeill, who was long tacksman of St Kilda informed me that it occurred there at irregular intervals of two or three years, but I have not heard of its having been seen on the coast of the Outer Hebrides.

In July 1840, MacGillivray's 18-year-old son John visited St Kilda where he was told:

... by several of the inhabitants [that the great auk was] of not unfrequent occurrence about St Kilda, where, however, it has not been known to breed for many years back. Three or four specimens only have been ever procured during the memory of the oldest inhabitant.

Professor Alfred Newton wrote to Harvie-Brown about a curious incident on St Kilda, his synthesis of various accounts being quoted in *A Vertebrate Fauna of the Outer Hebrides* (1888). It is worth giving in full since it included the important event that has elevated the great auk to such an iconic bird in St Kilda's avifauna. The first incident took place in 1821 and has already been referred to above:

The bird, frightened by men on the cliff jumped into a boat in which was a boy of fourteen years of age, named Donald MacQueen, whose son of the same name – now a man of from fifty to fifty-five years of age – gave Mr Henry Evans these particulars, and heard his father say he caught the bird thus. It was on the main island, ie St Kilda itself [Hirta].

But it also seems, from Mr Evans's information, that another bird was caught on Stac an Armine, in or about 1840, by some five men who were stopping there for a few days. Three of them were Lauchlan McKinnon, about thirty years of age – and now, or till recently, alive – his father-in-law, and the elder Donald MacQueen before mentioned – both now dead. McKinnon told Mr Evans that they found the bird on a ledge of rock, that they caught it asleep, tied its legs together, took it up their bothy, kept it alive for three days, and then killed it with a stick, thinking it might be a witch. They threw the body behind the bothy and left it there. McKinnon described the bird to Mr Evans, so that the latter has no doubt about its having been a Garefowl.

It was Malcolm McDonald who actually laid hold of the bird, and held it by the neck with his two hands, till others came up and tied its legs. It used to make a great noise, like that made by a gannet, but much louder, when shutting its mouth. It opened its mouth when any one came near it. It nearly cut the rope with its bill. A storm arose, and that, together with the size of the bird and the noise it made, *caused them to think it was a witch.* It was killed on the third day after it was caught and McKinnon declares they were beating it for an hour with two large stones before it was dead: he was the most frightened of all the men, and advised the killing of it. The capture took place in July. The bird was about halfway up the Stack.' ('This last statement,' says Professor Newton, 'is, to me, conclusive that the bird could not have been a Great Northern Diver, as some have suggested.') That side of the Stack slopes up, so that a man can fairly easily walk up. There is grass upon it, and a little soil up to the point where they found the bird. Mr Evans says that he knows there is a good ledge of rock at the sea-level, from which a bird might start to climb to the place. Mr Evans tried in vain to fix the exact year in which this event happened, but could only get 1840 as an approximate estimate.

Professor Newton was to add:

I have an extract from the *Glasgow Herald* of 14th June 1886 (sent me by Robert Gray) containing among other things, a version of the 1821 story, which differs in some slight particulars from Mr Evans. This I sent to him, and he (Mr Evans) prefers his own.

Sadly, the '1840' bird was the last British example and one of the very last great auks in existence. It is curious that neither John MacGillivray in 1840, James Wilson in 1841, nor William and Henry Milner in 1847 mentioned this particular incident. Indeed, only MacGillivray referred to the great auk at all. Nor did the Reverend Neil Mackenzie mention this last great auk. Amongst his notes, his son the Reverend J. B. Mackenzie could find nothing about the species:

... but from conversations I had with him I know that he made all possible enquiry. None of the natives then living had ever seen it, but they had heard of a bird of that kind, which they vaguely described. After consideration of all that he could ascertain about it, his conclusion was that at the time when the island was uninhabited it did breed there in some numbers, but that after the island was inhabited it gradually got exterminated by the frequent robbing of its eggs.

This could very easily be done, as the places where it could land and breed were very few, and all on the main island and near the village.

We know from later visitors that one or two of the men from the 1821 incident would still have been living during Mackenzie's tenure on St Kilda so it is strange that they never seemed to have confessed this to their minister. Yet accounts would indicate that the last great auk would seem to have been killed just before Mackenzie's departure for the mainland in 1844. Or was it?

Henry Evans reckoned that the garefowl had been killed around 1840, but it is just possible it happened *after* the Reverend Mackenzie left St Kilda in 1844. If this was the case, then it might qualify as the last great auk on the planet! Or perhaps, as Mary Harman has suggested in an article in the *Hebridean Naturalist* (1993), the islanders were ashamed to admit to it, knowing in retrospect the importance of the bird and conscious that the good Reverend might not have approved of their killing it as a witch. It is known that Malcolm (or Calum) MacDonald, the perpetrator, died in October 1846.

It is interesting to add a note of scepticism. Charles Dixon, in his 'Ornithology of St Kilda' published in *Ibis* 1885:

> … was convinced that much of the information which has been gathered at St Kilda respecting the great auk is very unreliable. I think that the great northern diver has been its proxy more than once; and that the bird which the St Kildans stoned to death (as I was informed) forty years ago [1845?] on Stack-am-Armain, thinking it was an evil spirit, was nothing more than a *Columbus glacialis* [great northern diver] I must however, state that the old man who assisted in this orthino-logical sacrilege recognised the plate of the great auk which I had brought with me. None of the young men know anything about the species, not even by name. The great auk's only link with the present day is the grey-haired weather-beaten old St Kildan with whom I conversed respecting its visit so long ago.

Newton has convincingly argued that the bird could not have been a great northern diver, which just would not be capable of landing on such a rocky shore let alone moving up the slope. Nor would it have any reason to do so. The man with whom Dixon spoke could only have been Lachlan McKinnon (1808–95), the sole survivor of the incident, and who had been 30 at the time. It was he who, to allay his superstitions, had advocated killing the bird. Intriguingly, Dixon claimed the event had taken place 40 years earlier, which tantalisingly might put it at 1845! Maybe that is why MacGillivray, Wilson and the Reverend Mackenzie did not mention the incident; it might just have taken place after they all left. Whatever the date of the incident, if indeed it took place at all, it could just vie with the last two great auks killed on the island of Eldey, off south-west Iceland, in 1844 as the acknowledged final extinction event of the species.

Although the last Faroese great auk had been killed on the island of Stora Dimun on 1 July 1808, a young ornithologist named John Wolley (1825–59) went to Faroe in 1849, convinced that the species might still exist:

About *Alca impennis* I made enquiries wherever I had opportunity, but I could learn very little. An old man, Paul Joensen, had seen one fifty years ago ...

Wolley travelled extensively in northern Europe, but considering his abiding fascination with the great auk, it is surprising that he never got to Iceland until 1858. Seven years earlier he had befriended Alfred Newton, who was five years his junior and partially lame since boyhood. In 1858, the pair journeyed to Iceland in quest of great auks. The steep cliffs of Eldey present an unlikely situation for the great auk to choose to breed, but apparently they used to nest on the appropriately named Geirfuglasker 14 miles (22 km) beyond until that island was obliterated in a volcanic eruption in 1830. There are several more islands around Iceland that bear the name Geirfuglasker, including one in the Westmann Islands quite near Surtsey.

The same year that the eruption destroyed their former home, a dozen or more great auks were found for the first time, and slaughtered, on Eldey. Landing there was never to be easy, even for humans. In two months the sea was never calm enough for Wolley and Newton to set foot on Eldey and so:

... we have come back knowing no more than when we started whether the great auk is living or dead.

Wolley died the following year from a brain tumour, still in his thirties. However, while in Iceland, he and Newton had succeeded in interviewing the men involved in the demise of the last great auks. From Wolley's notebooks three years later, Newton was able to present this poignant account of the tragedy on Eldey, that fateful day in early June 1844:

In form the island is a precipitous stack, perpendicular nearly all round ... at the foot of this inclined plane is the only landing place; and further up, out of reach of the waves, is the spot where the Gare-fowls had their home ... As the men ... clambered up they saw two Gare-fowls sitting among numberless other rock birds [guillemots and razorbills], and at once gave chase. The Gare-fowls showed not the slightest disposition to repel the invaders, but immediately ran along under the high cliff, their heads erect, their little wings somewhat extended. They uttered no cry of alarm, and moved, with their short steps, about as quickly as a man could walk. Jon with outstretched arms, drove one into a corner, where he soon had it fast. Sigurd and Ketil pursued the second, and the former seized it close to the edge of the rock, here risen to a precipice some fathoms high, the water being directly below it. Ketil then returned to the sloping shelf whence the birds had started, and saw an egg lying on the lava slab, which he knew to be a gare-fowl's. He took it up, but finding it was broken, he put it down again. Whether there was not another egg is uncertain. All this took place in much less time than it takes to tell it. They hurried down again, for the wind was rising. The birds were strangled and cast into the boat ...

In 1853, it was a close friend and colleague of the Reverend Fleming (the recipient of the Scalpay great auk), namely the Reverend James Wilson, who had been at St Kilda in 1841 who summed up the great auk's situation in the May 1853 issue of the *North British Review*. He lamented:

So infrequent has this great sea-bird become of late years that many considerate people begin to question the continuance of its existence upon earth.

He added that it had not bred anywhere in continental Europe for a century, it was now unknown in Iceland, had not been observed or heard of either in Greenland or the Faroe Islands for many a day and had ceased to frequent St Kilda. Gray (1871) ended his rather rambling, and in places inconsistent, account of the great auk with this final, gloomy observation:

Whether, however, the species be extinct or not, the fate of the Garefowl has still much interest. If it still exists, its doom will probably be sealed by its re-discovery.

Fig. 13. John Wolley.

For all practical purposes, therefore, we may speak of it as a thing of the past ...
the place thereof knoweth it no more.

On 22 May 1868, Captain Henry John Elwes (1846–1922) of the Scots
Fusilier Guards landed on Hirta from the paddle-steamer HMS *Harpy*. He
said he was the first naturalist to visit in 20 years. He was President of the
British Ornithologists' Union when he died in 1922. In this august body's
journal *Ibis* (1869) he described his St Kilda visit in 'The Bird Stations of the
Outer Hebrides', giving special mention to the great auk:

> I showed a picture of the great auk ... to the people, some of the oldest of whom
> appeared to recognise it, and said that it had not been seen for many years; but
> they were so excited by the arrival of strangers, that it was impossible to get
> them to say more about it; and though Mr Mackay [the minister] promised to
> take down any stories or information about the bird that he could collect when
> they had leisure to think about it, he has not as yet sent me any. I do not think,
> however, that more than two or three examples are at all likely to have been seen
> in the last forty years, as Mr Atkinson of Newcastle, who was there in 1831, does
> not say a word about it in his paper beyond mentioning the name, and neither
> John MacGillivray, who visited the place in 1840, nor Sir W. Milner, says that
> any specimens had been recently procured. I believe that Bullock was also there
> about 1818; and, as he had not long before met with the species in Orkney, there
> is little doubt that he would have mentioned it to somebody if he had heard of
> any having been recently procured at St Kilda.
>
> I made every inquiry about this bird on the north and west of Lewis and
> showed pictures of it to the fishermen; but all agreed that nothing of the sort
> had ever been since they could remember. Indeed the only specimen of which
> we know for certain that has been seen in the present century is the one that
> Dr Fleming had in 1821, which was captured alive by Mr Maclellan of Scalpay,
> somewhere off St Kilda.

Strangely, Newton was later to report, in 1861, that Sir William Milner had
been presented with a fine specimen, stuffed with turf, that had been killed
in the Hebrides a few years previously. However, the date, if not the incident
itself, must be suspect.

On 24 May 1880, a rather remorseless East Lothian farmer and ornithologist
called R. Scott Skirving reached St Kilda on the *Dunara Castle*. Keen to find
out about the great auk, he interviewed some local 'cragsmen' whom he claimed
had heard much about the great auk and took some interest in its history
– which seems at odds with the islanders' normal reticence about the bird.
They introduced him to an old man who, they said, had been the capturer of
the now historic auk secured alive in 1821:

The man was brought to me, a very little old fellow called [73-year-old Donald McQueen]. He said he was about 70 but he looked 80 at least. He said the people were wrong when they said he personally caught the Auk. He was one of four young men who caught it. They were in a boat when they saw the Auk on a low ledge of rock on the East side of the Island and they resolved to try to catch it. One man was landed at some distance from the bird and a second as far off on the other side of it. Then the boat was rowed slowly towards the bird and right in front of it, while the two men crawled along the rock towards the last of the Auks. It finally leapt down to the sea just as one of the men got directly under it, and it absolutely sprang into his outstretched arms.

The old man showed me how his companion clasped it . . .

In 1895, Steele Elliott reported on the second, more recent (1840) incident:

When we were on the island [1894] one of the oldest inhabitants was still living who helped in the slaughter of one of the last birds ever seen there, and probably one of the last specimens ever obtained. But, unfortunately it was destroyed. This useless destruction of birds and eggs is still a very weak point with the natives; they destroy numbers of young [seabirds] by throwing them out of their nests without any apparent reason, and the eggs that are highly incubated, or as they term them 'sun struck', are destroyed by being thrown from the cliffs into the sea beneath.

In his 'Observations on the fauna of St Kilda' (also dated 1895) Steele Elliott added:

The old grey-haired man, Lachlan McKinnon, mentioned by Mr Dixon as having taken part in stoning to death a great auk in Stack an Armin, was, I am sorry to say, dying when I left the island. An interview with him during my stay would have been useless, as I was informed that his memory had left him for some time.

Lachlan McKinnon died the following year (1896).

In the *Oban Times* of 11 July 1896 the groundsman Donald Ferguson and his son Alexander (later a tweed merchant in Glasgow) claimed to have seen a pair of birds at St Kilda similar in shape to a razorbill but twice the size. There is no indication when this was and, besides, great auks were eight times larger than a razorbill. So this report must lie alongside countless other wrong sightings. Norman Heathcote (1900) was told that a rock where the great auk used to breed was still called 'the rock of the garefowl', which Henry Evans (in Harvie-Brown and Buckley, 1888) placed in Glen Bay, Hirta. Elliott (1895) noted a ledge on Soay was similarly named after the great auks which bred there. He also mentioned another site on 'Stac Lii' – which surely must be an error for Stac an Armin.

It is generally accepted that it was on Eldey in 1844 that the great auk officially became extinct, when the lone pair, with an egg, were killed. Only skins, bones and eggs remain for posterity. The Eldey egg was damaged so was thrown away, but the internal organs of both adults were preserved in spirit and are in the University of Copenhagen Zoological Museum. The whereabouts of the two skins is not known. Sadly, when and where many other museum eggs and skins were collected has been lost through time, which reduces their value to science.

While many specimens originally lay in the hands of private collectors, most of them nowadays have ended up in museums. In 1844, a skin might only fetch a few pounds on the open market; the last ones to change hands in the 1970s fetched about £9,000. Eggs were most in demand in Victorian times, during the heyday of egg-collecting, when they might fetch around £250 each; by the 1930s they were worth £400. In Britain eggs can no longer be sold between private dealers and thus usually come to be deposited in museums.

In *Ibis* 1871 Newton reviewed 'the existence of 71 or 72 skins, 9 skeletons, detached bones of 38 or 41 different birds and 65 eggs'.

Of these relics Newton reckoned that Britain held by far the largest share, namely 22 skins, 4 skeletons, 13 detached bones and no fewer than 41 eggs. This does not mean that Britain was a stronghold of the species in the past,

Fig. 14. Cartoon by Ian Lyster.

and Newton's analysis probably reflects merely the acquisitiveness of British collectors in Victorian times. Indeed, the figures can be revised slightly now. In actual fact, there are in existence 81 mounted skins, 24 complete skeletons and 75 eggs. The species was undoubtedly more common in eastern Canada (where many bones can yet be picked up on Funk Island, for instance). As the American ornithologist F. A. Lucas put it in 1890:

> Here … the bones of myriads of Garefowl lie buried in the shallow soil formed above their mouldering bodies, and here, in this vast Alcine cemetery, are thickly scattered slabs of weathered granite, like so many crumbling tombstones marking the resting place of the departed Auks.

Being flightless, great auks had been easy prey for generations of hungry sailors and bird fowlers alike, factors which undoubtedly brought about their extinction. It was the Breton navigator Jacques Cartier who, on 21 May 1534, discovered large numbers of flightless great auks on Funk Island off Newfoundland. He noted they were 'exceedingly fat' and:

> … in less than half an hour we filled two boats full of them as if they had been with stones: so that besides them that we did eat fresh, every ship did powder and salt four or five barrels full of them.

When hungry Antarctic sailors in southern oceans finally encountered what we now refer to as penguins, they were quick to slaughter them too.

If the great auk ever did nest in any numbers on St Kilda, it is likely that the islanders had brought about its extinction there too. It would have been easy meat for them. Collectors in the 18th and 19th centuries merely mopped up the last remaining birds, who were by then too few and scattered to stage any sort of recovery anyway.

So are we left with just bones and feathers? What exactly do we know about that lost seabird known as the great auk or the garefowl? In his fascinating book *Great Auk Islands* (1993) Professor Tim Birkhead summed it up:

> The Great Auk was an impressive, flightless bird, standing about 70 cm high and weighing in at about 5 kg, five times as much as a common guillemot and almost eight times that of its closest relative, the razorbill. We can be fairly sure that in the absence of man, great auks were long-lived birds. Considering all bird species, as a general rule, the largest have the highest survival rates. The pattern also occurs in the auk family, and indicates that great auks may once have been among the longest-lived birds …
>
> What we know about the great auk is pieced together from a variety of sources, some based on written accounts, some based on educated speculation. The species was confined to the north Atlantic and we know of at least seven locations where it bred and several other places where it might once have bred …

We know from contemporary accounts, that like its closest relatives the two guillemots and the razorbill, the great auk was a colonial species, and that like them it laid a single egg.

Knowing the dimensions of its egg, and extrapolating from its nearest living relatives, Birkhead deduced that when fresh its egg would weigh about 327 g, requiring to be incubated for 43 days or 6 weeks. From the size of the egg a great auk hatchling would have weighed about 236 g. If Martin was correct in saying that the great auk's breeding season lasted 7 weeks in total, then its young must have left the colony when only about 5 days old, much sooner than most other auks. The ancient murrelet, however – a little smaller than our black guillemot – has a chick that takes to sea only 2 days after hatching and weighing a mere 27 g. Sadly, amongst all the skins and bones, there is not a single great auk fledgling preserved. Old accounts of adults at sea do indicate they carried their young on their backs.

Being flightless, great auks would not have been able to make such long foraging trips as their cousins, so it made sense for great auk chicks to have been so precocious and thus able to accompany their parents out to feeding grounds at the earliest opportunity.

Perhaps techniques yet to be devised by modern science will one day tell us more about the extinct great auk's life-style. But for now we can only ponder its mysteries. When a stuffed great auk came up for sale in the 19th century, a newspaper reported:

This relic of the sea is ... one of the seventy-nine [*sic*] which remain to stir spectacled old men to frenzy and inspire awe in the bosoms of those to whom the unattainable is the pinnacle of desire.

When some great auk eggs were being shown in Edinburgh in 1880, one perplexed member of the public is said to have muttered:

But the eggs are of no use; they will never hatch.

.8.

Fowling

The island of St Kilda may be ranked among the greatest curiosities of the British Empire. The situation of the place, the genius of its inhabitants, their manners and customs, the constitution of their little Commonwealth, that amazing dexterity with which they manage the most important branches of their business, that unexampled courage, with which they encounter dangers insurmountable to any other race of men, and that perhaps happy ignorance, which renders them absolute strangers to those extravagant desires and endless pursuits, which keep the great and active world in a constant agitation.

Kenneth MacAulay 1758.

IN 1865, the Lismore-born folklorist Alexander Carmichael reached St Kilda where he was excited to meet old Euphemia MacCrimmon (1788–1869). Despite acute disapproval from the island minister, not to mention competition from barking dogs and noisy children, she gave him many poems, songs and stories which he included in his monumental *Carmina Gadelica*. The most poignant must be her account of a tragedy on the cliffs:

Unfortunately, my father died shortly after he and my mother were married. He went with my grandfather to catch birds. Being young and active, he was the one below on the end of the rope killing the birds. The rock on which my grandfather was standing at the top of the cliff crumbled and both men plunged into the sea. The seabirds they had tied round their waists kept them afloat, but they were soon blown out to sea and lost.

Effie's mother went on to compose a heart-rending lament for her dead husband (quoted in Chapter 7). Fortunately, such fatalities were not that common, but images of St Kildan men risking their lives on ropes over precipitous cliffs or clutching handfuls of harvested seabirds remain amongst the most iconic of their culture.

The fact that the islanders were famous for catching and eating fulmars and were doing so until as recently as the 1930s has left the impression that St Kilda was unique in exploiting seabirds, at least in a British context. This is, however, far from the case. A similar culture prevailed on Mingulay, for instance, an island south of Barra and the most southerly but one of the Outer Hebridean chain. In the latter half of the 19th century up to 150 people lived there, but only 11 when the island was finally evacuated in 1912 (Buxton 1995).

In 1698, in his book on the wider Hebrides, Martin Martin affirmed how the Mingulay folk:

> ... take great numbers of sea-fowls from the rocks, and salt them with the ashes of burnt sea-ware in cows hides, which preserves them from putrefaction ... The rock Linmull ... abounds with sea-fowls that build and hatch here in summer; such as the Guillemot, Coulter-neb [puffin], etc

The range of seabirds available was more limited than on St Kilda. Mingulay and its neighbouring islands had no nesting gannets for example, nor – in those days – fulmars. The folk on the Barra Isles (Pabbay, Mingulay and Berneray) took adults and eggs of guillemots and razorbills, together with young puffins, shearwaters and 'cormorants' (probably more likely to have been shags). There are so many parallels between the two islands that Mingulay is often referred to as 'the other St Kilda'. The cliffs of St Kilda, however, tower twice the height of those on Mingulay, and the islanders fearlessly danced about them on ropes of hemp or horsehair. In hair-raising contrast, the fowlers in Mingulay:

> ... do not seem to have used ropes as they do in St Kilda, but to have clambered among the rocks like goats.

One of the most famous of Mingulay's fowlers was the barrel-chested Roderick MacNeill who died in 1875 aged 96. The folklorist Alexander Carmichael had met him in 1883:

> He had been an extraordinary 'rocker' after birds, moving about on precipices of eight hundred feet sheer down to the sea, where a goat might hesitate to go. So powerful was the man that wherever his fingers could get an insertion in the crevices of rock, he could move his body along the face of the precipice without any other support.

At the opposite end of the Hebridean chain, for hundreds of years the men of Ness in Lewis have been sailing north to Sulaisgeir every autumn to harvest young gannets or 'gugas'. They still do so to this day. The folk who until 1844 lived on neighbouring Rona had no boat, and could only harvest the birds on their own cliffs. So too did the community on Handa, an impressive seabird island off the west coast of Sutherland. Fowling was common in the Shetland and Orkney Islands and on the cliffs of Yorkshire.

Not only was the practice widespread it was also an ancient one for seabird bones have been found in kitchen middens dating back thousands of years throughout the length and breadth of Britain and Ireland. In 19 such archaeological excavations spread from Shetland to Ayrshire, James Fisher (1966) mentioned great auk bones in ten of them, gannets and cormorants in eight, guillemots in six, razorbills in four, puffins in three and petrels/shags/kittiwakes/terns in one each. There are many more recent excavations that could now be added to this list. The flightless great auk was obviously easy and rewarding fare. Many of these birds were probably taken in winter away from the breeding colonies. We know of some fowling techniques that were employed offshore in more recent times, St Kilda and the Faroes being especially revealing.

Seabirds congregating in traditional colonies have always been vulnerable to exploitation by humans. Nesting on inaccessible cliffs and islands and at high densities, they are relatively secure from ground predators and usually turn out to be relatively fearless of humans. Furthermore, seabirds tend to be ungainly on land, and a few are even flightless. So if fowlers overcome weather and rocks to reach seabird colonies, they find relatively easy prey. The temptation to kill large numbers in the birds' short breeding season does, however, generate a storage problem for winter consumption. Preserving seabirds and their eggs in draughty and dry, turf-roofed stone huts called *cleitean* may well have been a unique St Kildan development. Some 1,200 *cleitean* in various states of repair are to found on Hirta alone, with a further 78 on Stac an Armin, 50 or so on Boreray, 40 on Soay, and even one on Stac Lee that seems to have served as a bothy.

Reaching seabird colonies usually requires considerable climbing or boating skills, but also demands an element of bravado! Malcolm MacDonald from Ness seemed to have been first to have set foot on the summit of the great stack of Handa where he collected gull and puffin eggs. It is likely, however, that he cherished the challenge as much as the reward. It was in keeping with this heroic character that in 1884, some months after his only companion Murdo Mackay had died there, he too came to end his days on Rona, the most isolated inhabitable island in Britain.

Back on St Kilda around 1830 the Reverend Neil Mackenzie was aware of the risks:

> That a rope may break is not a very common source of danger; much more common is a tuft of grass slipping from the rock under the foot, or a stone

Fig. 15. A fowler, Alex Ferguson, poses on a rope for the photographer (R. Kearton).

loosened either by the foot or the rope falling upon those below. Once when I was with them I had to dress a wound in a man's head from which the brain was protruding, caused by a stone falling upon him when fowling on Soay. He fortunately recovered.

It was obviously a dangerous undertaking and fatalities were not unknown. In 1678, Robert Moray noted how St Kildan men seldom grew old, most either drowning or breaking their necks on the cliffs. Later authors often refuted this melodramatic statement, observing how the men could in fact live to a great age. Cliff deaths do seem to have been remarkably few. Mary Harman (1997) listed only a dozen deaths on St Kilda's cliffs in a little over a century.

Some traditional tales exhibit heroic self-sacrifice and extraordinary life choices. As an example, in 1838 Lachlan Maclean recounted the tale of a father and his two sons on a cliff when they noticed with horror that the rope holding them had worn against a stone. It was not going to support them for much longer so the sons made their father climb up to safety, just before the rope gave way. Both sons fell to their deaths.

A few years later, the Reverend Wilson told of two men on another rope which was badly frayed and about to give way; the top man cut the rope beneath him and let his companion below plummet to his death. Even young women could succumb; one lost her footing whilst checking fulmar snares. On another occasion, Murdoch Gillies and his daughter opted to overnight on a ledge to await the arrival of early-morning guillemots but were never seen again. According to the Kearton brothers, a girl watching men collecting eggs on Dun in 1892 was blown over the cliff. Miraculously she fell head first into a puffin burrow on the earthen slope below and survived!

In the 1930s, in South Uist, the American folklorist Margaret Fay Shaw (1903–2003) was told of a strange Gaelic proverb:

> *Biodh a ch-uile duine toirt sgairbh a creig dha fhéin.*

It translates as 'let every man take his own shags from the cliff'. Reputedly it recalled two St Kildans who went to the cliffs to gather shags. One held the rope while his companion descended. But after some time the man above shouted that it must now be his turn. The man below foolishly replied: 'Let every man take his own shags from the cliff.' 'Well,' countered the man above, 'if that is the way things are to be, let every man be at the top of his own rope!' With that he let loose the line, leaving his greedy companion to his fate. Undoubtedly this must be apocryphal for, in such a egalitarian and altruistic society, surely no St Kildan would mete out such wilful treatment to a companion.

There were other noteworthy incidents whilst fowling. We have already heard of the three men and eight boys who survived the 1727 winter on Stac an Armin, while back on Hirta and unable to retrieve the party the population was being decimated by smallpox from about 125 souls to only 30. Similarly, in October 1759, ten men were landed on Boreray from the islanders' only boat, just before a storm came up. The boat then had to shelter below the cliffs for three days before getting back to Hirta where it was dashed to pieces in Village Bay and all nine of the crew were drowned. The men on Boreray had to survive the winter in a bothy until finally rescued by the Steward in June. As the Reverend MacAulay recorded:

> Before they quitted this prison, the skins of sheep, and of the larger fowls tacked together with feathers, were all the clothing that some of them wore. What a grotesque figure they made in this distressful situation, one may easily imagine.

The men survived by killing sheep or harvesting seabirds to store for the winter. The 50 *cleitean* on Boreray and no fewer than 78 on Stac an Armin could all have been stuffed full of drying seafowl before winter, while, on Boreray at least, there were sheep and abundant freshwater springs. A few sheep were sometimes grazed on Stac an Armin, while Martin reported that a 'fountain of good water' was to be found there also. Nonetheless, just how the eleven marooned men and boys survived the winter months on Stac an Armin beggars belief.

In a British context, seabird harvesting has nowhere been better documented than on St Kilda. At the same time, Ken Williamson's *The Atlantic Islands* (1948) and Arne Nørrevang's *Fuglefangsten på Faerøerne* (1977) are classic studies on fowling in the Faroes. Along with parts of Iceland and Norway, these are some of the best-known fowling communities (Randall 2005), but there are others throughout the world. Indeed, coastal-dwelling humans have exploited seabirds as food ever since they first adopted a hunter-gatherer life-style. There are lively depictions of what must surely be great auks amongst prehistoric cave paintings at El Pendo in northern Spain. Similarly, bushmen in southern Africa have scratched on rock surfaces the outline of penguins and a range of other mammal quarry. Maoris and Aborigines harvested shearwaters or 'mutton birds' from islands off southern Australia and New Zealand, and so on.

In historic times seabird colonies all over the world were being visited by naval ships seeking convenient sources of fresh meat, and hence vitamins, to stave off scurvy. Corrals for herding rockhopper penguins which were then rendered down for oil can still be seen in the Falkland Islands, where the collection of their eggs remained a popular pursuit until recently. Harvesting eggs is still practised in other places, notably for instance the annual take of sooty tern eggs in the Seychelles.

Fishing communities frequently utilised carcases of seabirds as bait for hooks and creels. For example, natives of Newfoundland long used great auks and guillemots from Funk Island for bait.

Remote island communities like St Kilda did not just rely on seabirds as food, but also used the stomachs for storing oil, bones as pins or scoops and various other domestic implements, feathers for bedding or to pay rent, skins to make shoes or even clothing. In 1853, Osgood Mackenzie (1842–1922) noticed how the thatch of the roofs of the houses on St Kilda was pinned down with gannet beaks. In 1697, Martin observed the inhabitants wore socks of old rags sown with feathers instead of thread and also described how the St Kildans made their shoes from gannet skins:

> Their leather is dressed with the roots of Tormentil ... their ordinary and only shoes are made of the necks of Solan Geese, which they cut above the eyes, the crown of the head serves for the heel, the whole skin being cut close at the breast, which end being sowed, the foot enters into it, as into a piece of narrow stocking;

this shoe does not last above five days, and if the downy side be next the ground, then not above three or four.

In a letter to James Fisher in November 1947 the St Kildan Alex Ferguson confessed that the fulmar was his favourite seabird:

In my young days it supplied chicken for the table, feathers for my bed and oil for the crusy lamp.

Fulmar oil was burned in iron lamps on St Kilda late into the 19th century and later still if paraffin ran out; candles were made from sheep tallow. It was sold to the Factor at a shilling per St Kilda pint, which was equivalent to five English pints. Furthermore, the St Kildans also held fulmar oil in high regard as a medicine.

Martin described the method of its collection. Young fulmars will spit out oil to deter anyone approaching, but the St Kildans learned to surprise them from behind, enabling the oil then to be carefully drained into a dish; or else they killed each bird and tied its throat to contain the oil until they got back home with their prize.

This oil is sometimes of a reddish, sometimes of a yellow colour, and the inhabitants and other islanders put a great value upon it, and use it as a Catholicon for diseases, especially for pains in the bones, stitches etc, some in the adjacent Isles use it as a purge, others as an emetic.

The Reverend MacAulay went into more detail:

How soon the young Tulmer [fulmar] is attacked in the nest, he endeavours to disconcert the enemy, by spouting out a quantity of oil at his wide nostrils, which he squirts away directly into the face and eyes of the fowler; and this instinctive stratagem gives him frequently an opportunity to make his escape. But those who are versed in this diversion, take all possible precautions to surprise him; the more so, that they think the oil, furnished by this fowl, incomparably precious, and for that reason will exert the whole power of their skill and dexterity to save it. Yet in spite of all their care, the fowlers are totally besmeared with it, and any part of their cloaths, that is touched by an oil so spiritous, will burn like a candle. Every Tulmer yields near an English pint of this liquid substance, which drops out at the nostrils of the fowl while warm and a considerable quantity of it is annually preserved in the isle. Of the fowls themselves, every family has a great number salted in casks for winter provisions, and the amount of the whole is about twelve barrels.

In 1549, Dean Monro mentioned how dried birds were used by the St Kildans to pay their rent. Feathers also contributed. Each year the Factor received no less than 140 St Kildan stones (240 Imperial stones). Figures vary as to how many birds were required per stone – from 80 to 150 gannets, or 80 to 160 fulmar, but most agreed that it took 800 puffins, which also provided the best product. In 1887, Robert Connell noted that the Factor bought puffin feathers at five shillings the St Kilda stone of 24 pounds weight. Feathers, fumigated with sulphur, could be sold on to the British army for bedding, for example. The price fell significantly by 1890, by which time the women had stopped 'making feathers' on Boreray and they became only a by-product of harvesting for food (Harman 1997).

It was, of course, as food that seabirds were most valued – either eggs, plump chicks, or adult birds. With such a large annual harvest, it is hardly surprising that the most numerous colonies were to be found on the most inaccessible islands of Soay, Boreray and its Stacs nearly 5 miles (6.4 km) away from the inhabited island of Hirta. Not only did the islanders need a boat and favourable conditions, they had to be expert enough to approach and to land. Then the fowlers needed both the equipment and the skills to climb the steep cliffs. Martin was amazed at their prowess:

> The inhabitants, I must tell you, run no small danger in quest of these fowls and eggs, insomuch that I fear it would be thought an hyperbole to relate the inaccessibleness, steepness, and height, of those formidable rocks which they venture to climb. I myself have seen some of them climb up the corner of a rock with their backs to it, making use only of their heels and elbows, without any other assistance; and they have this way acquired a dexterity in climbing beyond any I ever yet saw ... from the age of three the young boys begin climbing the walls of the houses.

MacAulay witnessed for himself the ritual of landing:

> After having laid by all incumbrances, his upper cloaths and his shoes, [the first man] fastens a strong rope around his waste, the other end of it being in the boat; and as soon as the wave rises to a proper height, he springs out towards the rock with all the agility he is master of, and employs the whole power of his hands and feet, sometimes of his teeth and nails, to settle himself there; if he falls back into the sea, the affront gives him infinitely more pain than the severe drenching; his fellows haul him in, and he repeats the experiment ...
>
> 'I was foolish enough to engage in an adventure of this kind in Stack-in-Armin, but dare not recommend the same operation to any friend, however strong his curiosity may be. I was towed up against the face of a rock forty feet high.

One of the earliest detailed accounts of fowling on St Kilda was given by Robert Moray. His 'Description of the Island of Hirta' in the *Philosophical Transactions of the Royal Society of London* was probably gleaned from a visit

PLATE 17. Stac Biorach (left) and Soay Stac in Soay Sound with Stac an Armin, Stac Lee and Boreray behind. (J. Love)

PLATE 18. An aerial view of The Gap, Conachair and Mina Stac. (A. R. Mainwood)

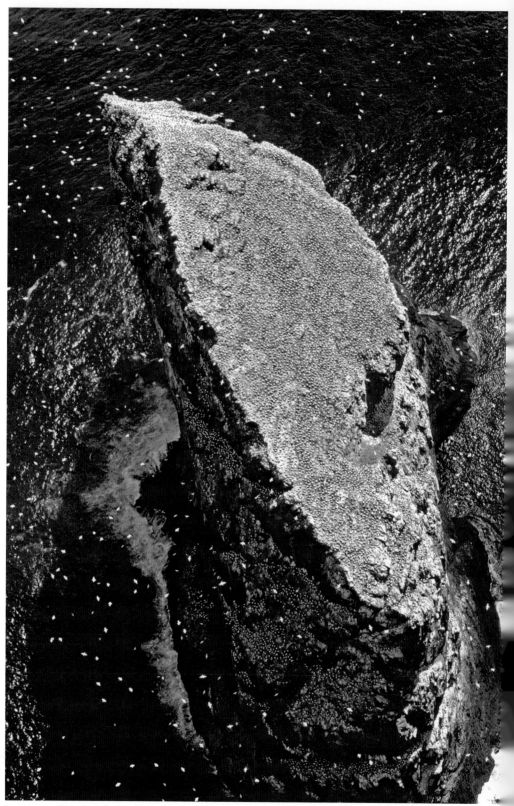

PLATE 19. Stac Lee from above, during the ten-year gannet count. (Stuart Murray)

PLATE 20. A pair of gannets fighting. (J. Love)

PLATE 21. Gannets on Boreray, with Stac Lee, Hirta and Soay beyond. (Jim Vaughan)

PLATE 22. Off–duty puffins on a rock. (J. Love)

PLATE 23. A puffin with thrift or sea pink. (J. Love)

PLATE 24. Lofoten puffin dog or Lundehund in Bodø northern Norway. (J. Love)

PLATE 25. A group of guillemots (one bridled) with their young, almost ready to fledge. (J. Love)

PLATE 26. A great skua (bonxie) divebombing the camera. (J. Love)

PLATE 27. A pair of fulmars calling. (J. Love)

PLATE 28. A flock of Boreray sheep on Boreray. (Peter Duncan/Scottish Natural Heritage)

PLATE 29. Passengers landing from the cruise ship *Meteor* in 1963. (Scottish Natural Heritage)

PLATE 30. An army landing craft begins Operation Hardrock in 1957.
(J. Morton Boyd/Scottish Natural Heritage)

PLATE 31. The supply vessel MV *Elektron* aground in Village Bay on 14 October 2000.
(David Maclennan)

to Uist, just before his death in 1673. He particularly mentioned landing on Stac Biorach which was only achieved:

> ... with much difficulty, a man having room for but one of his feet, he must climb up twelve or sixteen fathoms high. Then he comes to a place, where having but room for his left foot and left hand, must leap from thence to another such place before him; which, if he hit right, the rest of the ascent is easie; and with a small cord, which he carries with him, he haules up a rope, whereby all the rest come up. But if he misseth that footstep, (as oftentimes they do) he falls into the sea, and the company takes him in by the small cord, and sits still until he be a little refreshed, and then he tries again; for every one there is not able for that sport.

MacAulay described how:

> ... the St Kilda community have no more than a single boat, which must lie idle all winter, and is filled up with stones and earth in a secure place, to prevent the greatest of all public calamities, that is of its being swept away into the sea, or dashed against a rock by a violent gust of wind.

Boats had to be large enough to accommodate the crew, the fowlers and their catch, but small enough to be manhandled up the beach on Hirta. The community could not really survive without a boat, and at times even possessed as many as four or five, all usually about 25 ft long with six or eight oars. Such boats were hardly suitable for longer journeys, however, so the islanders themselves could never really have control over their contacts with the outside world. This did not stop them trying – albeit rarely – and we know that the 30-ft *Dargavel* went down on a voyage to Harris in April 1863, with the loss of seven men and a woman.

Ropes were essential for fowling and were prized possessions. The men often worked in small groups, descending the highest cliffs in stages using long ropes made of hemp or horsehair. The women and children often helped deal with the catch at the clifftop. The lower sections of cliff were scaled from a boat. Martin described the ropes:

> There are only three in the whole Island, each of them twenty four fathoms in length; ... the chief thing upon which the strength of these ropes depends is cows hides salted, and cut out in one long piece; this they twist round the ordinary rope of hemp, which secures it from being cut by the rocks; ... they tie [one end] about the middle of one climber, and [the] other about the middle of another, that these may assist one another in case of a fall; but the misfortune is, that sometimes the one happens to pull down the other and so both fall into the sea; but if they escape, as they commonly do of late, they get an incredible number of eggs and fowls.

The ropes belong to the Commonwealth and are not to be used without the general consent; the lots determine the time, place, and persons for using them; they get together in three days a much greater number of fowls and eggs than their boat is able to carry away, and therefore what is over and above they leave behind in their stone-pyramids.

The Reverend MacAulay said the best ropes were plaited strips of cowhide protected by sheepskin:

The St Kildians, besides the more costly and valuable rope already described, have another kind, made of horsehair, which is generally about nine or ten fathoms long. This they use in places more accessible, where the game is of a more ignoble kind, and so much the more easily mastered.

The islanders had also developed ingenious snares and nooses made of horsehair, occasionally stiffened with a gannet feather to keep them open. These were pegged to the ground or fixed individually to the end of a long pole.

Sometimes the islanders used long poles to strike at flying puffins, or at fulmars hanging on updraughts near the top of a cliff. Nets – either draped over rocks or attached to a long handle, common implements on the Faroes – do not seem to have been employed on St Kilda. The Faroese also attached nooses to a floating plank of wood, on which auks would alight to rest and so become entangled.

Boreray, Soay and the stacs were deemed common property and the harvest shared, whilst particular sections of cliff on Hirta and Dun were allocated each year to particular individuals – a habit common throughout the Faroes. The despatched birds were often dropped into the sea to be retrieved later by boat.

Having been deprived of fresh meat all winter, the islanders could not resist catching some adult birds as soon as they returned to the island in spring. According to Martin:

The Lavie visits them most seasonally in the month of February, when their fresh mutton and bread are perhaps nearly exhausted, and continues to furnish plentiful repasts till the Solan Geese appear in March . . .

MacAulay described the islanders' excitement at their arrival:

No sooner do these thrice welcome harbingers of plenty and universal happiness appear on the coast, than the most considerable persons in this small state assemble together, to congratulate one another on this great occasion, and withal to settle the operations of their campaign. With this view they divide their people into parties, made up of their ablest fowlers ... On the first acquisition of this prey, the people feast very lovingly together, the heart of every one overflowing with joy.

Guillemots huddling tightly together along broad ledges were easier prey than the less sociable razorbills. As long ago as the 1670s Robert Moray gave an interesting account of how the St Kildans captured them:

> Some of these fellows lie beside the door of the little houses they have in their islands, flat upon their backs, and open their breasts. Which, when the fowls perceive, they sit upon them, and are presently catched, and their necks broke. One fellow has kill'd hundreds of fowls in one night, after this manner . . .

The Reverend Kenneth MacAulay expanded on this:

> As soon as the Lavie is discovered on the coast, the heroes who have formerly distinguished themselves by such feats, go down, with the help of their ropes, into the well known shelves of those rocks, each having a broad piece of linen, or any thing remarkably white, fixed on his breast. This operation is done in the night time: The bird mistaking an object so conspicuous for a part of the rock, endeavours to cling to it, and is immediately caught and dispatched. In this posture the fowler continues till about the dawn: . . . [the catch] sometimes consists of no less than four hundred Lavies.

Robert Connell scoffed at this and considered that the St Kildans were merely wrapping up warm for their night on the cliffs, and rarely caught more than 30 birds in a morning. He judged that as food the St Kildans did not rate puffins as highly as fulmars, the feathers being sold and the carcases often ending up as fertiliser. Similarly, the Reverend Neil Mackenzie judged that adult guillemots:

> . . . are of no great value. They are not much esteemed as food, and their feathers neither bulk much nor are very valuable . . . One gannet will yield as much as ten of these and of better quality.

The cliffs of Hirta afforded the first opportunity for fresh guillemots, but, if weather allowed, the islanders might venture across to Boreray or Stac an Armin. By this time the auks were laying eggs and the gannets were well established. MacAulay noted the excitement at the commencement of the gannet season:

> About the middle of March, a select band of adventurers . . . go to the neighbouring isles, upon an expedition to them of very great importance. This is the season for catching the old Solan-Geese before they begin to lay; they hunt them in the night time, through steep and (to all other men inaccessible) precipices; as many as are not intended for immediate consumption, are secured within the little houses or barns, more than once mentioned, without salt, or using any other art to preserve them, than opening their backs, and washing them clean.

Mackenzie added:

The Gannet is here called 'suileire', the sharp-eyed. A few birds will sometimes come as early as the 13th January, and from that time more and more gradually arrive. By the end of February only about a third of the birds will have come, and it is not till the end of March, they are caught in any numbers and then only if the weather is suitable. When they arrive they are fat and very good eating.

After postulating the role of a 'sentinel' gannet, Martin outlined an equally improbable mode of capture:

Besides this way of stealing upon them in the night-time, they are also catched in common gins of horse-hair, from which they struggle less to extricate themselves than any other fowl, notwithstanding their size and strength; they are also caught in the herring loches with a board set on purpose to float above water, upon it a herring is fixed, which the goose perceiving, flies up to a competent height, till finding himself in a strait line above the fish, bends his course perpendicularly piercing the air, as an arrow from a bow, hits the board, into which he runs his bill with all his force, and is irrecoverably taken.

While gannets were obviously paramount to the St Kildans' survival, MacAulay also recognised the value of puffins:

Incredible flights of these Puffins flutter ... like a small cloud of locusts in another country.
    During the summer season the women of Hirta ... are much employed in fowling: The principal game that falls to their share, is the small sprightly bird called the Puffin. This fowl hatches under ground ... The wife or daughter of a family makes a short excursion from home in a morning, attended by a dog, and catches what may be a sufficient provision for the whole family, at least for one day.

Mackenzie added:

... by far the most numerous of all the birds which frequent these islands. There is not a suitable spot anywhere which does not swarm with them. Everywhere you see them in thousands, while at the same time the air is full of them coming and going. I estimate that there cannot be fewer of them than three millions.

Adult Atlantic puffins could be taken in May, June and July, after which the fledglings then became available, along with the young gannets or gugas, shearwaters and northern fulmars. Snares made of horsehair were effective, one woman catching 127 Atlantic puffins in three hours and another 280 in a day! Nooses attached to long poles extended the reach of the fowlers, while dogs were also useful in catching adult puffins and shearwaters, a good hound catching 60 or 70 in one night. Mackenzie elaborated:

> The number of birds and eggs of this species taken during a season is incredible. Men and women, boys, girls, and dogs pursue them incessantly. The dogs show which holes are occupied, when they are in general very easily got at.

Mackenzie also described how the St Kildans caught adult shearwaters:

> It is because of their way of alighting that the shearwaters are most easily and frequently caught. The fowler, with his trained dog, waits near a place where he knows that there are several nests. During this momentary halt the dog pounces upon them and brings them to its master. In this way a clever dog may catch sixty or seventy in a night.

I have always been intrigued by these dogs. After seeing so-called Norwegian puffin dogs or *lundehund* in northern Norway, I realised how similar they were to the earliest descriptions of St Kildan hounds (Plate 24). Like St Kildans, the people of Lofoten and other Norwegian communities harvested seabirds. On the southernmost island, Røst, nets were spread over the boulder fields to entrap nesting puffins, whilst in the neighbouring island of Vaerøy they bred special puffin dogs to dig out burrows. It is curious that the harvesting technique should be so different on two islands only a few miles apart.

Curiously, the puffin dogs of Vaerøy have been specifically bred to bear an extra toe on their front paws which enhances their digging ability. They also have a very flexible spine for wriggling in and out of burrows and can close off their ears to keep out soil and grit. Two other islands further south (Løvenden and Fugløy) also had these dogs, but none are used nowadays; indeed, there are now no puffin dogs on Vaerøy.

Martin, Clarke, MacAulay and Mackenzie all mention the St Kildans utilising dogs to lay hold of burrow-nesters such as puffins and shearwaters. Whether the dogs on St Kilda were a relic of ancient Norse fowling traditions or were especially bred for the purpose may never be known. Martin again:

> Their dogs are likewise very dextrous in climbing and bringing out from their holes those fowls which build their nests under ground, such as the Scraber, Puffinet, etc which they carry in their teeth to their masters, letting them fall upon the ground before them, though asleep.

While Martin said that the dogs were speckled, in 1797 Edward Daniel Clarke found them to be:

> ... a small rough hardy race, with long back, very short legs, black hair mixed with grey, tan-coloured visages, and erect ears.

He also encountered 'Pomeranians or fox-dogs', while MacAulay described the St Kildan dogs as small and rather terrier-like. These accounts are a pretty fair description of Norwegian puffin dogs. MacAulay reiterated how the women valued dogs for catching puffins:

> Every family in the island is furnished with one or more of those extraordinary dogs. They are a mixture of the tarrier, spaniel and those that take the water: Of their own accord they sally out early enough and soon return, bringing five or six puffins at a time.
>
> Sitting on the side of a hill with some of the people, I saw one of these little dogs stealing away from us: The men told me he would soon return with a considerable booty, accordingly he came back in half an hour and laid down his prey at this master's feet; ... he went off the second time, and had much the same success.
>
> These dogs have a wonderfully sagacity, and are so trained, that they neither destroy the fowls themselves, nor part with them till they meet the people of the family to which they belong, in spite of threatenings, flattery or bribes.

Later authors such as George Clayton Atkinson and John Sands commented upon more variability, a cross between collie, terrier, Dutch pug, lurcher, or lanky creatures like terriers but with long tails and a dash of sheepdog, looking a bit like jackals. By 1876 Sands added how 'the native breed of dogs', similar to cream-coloured collies, were nearly all extinct. By then a lot of mongrels had been imported from Harris, trained more to herd sheep than to catch seabirds.

As well as puffins, the St Kildans occasionally ate adult fulmars. The islanders managed this valuable resource carefully, since they were to depend upon it most later in the season. Martin noted:

> The inhabitants prefer this, whether young or old, to all other; the old is of a delicate taste, is a mixture of fat and lean; the flesh white, no blood is to be found but in the head and neck; the young is all fat, except the bones, having no blood but in the head.

Martin also provided us with a rather endearing observation on the St Kildans' pursuit of seabirds:

> When they have bestowed some hours in fowling about the rock, and caught a competent number, they sit down near the face of it to refresh themselves, and in the mean time they single out the fattest of their fowls, plucking them bare, which they carry home to their wives, or sweethearts, as a great present ...

While it is likely that the St Kildans would not turn up their noses at some other seabirds, such as fat young shags, Mackenzie only highlighted the kittiwake as:

... the only one of the gulls which is at all eatable, but as it is only fair eating and always rather lean, it is very seldom cooked.

As everyone knows, birds' eggs make particularly good eating. Colonial seabirds have long afforded rewarding and convenient opportunities for collecting them and, in 1953, the ornithologist Hugh Cott estimated that 82 species of seabirds throughout the world were exploited for their eggs.

On St Kilda the choice was reduced to five. At one time the St Kildans might have had the option of harvesting great auk eggs. These were five times larger than a hen's or a puffin's egg, at only 50 ml or so in volume. Those of razorbill, guillemot, fulmar and gannet range from 75 to 105 ml. But guillemots were by far the most favoured as the Reverend Neil Mackenzie attested:

I have seen seventeen basketsful of eggs taken at one time from Stackbiorrach, and at another time the same season fourteen ... These eggs are very good eating when fresh. After they are incubated for a few days most of the eggs appear when boiled to be changed into a rich thick cream, and in this condition they are also relished. Sometimes eggs, not only of this species but of some others which have not been hatched, are found late in the season. Some of these when cooked look like a piece of sponge cake, have a high gamey flavour, and are esteemed a great delicacy. Others are as bad as the most vivid imagination can depict.

[The Razorbill] is not so social as the guillemot, often breeding in solitude, but more frequently, when the space admits, in colonies. The egg when fresh is considered very good eating, but the bird even when in condition only fairly so.

Common guillemots could be harvested twice, with a gap of 18 days, and sometimes even a third time, as they would usually lay a replacement egg.

Atlantic puffin eggs could be scooped out of burrows with a spoon on the end of a stick.

MacAulay noted the next event in the St Kildans' calendar:

They go upon another expedition to [Boreray and the stacs] about the middle of May. This is the season for gathering eggs of the Solan-Geese ...

While the rocks of Boreray and Stack-in-Armin are thus plundered, all the eggs laid in the rock called Lij, are held inviolably sacred. This is an anciently established custom; and should any one break it, it is the universal opinion, that the whole constitution is entirely subverted.

It is interesting that the islanders maintained a taboo on collecting gannet eggs from Stac Lee, suggesting elements of management and sustainability to the gannet harvest. The St Kildans were also aware that the taking of eggs from Boreray and Stac an Armin forced the gannets to re-lay which then extended the guga harvest.

Mackenzie had noted this but added an interesting caveat:

They begin to lay about the 10th ... If the first egg is taken away it will lay a second, and if it is again robbed it will lay a third time. All of them will not lay again.

Martin had already concluded:

Every fowl lays an egg three different times, except the Gair-fowl and Fulmar, which lay but once.

He went on to note the beneficial effects of gannet eggs in particular; the islanders:

... have generally good voices, and sound lungs; to this the Solan Goose egg supped raw doth not a little contribute.

On the other hand, MacAulay was not much impressed:

... They keep [them] in their little stone houses. Great numbers of these eggs lie there, till the month of July, without any care taken to preserve them, an art which this indelicate people would most heartily despise, should one be at the pains to instruct them in it. By that time these eggs must unavoidably be offensive, and intolerably so, to the senses of any other race of men ...

To Hugh Cott's panel of Cambridge University egg tasters fresh gannet eggs were considered to be 'relatively unpalatable'. When the scientist then employed hedgehogs and rats as tasters, gannet came second in the popularity stakes! (Cott 1951–2).

In 1697, every single person in the Factor's party, including Martin himself, enjoyed a daily allocation of food which:

... beside barley cake, was eighteen of the eggs laid by the fowl called by them Lavy, and a greater number of the lesser eggs.

After a three-week stay, Martin calculated that the 50 or 60 visitors alone accounted for 16,000 eggs. With an indigenous population of 180, Martin could only marvel at the number of eggs that were needed to sustain everyone. Those of the guillemot were the most commonly eaten, visitors preferring them fresh, whilst the islanders liked them 10–12 days old, once embryos were forming inside.

Martin explained:

They preserve their eggs commonly in their stone-pyramids [cleits], scattering the burnt ashes of turf under and about them, to defend them from the air, dryness being their only preservative, and moisture their corruption; they preserve them six, seven, or eight months, as above said; and then they become appetizing and loosening, especially those that begin to turn.

Gathering eggs is perhaps the most sustainable way to harvest seabirds. The adults have thus far invested relatively little into reproduction and, if early enough in the season, there is every chance that the egg will be replaced. In this way the fowling season might be prolonged since these late eggs will be last to hatch and to fledge young. It is possible though that birds which fledge late in the season may not survive as well thereafter.

Having maximised the auk egg harvest, the islanders knew that guillemots and razorbills were then of little further use. These species take their chicks to safety out to sea when only three weeks of age (even earlier in the case of great auks) and at just one-quarter of the adult weight they never provided fatlings for the pot. So the only young auks the St Kildans had to harvest were puffins. According to Martin, 'the young Puffin is fat as the young Fulmar'. Mackenzie confirmed:

The young are generally very fat, but some seasons when food seems to be scarcer not so much so. It is much relished by the natives. As soon as it is quite fledged, which, if the nest has not been robbed, will be about the end of July, they leave the island.

Dried puffin was said to be as tasty as smoked ham, the young ones especially. In 1899, on Mingulay, Finlayson (in Buxton 1995) recorded:

This season the young puffins were in such a lean condition as to be unfit for the kitchen. One year all the birds were inedible – too dry; even the dogs would not eat them. This is due to scarcity of spawn on the fishing grounds.

Such lean years still occur, and probably more frequently nowadays with the adoption of modern fishing methods and overfishing of sandeels in particular (see Chapter 5).

In the autumn the St Kildan palate turned to gannets. An earlier crop of their eggs would prolong the harvest of fat youngsters, as MacAulay attested:

The young Solan-Goose is fit for use in the month of September, if the first egg laid by the old one remains untouched. If otherwise, the young fowl is not fit for the table till the month of October ...

Before the young Solan-Geese, which they call Goug, fly off, they are larger than the mothers, and excessively fat. The fat on their breasts is sometimes three inches deep; The inhabitants of Hirta, have a method of preserving their greese in a kind of bag, made of the stomach of the old Solan-Goose caught in March. In their language it is called Gibain; and this oily kind of thick substance, manufactured in their way, they use by way of sauce, or instead of butter, among their porridge and flummery.

Mackenzie added:

Martin says that in his time twenty-three thousand 'gugas' were killed annually, but probably this is only a very vague estimate. Nothing like that number are killed now. Never since I came the island have they killed in any year more than two thousand 'gugas', and about the same number of old birds ... It takes on an average eighty 'gugas' when salted to fill a barrel. In general they are very fat, but some years they are quite lean and comparatively worthless. This is also true of all the birds which frequent the islands; some years they are much leaner than others.

From the information which I got from the natives, I do not believe that they ever in any one year killed more than five thousand 'gugas' and four thousand old birds. As their bills are very sharp and they take a firm hold, it is not sage to seize them incautiously, or you may get your hand badly cut. It is only on dark damp nights that it is easy to catch many of them. The natives of course select such times for their capture, and in the twilight ascend the rocks very quietly so as to cause as little alarm as possible ... As soon as it is day, the birds which have been caught are all thrown down into the sea and secured by the boat below. They are now off for home, and on arrival the birds caught are divided equally among all the families in the island, As no rope can be ordinarily used, this fowling is rather dangerous work, They may slip in the dark, or if the wind suddenly rises they may be blown off the ledges.

Fatling shearwaters also provided succulent eating as the Reverend Mackenzie recorded:

The young bird, which is called 'fathach' is fed in the nest till it is fledged. It, like the young fulmar, is also very fat and is much relished as food. The old birds when fat, which they often are, are also considered good eating. As they never leave their holes by day, but always by night, it is difficult to estimate their numbers, but I believe that they are about as numerous as the fulmar.

The Mingulay folk also harvested them, from the 123 m stack of Lianamul – both as food and to pay rent – until late in the 18th century. Young shearwaters were also relished in the Faroes.

There is a unique colony of Manx shearwaters, nesting in burrows on the summits of the mountains, above the 600 m contour on the island of Rum, in the Inner Hebrides. The hill with the greatest density of burrows is still known today as Trollval, a name it probably gained from the Vikings a thousand years earlier. Unfamiliar with shearwaters in their native Scandinavia, these sea-going adventurers would have likened the eerie nocturnal cries from beneath the earth to trolls. Similar placenames incorporating the word 'troll' occur at known shearwater colonies in the Faroes. Historical records indicate that the young of these shearwaters – known in Gaelic as *fachaich* – were harvested in Rum until at least the 18th century and perhaps even until the island was cleared of its entire human population in 1826. On the smaller island of Eigg nearby, shearwaters were still being taken into the 20th century, until they were wiped out there, and on the Isle of Canna nearby, by rats. Shearwaters, like most other 'small' petrels, have become nocturnal to avoid the worst attentions of avian predators – though it is interesting that even golden eagles in Rum can catch them (Love 2001).

I have deliberately left more detailed treatment of the fulmar harvest to the end of this section, for reasons which will become apparent. The Reverend MacAulay concluded the fulmar to be one of the most important seabirds in the economy of St Kilda:

> Another sea fowl highly esteemed in this island, is the Tulmer [fulmar]. I was not a little entertained, with the encomiums they bestowed on this bird. 'Can the world,' said one of the most sensible men at Hirta to me, 'exhibit a more valuable commodity? The Tulmer furnishes oil for the lamp, down for the bed, the most salubrious food, and the most efficacious ointments for healing wounds, besides a thousand other virtues of which he is possessed, which I have not time to enumerate. But to say all in one word, deprive us of the Tulmer, and St Kilda is no more.'

Only a few adults may have been caught, early in the season, while the St Kildans knew that fulmars would not re-lay so they rarely harvested their eggs. It was really the fledglings that the islanders relished. Thus they were careful not to interfere too much with the breeding cycle and so risk diminishing the fulmar harvest at fledging time. The Reverend Mackenzie summed up the situation:

> At times a few old birds are caught by means of the snaring rod, like the puffin and the Guillemot, but not many, as they wish to get as many young birds as possible. For the same reason also very few of the eggs are taken.
>
> It lays one egg, which the parents hatch by turns for about six weeks. If the nest is robbed they will not lay a second time. When the chick is hatched both parents take great care of it and feed it most assiduously for six or seven weeks, so that it is generally very fat ...

The Reverend MacAulay noted how:

The young ones of this species, are in season about the beginning of August.

The Reverend Mackenzie went further:

About the beginning of August the young fulmars are about fully fledged and ready for killing. During the preceding week an unusual excitement and alertness pervades the village. Every possible preparation is being made. The women bring the cattle home from the sheilings, and grind sufficient meal to last the killing time, while the men test the ropes, make good deficiencies and provide barrels and salt. Other fowling is really hardly anything more than amusement, and may almost be prosecuted or not as you like, but for ten days at this time it is quite different … A large and valued portion of the winter's food must now be provided or you have to do without it. The breeding places have all been carefully examined some time before, and an estimate made of the young birds which they respectively contain. They are now divided into as many portions as there are groups of four or five men who are to work together. These portions are now assigned by lot to each group, and all is ready.

When the day considered most suitable comes all move off to the rocks, and the men either climb down to the breeding places or get lowered by rope if necessary. The birds must all be caught by hand, and skilfully too, or much of the valuable oil will be lost. They must be caught suddenly, and in such a way as to prevent their being able to draw their wings forward, or they will squirt the oil. It cannot do this easily while you are holding the lower joints of its wings back against each other. Caught in the right way its neck is speedily twisted and broken and the head passed under the girdle, When the man has got strung about him as many as he can conveniently carry, they are passed up to the women who are waiting above.

Fig. 16. Women and children with the fulmar crop (David Wilson collection).

At once they are divided into as many shares as there are men in the group, when the womenkind and children seize upon their shares and begin to drain out the oil into receptacles, which are generally made of the blown-out and dried stomachs of the gannet. This they do by the very simple means of holding the bird bill downwards and gently pressing, when about a gill of oil flows out by the bill. This oil is much valued, some used by themselves for various purposes and the surplus sold.

Only gannets and fulmars – carcases, feathers and eggs – were divided equally amongst the 16 crofts on the island. According to Connell, puffins, guillemots and razorbills belonged to whosoever had collected them.

Mackenzie continued:

When all got home, plucking off the feathers, disposing of the internal fat, and salting the carcases for winter use, goes on till far in the night. Early next morning the same round begins, and so on from day to day till all the accessible breeding places are visited. All this time there is nothing but birds, fat, and feathers everywhere, Their clothes are literally soaked in oil, and everywhere, inside and outside their houses, nothing but feathers; often it looks as if it were snowing.

This blizzard scenario was also witnessed by John MacCulloch in 1815:

The air is full of feathered animals, the sea is covered with them, the houses are ornamented by them, the ground is speckled with them like a flowery meadow in May. The town is paved with feathers, the very dunghills are made of feathers, the plough land seems as though it had been sown with feathers, and the inhabitants look as though they had been tarred and feathered, for their hair is full of feathers, and their clothes are covered with feathers.

Many visitors commented on the smell around the village while the seabird harvest was being processed, whilst others noticed how the aroma of fulmars could be detected in some cleits long after the island had been evacuated. It was largely the women who plucked and drew the bird carcases ready to store for the winter. This was also the case in Iceland and in Faroe. Not surprisingly, from time to time, this seems to have turned out to be a rather unhealthy duty.

Each September between 1933 and 1937 no fewer than 165 people living in the southern isles of the Faroes were diagnosed as suffering from ornithosis, also called psittacosis. All but 24 (14.5 per cent) were women, most of them engaged in the fulmar harvest; 32 of the cases (19.4 per cent) were fatal. In 1939, a similar outbreak occurred in Iceland. James Fisher was sent a first-hand account which he quoted in his monograph on the fulmar:

The fulmar catch in Vestmannaeyjar in 1930 began on August 22nd and lasted

Fig. 17. Plucking the fulmar catch (David Wilson collection).

for two or three days. It seems that 79 men and 225 women took part in plucking and otherwise preparing the catch [some 7,600 birds]. About 8 to 10 days [later] 5 women aged about 20 to 60 years and one man aged 70 years developed an unusual type of pneumonia ... A clinical description of the cases is given that fits in very well with the ordinary picture of psittacosis. Fever lasted for about four to five weeks and recovery was slow. No deaths occurred.

The following year, harvesting of fulmars was made illegal in Faroe and Iceland until 1954 (when a cure for ornithosis was discovered), but the incidence of the disease in fulmars apparently increased noticeably. Ornithosis had been first recognised in parrots in the late 1920s. Indeed, James Fisher (1952) invoked a shipload of diseased parrots from Argentina being thrown overboard and washing up in Faroe as the cause of the outbreak in the first place. This seems altogether too neat.

Ornithosis has since become a serious disease amongst domestic turkeys in the United States, domestic ducks and geese in central Europe, and is common amongst domestic and feral pigeons worldwide. It has now been known to infect some 160 species within 20 orders, including seabirds such as gulls and terns. The disease is caused by a bacterium initially known as *Chlamydia psittaci*, an organism found in the faeces and nasal discharges of infected birds which can be picked up by inhaling airborne particles. Outbreaks still occur amongst captive birds, sometimes transferring to poultry slaughterhouse workers for instance, but now, with modern antibiotics, the infection rarely proves fatal.

Although ornithosis was not clinically diagnosed until the 1920s, it could well have been occurring in wild bird populations long before this. Island communities who regularly harvested seabirds such as fulmars may have been largely immune to it and it may have taken a particularly virulent strain from the pet trade that somehow manifested itself in the Faroese and Icelandic outbreaks in the 1930s. However, it might well be significant that the bacterium, now called *Chlamydophila abortus*, is the same organism that causes enzootic abortion in ewes. Pregnant women are widely advised to avoid contact with sheep during lambing since it may affect their own health or that of their unborn child. Fortunately, only one or two related incidents of abortion in humans are reported each year and there has only been one death in the last three decades.

It is worth highlighting, however, the tragically high infant mortality that was known on St Kilda during the 18th and 19th centuries. This has already been well described by other authors, its cause being put down to neonatal tetanus, a condition also known at the time from Greenland, Iceland and Faroe. These are all places where seabird harvesting was a common pursuit. In Iceland alone some 4,478 infant deaths were attributed to tetanus in the century leading up to 1937. This accounted for a third of all infant deaths, with the fowling community of the Westmann Islands one of the places singled out for special mention. It was also known in the west of Scotland, in parts of Lewis and islands such as Barra and Tiree, but only on St Kilda was it seen as a critical problem. Out of 225 births listed by Dr Richard Collacott (1984), no fewer than 97 of the infants (43 per cent) died within a month, usually after the first week or so. One man is said to have lost nine of his 13 children and another man 12, to be left with only two.

It was G. Gibson (1926) who first suggested the infant tetanus resulted from the St Kildan midwives' habit of dressing the umbilical cord with a rag soaked in fulmar oil, which would have been stored in a gannet's stomach. He seems to have had little direct experience of this, yet his thesis remains popular to this day. Certainly standards of hygiene left a lot to be desired and it was only after the Reverend Fiddes and a Nurse Chisnhall managed to introduce a more aseptic treatment of the umbilicus in the 1890s that the deaths finally stopped.

But the matter has never been resolved satisfactorily. It was the women who plucked the fulmars and proved to be most at risk to ornithosis in Faroe and in Iceland. None of the accounts makes any mention of infant mortality, though a closely related organism is now known to affect pregnant women. So, I wonder, is it just possible that the *Chlamydophila* bacillus was in some way implicated in the high infant mortality on St Kilda, normally attributed to tetanus?

Some seabird populations on St Kilda exhibited an increase in numbers at the beginning of the 20th century, as the number of islanders – in tandem with their requirements – diminished. This would suggest that fowling had in fact been imposing a limit on seabird numbers. It might be significant that the best seabird colonies were to be found on Dun, Soay, Boreray and the stacs, with the fewest on Hirta where all the people lived. On the other hand, that harvesting had continued on St Kilda for centuries would indicate how, in the longer term, the activity was indeed sustainable. Numbers being taken each year were probably balanced by recruitment of birds into the population, whether through reproduction or immigration. Before going on to discuss this further, it is worth pausing to consider aspects of seabird population dynamics.

In stable, undisturbed habitats bird populations tend to remain within certain limits, give or take a little each year. Breeding numbers tend to be limited by the amount of food available and/or the available nest sites. If there is a temporary shortage of food, more birds than normal perish. Others can then find nests and perhaps even breed at an earlier age. If, on the other hand, *more* food becomes available, then more birds can enter the population until a limit is imposed by suitable nest sites. This is termed density-dependent regulation.

From time to time other, external, factors come into play, quite *independent* of the density of birds in the population. The sudden and acute shortage of food during El Niño events in Peruvian waters is one example when, for instance, millions of seabirds may starve. Also persistent storms can inhibit any seabird's ability to find food. Pollution, disease, exploitation or the introduction of alien predators are other typical density-independent factors. Outbreaks of avian botulism have, from time to time, caused many deaths amongst gulls in northern England for instance, while toxic algal blooms have killed breeding shags. New commercial fishing techniques can sometimes threaten seabirds, such as auks drowned in monofilament nets, or albatrosses and petrels killed on the baited hooks of long-line fisheries. New techniques, or economic demands, or even the over-exploitation of fish stocks, can quickly reduce stocks of species that were hitherto ignored at market and thus freely available to seabirds as prey. The recent sandeel fisheries around Shetland provide an example. Once these external factors cease to impact, density-dependence should allow the population to recover to its normal carrying capacity.

Fowlers would have been aware of fluctuations in seabird numbers and breeding success, although they may not have understood why these were happening. They would also have appreciated how they must regulate their own activities to safeguard this vital resource for future years.

Seabird population dynamics differ from those of landbirds in several crucial ways (Love 2005b). Firstly, adult survival is normally high – between 80 and 95 per cent. Adult auks, gannets and petrels live longer than cormorants, shags, gulls and terns. On the other hand, juvenile survival is low (30–70 per cent) and more variable. Secondly, in seabirds sexual maturity is delayed – for two to three years in cormorants and black guillemots, four to five years in other auks, gannets and gulls, seven in great skua and up to nine in fulmars. Thirdly, productivity is low; gannets, petrels and most auks lay only a single egg; cormorants and shags up to five. Most seabirds can only produce the one brood each year. Finally, breeding adults, once established, tend to be faithful to that colony for life, preferring the one where they themselves were reared to striking out anew.

Low productivity means that seabird population may take several years to recover. On the other hand, deferred maturity means that there is a large reservoir of non-breeding birds in seabird populations which can help to buffer disaster events and limit the impact. It is events that kill off large numbers of *mature, experienced breeders* that can have the most serious impact upon the population.

Fowling communities have long recognised the risks in exploiting adult seabirds – of killing the solan goose that laid the golden egg. It is well documented how the Faroese imposed restrictions on this activity (Nørrevang 1977; Olsen and Nørrevang 2005). It is understandable though, after a long, lean winter, they could not resist one or two meals of fresh puffin as soon as the birds arrived back on the cliffs. They also recognised – quite rightly – that the spectacular wheels of puffins around a colony at the height of the breeding season consisted largely of immature birds, which were more expendable. These were snatched out of the air with a long-handled net called a 'fleyg'.

Experienced fowlers could also age puffins up to the fourth year from grooves on the bill so they could avoid killing adult birds. They also avoided killing birds returning to their burrow with mouthfuls of fish. Furthermore, the Faroese were tentative about pulling adults from burrows – usually limiting this to one bird per burrow early in the season, also by marking those burrows already visited and then not returning to that part of the colony for a further two years. In addition, Faroese fowlers imposed annual limits on the number of adult guillemots that could be taken and particular stretches of cliff tended to be allocated to the care of individual fowlers. Presumably similar restrictions on judicious harvesting might have applied amongst other island communities, and, of course, amongst the St Kildans.

In such ways, harvesting seabirds could be rendered a sustainable activity, for after all the islanders' very survival depended upon it. Certainly we know of only one seabird in the North Atlantic that has become extinct due to direct human activity – the great auk. Being flightless, it was especially vulnerable.

It is probably pointless to speculate upon the impact of St Kilda's annual seabird harvest. Besides, those few accounts that mention numbers killed tend to be highly variable, speculative and distinctly unreliable. It is interesting on the other hand to appreciate just how many seabirds the St Kildans required each year and just how much time and effort this would require.

Predictably, we find Martin Martin to have been one of the first commentators:

> We made particular enquiry after the number of Solan Geese consumed by each family in the year before we came there, and it amounted in the whole to twenty two thousand six hundred, which they said was less than the ordinary number, a great many being lost by the badness of the season, and the great current into which they are obliged to be thrown when taken, the rock being of so extraordinary an height, that they cannot reach the boat . . .

It seems that never more than 4,000 northern gannets (including gugas) per year were being collected in the 1830s, but supplemented by 12,000 to 20,000 northern fulmars. In one single exceptional day on Boreray in the 1880s 1,000 gannets were harvested and the incredible figure of 89,600 adult Atlantic puffins has been calculated for the year 1876. By the early 1900s the annual average harvest seems to have been about 7,500 northern fulmars and 5,000–6,000 common guillemot eggs.

It is difficult to estimate the impact such a harvest may have had upon seabird numbers on St Kilda. The increase in fulmars and gannets after harvesting ceased could have been as much a reaction to an improvement in food availability, as to relaxation of hunting pressure. James Fisher preferred to put the spread in fulmars around Britain down to increased offal and discards from the fishing fleet rather than to any decline in harvest and the eventual evacuation several decades later.

The St Kildans despised and persecuted black-backed gulls, so this species too was able to increase between 1930 and 1958. By that time, Ken Williamson (1958) was particularly concerned about the effect increasing gull predation might have been having upon other seabirds. However, gull numbers then appeared to stabilise before decreasing by 75 per cent during the 1980s. This trend tends to have been mirrored, albeit on a smaller scale, by lesser black-backs and herring gulls, possibly due to food shortages at sea (perhaps related to a reduction in offal from fishing boats). Kittiwakes are now at their lowest ever, probably through human over-fishing. It is really the commercial exploitation of a resource that introduces the greatest risk.

Direct exploitation of seabirds in Britain and Europe probably reached a peak during the 19th century, as the human population increased. This was less due to the impacts of harvesting and more to a demand for other seabird products. Victorian gentlemen were seeking eggs and stuffed birds for their private collections, whilst their fashionable wives sought to decorate elaborate hats with feathers.

It was wanton slaughter to supply the millinery trade that stimulated the passing in Britain of the Protection of Birds at Sea Bill in 1869. Realising the dependence of St Kilda upon fowling, specific provision was made in the legislation to exempt St Kilda. The Bill helped save many British seabird colonies, such as the massed kittiwakes on Flamborough Head, but attention then turned to other countries to satisfy demand. Terns – and their eggs – suffered heavily elsewhere in northern Europe, North America and the Tropics before, in Britain at least, the Importation of Plumage (Prohibition) Act of 1922 finally put a stop to the plume market (Love 2005b).

We have already discussed how the Leach's petrel and the St Kilda wren attracted quite a bit of attention from naturalists, museums and collectors in Victorian times. The sale of eggs and skins provided the St Kildans with a handy supplement to their meagre income. This was in effect commercial exploitation, and, in 1904, Parliament passed a special Act to protect these two species alone. Ultimately, it was the Protection of Birds Act of 1954 that introduced more effective measures and for a wider spectrum of species. The following year, the Wild Birds (Gannets on Sula Sgeir) Order gave the men of Ness in Lewis a right to continue their centuries-old harvest of young gannets – 2,000 per annum. Unfortunately, no amount of protective legislation on a local scale can counter impacts on their prey from overfishing and pollution on a global scale. But that is another story.

.9.

Land birds

Perhaps no part of the British Isles is more interesting to the ornithologist than St Kilda. On this bleak and sublimely grand ocean-rock some of the rarest and the most interesting birds in our fauna find a congenial home; here alone they may be studied at their breeding places ... It is very strange that no complete list of the birds of St Kilda has ever been compiled by any modern ornithologist, and stranger still is the indifference with which the place and its bird-treasures have been treated by British naturalists during the past forty years. Perhaps the difficulty of reaching St Kilda and the hardships, real or imaginary, which must of necessity be endured, if the sojourn on its by no means hospitable shores is for any length of time, are the chief reasons for its having been so much neglected. Strange it seems that while British ornithologists have journeyed far and wide over all parts of the known world in the interests of their favourite science, St Kilda, the remotest part of the United Kingdom, has been disregarded ...

Charles Dixon 1885

WITHIN THREE YEARS of the appearance of Surtsey above the sea surface, and even before volcanic activity had ceased, kittiwakes and black guillemots were seen roosting on the island. Black guillemots and fulmar were the first to nest, in 1970. Six more species of gulls and terns quickly followed. It was not until 1996 that the first land birds nested – two pairs of snow buntings that have now increased to 11 pairs. A couple of greylag geese set up home in 1999 and fledged young three years later. In 2001, meadow pipits raised a brood, two pairs of white wagtails bred the following year and ravens have built a nest though have not yet bred. This story is probably not dissimilar to that on St Kilda, although, from the outset, its hard rocks would have offered more opportunities than Surtsey for cliff-nesting seabirds

The complement of breeding birds on Surtsey has grown only gradually. The actual checklist of vagrants turning up there increases apace however. By 2005 there were still only 13 breeding species on Surtsey. On the other hand, a further 76 species have been recorded as migrants – thus far. Additions to this list have depended entirely upon human presence, which to date has always been sporadic.

Almost any bird that flies has the capability of reaching offshore islands, especially if assisted by favourable winds. St Kilda is typical in this respect although only the main island of Hirta has had continuous human presence so boasts a more complete list than its neighbouring islands and stacs. However, this bird list has also depended upon the identification skills of the residents. The Reverend Neil Mackenzie was unusual in keeping records; the Reverend Fiddes although observant enough, was, however, less skilled.

Mackenzie was undoubtedly an important ornithological presence. He is known, for instance, to have sighted a ptarmigan on a hill top one winter after a succession of easterly gales. He also noted a swan but it is not clear which species (probably a whooper):

> One day some village boys noticed a swan in the broken water at the head of the bay and would not allow it to land. As the day was quite calm with a heavy surf it never could rise high enough to overtop the curling surf. It swam about for hours in the space between the sand and the breakers, but at last, quite exhausted, it laid down its head and floated ashore. It lay so quiet that I thought it could be tamed, and brought it home and shut it up for the night in a bedroom. Fortunately, I tied it by the foot to a bed-post, for next morning when it revived it smashed everything within reach, and was so furious and aggressive that it had to be destroyed.

In the summer of 1841 Mackenzie also saw a European roller, which today's powers that be are reluctant to accept. Personally, I see no reason to doubt Mackenzie's record. His bird remained for several weeks, but, as he had no powder, he was unable to shoot it! The Reverend Wilson, an accomplished naturalist, told how:

> ... it was of a lustrous green and blue colour, extremely brilliant when the sun shone upon its glancing plumes. From his description of its size, form, and general aspect, we have no doubt it was the roller *Coracias garrulus*, a species well known in Germany, and a summer migrant as far north as Sweden.

On 14 June 1894, Steele Elliott 'obtained' the first British specimen of sub-Alpine warbler. There is no doubt about this record as the unfortunate warbler is now in the British Museum of Natural History, where it was recognised as being of the race that occurs in Iberia, southern France, and Italy. Elliott had spotted it in the minister's garden, but in his 'St Kilda and the St Kildans' (1895) the frustrated naturalist admitted:

> It was first noticed the previous day, but that being a Sunday and under the very walls of the church I was obliged to refrain from securing it till the morrow. Fortunately enough it was still haunting the Manse garden, but to my disgust an early morning service was going ahead, which meant another few hours before I was able to lay my hands on this record bird . . .

He gave more detail in his 'Observations on the fauna of St Kilda' (also published in 1895). The hapless sub-alpine warbler was:

> . . . busily employing itself seeking for food along a row of young peas, and it frequently flew to a parsnip in seed that grew in one corner of the garden; the latter plant seemed to attract a greater number of insects, and it was my particular spot for securing various Diptera, etc. This little bird allowed people to approach quite close to it, and I was able to take full particulars of its plumage within a few feet. It remained throughout Sunday till the following day, when I shot it in the presence of Mr Fiddes [the minister] and Mr Mackenzie, the factor. Its presence on the island was probably caused by the great gale that blew across the island the previous day (June 12th) from the S.W. It is remarkable that the species should be first obtained in the British Islands in such a northern and out-of-the-way locality as St Kilda.

It was largely left to naturalists to spot migrants, although such observers only visited in the summer months. In 1895, Steele Elliott lamented:

> Little could be gleaned from the natives respecting birds seen during the migration and winter periods, owing chiefly to the difficulty of their speaking only Gaelic. Although they have some notion of how to skin any strange species obtained, owing to the want of a gun on the island rarities are seldom secured. The minister of the island [Mr Fiddes] cannot be said to render much service to the ornithologist for he does not profess to know anything beyond what relates to the common breeding species on the island.

Every year since 1957, Nature Reserve wardens (who are now employed directly by the National Trust for Scotland) have spent April to September inclusive on Hirta. In that time they kept detailed records, supplemented both summer and winter by birds seen by researchers and also, initially, by the army detachment at the base and then civilian staff who replaced them. The St Kilda warden in 1993, Jim Vaughan, summed up a fairly good September for autumn migrants (Vaughan and Love 1994):

> There were 2 herons and the wildfowl included a merganser, a female tufted duck, a female mallard, wigeon and 2 brent geese. Daily sightings of waders

included turnstone (max 43), golden plover (max 34), ringed plover (up to 7), dunlin (up to 6), and sanderling, one of which was killed by a merlin. Other records included a few oystercatcher and curlew, 2 little stint and single Jack snipe, whimbrel and knot. But it was the passerines that excelled. Regulars included meadow pipits (up to 600), rock pipits (100 regularly), wheatears (up to 63), siskins (up to 25), willow warblers (up to 5) and chiffchaff (all singles). The first snow buntings arrived on the 15th and there were 27 by the 26th. Lapland buntings were present with up to 10 on the 15th.

In addition a tree pipit and a wryneck turned up on the 8th, a bluethroat and a swift. Three days later we saw a house martin, a rosefinch, a skylark while a naughty red-backed shrike killed and ate a St Kilda wren! Another yellow wagtail arrived on the 18th and stayed two more days. There was a whinchat and a pied flycatcher on 19th. But it was the 21st which brought two gems – a barred warbler followed by a White's thrush – the first for the Western Isles. The next day was slack by comparison with only a reed warbler, a third yellow wagtail, a blackcap and a robin, things calming down considerably thereafter. Three skylarks and a second bluethroat arrived on the 24th, a goldcrest two days after, a redpoll the next day and a garden warbler on 29th. The last day saw the first of the autumn redwing.

Over a hundred species turn up in any one year and up to the year 2001 a total of 228 species has been recorded on the island (Murray 2002). Since the first checklist was compiled by Mike Harris and Stuart Murray in 1978, 23 years earlier, 50 new species have been added to St Kilda's list – about two a year on average. Forty-five of these birds have only ever been recorded once, while a further 54 have been recorded no more than five times.

Twenty of these rare vagrants are American in origin; others have originated from Europe or Asia. All were far off course and would have been unlikely ever to have made it back home. Some species turn up regularly every year, *en route* to and from more northerly breeding grounds. Whooper swans from Iceland, for instance, together with skeins of various geese from both Iceland and Greenland, are regularly seen on passage.

Single snowy owls from the Arctic have been seen on Hirta. The first was recorded in November 1962, with others in March and April 1968, 1972, 1973 and 1975. These conspicuous birds became more regular in the late 1990s and into recent years, especially in spring. W. Miles and Sarah Money (2008) recorded at least five different individuals during 2007 alone, noting how they fed almost entirely on St Kilda field mice and adult puffins. In one owl pellet a ring was found that had been placed on a puffling 27 years earlier! The only other bird remains detected were those of a juvenile great skua.

There seems to be a link between snowy owls seen in Uist, which then disappear only for a bird (or even birds) to appear on St Kilda, and vice versa.

The sexes would indicate that these often involve the same birds, as the warden Andy Robinson (2004) deduced:

> The next day the wind had eased a little by the afternoon and there, at the head of the valley, was a beautiful male snowy owl. The bird had left South Uist on its way north – breaking its journey on St Kilda from 19th to 22nd May. Equally as impressive was a gyr falcon on 9th April 2000 – a sight not to be forgotten.

The gyr is another Arctic wanderer. In 1841, MacGillivray also made a puzzling reference to an Arctic falcon:

> Of *Falco Islandicus*, the Iceland [gyr] falcon, sometimes reported to breed in St Kilda, I could obtain no information from the inhabitants, who could scarcely allow so conspicuous a bird to escape their observation. That they may breed there, however, is possible, as a friend of mine in North Uist shot and procured a beautiful specimen, and another was seen and fired at about the same time in the adjacent island of Pabbay.

There are nine recent records of this handsome falcon on St Kilda, all in late winter/early spring, while in 1964 one individual remained around the island for no less than 55 days!

Nor are northern migrants on St Kilda confined to raptors. On Hirta in September 1911, W. Eagle Clarke shot a Baird's sandpiper, the first ever known to have crossed the Atlantic to Britain; it would be another 60 years before anyone saw another. More have been seen in recent years, 38 of them in Scotland, of which six have been reported from St Kilda alone. Indeed, September 1997 proved a remarkable month for American waders as Andy Robinson (2004) explained:

> The most staggering wader experience in my three seasons began in late August 1999 with the appearance of a Baird's sandpiper. But this was just a foretaste of what was to come. Westerly gales predominated the weather patterns through the end of August and into early September. On the 3rd as I neared the top of Mullach Sgar, a bright looking golden plover flew up. Continuing onwards I approached the small lochans between Mullach Sgar and Am Blaid, where the cloud drifted in and the wind gusted. Two small waders got up in front of me and landed by the lochans. Through my tears from the wind and the shaking binoculars they were confirmed as Baird's sandpipers; on closer approach – brilliant. Whilst watching them the weather cleared and the sun started to shine. So, proceeding on my way, I noticed the same bright-looking golden plover but on closer inspection it turned out to be a moulting summer-plumaged American golden plover, looking quite stupendous in the sunshine! Nearing the road back to Village Bay yet another surprise was waiting – a pectoral sandpiper! An amazing day's birding – four waders all from across the Atlantic.

The next day I headed back to see if the birds were still present. I located the two Baird's sandpipers and the pectoral sandpiper, but on heading towards the radar I thought my eyes were deceiving me – two American golden plover – the summer-plumaged bird being joined by a female in extensive moult! Not to be outdone the pectoral sandpiper was then joined by a second individual on the 6th. An unprecedented concentration of Trans-Atlantic waders with 6 birds of 3 different species!

Other trans-Atlantic migrants include an evening grosbeak (March 1969 – the first for Britain and Europe), an American robin present for a month early in 1975, a bobolink (September 1985), a hooded warbler (September 1992 – the second for Europe), a Tennessee warbler (September 1995) and a ring-necked duck on 19 September 2000 (Forrester *et al.* 2007). On returning to the base that day with news of his American duck, the warden Andy Robinson got a totally disinterested reply from the staff: 'What's its name? – Donald?' Another rare American duck, a Harlequin, probably from Iceland where it also breeds, turned up in Glen Bay on 18 June 2007. Three-quarters of the score or so British records emanate from Scotland, especially the Outer Hebrides, but this was a first for St Kilda.

In early June 1884, Charles Dixon had been delighted to discover the presence of two pairs of king eider in St Kilda, which he felt sure were nesting on Dun. He eloquently described what they were up to but, lamenting the fact that he 'failed to secure an example', he also failed to offer any description of the birds themselves. Doubt must remain attached to this sighting, although one single female was seen by the warden and skilled observer, Jim Vaughan, in June 1992.

Many unusual passerine migrants turn out to be of Scandinavian origin, such as the common rosefinch, red-breasted flycatcher, bluethroat and Lapland bunting. Indeed, Andy Robinson remembered 2000 as 'the year of the bunting' with the usual snow and Lapland buntings from the north and west, but also reed, rustic, and yellow-breasted buntings and a yellowhammer from the north and east.

It is testament to Eagle Clarke's field skills that on 30 September 1910 he made out the call of a buff-bellied pipit amongst a group of meadow pipits. He later caught the bird in a burn near the village. Its stuffed and mounted skin is preserved in the National Museum of Scotland. Normally occurring in the tundras of Siberia or in Arctic Canada, this proved to be the first British record. Another turned up on St Kilda on 20 September 2005. This one happily escaped a museum drawer, and is still only the third Scottish record. Other Siberian rarities on St Kilda have been rock thrush (June 1962), grey-cheeked thrush (found dead on 29 October 1965), White's thrush (September

1993), Blyth's reed and dusky warblers (October 1993), and eye-browed thrush (October 2001) (Forrester *et al.* 2007).

From a different quarter altogether, a Mediterranean gull turned up on Hirta (6 October 2001), an Alpine swift (May 1974), a hoopoe (May 1977) and a collared flycatcher (May 1992). In addition, there have been two adult male golden orioles; Stuart Murray found the mummified corpse of one down a puffin burrow in July 1975, while Jim Vaughan had a live one in May 1994. In May 1992, an adult little egret was found dead after surviving three days on Hirta, while a single common crane summered in 1997. A Calandra lark from North Africa found on 21 September 1994 was the second Scottish record, only the third seen in Britain, and still the only British specimen to have turned up in autumn.

But it is not just extreme rarities that cause excitement on St Kilda. A single great tit turned up in April 1981 (still St Kilda's only tit), a little grebe (September 1994), a partridge in May 1993, and a couple of red grouse (December 1959 and July 1970). Even house sparrows, chaffinches and mallard are cause for comment. The Reverend Neil Mackenzie made a curious reference to 'rooks' in 1840 which his son interpreted as a mistake for carrion crows. However, in June 1894, Steele Elliott (1895) got this interesting observation from the Reverend Alexander Fiddes (resident on the island from 1889 to 1902):

> ROOK. – Mr Fiddies informed me that hundreds of these birds passed over the islands last winter, great numbers of which perished. Five individuals frequented the island during our stay, the remnant of the above flock. I could not hear of their having nested anywhere.

In his 'St Kilda and the St Kildans' Steele Elliott was able to place this event in the early part of 1895. None of the islanders had ever seen rooks before, though up to three birds have been recorded in 14 years of recent decades.

The name W. Eagle Clarke (1853–1938) has already been mentioned several times and it will always be associated with bird migration. Born in Leeds, he gave up a career in civil engineering to become curator of his local museum. Four years later he moved to Edinburgh and, through the influence of Harvie-Brown, became curator of birds at the Royal Scottish Museum. Like his mentor, he had a passion for migration and, while still maintaining regular contact with lighthouse keepers, etc., he was able to visit many remote islands himself.

In 1904, Eagle Clarke visited the Flannan Isles with Harvie-Brown, but judged that Fair Isle would prove much more productive for watching migrant birds. He went there the next year and became convinced. He befriended a local teenager George Wilson Stout of Busta (1888–1916), who became a skilled ornithologist in his own right and reported many more rarities before

his untimely death in war-torn France. Together they visited St Kilda in 1910 where they 'met with quite unlooked for success'. Another lengthy visit in 1911, as we have seen, turned up many interesting rarities. Although Clarke was a proficient observer, field identification was still in its infancy then, so rare birds had to be shot to gain acceptance, hence the cliché 'what's hit is history, what's missed is mystery!' Eagle Clarke was to have the British subspecies of song thrush *Turdus philomelos clarkei* named after him, and went on himself to describe the Hebridean subspecies *T. p. hebridensis*.

In 1912, Eagle Clarke wrote his seminal two-volume *Studies in Bird Migration*. He died in 1938, seven years after David Lack visited St Kilda, and in 1959, Lack commented on Eagle Clarke's distinguished career:

> He was the first to study visible bird migration in Britain, the first British ornithologist to watch regularly at lighthouses and on small islands, the 'discoverer' ornithologically speaking of Fair Isle and the first to discuss the weather factors responsible for the arrival of night migrants.

In 1948, the Edinburgh ornithologist George Waterston (1911–1980) bought Fair Isle to set up Britain's most famous bird observatory, appointing Ken Williamson (1914–1977) as its first director. While Eagle Clarke thought that birds followed favoured routes whilst on migration (with Fair Isle on a convenient crossroads) and recognised the importance of weather, Ken Williamson developed a theory of drift migration which was significantly affected by wind direction. Birds arrived at Fair Isle and elsewhere in Britain on a following wind, which was why south-east winds proved particularly productive. The east coast of Britain has always yielded more continental rarities than the west, thought the west scores better on those individuals which have been blown all the way across the Atlantic. Fair Isle, in particular, is well placed to benefit from both. During the war David Lack himself had been responsible for realising that the worrying 'angels' which appeared on the first radar screens were in fact flocks of migrating birds. In the 1960s, he was able to put his radar experience to good use to modify and improve all these early ideas on bird migration.

By 1956 it was clear that St Kilda was to become a National Nature Reserve. On a visit there from 11–14 June 1956 on behalf of the Nature Conservancy, Max Nicholson and James Fisher summarised its suitability as a bird observatory (Nature Conservancy files):

> It would probably yield most interesting results in connection with the migration between the British Isles, and Iceland/Greenland, and could also be expected to give some interesting transatlantic records, as well as a number of drift migrants from Europe and Asia, although they might be expected to be far fewer than on Fair Isle. Apart from migration studies the island is exceptionally well situated for intensive researches into oceanic birds, including the fulmar, gannet, Leach's petrel and the auks, and of course into the resident sub-species, the St Kilda wren.
>
> Any bird observatory on the St Kilda group would have to be on Hirta and to be centred on Village Bay. There appears to be a very satisfactory site for the main operations in the large field containing Lady Grange House, between the village street and the shore on the west of the valley. As there are absolutely no trees on St Kilda, it is thought that the provision of a small plantation here would act as a magnet to pull in any cover-loving species which find their way to the island ... it is thought that a satisfactory growth could be obtained by such species as sallow, rowan, birch, alder and possibly a mixture of Scot's pine. Among exotics it is just possible that Escallonia ... might be able to stand the comparatively frost-free oceanic climate, and to make a useful hedge ... The Heligoland trap might be placed at the bottom end ... and if necessary, another can be placed on the top end. At the south-western corner ... there is a very attractive piece of boggy ground, which with a little earth banking could be made into a resting place for waders. It is already frequented by snipe and a wader trap here might give interesting results.

Obviously inspired by experiences on Fair Isle, Nicholson and Fisher went on to explore the potential for further traps in Glen Mor, suggesting a hut so that the wardens could overnight there. They accepted, however, that none of this would be possible if the army decided not to pursue their radar base on

St Kilda. Strange as these development ideas might be considered nowadays, bird migration was the 'growth industry' of the time, rather than pure conservation, so this had been used as additional justification for the establishment of St Kilda as a National Nature Reserve.

Once the military presence was assured, the Nature Reserve required a counter-presence of its own. The Nature Conservancy decided to appoint a summer warden and, not unnaturally perhaps, the Director of the Fair Isle Bird Observatory, Ken Williamson, was head-hunted for the job. The Fair Isle observatory was in dire financial straits at the time so St Kilda offered Ken a stop-gap opportunity. In the June 1957 edition of the *Scottish Field* Williamson explained:

> I had already served a long apprenticeship to island life [with the Yorkshire Regiment during the Second War] among the awe-inspiring ocean peaks of Faroe three hundred miles to the north. There I learned the first and greatest lesson about islands, that an island without people is like a cask without wine … It was only logical that when the newly-formed Fair Isle Bird Observatory Trust were looking for someone to set up their migration station in 1948, my wife and I should jump at the chance. To Esther, born and bred in Faroe, going to Shetland became the next best thing to going home … Perhaps the bird observatory could be the key to a new prosperity [for Fair Isle] … The time to set about improving the life conditions in remote areas is when there is still a vigorous population there to enjoy them. I would that we could get a glimpse of the Uists, without their rocket-range, in fifty years' time. I would that we could see today a St Kilda that had been offered some similar development away back in the early twenties.

Although coming from a museum background like Eagle Clarke, Ken was very much one of the new breed of field ornithologists and bird ringers, employing binoculars, field description and live traps to verify the identification of rarities. On taking up his post in 1957, Ken Williamson provided a diplomatic liaison with the army during the construction of the radar base. His military service on the Faroes during World War II stood him in good stead. In addition, he carried out a full programme of research into St Kilda's migrants, its breeding snipe, wrens, mice, etc. Williamson and Morton Boyd described their experiences with the military during Operation Hardrock, the construction of the radar base, in *St Kilda Summer*, and Ken's books about the Faroes and about Fair Isle remain classics to this day. As we shall see later, Ken's legacy to St Kilda will always be significant – though it has to be said with some relief that the trees were never planted. St Kilda never became a designated bird observatory of world-wide repute like Fair Isle, even Ken Williamson realising that it might never aspire to that.

Dr David Boddington was a friend of Ken Williamson's and a keen birdwatcher who engineered his national service posting to St Kilda as medical officer in 1958. The Nature Conservancy made use of his unique abilities by nominating him as warden. David told me how he found that the island's radar installation could track foraging gannets all the way to Barra Head. He also used military communications to radio in his bird records, using the species number on the British Ornithologists' Union British List followed by the date in numerals. He later discovered that the Russian spy vessels patrolling the North Atlantic at that time were intercepting his messages and were totally perplexed by the code being used! Subsequent wardens have, of course, carried on this noble tradition of bird recording, as have researchers and staff at the base (though employing standard terminology).

While St Kilda has a long list of migrants, as far as we know only 34 species have ever bred on the islands. A few, such as white-tailed sea eagle, peregrine, corncrake, dunlin, and rock dove, with perhaps twite and corn bunting, were probably regular breeders in the past but are now extinct. Others, such as red-breasted merganser, skylark, song thrush and tree sparrow, may only have nested sporadically. More than likely, as with various plants, some of the breeding birds, such as corncrake and corn bunting, might have given up as soon as cultivation ceased after the 1930 evacuation.

In 1840, MacGillivray suspected that corncrakes were breeding, a few 'always to be found among the corn, and their cry may be heard all night long, and occasionally during the day'.

A year later James Wilson 'only perceived … the corn-crake or land-rail *Rallus crex* by sound'.

By 1884 Charles Dixon reported:

> I neither saw nor heard this species, and do not think it breeds there. It cannot be very common, for I could not learn that the natives have any Gaelic equivalent for it.

On the other hand, corncrakes were breeding in 1915 when Eagle Clarke found chicks. Lack did not hear any in 1931 and the species became a rare visitor. Single calling birds have been heard in only a few summers subsequently. These records included two birds on Dun in 1982. There have been only three autumn records, one as late as 20 October 1982. This secretive rail has declined significantly throughout Britain, although it persists in the Outer Hebrides, Coll and Tiree where the effects of grazing and haymaking are tempered through agri-environment schemes. It is possible that on St Kilda grazing pressure from sheep within the village area throughout the summer limits the options for corncrakes to re-establish.

Corn bunting, as its name suggests, is another bird of the cultivations. It probably bred in the past, MacGillivray finding them 'common' in 1840. The following year James Wilson confirmed that they were 'well-known'. They were also present in 1879 and 1896. Only single birds (on three occasions) have been seen since, and this species proved the most vulnerable to the loss of cultivation after the evacuation. It is a common breeder in those parts of Uist where cropping in a traditional manner is still a regular practice.

In 1841, James Wilson had reported how 'the only linnet was the twite *Linota montium*'. In 1931, only a year after the evacuation, David Lack's party recorded 13 pairs of twite breeding on Hirta, and Harrisson even found a pair on Boreray. Numbers appeared to hold their own until the 1970s, by which time birds were only ever heard singing around the village and only a few might now remain during the summer. Two pairs have been recorded in Dun.

Dunlin were suspected to breed on several occasions. In 1840, MacGillivray noted 'several pairs on the hillside where they doubtless had young' and Wiglesworth also recorded them in 1902. In actual fact, nests, eggs or chicks have never been found to prove breeding on St Kilda once and for all. Up to 56 have been recorded on spring passage, however, with fewer birds passing through in autumn. This wader has also been recorded from Dun, Soay and Boreray.

Rock doves have an enigmatic history on St Kilda. In 1884, Charles Dixon confirmed:

> There can be little doubt that the rock dove breeds on St Kilda, but it is certainly not a common bird. I never saw more than a pair; but it may be more numerous on Soay, Boreray and the adjacent stacks.

Ten years later Elliott could find none. By 1910 the islanders did not know the bird. Nonetheless, rock doves were breeding in 1930, with up to five birds present the following year and two in 1939. Odd birds have been recorded since, but none now breed.

Considering the huge seabird colonies as potential sources of prey, breeding raptors have always seemed remarkably scarce in St Kilda. Peregrines and white-tailed sea eagles should surely have been attracted to the well-populated cliffs of St Kilda and, indeed, Martin referred to both 'hawks and eagles' on St Kilda. By 'hawks' he undoubtedly meant peregrines. In his *Description of the Western Islands of Scotland* (1698) he went as far as to say:

> This Isle produces the finest hawks in the Western Isles, for they go many leagues for their prey, there being no land fowl in St Kilda proper for them to eat, except pigeons and plovers.

Pigeons and plovers are typical peregrine prey. Our smallest falcon, merlin, on the other hand, selects smaller species, such as pipits. Steele Elliott (1895) was told by the Reverend Alexander Fiddes that merlin occurred frequently and of how he had secured one that flew in the Manse window. There are now some 150 records, two-thirds of them on northward spring migration; the remainder are autumn records, and none have yet summered on St Kilda.

In 1831, George Clayton Atkinson read a paper to his local natural history society in which he listed goshawk (and, erroneously, great auk!) as 'having been seen' whilst he was on St Kilda, but the goshawk must have been an error for peregrine. He does not mention peregrine in a short list published in his book, but in his journal he explained how the peregrine, which:

> ... the minister, I know not on what authority, called the goshawk, has two eyries on the islands; one on the east side of St Kilda [Hirta], in descending to which as I have mentioned before, a lad a few years since broke his neck, and another on a small cliff on the west side of Borera, from whence we procured two young ones, a drawing of one at three months old graces these pages ...

> 1st June: We then proceeded to a small inland cliff on the W side of the island [Boreray] where the Falcon breeds, and had soon the satisfaction of being put in possession of two young birds by a couple of lads who accompanied us. The old birds I hope reared in a satisfactory manner the two remaining youngsters which the lads told us occupied the nest.

> ... I intended to have taken some pains in noticing their progressive changes of plumage, which, even though they be but the Peregrine Falcon, as I shrewdly suspect, would have been interesting; they have however saved me the trouble, as one escaped in September and the other in October.

Ten years later John MacGillivray mentioned:

> *Falco peregrinus* and *tinnunculus*, the peregrine falcon and kestrel, both breed in the precipices, but in small numbers. I procured an egg of the former from the same nest which several years ago had furnished two young birds to the Messrs Aitkinson of Newcastle.

In 1841, James Wilson reported both peregrine and kestrel. Milner saw a peregrine on 15 June 1847, while in 1884 Charles Dixon observed:

> The peregrine breeds sparingly on the cliffs, two or three pairs only tenanting the most inaccessible portions of the island. The lofty pinnacles of Doon are the bird's favourite haunt.

Ten years later J. Steele Elliott added:

> One peregrine falcon only was noticed soaring above Mullach Oiseval; several pair are said to breed on these islands yearly, their eggs being taken from Borrera and Doon.

So, up to two or three pairs of peregrines were often to be found breeding in St Kilda, with eyries known on the cliffs of Dun, Hirta, Soay and Boreray. Some may have been alternative sites of the same pair. Two pairs were still present on Hirta in 1931, but they seem to have disappeared by the 1950s at the time that they were suffering from pollutant effects on mainland Britain. They were spotted several times in 1962 and again during the 1970s, but they did not breed. Records increased in the 1980s, with breeding confirmed in 1987 and 1988. A female was found dead on Dun in May 1989 and if breeding had been attempted that year, it certainly did not succeed. A pair then nested annually until 1997 and although two were seen on the Dun cliffs the following year, and back on Hirta in 1999 and 2000, there has been no further breeding on Hirta. Three single birds have been reported on Boreray over the last two decades.

In his *Description of the Western Islands of Scotland* (1698) Martin Martin mentioned:

> There's a couple of large eagles who have their nest on the north end of the Isle; the inhabitants told me that they continuously make their purchase in the adjacent isles and continent, and never take so much as a lamb or hen from the place of their abode, where they propagate their kind.

In 1831, William MacGillivray quoted a poem from a book popular at the time called *The Seasons* by James Thomson, which celebrates the eagles, nesting on St Kilda. Thomson had never visited St Kilda, but in 1747 had read Martin's book.

> High from the summit of a craggy cliff,
> Hung o'er the deep, such as amazing frowns
> On utmost Kilda's shore, whose lonely race
> Resign the setting sun to Indian worlds,
> The Royal Eagle draws his vigorous young ...

It may be no coincidence that these birds would be catching the self-same seabirds upon which the St Kildans themselves depended. The islanders probably saw sea eagles as competition. Furthermore, they would have been well capable of reaching even the most inaccessible eyries to destroy the eagles and their eggs.

But, rather than noting any possible rivalry over seabird prey, most visiting naturalists seemed more obsessed by the threat that eagles might pose to the islanders' sheep and lambs. Previously, Martin – as we have already seen – and then MacAulay were careful to point out that eagles did not in fact pose any such risk on St Kilda:

> At Hirta are some ravens of the largest sort, and a few eagles, which though very

pernicious elsewhere, are perfectly harmless here, the reason I conceive must be that their necessities are more than sufficiently supplied by the inexhaustible stores of eggs, that must every other moment fall in their way. This must be the case in summer. How they procure their food in winter is a question which one will find some greater difficulty in resolving, unless we take it for granted that they make frequent excursions to the neighbouring isles.

Compared with the rest of Scotland, sea eagles disappeared early from St Kilda. Almost certainly Mackenzie would have mentioned them had he known them to be present, or even had he heard any reference to eagles. MacGillivray did not mention eagles in 1840, nor did Elwes in 1869. In 1841, Wilson was more categorical: 'there are now no eagles'. Milner reported one on 14 June six years later, probably a passing immature. So it seems likely that the white-tailed sea eagle was extinct as a breeding species, at least by 1840, and probably some time prior to Mackenzie's arrival in 1829. It is no coincidence that the skilled cragsmen on the Faroe Islands, another fowling community just like St Kilda, were responsible for bringing sea eagles there to an early extinction, probably more for their impact on seabirds than on sheep (Love 1983).

In 1884, Charles Dixon elaborated on how the extermination came about on St Kilda:

The white-tailed eagle can only be regarded as an accidental visitor to St Kilda. It would probably breed there regularly were it left unmolested; but as soon as the birds have made a nest, the natives draw lots as to who must undertake the perilous task of descending the cliff and setting fire to the structure. The St Kildans are afraid that the eagles would destroy their sheep and lambs.

Ten years later Steele Elliott commented:

The white-tailed eagle has not bred for some forty years [1850s??]. It formerly had an eyrie on the Conachair cliffs, but upon the natives destroying the nest with fire it never returned again.

There have been several recent records, all of them immatures, and all since the recent reintroduction to mainland Scotland and subsequent breeding in the Hebrides and elsewhere. But it is amazing how such large birds can be completely dwarfed amongst the awesome cliff colonies of a seabird capital like St Kilda. Maybe one day white-tailed eagles will be found nesting there again. Several pairs of white-tailed sea eagles are now breeding in the Outer Hebrides but 40 miles (64 km) of open sea to St Kilda is a large gap for any sea eagle to cross. Nonetheless, it is by no means impossible, as several recent sightings would indicate. There have also been five records of golden eagles reaching St Kilda, but only between 1955 and 1976.

Of the two eagles, the white-tailed is by far the better equipped to make a

Fig. 19. A sea eagle in flight (John Love).

living along coastal cliffs. Golden eagles took up old eyries on Hebridean sea cliffs only after the white-tailed sea eagle became extinct. Goldies may hunt seabirds but never fish, and they always resort to flying inland for rabbits or hares as preferred prey. Both eagles and peregrines will prey on fulmars, but run the risk of being spat at and having the oil matt the plumage. One sea eagle set free by George Waterston on Fair Isle in 1968 actually died from this, having found it too easy merely to walk up to young fulmars sitting enticingly on ledges – with the inevitable result. It seems, however, that older eagles are well practised at catching adult fulmars, probably swooping from behind as the prey tries to rise from the surface of the sea and thus evading a fusillade of oil. If sea eagles should settle to breed on St Kilda again, they can surely cope easily with the presence of so many fulmars (Love 1983).

With sea eagles gone, the Reverend Mackenzie found that the largest land bird on St Kilda in the 1830s and 1840s was the raven. Steele Elliott (1895) noted:

Their eggs are seldom taken, as they breed so early in the year that the storms prevent the inhabitants from visiting their nesting sites in the adjoining islands.

In May 1959, the Cumbrian naturalist Ernest Blezard (1902–1970), visiting St Kilda with his botanist friend Dr Derek Ratcliffe, was able to investigate the diet of ravens. He collected and examined 24 raven pellets at Ruaival (Nature Conservancy files). Most consisted of more than one prey type. Sixteen contained puffin remains, and 15 sheep's wool and/or bones; seven had fragments of shag eggs; and seven the remains of sexton beetles. Finally, one had fragments of a mollusc and another the jaw bones of a St Kilda field mouse.

In 1841, James Wilson mentioned how the raven's smaller cousins, hooded crows, 'were very troublesome, taking the thatch off the houses, seeking for grains and insects which rest in the thatch'.

In 1895, Steele Elliott had this to say about them:

Hooded crows are very common and absurdly tame; you get within shot of one on the mainland quite by accident, but here they can be seen all about the village picking amongst the refuse within a few feet of you. I must own I really thought the first few were tame ones with clipped wings, as they never offered to fly, but moved off with their series of jumps, until our friend from the steamer approached too closely in order to give them the usual biscuits. I am greatly indebted to these birds for relieving me of some very fine varieties of guillemots' eggs. Whilst blowing out the contents in the immediate proximity to the house I was called away to dinner, and left my specimens outside, some to dry and some still unblown. The only traces I ever found of them afterwards were small pieces of shell scattered about.

In 1927–8, the geologist Alexander Cockburn had seen a flock of 40 hooded crows and reckoned there to be about ten pairs. No more than three pairs nest on St Kilda nowadays, with single pairs perhaps on Dun, Boreray and Soay. Nests are rarely found and breeding is usually confirmed only by the presence of juveniles having fledged.

Having considered the birds that formerly bred on St Kilda, we now come to the species that breed only intermittently. There were several times when whimbrel were thought to breed. In 1884 for instance, Dixon 'saw a pair on the rocks below Mullach scaill; they were very wild and noisy'. In 1905, James Waterston reported five or six pairs but that 'one collector told me he had taken and sold the eggs'. In May 1914, the Duchess of Bedford found them all over Hirta, both on cultivated and uncultivated ground. There are also breeding records from 1956, 1961 and 1963, but breeding was not fully confirmed until 1964. Nesting probably happened every year thereafter until 1980, usually involving a single pair but three pairs in 1972. In 1979, two females laid eight eggs in a single scrape. Young hatched in at least four years, but it seems that none ever fledged. Whimbrel are, of course, regular spring migrants (never more than 25 at a time and usually only a few individuals); they are more scarce in autumn.

Since 1947 golden plover have also been recorded breeding, but only a few times in recent years, and usually a single pair. Up to 40 may be seen during autumn migration.

Other species that have bred only once include red-necked phalarope (in 1972) and teal (1974). A pair of greylag geese laid five eggs in a nest on the Cambir in early June 2002, but the clutch was predated. Several small passerines have also bred only once – snow bunting (1913), house martin (1990), stonechat (1975), pied wagtail (1993) and yellow wagtail (1998). In June 2001, an immature black redstart built a nest in one of the garages at the base; there have been no records of black redstart nesting anywhere else in Scotland.

Only nine species of landbirds now nest annually on St Kilda, the lowest total since records began. About 50 pairs of eider nest, some 300 pairs of starlings, 100 pairs of rock pipits and 20 pairs of meadow pipits. Thirty to 60 pairs of wheatear breed, and probably several pairs of hooded crows and ravens, although their nests are rarely detected amongst the huge cliffs. The population of oystercatchers has halved in recent years to about 25, perhaps due to predation by great skuas. On the other hand, snipe have become more abundant, though fluctuate from year to year, with about 100 pairs in good seasons. They also nest in Dun, with about ten pairs on Soay, though seem to be scarce on Boreray.

Snipe on St Kilda present rather an interesting story. The Reverend Neil Mackenzie had noted a few pairs in the 1830s and John Sands noted a fair number 40 years later. However, in June 1884, Dixon made a determined search through all the marshy places around Hirta but failed to find any snipe. He noted that none of the islanders had ever seen a nest. It was Wiglesworth who located the first nests in June 1902. Numbers seem to have remained scarce, especially around the croft land, until after the evacuation in 1930. When James Fisher and Max Nicholson searched Hirta in June 1939, they found:

> The abundance and widespread distribution of [snipe] was surprising ... The number of breeding pairs could hardly be put at less than 30 and was probably more ... In the fields around the village, density appears to have exceeded one pair to the acre and the birds were commoner in dry grass than in the island's few typical snipe situations. Attention must be drawn to this remarkable change in habitat; the small fields round the village would appear to be a most un-snipe-like situation.

Ten years later, however, Fisher struggled to find many snipe, attributing the short sward, heavily grazed by the Soay sheep, to have rendered the habitat

Fig. 20. Neil Gillies finds a snipe nest (R. Atkinson/School of Scottish Studies).

unsuitable. By 1952, however, the warden Tim Bagenal found that the numbers had recovered again.

It was Eagle Clarke who first noticed how the snipe breeding in Orkney and Shetland, and on Fair Isle in between, were darker and more rufous in colour, in fact just like the Faroese subspecies. Visiting St Kilda during September and early October he had noted many snipe on migration, even seeing them on Soay. He collected two specimens; one on 12 September 1910 and the other on 30 September 1911. Only later, back at the Royal Scottish Museum, did he attribute the skins to the Faroese subspecies, but he dismissed them only as birds on passage through St Kilda.

In 1957, while Ken Williamson was warden on St Kilda, he took Eagle Clarke's two skins and another of his own that he had collected on Faroe during the war. That spring and summer he caught over 70 snipe in mist nets and all matched his three skins perfectly. Now he could explain Fisher's puzzlement at the snipes' odd habitat on St Kilda. From his own experience Williamson knew that, on Faroe, snipe preferred drier ground to marshes (Williamson 1959). He went further:

> It also suggests, in the light of the recorded history of snipe at St Kilda, that this group of islands has been colonised in comparatively recent times (and largely since the evacuation of 1930) by a migratory population from the north-west,

and not, as might have been expected, by a population expanding outwards from the mainland of the British Isles.

In 1957, Williamson estimated about 40 pairs nesting within the village fields and found 20 nests. He made detailed observations on their breeding habits. The clutch size averaged 3.7 eggs. Two newly-hatched chicks weighed 11 g each, and after one week, 30 g. They fledged about 3–4 weeks after hatching, but did not attain full adult weight (110 g or so) for a further fortnight. The St Kilda snipe probably rear two broods each season.

Williamson found one snipe nest right beside the quarry that the airmen had opened up whilst constructing the military base. Despite all the noisy activity only a few feet away, the determined snipe successfully hatched her chicks. Another bird was not so lucky. She had apparently mistaken freshly-laid bitumen for a mud pool and the tar had caked around her legs. Williamson managed to net the bird and although he laboriously cleaned her up, she deserted her nest.

Sheep's wool wrapping around the legs of snipe constituted another problem. Ken caught one bird that was completely hobbled, but she had continued to incubate. Sadly her legs had become so tightly bound together that one tarsus had snapped and the tendons had severed. The RAF medical officer successfully amputated the foot and dressed the wound in the hope that the bird might survive. This problem with sheep's wool seems to be a not uncommon occurrence amongst wading birds that nest wherever sheep graze. The feral Soay sheep on St Kilda cast their fleeces annually, rather than being clipped, so the amount of wool lying around these islands seems to present a particular hazard to its ground-nesting birds. Subsequent wardens do not seem to have reported a problem, however, but then none have studied the snipe and other waders in the detail that Williamson did.

Another of Williamson's ornithological passions was the wren, but St Kilda's celebrated birds deserve a chapter to themselves.

.10.

The St Kilda wren

Wrens make prey where eagles dare not perch.

William Shakespeare, *Richard III*

As well as its unique mammals, St Kilda has a unique bird, the St Kilda Wren, *Troglodytes hirtensis*, described by Seebohm in 1884. It is somewhat larger than the common Wren of the mainland, has a thicker and stronger bill, and paler plumage more distinctly marked with bars. It makes a ruder nest than its Scottish relatives, its eggs are slightly larger, and it has the distinction of having had an Act of Parliament passed solely for its protection.

Professor James Ritchie 1930

THE ONE BIRD, and a land bird at that, for which St Kilda might be said to be world-famous is its wren. Its presence has long been known. Martin Martin first mentioned them on St Kilda in 1697, and in 1758, the Reverend Kenneth MacAulay astutely speculated 'how these little birds ... could have flown thither or whether they went accidentally in boats, I leave undetermined'. Almost certainly they flew.

Indeed, modern studies of ringed birds have revealed that wrens are capable of quite respectable journeys on migration. Kenneth Williamson considered that the wrens that were trapped at the Bird Observatory on Fair Isle every spring and autumn – as distinct from the resident island wrens – were probably Norwegian birds on passage. Up to a dozen are recorded some years, and an unprecedented 35 on 4 October 1976 (Pennington *et al.* 2004). There have not, as yet, been any ringing recoveries to prove these wrens' Scandinavian origins, but birds ringed in Britain, perhaps immigrants in the first place, have turned up in continental Europe. Two ringed in England have been recovered in Sweden and another in the south of France. In turn, continental birds have turned up in Britain (Werham *et al.* 2002). So we know beyond all doubt that it is perfectly within the capabilities of such tiny and seemingly unlikely long-distance fliers like wrens to reach offshore islands.

All that the Reverend Neil Mackenzie offered was that the wren was resident, while around the same time George Clayton Atkinson similarly dismissed it:

> The Kitty Wren we also saw shirking about among the large stones. And this, I think, concludes the ornithological zoology of the island.

John MacGillivray failed to see a wren in 1840, while, a year later, the Reverend James Wilson, whether or not he actually saw any, chose to doubt his clerical colleague Mackenzie's observation that wrens remained on St Kilda all the year round. The St Kildan Lachlan Macdonald (1905–91) commented how one rarely saw the secretive wren in the winter and, needless to say current knowledge confirms that the good Reverend Mackenzie was perfectly correct when he said they were resident all year.

This more or less sums up the world interest in wrens on St Kilda until, that is, 1882, when the great Irish naturalist Alexander Goodman More (1830–95), mentioned to his friend Richard Barrington that he thought the St Kilda wren seemed quite distinctive. Barrington went to St Kilda the following year resolving, firstly, to compile a plant list for the island but also to procure a specimen of the wren to look into More's claim.

In fact, Barrington only saw a wren six times in three weeks. He managed two shots, but both his targets disappeared never to be seen again, dead or alive. One day, armed with his vasculum (for collecting plants) and his gun, he went botanising on the summit of Conachair. There he came across a rope dangling over the edge of the clifftop and realised that some St Kildans were catching fulmars down below. Having just made a historic ascent of the seemingly impossible Stac Biorach with the St Kildan cragsmen, Barrington obviously did not lack courage and bravado. Despite the dubious peg to which it was attached, he descended the rope hand over hand to join the fowlers. Three or four hundred feet down a wren flew out of a crack, so Barrington paused to watch it for a few minutes:

> ... hopping among the luxuriant herbage which grows here in every cleft and fissure. I may here correct a common impression that St Kilda is extremely barren. Some regard it as an igneous rock with precipitous sides, whose summit has less vegetation than the lava-beds of Iceland; and Mr Seebohm says it does not possess a 'tree or shrub, or even a bush of heather.' There are 110 phanerogams [higher plants] on St Kilda ... On three islands, Borrera, Soa, and the Doon, the

grass is long and plentiful between the rocks, and though St Kilda proper has a very barren look from the sea, a short examination will show that, although the flowering plants are comparatively few, yet some of them grow with exceptional luxuriance on the cliffs where they are beyond the reach of sheep ... The wren has therefore plenty of cover, and I should say insects also ...

So in the end, Barrington failed to bring back his wren and thus missed making a historic discovery. In the meantime, Henry Seebohm (1832–85) had arranged for Charles Dixon to visit St Kilda in June 1884:

> ... to procure some notes respecting the birds of that interesting island for my forthcoming volume [*History of British Birds 1883–5*]. Amongst other valuable information he had ascertained the existence of a Wren on St Kilda ...

Seebohm was a Sheffield steel man, a supreme example of the academic amateurs of his time. He was a robust Arctic traveller (often in the company of J. A. Harvie-Brown) and a tireless collector who presented 16,000 specimens to the Natural History Museum. His *History of British Birds* became a classic reference book. Seebohm's friend Charles Dixon is now credited with discovering that the St Kilda wren was indeed distinct, and in his own 1885 paper 'The Ornithology of St Kilda' he acknowledged Seebohm's input. It is worth quoting Dixon's observations in full:

> The most interesting result of my trip to St Kilda was the determination of its Wren, called 'Dhra-in-doun' by the natives. Although this little wren was known to Martin nearly two hundred years ago, neither he nor any subsequent naturalist had the least idea that the bird was different from the Wren inhabiting the rest of the United Kingdom. This little stranger was introduced to the notice of ornithologist by Mr Seebohm (Zoologist 1884, p. 333). He writes:- 'The St Kilda Wren ... is much more distinctly barred on the back and head, and almost free from any traces of spots on the throat and breast. In general colour it is quite as pale and slightly greyer ...'
>
> I [Dixon] had not been on St Kilda long before the little bird arrested my attention, as it flew from rock to rock, or glided in and out of the crevices of the walls. It differs very little in its habits from its congener; only instead of hopping restlessly and incessantly about brushwood, it has to content itself with boulders and walls. It was in full song, and its voice seemed to me louder and more powerful than that of the Common Wren. I often saw it within a few feet of the sea, hopping about the rocks on the beach; and a pair had made their nest in the wall below the manse, not thirty yards from the waves. I also saw it frequently on the tops of the hills and in many parts of the cliffs. It was especially common on Doon, and its cheery little song sounded from all parts of the rocks.
>
> As there are no bushes nor trees on St Kilda (except those the microscopic

eye of a botanist might discover), the Wren takes to the luxuriant grass, sorrel, and other herbage growing on the cliffs, and picks its insect food from them. It also catches spiders and the larvae of different insects in the nooks and crannies which it was incessantly exploring. It is a pert active little bird, by no means shy; and I used to watch a pair that were feeding their young in a nest not six yards from our door. Its breeding season must commence early in May, for the young were three parts grown by the beginning of June. It makes its nest either in one of the numerous 'cleats', or in a crevice of a wall, or under an overhanging bank. The nest is exactly similar to that of the Common Wren, and abundantly lined with feathers. I had not the good fortune to obtain any of its eggs, but I presume that they resemble those of its near congener.

On 7 June Dixon shot a female St Kilda wren and Barrington would have been able to take a little consolation in knowing that it had been his own companion, the islander Sandy Campbell, who had been instrumental in the act, the only man on the island other than the minister who could speak English. From his time pursuing wrens with Barrington, Campbell had realised how important it might be for Dixon to procure a specimen. Henry Seebohm (1884) took up the story:

Amongst other valuable information, [Dixon] has ascertained the existence of a Wren on St Kilda, and has brought home a skin of one of them, which differs in many important respects from either the European or the Faroe Island forms. Those ornithologists who regard the climatic races of this bird as distinct species, will probably come to the conclusion that the St Kilda Wren is one of the most distinct, and I propose to name it *Troglodytes hirtensis*, Hirta being the Gaelic name of St Kilda ... These various forms of Wren appear to differ in colour according to climate, and not according to geographical distribution, except so far as it a happens to be connected with climate ... The St Kilda Wren has been obliged by force of circumstances to change its habits, as well as the colour of its dress. Stranded on an island where there is not a tree or a shrub, not even a bush of heather, it picks up its food on the water and rocks, and has, in fact, become a rock wren. In all probability it has gradually acquired its grey colour and barred back by the slow process of protective selection, and is now almost invisible to the eyes of hungry hawks that visit St Kilda, as it flits about the grey lichen-pitted rocks. It would be interesting to know how many thousand years ago the accident happened which gave St Kilda a Wren. Doubtless some flock of Norwegian birds, migrating southwards to find a milder winter in Great Britain, were driven out of their course and took refuge on the lonely Atlantic island, where their descendants, modified by time and circumstances, still survive. Let us hope that they will succeed in baffling the skill of all persecutors of rare birds, and for ages yet to come enjoy their barren home.

While it may be lamented that scientific journals have lost such eloquence, they are nowadays much more succinct and discerning both in content and speculation. It is extremely unlikely many 'hawks' would ever have managed to secure a wren, so Seebohm's charming idea holds little water today. Having failed in his own quest to procure a specimen, Barrington chose to invoke 'exposure to a more maritime climate' as a possible factor for the St Kilda wren's distinctive appearance, which sounded a bit more plausible.

Although Seebohm later received four more specimens from Mr Mackenzie, St Kilda's Factor, his taxonomic conclusions were short-lived. One of his specimens he 'courteously' gave to the obsessive collector Henry E. Dresser (1838–1915) whilst also permitting him to examine the others. Dresser was not universally liked and Sir Philip Manson-Bahr in the centenary *Ibis* volume (1959) described him as possessing:

> ... demoniacal energy, boundless enthusiasm and immense application ... [He also had] a striking appearance which was arresting in company ... heightened by a rather ill-fitting wig, because he was completely bald.

An obituary also noted:

> He was one of the old order of systematic ornithologists who did not believe in subspecies or trinomials.

One wonders too whether there was some rivalry between the two amateurs Seebohm and Dresser, both of whom were in the metal industry. Not surprisingly perhaps, Dresser (1886) was quick to conclude 'that I do not consider the St Kilda bird worthy of specific rank'. He made light of the size of the bill and maintained, unreasonably, that the pale plumage of Seebohm's St Kilda wrens was the result of their having been preserved in spirit. Ironically though, he was partially right. The differences were indeed insufficient to justify full specific status, so the St Kilda wren was relegated to a subspecies, a status it still holds to this day. In 1915, Eagle Clarke finally resolved the situation:

> The majority of the ornithologists of the present day regard it, however, as a race of the Common Wren, and it rejoices in the trinomial name of *Troglodytes troglodytes hirtensis*. Whether or not it should be regarded as a distinct species is a matter of opinion rather than of rules ... The descriptions of the St Kilda Wren by Seebohm and others have all ... been based upon specimens in the well-worn plumage of summer. This fact led Seebohm in 1885 to remark in his *British Birds* (vol iii, p 665) that 'the young in first plumage and adults after the autumn moult are unknown ... To furnish these desiderata towards the knowledge of these plumages is the main object of the present contribution ... In the autumns of

1910 and 1911 the writer spent nearly twelve weeks at St Kilda, devoting his time to the observation of its bird-life, resident and migratory.'

The abrasive Dresser would have abhorred Clarke's trinomial! In actual fact the St Kilda wren is not so unusual. Small populations of wrens have established on many offshore islands in the North Atlantic (notably Fair Isle in Shetland), where they have quickly become quite distinctive in appearance and habits. Both St Kilda and Fair Isle wrens are larger than those living on mainland Britain, though not as large as Icelandic wrens (Table 4). According to available figures, St Kilda wrens also lay larger eggs. In 1931, Tom Harrisson noted how the St Kilda wrens:

> ... exhibited a marked dimorphism, with light and dark forms often very distinct in the field. This is clearly demonstrated in some of our photographs, and has not previously been recorded.

Some 43 subspecies of the winter wren, as *Troglodytes troglodytes* is now called, are currently recognised throughout Eurasia, North Africa and North America. Eleven of these occur in Europe – *zetlandicus* in Shetland, *fridariensis* in Fair Isle, *hebridensis* in the Outer Hebrides, *hirtensis* on St Kilda, *indigenus* in Ireland, Wales and much of England, *troglodytes* in south-east England – with five more races in Iceland, Faroe and the Mediterranean islands (Forrester *et al.* 2007). In passing it may be said that, so far, the Icelandic wren has not colonised Surtsey, the island still being too sparse in vegetation should the wren turn up there.

We will return to the subject of just how the wrens of St Kilda, and indeed those of other islands, came to be so distinctive when we come to consider St Kilda mice in the next chapter.

Table 3. Comparison between island races of wren (various sources)

	Mainland	St Kilda	Fair Isle	Iceland
Body weight (g)	8.9–11	12.5–14.5	10–15	13.5–20
Wing (mm)	47.5 (45–52)	50.2 (48–52)	49	56.3
Bill (mm)	13.3–14.8	13.5–16		
Tarsus (mm)	16.6–19.1	18–21		
Egg (mm)	16.4 x 12.6	18.6 x 13.9		
Egg weight (g)	1.32	1.84		

Whether species, subspecies or mere race, the St Kilda wren was now to attract quite a bit of attention from naturalists, museums and collectors. This enabled the opportunistic human inhabitants of St Kilda to supplement their meagre income by selling skins and eggs. Soon fears were being expressed that the subspecies could become extinct. So, in 1904 (when a skin was fetching as much as a guinea), a special Act of Parliament was passed to protect the St Kilda wren, together with the rare Leach's storm petrel which was equally prized.

In 1894, Steele Elliott found wrens on Hirta, Dun and Boreray, and assumed them to be on Soay also, although he did not reach there. He confirmed how they differed from the dark, rufous-brown mainland wren in having a paler greyish-brown plumage, larger bill and feet. The Reverend Fiddes told him that they used to be much more common, especially about the village. Elliott found several nests, one of which contained recently hatched young, and he took one to send to Cambridge University Museum. He did not admit to the fate of the eggs from the other nests he found.

Perceptively he summed up the future for the St Kilda wren:

> Its eggs are known to the natives as being well worth securing, always finding a ready sale among the English and other dealers ... It rests entirely with collectors whether this bird is to be exterminated, or remain one of the greatest attractions of the island to the ornithologist of the future.

One such collector was Charles Henry Wells from Sheffield, who visited St Kilda from 6 to 20 June 1907 (D. Clugston, personal communication). His diary recorded how the St Kilda wren:

> ... could be ranked a distinct species. It is still fairly numerous, tho' much persecuted on account of its rarity. It frequents the cliffs and stones of the main island, Doon, Borera and Stack-an-Armin. Its song is loud and shrill, but sweet, and in the general absence of bird song is very striking ... I only saw one nest with eggs and this contained five, rather larger than the mainland bird, and with much bigger spots. I found another nest myself but no eggs ...

Numbers of wrens do seem to have declined around the Village in Hirta, where nests were easily accessible to meet the collectors' illicit trade. In actual fact, the islands' wren population was unlikely to have been in much danger since it was secure and numerous on the steep, dangerous cliffs. Barrington summed up the situation when he said 'it would take some of the best cragsmen in the Alpine Club to extirpate it'.

Notwithstanding, in 1894, W. H. Hudson (1841–1922) chose an engraving by A. D. McCormick of a St Kilda wren perched upon the skull of a great auk, as the gloomy cover of his 32-page Royal Society for the Protection of Birds pamphlet Lost British Birds, claiming both were now extinct:

> When one considers that this small feathered creature is a dweller among the rocks near the sea, and frequently nests in crevices and holes just above the

high-water mark on the shores of that 'habitacle of birdes' which the Great Auk once haunted, he will not regard the drawing as a representation of something purely fanciful ... No sooner had the news gone abroad that 'lone St Kilda's isle' possessed one little song-bird of her own – a wren that differed somewhat from the familiar wren – than it was invaded by the noble army of collectors, who did not mind its loneliness and distance from the mainland so long as they secured something for their cabinets; and the result of their invasion is that the St Kilda wren no longer exists.

Fortunately, of course, he was wrong, though it has to be said that it was the St Kildans themselves who soon began to feed those amongst 'the noble army of collectors' who were not prepared to voyage out for themselves.

In effect, it was only after the evacuation that the St Kilda wren began to enjoy some respite from the depredations of collecting. Nonetheless, in 1931, the Cambridge ornithologists Tom Harrisson and John Buchan had known of a clutch of St Kilda wren eggs being sold for £5, their informant having been offered only the previous year a single egg for the sum of seven shillings and sixpence. Furthermore, their informant had claimed to know of a dozen or so nests being robbed annually. Harrisson and Buchan acknowledged that Lord Dumfries, St Kilda's new owner, employed a bird warden during the summer, but it was a position they considered 'far from satisfactory'. They obviously had their suspicions as to who the supplier of St Kilda wren eggs might be!

But by now, on the whole, *bona fide* naturalists were becoming much more interested in the wren's biology than in procuring specimens. Harrisson and Buchan themselves undertook the first serious investigation into the wren population in 1931. Tom Harrisson was able to visit North Rona and the Flannans later that same year. Ironically, Harrisson went on to have a glittering and varied career in an astonishing array of activities, which led to his pioneering ornithological work being largely forgotten. After he was killed in a motor accident in Thailand in 1976, one observer remarked:

> It is one of the absurdities of our science that T. H. Harrisson – who as ornithologist, anthropologist, sociologist, biologist, museum curator, conservationist, and adventurer became one of the great polymaths of his time – is largely unknown to birdwatchers today.

Men like Tom Harrisson, Ken Williamson and Max Nicholson had dragged birdwatching out of the Victorian era of guns and museums and into the field where birds could be observed in their proper context. This not only led to a deeper knowledge and understanding of birds, but even more importantly helped to popularise birdwatching as a hobby.

Harrisson and Buchan only censused some 68 pairs of wrens on the whole St Kilda archipelago, 45 of them on Hirta, 11 on Dun, 9 on Soay and 3

Fig. 21. St Kilda wren eggs in Kelvingrove Museum, Glasgow (J. Love).

on Boreray. This was probably an underestimate. They reckoned that 82 per cent of them were living on the cliffs or puffin slopes, with twice as many on the puffin slopes. The remainder (12 pairs) nested in buildings around the village on Hirta. The territories were regularly spaced and, in the Village, ranged from 17,000 to 30,000 square yards in extent. The nests around the village were usually about 90 yards apart, those on the cliffs usually twice this distance.

Clutches usually range from four to six eggs. Harrisson and Buchan found one brood of four chicks but no wren pairs fledged more than three. Making 10–13 visits to feed young every hour between 7 a.m. and 8.30 p.m., a wren might fly over 4 miles each day. They even clocked three wrens flying about 12 miles per hour. Nonetheless, the Oxbridge duo deduced that the birds spent only 2 per cent of their time on the wing. It is obviously advantageous for such a small bird (or indeed any small animal) to spend as much of its time on the ground or underneath it, safe from the strong winds that persist on any offshore island, let alone one as exposed as St Kilda. Indeed, the St Kilda wrens might even be considered subterranean, creeping within the walls and buildings like mice.

During their three-week stay the Oxbridge expedition encountered four dead birds, two of them – lamentably – in their mouse traps; another killed itself against a window, while the fourth had alighted on some tar on a hot day. Before they departed, the team, with the blessing of Lord Dumfries, exterminated the last of the feral cats on St Kilda – two females, one with kittens, leaving only a single male to die alone. Until the evacuation, cats may even have proved much more of a threat to the St Kilda wren's survival than the collecting of eggs and skins for sale.

Amazingly, as long ago as 1896, Richard and Cherry Kearton had managed to photograph St Kilda wrens. The nest was in a hole above a lintel stone, inside a cleit, so they had to devise a system of mirrors to provide enough light. Later, during July and August 1938, with the benefit of flashbulbs, Robert Atkinson was to take an even better set of monochrome photographs at the nest, which were published ten years later in the magazine *British Birds* (1947). Just exactly how he achieved this is described in his book *Island Going* (1949).

Harrisson and Buchan had found that the first brood of wrens did not fledge until the end of July, with no sign of any earlier broods. Nonetheless, they suspected that the wrens were double-brooded. Neil Gillies, the bird warden, told Atkinson that he had found his first nest with five eggs at the end of May – we may wonder what he did with it. Atkinson went on to find 15 empty nests in the village, and then three nests with young which he now felt certain were second broods. The Ulster-born Reverend E. A. Armstrong (1900–78), however, who visited St Kilda in 1951 and went on to write the

Fig. 22. Richard Kearton
(C. Kearton).

New Naturalist monograph *The Wren* (1955) considered second broods to be rare. Like mainland wrens, each cock bird may build several nests.

Atkinson noted a distinct smell of fulmars in his wren nest! With three or four St Kildans back each summer during the 1930s, fulmars were still being caught and eaten. Plucked feathers, which the wrens gathered to line their nests, lay all round the Village. Atkinson also added to the list of mortality factors by finding a St Kilda wren drowned in Mrs Gillies's washtub!

In 1939, Max Nicholson and James Fisher had estimated 31 pairs of wrens on Hirta, 12 on Dun and another five or more on Boreray. Eight years later James Ferguson-Lees, with James Fisher, found about 48 pairs of wrens on Hirta, and another 14 or 15 on Dun. Censuses throughout the archipelago can be notoriously difficult for any visiting naturalist to achieve, so several have confined their efforts to the village area. There the numbers seem to be remarkably consistent. Harrisson identified eight pairs there in one paper co-authored with David Lack, but claimed 12 pairs in another paper with John Buchan. Atkinson reckoned 12 pairs in 1938, as did Nicholson and Fisher a year later. Fisher found 10 pairs in 1947 and Ferguson-Lees 11 pairs the following year. Then Fisher found ten again in 1949, as did Armstrong in 1951. The next year, Morton Boyd, with Timothy Bagenal, found 12 pairs, with another just behind the head dyke. Boyd and various other workers only found six pairs in 1955 and five to eight pairs the following year.

In 1957, St Kilda became a National Nature Reserve and Ken Williamson arrived as the first warden. Coming from Fair Isle, he had already developed an interest in wrens, and, indeed, was the first to realise the Fair Isle wren was different from the Shetland wren. In 1951, he had described it as a new subspecies *Troglodytes troglodytes fridariensis*. In 1957, in the light of his experience on St Kilda, Williamson revisited his 1951 census of the Fair Isle wren and estimated about 50 pairs – its total world population. This dropped to as low as ten pairs in the 1970s and has since stabilised at around 30–40 pairs (Pennington *et al.* 2004).

Not surprisingly, on his arrival Williamson was keen to see how the Fair Isle wren compared with its St Kilda counterpart and immediately set about undertaking the first comprehensive survey of Hirta:

> There is only one way to census satisfactorily so inconspicuous a mite as the wren, and that is to count the singing males at a time when one can be reasonably sure that all of them are in song. This means counting them in spring within a couple of hours of first light, when, like their cousins in mainland woods, the St Kilda wrens have their traditional 'dawn chorus' in serenade to the rising sun. During the remainder of the day, when the birds are primarily concerned with feeding, preening, nest-building and the like, their song is desultory, so that day-time estimates such as have been made in the past are inevitably far from accurate.

Since it is manifestly impossible to encompass Hirta's seven miles of rugged coastline during one brief spell of early light, I divided the island into different sections, and tackled each in turn between 4 and 6 am on successive days. This necessitated rising at 3.30 British Summer Time, or earlier if I had first to climb to a distant point before making a start. A week of such activity is arduous only in contemplation – in the event, it brings many compensations, such as that memorable sunrise over the dark stacs and minarets of Boreray (surely the most attractive small island in Britain), with the Seven Hunters [the Flannan Isles] sprawled sleeping across the divide of grey seas and crimson sky 40 miles beyond, and the gentle hills of the Outer Hebrides bold and clear in the east. And there was the fly-past of the puffins at the Carn Mor in the dawn, wheeling in their thousands above the crazy jumble of jagged boulders which lie strewn across a once-grassy terrace in the lap of Mullach Bi. What a strange and fascinating dawn chorus, with the wrens singing and counter-singing amplified by the great rocks, mingling with the croaking fulmar voices and the groans of puffins in holes and crevices at one's feet. Occasionally, a rock pipit or a wheatear would compete but the wren is the only real songster St Kilda has.

Between 21 and 31 May 1957 Ken Williamson counted 115 singing males on Hirta, with nine pairs in the village area. He then postulated how Boreray and Soay might hold a further 40–50 pairs, with rather fewer on Dun, say 25–30. Thus he estimated a total of 230 pairs for the archipelago – effectively the world population of this unique race.

He added:

Since the St Kilda wren has no natural predators, and a normal clutch size is five or six eggs, it is probable that in most seasons the population of *Troglodytes t. hirtensis* soars to the 1,500 mark by the end of August, only to be reduced by an Atlantic winter's fearful gales to a breeding potential of about 450 birds by the following spring.

Williamson went on to compare the biology and habits of St Kilda and Fair Isle wrens and came to the following conclusions. The St Kilda wren's distribution is closely linked to the puffin and the highest densities are to be found on Dun and at Carn Mor on Hirta. The wren is less abundant on the slopes of Oiseval, but a few are to be found associated with the small puffin colonies in Gleann Mor and on Stac an Armin. Sandeels dropped by puffins, carcases from adults predated by gulls and dead chicks at the mouth of nest burrows all support an abundance of carrion-eating insects upon which the wrens feed. The Village and the slopes above it are the only inland situations in which wrens are to be found but constitute suboptimal habitat. It is likely that the birds benefited from the middens and food stores around the houses (and nowadays the Army Base) and from rotting sheep carcases in the cleits.

St Kilda wrens are never seen on the shore or the tideline (except perhaps in Village Bay), which is in stark contrast to the Fair Isle subspecies in Shetland. On this island, larger than Hirta, big concentrations of nesting seabirds are lacking so the wrens seek out sheltered inlets and geos in the cliffs, where the beaches are strewn with cast seaweed (a habitat that is absent in St Kilda). Fair Isle cliffs are more uniform, ranging only from 100 to 500 ft high with very much less of a vertical aspect than St Kilda's 7 miles of cliffs, some 1,200 ft in height. Thus the Fair Isle wrens have a more linear, low-level distribution, totalling no more than 50 pairs, despite the island's greater area (525 ha) and 25 miles of coastline. There they take small marine insects and larvae from the seaweed. The wrens' diet on St Kilda is mainly terrestrial insects, especially carrion-feeders, chiefly small beetles but also flies, spiders, and a few small seeds, also a few moth caterpillars, centipedes, earwigs and thysanurids; on occasions the wrens may even venture inside houses to take flies and other small insects.

Thus the St Kilda wren retains a plasticity in behaviour that the Fair Isle wren has lost. Fair Isle wrens avoid the crofts for instance, despite winter storms rendering the geos rather austere, inhospitable places. Amongst the towering cliffs of St Kilda, on the other hand, wrens gain considerable choice of shelter from strong winds amongst rock chimneys, complex outcrops and boulder slopes. Yet they are not so rigid in their requirements that they would shun the drystone structures of the Village, and will even venture inland up into Village Glen (although this has never been an optimum habitat).

Estlin Waters was medical officer with the army on St Kilda from May 1961 to September 1962, a worthy successor to David Boddington. During his time on St Kilda, being a keen ornithologist, Waters undertook several important studies, especially of the wrens. First he carefully repeated Williamson's survey on Hirta at the same time of year but in 1962. He mapped 92 singing males (with one less pair in the Village area) which he considered to be a genuine decrease, agreeing with Williamson that 'the troglodyte existence of the St Kilda wren is a good protection against both wind and snow'.

In his brief summer sojourn on St Kilda, all Williamson had been able to conclude was that the total incubation and fledging period in one St Kilda wren's nest was 40 days. Waters was able to study three more nests, measuring two incubation periods of 19 and 20 days (three or four days longer than mainland wrens), and three fledging periods of 16, 16 and 17 days (one or two days longer than the mainland) – roughly consistent with Williamson's figure. Whilst acting as relief warden for Ken Williamson in 1957, Tim Bagenal (1958) had suggested that the longer incubation period of the St Kilda wren was due to its larger egg. However, Waters noticed not only that the eggs of the Shetland subspecies are hardly any smaller than the St Kildan ones, but

Fig. 23. Robert Atkinson with Finlay MacQueen, Neil Gillies and Mrs Gillies
(R. Atkinson/School of Scottish Studies).

the incubation period in Shetland is shorter even than that of the mainland wren. Waters found one pair of St Kilda wrens that had delayed the onset of incubation for three days, a habit which could easily have accounted for the inconsistencies. He agreed with Armstrong that the northern subspecies, perhaps living in less optimum conditions, had to extend the fledging period over that of birds living on the mainland.

In 1990, the warden S. G. Holloway estimated 145 to 157 pairs in Hirta and, three years later, the next warden Jim Vaughan found 113 to 117 pairs (Scottish Natural Heritage files). These two surveys found between 19 and 27 pairs in the Village area. Nowadays, numbers on St Kilda may vary slightly from year to year but probably total around 230 pairs, with over a hundred on Hirta, about 50 pairs on Boreray and on Soay, another 25 or so on Dun, and even three to four pairs on Stac an Armin.

Interestingly, David Boddington told me that the wrens he encountered on Stac an Armin in 1958 did not seem to have any particular threat response when he was close to a nest; they just stood their ground and sang loudly at him! With no predators, birds on other islands seem to have little fear response. On the arid island of Española in the Galapagos, I have had the local mocking birds land on my knee trying to drink out of my water bottle. I have even had one perch on my shoulder to probe into my ear for insects; happily it found none!

It would be interesting to know whether the wrens on the other islands and stacs of the St Kilda archipelago differ in any way from the Hirta wrens and have progressed towards producing distinct races of their own. This is the situation that so intrigued Charles Darwin on the Galapagos Islands and other archipelagos he visited from HMS *Beagle* in 1831–36, ultimately leading to his theory of evolution and his historic synthesis *On the Origin of Species*.

Darwin first noted island differences amongst the Galapagos mocking birds but it is the finches that are the birds which have come to illustrate best how populations can diverge sufficiently on satellite islands so that they can no longer interbreed with the parent population should they ever meet up again. It was David Lack, who went to Galapagos just a few years after he had visited St Kilda, who unravelled the evolutionary complexities of Darwin's finches. Although St Kilda is an archipelago like Galapagos, it is likely that St Kilda's satellites are too close to one another to isolate effectively the wrens and their genes.

Far removed from prime habitats on the mainland, the St Kildan wren rarely raises more than one brood each season. They begin nesting later, in late May, once the puffins have got nesting well in hand, and they find ample insect food in the seabird colonies. Both sexes participate in rearing the chicks, whereas on the mainland male wrens can afford to abandon their first brood to court other females. On St Kilda the wrens have no real predators and can stay close to ample cover. Thus, although numbers may fluctuate from year to year due presumably to the vagaries of the weather and of food supply, the population of *Troglodytes t. hirtensis* seems secure.

St Kilda wren perched upon the skull of a great auk
(Engraving by A. D. McCormick).

.11.

St Kilda mice

The zoology of archipelagoes will be well worth examination . . .

Charles Darwin 1835

S T KILDA IS, of course, an archipelago within the larger archipelago
that is the British Isles. In Chapter 10 we discovered that our familiar
little 'jenny wren' of the British Isles is actually a mix of populations, mostly
on offshore islands, each of which has evolved slightly different from the
others in appearance and habits. On his voyage round the world the naturalist
Charles Darwin came to realise that archipelagos are particularly instructive
to evolutionary biologists.

St Kilda is not quite on a level with the Galapagos Islands, where Darwin
began his ground-breaking quest into the origin of species. We have already
seen that it possesses its own subspecies of wren, but St Kilda has in addition
given rise to two quite distinct subspecies of mice.

We recall that the scientist who in 1939 made a particular study of the
dozen species of Darwin's finches on the Galapagos Islands was none other
than David Lack, who had visited St Kilda only a few years earlier. Sadly,
Lack and his five companions were the last scientists to see the St Kilda house
mouse before it became extinct. But the long-tailed field mouse still thrives.
It is more frequently referred to as the 'wood mouse' nowadays, but this does
seem particularly inappropriate for a treeless island like St Kilda, so I adhere
to the original term 'field mouse'. Just how did a land mammal like a mouse
get to St Kilda in the first place?

Global sea levels have certainly altered through time. Just after the last Ice
Age, the British mainland is known to have been connected by a land bridge
to the Continent. Thus, as the ice retreated, the first mammals and many

other creatures could walk into Britain. Early naturalists tended to the view that mice could then have walked to even the most distant of the British Isles. However, nowadays, many of the more remote islands such as St Kilda are considered never to have been connected to the mainland. So just how did its mice reach St Kilda? The answer is simple. Where wrens could fly, mice had to rely on human assistance.

The house mouse could have reached St Kilda with some of the earliest human settlers, at the very most only a few thousand years ago, or – more likely – at some stage after that. Field mice would have arrived in the same way, though perhaps, as we shall see, in more recent times. The house mice in particular evolved in close association with the people on St Kilda where, doubtless they were considered at least a nuisance, if not a pest.

For long, visitors and naturalists alike considered the mice to be of little interest. Mice were mice, so ubiquitous and commonplace elsewhere that there seemed little reason for the little rodents on St Kilda to be any different. Thus there were few early references to them. Mice attracted no comment from John MacGillivray in 1840. Perhaps he missed them altogether during his short stay. But a year later the Reverend James Wilson did speculate how these rodents might have reached St Kilda:

> Besides sheep, cattle, one or two small horses, and the dogs aforesaid, the only other four-footed creatures are mice, introduced in vessels either from the Outer Hebrides, or the mainland.

John Sands was one of the first visitors to spend any time on Hirta and so became familiar enough with the mice. His is an interesting story. A qualified lawyer, he pursued a career as a journalist, enabling him to visit Shetland, Tiree and Faroe. In 1875, he went with Macleod's Factor to St Kilda and left six weeks later on the next available boat. He then returned in late June 1876 with a gift of a boat for the islanders, again travelling with Macleod's Factor in the *Janet*. Sands planned to leave when the Factor returned for a second visit in autumn, but this never took place. Sands was stuck for the winter.

He struck up a relationship with one of the local girls, but quickly fell out with the minister Reverend Mackay, later to write vindictively, and somewhat unreasonably, about the man's domination over the islanders. In the meantime Sands set adrift several pleas for relief inside floating 'mailboats' – little wooden containers attached to a float with the instruction 'Please open' painted in large letters. So began what is now thought to be an age-old St Kildan tradition for posting letters! Finally, in February 1877, whether in response to a St Kilda mailboat or not, the government ship *Jackal* arrived and offered to take Sands back to the mainland, along with nine shipwrecked Austrian sailors whom the islanders had been feeding for the past month. The *Jackal* left some food for the islanders, but no other vessels were to arrive until the Factor came the next April.

Back on the mainland, Sands went on take up the islanders' plight as a *cause célèbre* – though quite how effectively this abrasive journalist advanced their dilemma is best left to others to argue. Notwithstanding, in a disappointingly short book, he was in rather a unique position to describe the island of St Kilda and its inhabitants, human or otherwise. Although brief enough, his mention of the mice is useful:

> The only wild animal is the mouse, of which there are two species, the house and field. I have only seen one of the latter, and it was too distant for inspection. They swarm in Glen More I was told, and also in Dun. The people are careful not to carry them to Boreray or Soa, and I heard that a party of men who had gone to Boreray to pluck sheep happened to carry a mouse in their baggage, and dreading that it might be a female who would introduce the breed, they resolved to destroy her at any cost. They had, however, to take down seven cleatian [*sic*] before they accomplished their purpose.

This commendable effort must surely be one of the first recorded instances of biosecurity on islands!

It would be nearly a decade after Sands that Steele Elliott came to collect for science nine specimens of 'common mouse', mainly young, in the manse. He considered the house mice to be 'fairly numerous' among the dwellings but struggled to find any long-tailed field mouse:

> Unfortunately only one specimen was obtained, trapped near the top of a high stone wall. The coloration of this specimen was very handsome. Instead of the reddish brown fur on the back it was more inclined to grey, somewhat similar to the young of our type; the fur on the stomach was of a light red shade. Further particulars may be reserved until a series can be obtained for examination and comparison with the typical form *Mus sylvaticus*.

The following year, 1885, he reported:

> The whole of the mice taken are now in the British Museum, and I might add a supply of traps, etc, has been sent out [to St Kilda] by the authorities to obtain if possible further specimens. I hope in the future, if I am spared for another visit, to be able to obtain further specimens. The other Hebrides are likewise being trapped to obtain, if possible, any intermediate forms.

Where Dixon had given his ground-breaking St Kilda wren to Henry Seebohm for examination ten years earlier, Steele Elliott sent his St Kilda mice, preserved in spirit, to the Natural History Museum. They were eagerly examined by Gerald E. H. Barrett-Hamilton (1871–1914) who was both a distinguished soldier and an eminent mammalogist. In 1910, he embarked on his monumental *History of British Mammals* which was to be illustrated by Edward A. Wilson (1872–1912), but, of course, the artist died with Scott of the Antarctic two years later. Barrett-Hamilton's work ran to three volumes and was still only half complete by the time the author himself died of pneumonia, also at southern latitudes, in South Georgia, on an expedition to study whaling. But in 1899 he had this to say of the St Kilda rodents:

The existence of any wild species of Mouse on the isolated rock of St Kilda is an occurrence so apparently unlikely, that when in 1895 a specimen of a *Mus sylvaticus*-like species was found amongst some examples of *Mus musculus* sent thence to the British Museum in spirit, it was received with an amount of surprise certainly equal to the importance of the discovery. The specimen, a young male, had been obtained and was presented to the Museum by Mr J. Steele Elliott. It was a very remarkable one, and bore unmistakable evidence of having come from an out of the way part of the world. Its characteristics were a larger foot and a smaller ear than the corresponding organs of typical *Mus sylvaticus*, while, what was no less noticeable, the very characteristic snow-white colour of the belly of our common Field-Mouse was in this individual replaced by a uniform rufous hue shading imperceptibly through the flanks to the peppery reddish-brown of the upper surface.

All these peculiarities seemed to clearly point to a new species or subspecies of Mouse; but the animal having been in spirit, its colour was regarded as unsatisfactory, and the unusual proportions of its ears and tail were ascribed to individual variation. And so the specimen was put on one side in the hope that in due time further examples might be procured.

Early in the spring of the present year I happened to come across the specimen, and, being greatly struck by its remarkable appearance, I at once endeavoured to procure some more of these St Kilda Mice, with the result that my friend Mr Henry Evans, during the course of a yachting cruise among the Scottish Islands, put in at St Kilda and landed some traps for me on the island. Thanks to Mr Evans, I have now before me, in addition to Mr Steele Elliott's specimen, a fine adult pair, male and female, as well as a young female, of the St Kilda Mouse, all sent down in spirit . . .

In addition to the above mice, Mr Evans also procured for me five specimens of the House-Mouse of St Kilda, of which the Museum already possessed five specimens collected on previous occasions and now preserved in spirit. These are if possible, of even greater interest than the *Mus sylvaticus*-like species, since they are characterized by the possession of a buff-coloured underside clearly marked off from the colour of the upperside by a distinct line of demarcation, and are thus very different from the ordinary almost uniformly smoky-brown-coloured

House-Mice with which everyone is familiar … All these mice – even the very young ones – agree in presenting similar characters, and altogether are quite the most distinct local form of *Mus musculus* which I have ever examined.

In form and proportions these mice are well-developed large House-Mice, only differing in this respect from ordinary mice in being above the average size …

It is obvious, that, according to the custom of modern naturalists, these two form of mice need new names, which I therefore propose to give …

The names he proposed were *Mus hirtensis* for the field mouse and *Mus muralis* for the house mouse, opting for full specific status at this early stage rather than a trinomial subspecies. Barrett-Hamilton went on to suggest, in the accepted wisdom of the day, that the field mouse had reached St Kilda over a land bridge, but he was prepared to admit that humans had been responsible for bringing the house mouse, albeit perhaps, only a few hundred of years ago. He was willing to accept that its appearance could change in a comparatively short space of time. His final point was well made:

We have here a clear opportunity of studying the effect on two distinct species of the same genus of isolation side by side on the same island. Here we have on a circumscribed area two species in the course of evolution, the progress of which may be easily studied from time to time.

The following year Barrett-Hamilton published another paper in the *Proceedings of the Zoological Society of London*, downgrading the field mouse to a subspecies *Mus sylvaticus hirtensis*.

When James Waterston was on St Kilda in June/July 1905, he chose to concentrate on catching field mice. He noticed how they preferred traps baited with meal and biscuits but were totally disinterested in cheese!

With regard to trapping it was found that the most productive spots were cleits, especially when filled with hay. Traps laid in the open never brought a single mouse … The species is distributed fairly commonly round Village Bay and in the glen. On Dun it is abundant, and the men who sometimes sleep in a semi-underground house there say that at night the mice run over their bodies in numbers. They are agreed that no mice occur on Boreray, while as to Soay no evidence was forthcoming.

The house mice, on the other hand, he found to swarm in all the houses and cleits within the cultivated area. Waterston procured as many as he wanted by supplying the local lads with traps. He observed how omnivorous the mice were, and how prolific, with six to nine young to a litter.

Eagle Clarke at the Royal Scottish Museum showed Waterston's series to

Barrett-Hamilton in London who saw fit to reserve judgement on his original assessment until his British mammal book was published. In the autumn of 1910 and 1911, Eagle Clarke and the young Fair Islander George Stout of Busta spent 12 weeks on St Kilda. While more interested in migrant birds, they were able to trap no less than 60 field mice and 40 house mice, none of which were preserved in alcohol like previous specimens, so probably retained a truer colour to the fur.

Clarke (1914) noticed that the upper body of the field mouse was indeed a peppery reddish brown, but, while the underparts had been said to be creamy yellow, they were in fact white, at odds with Steele Elliott's initial description. There was a sharp demarcation line and the belly was only washed with brown along the central line. Furthermore, none of the house mice had a smoky underbelly, but were a bright buff in colour, with a clear line to the upper body, and paler than the mainland house mice.

Clarke also noted that the field mice were in fact larger than previously supposed. The head and body of the biggest male he caught was 130 mm long, with the tail another 100 mm. Similarly, his house mice were bigger than hitherto supposed, the largest being 111 mm long, with a 90 mm tail. He also added an interesting little observation – while the fur of the field mouse was long, soft and fluffy like that of a vole, that of the house mouse was hair-like and short.

By now all 11 Eurasian species of field mouse were included in the genus *Apodemus*. By the time Eagle Clarke wrote up his results in 1914, Barrett-Hamilton had just died, but Clarke chose to adhere to the great zoologist's specific status for both St Kilda mice: *Apodemus hirtensis* and *Mus muralis*. He did, however, qualify this:

> It is difficult to understand on what grounds these two mice have been given full specific rank ...

In 1910, a French zoologist had decided that the St Kilda house mouse was merely a robust and pale race of the common house mouse and so it became *Mus musculus muralis*. Its hind foot was broad and more robust than that of mainland mice, but the 10 cm tail seemed somewhat delicate, and could break easily if the animal was held by it. While there is a good series of body dimensions for St Kilda house mice, fewer body weights are available. The largest of 11 house mice caught by Harrisson and Moy-Thomas in 1931 was 32 g, twice as heavy as mainland house mice. The largest St Kilda field mouse they trapped was 50 g, similarly twice as heavy as its mainland cousin. Conveniently, the hulking St Kilda field mouse is quite placid and is usually reluctant to bite the hand that holds it!

The tension amongst biologists as 'splitters' or 'lumpers' was to continue for some time. Indeed, a new species – *Apodemus fridariensis* – was described from six adult mice caught on Fair Isle in 1906. But, by 1940, after reduced status gained favour, no fewer than 15 subspecies were postulated from islands all round the British coast. It was not until 1961 that some rationality was introduced to the problem, and the field mice from Rum were the most distinctive example – *Apodemus sylvaticus hamiltoni*. Furthermore, no longer was it speculated that the mice had reached these offshore islands by a complex system of land bridges or Ice Age refugia, but it was generally agreed that humans had been involved.

Detailed anatomical studies by Professor R. J. 'Sam' Berry (1969) highlighted how the island mice were more similar to those from Norway than to British mainland populations. So he proposed that the Vikings were the most likely agent of dispersal, especially since the St Kildan and Icelandic mice were the most Norwegian of all. This has now been confirmed by up-to-date DNA studies. Mice can easily stow away in the belongings, foodstuffs and animal fodder carried by seafaring colonists and so could reach anywhere the Vikings chose to voyage.

It seems that parallel evolution has since moulded the island mice to the specific environmental conditions offered by these diverse localities. Acting upon a limited gene pool from so few original colonists – known by geneticists as the 'Founder Effect' – the various populations became distinctive in both size and appearance.

Unfortunately, we will never now know much detail about the habits of St Kilda's house mice, only that they were once abundant around the Village, apparently to the exclusion of the field mice further inland, which seemed almost scarce by comparison. In 1928, John Gladstone noticed that there were more cats than dogs on Hirta and that they had almost exterminated the mice. He specifically mentioned the field mice but he most probably meant house mice, as the missionary's wife 'who does not keep a cat, occasionally sees them in the manse, and was able to trap two of them this year'.

At the time of evacuation in 1930, Alasdair Alpin Macgregor (1899–1970) was present on Hirta as correspondent for *The Times*. He noticed that every household on St Kilda possessed at least one cat and dog . As a vehement animal rights campaigner, and a vegetarian, he was horrified to hear that the dogs were to be drowned. Macgregor wished he had taken a humane-killer with him. While he was on the island a letter arrived from the National Canine Defence League expressing concern at the dogs' welfare, but by then Macgregor had convinced some of the islanders to take a few dogs to the mainland. In case the islanders could not afford it, the Defence League were offering to pay the seven shillings and sixpence for each dog licence. Some of the cats on the other hand were to be left to their own devices:

Several cats will be left on Hirta. Their fate will be a better one, for they are semi-wild in any case, and will be able to procure mice and birds for themselves. Nature is ruthless in her redness ... Circumstances now compel these creatures to return to a wild state.

For generations [the house mouse] has confined himself to the post office building ... Time will tell what fate awaits the post office mouse after St Kilda has been depopulated, and the natives' cats are obliged to forage for themselves. And there are no stores in the post-office building now – no sacks of sugar and the like.

Macgregor was probably referring back to Dr James Ritchie (1930) who was also of the opinion that the house mice were confined to the Post Office buildings and wrote:

With the willing assistance of the Postmaster we made several attempts a few years ago, to transport living specimens to Edinburgh in order to create a stock for experimental work in cross-breeding. But alas! None survived the journey beyond Oban. When the houses are deserted, how will the unique House Mouse of St Kilda fare?

Alasdair Alpin Macgregor went on to print an amusing epitaph apparently written by an unnamed London naturalist:

Oh, what will become of the Post Office mouse,
When the Post Office posts no more?
It will mope, it will mope in the Post Office house,
And die on the Post Office floor.

By August 1931, a year after the evacuation, Harrisson and Moy-Thomas of the Oxford/Cambridge expedition caught house mice in only two houses (No. 8 and No. 16), where some flour, dried fish and sugar had been left. None were caught in the Post Office however; nor did that building reveal any holes or other signs of mouse infestation. None of the islanders recalled house mice in the Post Office. So quite why that myth persisted is not clear. The islanders had always maintained that it had been No. 16 that was notorious for its mice. Harrisson and Moy-Thomas estimated that there could not have been many more than a dozen house mice left on St Kilda by 1931 and considered them doomed to extinction. Luckily John Buchan photographed an ailing house mouse out of their traps, just before it died. This seems to be the only photograph in existence, but sadly is not of great quality.

By 1931 there were only three cats left. Two females (one with kittens) were shot by Harrisson and his companions (under instructions from the owner), but a third – a male – escaped, and must have died soon afterwards. When

Fig. 24. Alasdair Alpin Macgregor (Oban Times).

the military moved into St Kilda in 1958, they had to include in their standing orders a ban on killing mice and on the introduction of pet cats and dogs. Mercifully, today St Kilda is free from feral cats. The seabird colonies and field mice thus can continue to thrive. But it was too late for the house mice.

So dependent had the house mouse become on humans and their dwellings that within a few years it had indeed become extinct. The scientists had been able to study the last few in the Village in 1931, but by 1938 the unique St Kilda *Mus musculus muralis* had vanished altogether. Robert Atkinson penned another, less frivolous epitaph in 1949:

> The house mice, it seemed, really were gone . . . It seemed a sad little story, tacked on to the human saga of St Kilda; common house mice had come in with man so long ago that their generations had gradually formed a new race; now the men had gone and their small camp followers were to be written off as extinct.

Interestingly, there seems no known case of field mice co-existing with house mice in the absence of humans. In the Faroes the equally distinctive house mouse abounds on the bird cliffs as well as the villages, but there are no field mice. On Lunga, of the Treshnish Isles in the Inner Hebrides, house mice have lived wild since the people left 140 years ago, but again there are no field mice. Thus, if there had never been field mice on St Kilda, it seems that the house mice would have survived. In retrospect, Morton Boyd considered it regrettable that no St Kilda house mice were transferred to Boreray or Soay where field mice had never hitherto established, doubtless due to the diligence of the islanders (as mentioned earlier in this chapter).

So the field mouse has inherited Hirta. And we know that it had also existed on Dun. Some of the islanders told Waterston how, if sleeping in a semi-underground house on Dun, field mice would be running all over their bodies during the night. They did agree that no mice occurred on Boreray and, as John Sands had revealed, they took great pains to ensure that it stayed that way. Eagle Clarke's contention that field mice occurred in Soay seems at odds with others. Harrisson and Moy-Thomas, for example, failed to find any runs on Soay or on Boreray, nor has anyone else since then.

So we have to conclude that field mice only ever occurred in Hirta and Dun. Back in 1884 Steele Elliott had found it hard to collect any in Hirta, but now they now abound all over Hirta, even to the summit of Conachair, although rarer in short grass and heather. They are, however, especially common in the old cultivations around the Village. The St Kilda field mice seem to have less of a burrowing habit than mainland field mice, preferring the shelter of stony

Fig. 25. *Probably the only photograph ever taken of a St Kilda house mouse (D. Lack).*

recesses, old walls, cleits and buildings. The desiccated body of a mouse has been found in an old wren's nest, where rodent fleas have also been collected, suggesting that bird and mouse, if not co-habiting, at least share the same living quarters from time to time.

In 1905, when house mice were still common, the field mouse seemed to spend most of its time in the neighbourhood of cleits, pens and dykes, especially those cleits filled with hay. It was fairly common around Village Bay and the glen behind. Waterston observed it to be very shy, never being detected far from cover, and never on the open hillside. In 1910, Eagle Clarke added how it was most abundant where coarse grass prevailed, but was to be found almost everywhere – in the crofted area, in the neighbourhood of the houses, on the faces of cliffs and on hillsides and hilltops. It found:

> ... congenial retreats in the rough stone-built 'cleits' (which are such a feature of the St Kilda landscape), and in the walls surrounding the crofts.

Eagle Clarke even caught some in the Feather Store. On Dun he encountered mice and their runs in fissures and holes in the face of rocks, where grass was growing close by on ledges or at the foot of crags. Waterston found one field mouse nest in an abandoned Leach's petrel burrow, with a petrel incubating its egg at the end of an offshoot tunnel, and a puffin sitting just through a wall of turf. The St Kildans told him how mice and petrels frequently inhabited the same burrow.

Both Eagle Clarke and Waterston noted that the field mouse was exclusively nocturnal and only one was ever seen in daylight – on Dun. The animals appeared to become active from about 10.30 p.m., with most of Eagle Clarke's captures occurring from then until midnight.

On the other hand, Eagle Clarke caught house mice by both day and night, and even caught one near the churchyard – where field mice were abundant. Furthermore, the house mice were 'omnivorous', while the field mice fed largely, if not exclusively, on grass and various seeds. In 1931 Harrisson and Moy-Thomas noted the staple diet of field mice to be Yorkshire fog *Holcus lanatus*, *Anthoxanthum*, *Festuca ovina* and seeds of scurvy grass *Cochlearia anglica*, *Statice maritima*, *Ranunculus acris* and *Rumex acetosa*.

An islander told the Oxbridge party that he had seen a field mouse on the top of Conachair at 1,400 ft, but they doubted this since they themselves had caught none above 550 ft. Below this height, however, field mice were fairly numerous over most of the island, but rare or absent in short grass or moorland. They were common in the arable land around Village Bay and where it graded into moorland, as long as there were walls or cleits in the vicinity. The writer and naturalist Robert Atkinson (1949) was able to come to a telling conclusion in 1938, only eight years after the evacuation:

In 1931 the scientists had caught no field mice inside the houses. Seven years later they were everywhere. I trapped them in the byres and houses, in the cleits, the old walls and in the long grass. At some time past, somehow, they had colonised Dun; Finlay [MacQueen] told in translation and by gesture, of a field mouse which had run up his sleeve there, when he was feeling down a petrel's burrow.

Where Ritchie had failed in bringing St Kilda mice into captivity, Atkinson was to succeed. He managed to deliver a single pair of St Kilda field mice to London Zoo, although a few others escaped in Mallaig on the way.

Where earlier observations had maintained the field mice to be strictly nocturnal, by late May 1938 Atkinson was seeing many field mice in daytime, as did James Fisher during several visits between 1939 and 1949, and again Morton Boyd in the 1950s. In the absence of house mice the field mice had radically altered their habits.

James Fisher was able to recount an amusing tale in a letter to the Natural History Museum dated 3 September 1948, a copy of which David Wilson has sent me. In 1938, the owner, Lord Dumfries, by then the Marquis of Bute, had spent a little time on St Kilda, leaving behind a barrel of salted mutton in the Manse byre. He wrote to Fisher:

> A large number of mice, probably between sixty and seventy, climbed down an overhanging net and got into the barrel, from which they were unable to escape. These unfortunate beasties, of course, perished, and when I returned in 1939 they were all pickled. I shall always kick myself for not having either examined or counted them, but, if my memory serves me right, I would say that about a quarter of the beasties were house mice.

Intrigued, Fisher did not to let the matter rest and enlisted the British Museum to comment:

> On St Kilda in 1948 I discovered what must have been the very barrel. Although the pickled fluid had dried out and the mutton had all gone, the skeletons of thirteen or fifteen mice, which are what are in the tin, remained behind stuck to the bottom of the barrel. I scraped them off, and you have them ...

Fisher had been wary of admitting what he had done since Lord Bute had expressly asked the expedition not to collect anything:

> I have taken it that he clearly meant that we were not to kill live animals, and I'm sure that he does not object to our having collected certain animals which we found dead, including these *Apodemus* skeletons. All the same, I would be glad if you could treat this correspondence as confidential.

T. Morrison-Scott of The Mammal Room at the British Museum replied:

I have now looked at the pickled specimens. As you thought, they are all *Apodemus* ... I wonder why Bute would say that about a quarter of the beasties were house mice? There are certainly none in your sample. Do you want the specimens back? If not I will keep some of the skulls and discard the rest.

When Morton Boyd made his second visit to St Kilda in May 1955, he repeated as closely as possible the trap effort that Harrisson and Moy-Thomas had undertaken in July/August 1931. With more efficient traps and more young around later in the summer, Boyd could still conclude that the field mice were now much more abundant. Also, by catching a field mouse on the summit of Conachair, he confirmed what the islanders had maintained all along. But Boyd added that the field mice might retreat to lower ground in winter. He even caught some in the boulder field of Carn Mor, but by far his largest catches were inside the perimeter wall of the Village area, in the vicinity of the street and immediately behind the beach. The mouse had less of a burrowing habit than mainland forms, perhaps because of the wet, shallow soils. Instead the animals sought cover in stony recesses, walls and buildings.

It was obvious that the field mice had indeed exhibited 'niche expansion' as soon as the house mice disappeared. They had moved into the houses, had become more numerous and were much less exclusively nocturnal.

Rats

Probably the greatest threat to any offshore island with seabird colonies is the appearance of invasive mammals. Strictly speaking, the mice would have come into this category originally. Now, of course, they are of sufficient biological interest to merit special consideration.

It is perhaps surprising, given the shipping traffic in the last century or two, that rats have never established in St Kilda. Fortunately, there is only one feasible access point – the beach at Village Bay where all the people live, and the pier was only completed by 1900.

In 1841, Wilson remarked:

The only other four-footed creatures are mice, introduced in vessels either from the Outer Hebrides, or the mainland. Rats are fortunately still unknown ...

In 1957, the Air Ministry were charged with establishing a radar base on St Kilda. Materials were to be shipped out by tank landing craft which would drop their ramps on the beach in Village Bay. Knowing how both house mice and field mice had reached St Kilda at some time in the past, the Nature Conservancy were only too well aware of the risk of rats getting ashore and decimating the seabird colonies (Nature Conservancy files). They quickly sought assurances from the Ministry who agreed to the following precautions:

1   All five tank landing craft likely to operate between Cairnryan and St Kilda were inspected and given rat-free certificates. If traces of rats were found, poison was to be laid. If that failed to eliminate them, the ships were to be closed down and fumigated.

2   Tank landing craft Commanders were to show up-to-date certificates on demand and ensure that their vessels remained rat-free.

3   Tank landing craft reaching St Kilda were to be unloaded swiftly and in daylight to minimise the time that the vessels were in contact with the beach.

4   Rat guards were fitted to hawsers, while special 'rat watchers' were to be on duty at the unloading ramps.

5   A careful watch would be maintained whilst the stores were being loaded and fresh food would be carried in sealed, refrigerated containers.

6   A careful watch would also be maintained while all crates and packages were being unloaded on the island.

7   Everyone responsible for the operations would be made aware of the importance of the issue.

On 30 April 1957, however, only a fortnight after such precautions were agreed, the warden Ken Williamson reported that the first landing craft still did not possess the required certificates and had not yet been inspected! It took a month for the Air Ministry to reply, apologising profusely and lamely attesting how there was nowhere on a tank landing craft for rats to hide. By then *all* the ships had indeed been certified rat-free.

There was, however, a scare in August 1959, which happily proved to be a false alarm. Someone claimed to have seen a rat swimming ashore, and to have seen 'rats' about 6 in long around the Village. Furthermore, Ernest Blezard of the Carlisle Museum, completely unaware that there were no rats on St Kilda, thought that the raven pellets he had examined from Ruaival contained rat remains. However, he looked at them again and later confirmed that the bits of skull were just field mice and the tail vertebrae were just the end of a lamb's tail!

The matter raised its head more seriously in July 1967 when a soldier moved a water tank in the Manse meadow, flushing a 'large mouse or a small rat'. It ran about 4 yards, apparently paused 'to give birth' to two young and then disappeared down a hole. In actual fact she may have been carrying two young from the nest and had to drop them in her haste. Under interrogation the soldier later admitted that he was familiar with rats and thought what he had seen was only a mouse. Swept up in the excitement, however, an army chef then claimed to have seen a rat in his vegetable store nearby.

The botanist David Gwynne, a postgraduate student from the West of Scotland College of Agriculture and a member of the sheep research team, was not convinced and so sent the two 'baby rats' to Edinburgh for examination. A Nature Conservancy staff member in Edinburgh considered that the babies were four times larger than mainland field mice he had seen and could indeed be rats. Traps were immediately despatched to St Kilda.

On 29 July, J. Barron Rochard, an officer from the Department of Agriculture's Rodent Control Division at East Craigs in Edinburgh – and a former colleague of mine when I had worked there a few years earlier – was sent to St Kilda but found no evidence whatsoever of rats (Nature Conservancy files). Nevertheless, he laid out an array of poison baits and traps in a cordon around the offending area. It is not known how many field mice succumbed to the poison but 19 field mice were trapped, including a pregnant female. She weighed 40 g and was carrying four 2–3 g embryos, which he collected to compare with the suspect babies. He also caught two more pregnant female mice which weighed 53 g and 64 g! A week later Rochard returned to Edinburgh, leaving the warden to continue precautionary trapping until mid-September.

In the meantime one of the babies had been despatched to the British Museum, who pronounced that it was indeed a rat. On receiving one of Rochard's foetuses, the mammal expert later had to retract his statement, having made it clear at the time that:

> I had no comparable material of *Apodemus sylvaticus hirtensis*. All I could say was that the size was such that rat could not be ruled out. I do indeed have here nestlings of *Rattus rattus* that match it in size.

So the panic was over. People who have no experience of St Kilda field mice do not realise just how large they can be. In 1959, the naturalist David Boddington, medical officer on the Army Base, had noticed how the mice could look almost as big as a small rat – a length of 6 or 7 in was not unusual. Hence the confusion with rats, whose presence, fortunately, has never been confirmed – yet. But the incident certainly highlighted the risk and served as a useful exercise for all concerned. It further emphasised the need for constant vigilance.

There is a small pier at Village Bay, built in 1899, and visitors have often wondered – on the very rare occasions it would have been feasible – why their charter boat was not permitted to tie up alongside. The fact that they must first decant into a dinghy is a measure designed specifically to reduce the risk of rats getting ashore. One evening a few years back, I was on one such charter boat heading for St Kilda, but tied up overnight at Leverburgh pier in Harris. A rat crawled down our mooring rope hoping to reach the fishing boat tied up alongside us, but fortunately the rodent failed and turned back. It brought home to me how any vessel wrecked in St Kilda need not necessarily be rat-infested; it only takes one pregnant female!

Rats were often reported around the mainland docks where the tank landing craft loaded up, for example Cairnryan, Rhu on the Clyde and Loch Carnan in South Uist. Although the Conservancy continued to remind the military of the dangers, it is perhaps surprising that none of the tank landing craft ever did carry rats to St Kilda. The fortnightly summer runs by tank landing craft finally fell out of service once the radar base was privatised in 1998. A less regular resupply was then offered by a civilian vessel called *Elektron*.

Bad weather had delayed the last resupply in the 2000 season, but *Elektron* did manage to beach in Village Bay at 11 p.m. on Saturday 14 October. Fuel and supplies were offloaded, but by 4 a.m. the next morning, very strong south-easterly winds had arisen which caused the vessel to drag her kedge anchor as she was attempting to pull off. The winds then rapidly turned her broadside to the beach ramp and she was lifted on to the boulder beach. Her engine rooms became swamped. Attempts to get the nine Serco staff and six crew ashore became so risky that the Coastguard helicopter from Stornoway had to be summoned to complete the rescue.

The storm then caused damage to her hull which, fortunately, was especially strengthened. Monday dawned reasonably calm, however, allowing the salvage operators to drain 40,000 litres of fuel oil from the ship's own tanks into containers ashore. The risk of pollution was further minimised when a crane working on St Kilda was positioned to lift off a further 7,000 litres of lubricating oils and 25 barrels of waste oil. The return of gale force winds on Tuesday pushed the *Elektron* a little further up the beach so the remaining gear and vehicles (including a council bin lorry!) had to be left on deck, while her empty tanks filled with sea water, to prevent her moving again.

On the next high spring tide, on Friday 27 October, at 8 p.m., after one unsuccessful attempt, the *Elektron* was finally towed off the beach by a chartered salvage tug. However, while the vessel was under tow to dry dock in Liverpool, she experienced further difficulties in high seas and the salvage crew had to be airlifted off 30 miles south-west of Barra. A decision was made to divert to Belfast, but then the stricken vessel developed a 20° list, so the local lifeboat had to deliver emergency pumping equipment before she eventually berthed safely.

The whole *Elektron* incident from beginning to end, and in appalling weather conditions, was fraught with difficulty, but the extreme professionalism of the personnel on St Kilda, the rescue services and the salvage team ensured that a major accident was averted.

By that time, however, the National Trust for Scotland and Scottish Natural Heritage had already reviewed the protocol, had updated rat measures and put contingencies in place. Nonetheless, rat measures on the island were immediately stepped up and it had indeed been fortunate that the *Elektron* had been rat-free.

On 4 March 1995, a trawler *Aeolus* went on the rocks near Boreray; one man died, but four others were rescued. Sheer logistics prevented any investigation into the possibility of rats getting ashore on the remote and inaccessible coast of Boreray. One can only presume they never did. Furthermore, media attention was minimal – that is, compared with the next major incident on Hirta 13 years later.

At 5.20 a.m. on 1 February 2008, during a force 9 storm, a Spanish fishing boat *Spinningdale* was dashed against the rocks near the Feather Store in Village Bay. No one died, but the true heroism of the Coastguard helicopter from Stornoway who rescued the 14 crew was overshadowed nationally by an Irish Sea ferry running aground on a sandbank at the same time. A violent storm in January 2009 broke the wreck in two. It is still hoped to salvage the crumpled remains. Most of the media attention to the St Kilda incident consisted of a huge over-reaction to the threat of rats getting ashore. Again though, the incident did serve to highlight the dangers.

And the risk is not just from rats. Mink or even otters are known to stow away on fishing boats tied up in port, attracted by fish remains in the nets. So the threat of any predator reaching St Kilda – or any other seabird island in the world – is very real indeed.

These were not the first wrecks in Village Bay. On 4 June 1960, the 72-ft gaff-rigged yawl *Avocet* came to grief there. Having landed a National Trust work party, the *Avocet* anchored overnight. The skipper was unable to sleep because of the rattle of the anchor chain and so replaced it with rope. A south-easterly gale blew up that night, the rope parted and the vessel went on the rocks. The army supply vessel RASV *Mull* later tried to tow her off, but the *Avocet* broke up. Her mast was recovered later to be erected at the head of the pier until finally removed for safety reasons some 35 years later.

Then on Saturday 13 June 1981, at 2 a.m., the 18-m MFV *Golden Chance* dragged both her bow anchors and drifted on to the boulder beach in Village Bay during a 90 mph south-easterly gale. At the same time two small army boats were washed up, but, fortunately, the crews were rescued before any damage was done. At the height of this storm one of the Trust houses lost its roof, and at first light it could be seen that the *Golden Chance* had broken her

Fig. 26. Spanish fishing boat Spinningdale on the rocks of Village Bay, February 2008 (A. MacEachen).

back, with wreckage strewn all over the beach. The army cleared up what they could, leaving the rest to wash out to sea in an offshore wind.

Going much further back in time, and on the other side of the islands, the St Kildans identified a rock on the north side of Soay as *Sgeir Mhic Righ Lochlainn*. This means 'the rock of the son of the king of Norway' and was where a ship of the said Viking was wrecked. There was a tradition on the island that the inhabitants slew the prince as he drunk from a well. We have already mentioned a possible Armada wreck and doubtless many other passing ships have come to grief in these dangerous waters.

Although Village Bay is the accepted harbour for St Kilda, there is an alternative anchorage in Glen Bay, where vessels may seek a modicum of shelter if a sudden south-easterly blows up. It is not good holding ground so it is not surprising that there have been accidents there too. Captain Otter almost came to grief there on 3 October 1860 for instance. Glen Bay is certainly another illicit point of entry for rats and other undesirable aliens.

Until recently, the details of only one Glen Bay incident were known so it is worth recording this particular sequence of events in some detail. Stuart Murray has assembled the facts, July 1997 being a good place to begin his tale.

A dive charter vessel *Poplar Diver* was anchored in Glen Bay. She had lost a ladder overboard and some divers went over to try to retrieve it. Instead they came across the wreck of a single-screw vessel. It was quickly identified as a beam trawler from the gear lying alongside the crushed hull. The only wreck of which Stuart was aware in the vicinity was that of a Fleetwood trawler *Briarlyn* which had gone aground in heavy seas near Geo nan Ron off Soay on 13 February 1928 with the loss of eight of its twelve crew (including the skipper, mate and engineer); their bodies were never recovered. The divers knew that the boiler of the *Briarlyn* still lay in Geo nan Ron so this Glen Bay wreck, with its boiler and parts of the engine lying in 15 m of water, had to be another vessel altogether.

Lachlan Macdonald (in Quine 1988) recalled the wreck of the *Briarlyn*:

> One winter night there was an awful gale and it was misty. There were several trawlers sheltering in Glen Bay. This fellow comes in; he was a great friend of ours from Fleetwood; he used to take the mails to the island and the groceries we wanted ... He knew the place well; he just came in right past the other trawlers, right into the bay, and he went into this cave, Geo nan Ron and he sank there. It's awfully deep – it was quite a big size of trawler too, and you would only see the top of one mast at low tide. Eight of the fishermen were lost. You could jump on to the rock there, but it must all have happened so quickly that they didn't know where they were. It was a sad tragedy, right enough.

One of the divers on the *Poplar Diver*, George Gillespie, followed up his find in Glen Bay with Lloyds Register and the Fleetwood Museum to find that the other wreck was the *Kumu*. A year almost to the day after the *Briarlyn*, she had run aground, in calm seas but thick fog, on 19 February 1929. The 12 crew and a small fox terrier were rescued by another trawler, the *Harry Melling*, which attempted to take the *Kumu* in tow. But she was badly holed and sank in the middle of Glen Bay 42 hours later. A crewman said the boat gave an eerie blast on her whistle as she went down. Over the years the event has been forgotten, obscured by the tragedy of the *Briarlyn* the year before. But there is a curious twist.

On 13 August 1998, a diving boat recovered a ship's bell from a trawler wreck in Glen Bay. Fortuitously, the *Poplar Diver* arrived in Glen Bay just as the diver surfaced with his trophy. Bob Theakston, the skipper of the *Poplar Diver* realised its significance and eventually persuaded the diver that it should be handed over to the warden on St Kilda, who happened to be Stuart Murray. On 29 September, Stuart passed the bell to Robin Turner, the National Trust for Scotland archaeologist, who in turn gave it over to Glasgow Museum for conservation. The name on the bell was not the *Kumu*, however, but the *Manor*. This was a trawler belonging to the same Fleetwood company, which was later sunk by German U-boats in the English Channel in 1939. How the *Manor* bell came to be on the *Kumu* remains a mystery, but I am told it was not uncommon for a new owner to rename a ship yet retain her original bell. Both Fleetwood vessels had been built in Aberdeen in 1913. But the *Manor* came to be sold to France in 1924 so perhaps the Fleetwood company did indeed retain her bell. She was bought back in 1937 and resumed the name *Manor*, but by then her original bell would have been lying at the bottom of Glen Bay in St Kilda. It is now on display in the island museum in one of the cottages on Hirta.

The moral of this interesting diversion is that, like Village Bay, Glen Bay could just as easily function as a feasible point of entry for rats, mink or any other ship-borne species to invade St Kilda.

.12.

St Kilda sheep

Siod a'chaora bha grinn,   That was the elegant sheep
Dh'fhàsadh an dath air a druim.   The colour would grow on her back.
Cha n-iarradh i crotal no sùith   She would require neither lichen nor soot
Ach snìomh na clòimh gu briogaisean.   But to spin the wool for trousers.

Siod a'chaora bha luath   That was the sheep that was swift
Nuair a thigeadh i mun cuairt,   Whenever she would come around
Cha robh h-aon anns an taobh tuath   Not one on the north country
An uair sin chuircadh it' aisde.   Could keep up with her.

'Cas na Caora Hiortaich' (The foot of the Hirta sheep). Song by Peigi
Macrae, South Uist, 1948.

SADLY THERE IS NOT much remaining of what once must have been a rich and ancient Gaelic oral tradition on St Kilda. Some of what has survived has sometimes been located within other communities, such as Peigi Macrae's South Uist. The people of St Kilda have long departed, but Peigi's song tells us of an equally ancient and unique biological survivor that happily still thrives on St Kilda – the Soay sheep.

Sheep and people share a common heritage on St Kilda. Sheep are farm animals, but exactly when people arrived to graze animals rather than just hunt them is still a matter of debate. In his monumental tome *Sheep and Man* Michael Ryder (1983) referred to the St Kilda sheep as 'prehistoric':

> A survival of this type is probably seen today in the Soay sheep which now lives feral only on St Kilda ... [They] are small in stature, the rams being only 56 cm and the ewes 52 cm at the shoulders, and their liveweights 25 to 35 kg and 22 to 25 kg respectively. Their primitive features include a short tail and a coloured

219

fleece, which undergoes an annual moult. Most Soays have a white belly, like wild sheep, and the fact that the Soay is virtually the only domestic sheep to retain this feature shows how truly primitive it is. The fleece is otherwise very variable – hairy, woolly, dark and light brown types being recognised.

In his great three-volume work the *Mammals of Great Britain* the eminent animal artist John Guille Millais (1865–1931) asserted how Soay sheep have all the habits and appearance of a wild sheep and, when galloping, look much like Mouflon. Their short tails, hairy throat and mane, and general markings all suggested Mouflon parentage. Furthermore, he said, they freely interbred with Mouflon and the wild Urial of the Punjab.

Soay is in fact a Norse word meaning 'sheep island', but whether this indicates that the Vikings found sheep already on the island of Soay, or that they put them there is not known. Certainly these sheep are older than the Vikings. In *Island Survivors* Peter Jewell described them as 'a remarkable survival of the type of domestic sheep that people kept in the Bronze Age'.

Indeed, bones excavated from earlier Neolithic sites in Britain seem identical to the Soays of St Kilda. If the flock on St Kilda's island of Soay is anything to go by, the sheep had to be 'hunted' rather than shepherded, preferring to scatter rather than be rounded up by dogs or men. A flock similar to Soays survived on a small island in the Faroes called Litla Dimun until they were shot out at the end of the 19th century.

The first written reference to St Kilda's sheep dates from the 14th century, when the sheep were already running feral on Soay. Some time prior to his death in 1384, John of Fordun had compiled a *Chronicle of the Scottish Nation* in which he stated:

> Hirth, the best stronghold of all the islands. Near this is an island twenty miles long, where wild sheep are said to exist, which can only be caught by hunters.

The sheep on St Kilda were also mentioned by Hector Boece (c 1465–1536), one of the founders and the first principal of Aberdeen University, in his *History of Scotland* (1527), but which is said to contain a large amount of fiction. There is no reason to doubt his comment about a large number of sheep on Hirta. He then went on to describe a particularly wild flock, not unlike sheep in shape, on a nearby island, presumably Soay, which could only be caught by surrounding them; their fleece was not as soft as that of a sheep nor as harsh as that of a goat. This suggests that by the 15th century there were two distinct types of sheep on St Kilda, the Soays already isolated on the island of the same name and another breed, probably the old Scottish shortwool, on Hirta.

Not long afterwards, in 1549, Donald Monro (1526–89), Archdeacon of the Isles, wrote in his own quaint way *Description of the Western Isles of Scotland*.

Although sketchy, it did contain some natural history, having this to offer about St Kilda and its sheep:

> Out of the mane Ocean seais be 60 mile of sea lyis ane Ile callit Hirta, mane laich sa far as is manurit of it, abundand in corn and girsing, namelie for scheip … The saids Stewartis ressaves thair maillis in maill and reistit muttonis, wild reistit foullis and selchis.

Alasdair Alpin Macgregor in *A Last Voyage to St Kilda* (1931) quoted a slightly later but equally impenetrable account by Bishop Leslie in 1578, where he pondered on their appearance, and in particular their likeness to goats:

> The Ile Hirth hes the name frome a certane scheip of the sam name, in quhilke this only Ile did abunde. This scheip may be comparet in heicht til a gait [goat], in gretnes til a buffil [buffalo], quhais hornes in lenth excelis the hornes of a buffil. Neist this lyis another Ile, bot nocht inhabited, quhair nae kynd of cattail is fund, excepte sum verie wylde, quhilkes to cal scheip or gait … for by thair wylde nature, nathir haue thay wol lyke a scheip; nathir beir thay hair lyke a gait …

Sometime between 1577 and 1595 an anonymous report about Scotland was submitted to the Crown, but mention of St Kilda is brief, noting principally the value of its sheep as rent to the landlord:

> Irt … is maist fertile of scheip and foullis, quhairof it payis ane great matter yeirlie to … McCloyd and his factors.

Macfarlane's *Geographical Collections* contained a more detailed account, written about 1675 and given to Sir Robert Sibbald by the Lord Register Sir George Mackenzie of Tarbat, later Lord Cromarty:

> Their sheep upon this Island of Hirta are very different from all other, having long legs, long horns, and instead of wool, a blewish hair upon them … Of the milk of these sheep, they make Butter, and a sort of cheese which my Lord Register saith, pleaseth his tast better then Holland's cheese.

It is obvious that the sheep were at least as prized for their milk as their wool.

Sibbald, of course, brings us to Martin Martin who provided the first and most comprehensive description not only of St Kilda, but also its sheep:

> The grass is very short but kindly, producing plenty of milk; the number of sheep commonly maintained in St Kilda, and the two adjacent Isles, does not exceed two thousand, and generally they are speckled, some white, some philamont, and are of a common size; they do not resemble goats in any respect, as [George?] Buchanan was informed, except in their horns, which are extraordinarily large, particularly those in the Lesser Isles.

This might be the earliest mention of sheep on Boreray, about which island Martin wrote:

> ... feeds about four hundred sheep per annum, and would feed more did not the Solan Geese pluck a large share of the grass for their nest.

Martin also reported how Soay lay 'within a pistol-shot' of Hirta, with a single hazardous landing, and was:

> ... furnished with an excellent spring, the grass is very sweet, feeds five hundred sheep, each of which generally has two or three lambs at a birth, and every lamb so fruitful, that it brings forth another before itself is a year old ... The sheep in the Isle Soay are never milked, which disposes them to be the more prolific.

Obviously, by this time the islanders were maintaining flocks totalling some 2,000, not just on Hirta where the people all lived but also on Boreray and Soay where access was limited. As usual, half a century later, the Reverend MacAulay was generous in his account, if a little melodramatic about the temperament of the sheep:

> To the west of Hirta, within a small distance, lies a third isle, called Soay, of much the same extent with Boreray, in which there are five hundred sheep. These belong to the Steward, as those of the isle just now described, are the property of his vassals. The rugged face of this island makes it very difficult to catch the sheep, either to shear, or bring them to Hirta. To pursue such wild creatures through declivities terminated by the deep, or into the shelves of vast rocks, is undoubtedly an adventure no less perilous than bold ... I am persuaded there are thousands who would sooner encounter an armed enemy, and face all the dangers and horrors of war, than attack the very sheep of Hirta, in those hideous fastnesses into which they very often make their retreat. The old rams if chased into dangerous places, and heated into a passion, turn sometimes desperately fierce; reduced to the necessity of yielding or tumbling over a precipice into the sea, they face about, and attack the pursuers ...
>
> The St Kildians owe a great part of their felicity to sheep and wild fowl. They have considerable flocks of sheep; it is hardly possible to ascertain the precise number of them in the main isle ...
>
> ... Since every householder has to pay the steward every second he lamb, every seventh fleece, and every seventh she lamb, they tend to conceal numbers! At Borera, are about four hundred sheep and in the main isle are, I may venture to affirm, a thousand more; they are all of the smallest kind, and their wool is short and coarse. It is rather softer than that in the other isles, and not so well mixed. The mutton had, I imagined, a peculiar taste, though agreeable enough. Every one of those sheep has two horns, and many of them four. They are wonderfully fruitful. One of the people assured me, that in the course of thirteen months,

one sheep had increased his flock with nine more: She had brought three lambs in the month of March, three more in the same month the year after, and each of the first three had a young one before they had been thirteen months old …

Both Martin's and MacAulay's figures for sheep on Soay and Boreray are remarkably consistent, although, of course, MacAulay had read Martin's book and was undoubtedly influenced by it. After commenting upon fecundity, interestingly, MacAulay added how a barren old ewe on Hirta would extend her reproductive life 'for a course of years' if moved to Boreray.

In 1815, the geologist John MacCulloch pondered upon the provenance of the island sheep:

> The sheep of St Kilda are of the ancient Highland, or Norwegian breed, so nearly extirpated everywhere else, and among them are many of the brown fleeced variety, natives alike of Iceland … The milk of the ewe is manufactured into cheese, being mixed with that of the cow and goat, this forming one of the articles of export.

His reference to the Norwegian breed is slightly misleading, although it could imply that the sheep on Hirta at that time were indeed of the old Scottish shortwool type, which still survive on Boreray and are similar to the North Ronaldsays of today. Although Ryder maintained a date of 1870, it seems from the Reverend Mackenzie's account in the 1820s that mainland blackface sheep were just beginning to be introduced to St Kilda half a century before, not so long after they are thought to have reached the Isle of Lewis:

Fig. 27.
A Soay ram
casting its fleece
(J. Love).

About the beginning of winter each family will kill a cow, and at intervals thereafter about twelve sheep, principally wethers, and what of the flesh is not consumed fresh is salted. The sheep on the main island are, to some extent, crossed with the black-faced variety. The only pure-bred ones are the property of the proprietor, and are kept by him on the islands of Soay and Dun. Those on the main island, belonging to the crofters, are not large, but they are fat and tender.

Apparently, pure Soay sheep were now only to be found on Soay and Dun. Overlapping with Mackenzie, John MacGillivray did not have much to say on the sheep:

The breed of horses, cattle, and sheep is of small size; many of the latter being of a dun colour, and remarkable for their length of legs and shortness of tail; the wool however, is very fine.

A year later Wilson added:

There are about 2000 sheep, including those of Borrera and Soay. The Soa sheep are chiefly of Danish breed, with brown and black wool, and one or two more horns than the usual complement.

By 1868, the ornithologist Henry Elwes implied that the introduction of blackface, so prevalent on the mainland, had not progressed far on St Kilda:

The sheep are of a peculiar sort, not unlike those which were kept by the crofters, in most of the Hebrides before the introduction of the improved breeds, and have very fine wool, which is sometimes of a light brown colour. This sort, however, is not very common; and the wool is in great request, as the rent is paid principally in wool and feathers.

By 1877, George Seton observed that most of the sheep on Hirta were white. That same year J. MacDiarmid assessed the sheep flock and gave more detail about cross-breeding with blackfaces. Indeed, he seemed to judge local husbandry against modern mainland practices, not realising that the Soay sheep did not in fact need much management. He confirmed that pure Soays were still being kept on Dun, in addition to the flock on Soay itself.

I found it impossible to ascertain the number of sheep on the island, but from what was to be seen in going over the hills, the number may be put down at over 400. There may be many more, but I do not think the number is less than that. Each family, it is said, should have between 20 and 40 sheep; but on enquiry it was found that some families had scarcely any at all, while others again had a good many more than that number. The sheep are badly managed, and receive very little attention. In winter they are allowed to shift for themselves, and a number are blown over the rocks in seeking shelter from the storms ... The size of a man's flock depend very much upon how they thrive and survive the winter's storm, and whether he gives them any attention. The sheep are very wild; and though it was just after the lambing season, appeared in very good condition, and able to climb the steepest parts of the tops.

The wild sheep are plucked about the beginning of June, and the ewes about the middle of summer. They sell neither sheep nor wool. From 2 to 5 sheep are killed by each family for the winter's supply, and the wool is made into blanketing and tweed, which they sell. They keep about 12 tups. Some black-faced tups were brought from Skye about six or seven years ago, from the same person who supplied the bull. The breed of sheep may be called a cross between the old St Kilda breed and the black-faced; but if fresh tups were annually introduced they would soon be all very good black-faced sheep. Nothing is applied to the sheep by way of smearing, and, so far as could be ascertained, they were quite free from scab and other skin-diseases common to the class ...

The proprietor has between 200 and 300 sheep on the Island of Soa, and between 20 and 30 of the native St Kilda breed on the island of the Dun. The latter I only saw at a distance, and they appeared of a light brown colour. All the tups were on the Dun island, and there was not an opportunity of seeing them. The sheep are said to be very fat in autumn when killed, which I well believe from the nature of the pasture; and the St Kilda mutton that was presented to us for dinner would favourably compare in flavour and quality with the best fed black-faced ... I understand they milk the ewes, and mix their milk with their cows', which they say gives the cheese a better flavour.

In 1896, Richard Kearton elaborated on how the Soay sheep were gathered.

On Soay exclusively is to be found a flock of from two to three hundred peculiar little brown sheep, supposed to be descendants of a few individuals left upon the island by Vikings, who called to renew their supply of fresh water. These sheep, like those of Iceland, which they are said to resemble closely, are liable to produce an additional pair of horns, although I failed to discover any evidence of the fact when I examined the flock through my binoculars.

... The St Kildans have an extravagant method of capturing them which I had the good fortune to see in operation ... we took a dog or two in the boat with us. These dogs had their fangs broken, and by the aid of their barefooted masters, who sprang from rock to rock with great nimbleness and not a little excitement, literally ran down one of the timid creatures. As the sheep raced madly round the little island, they came close past where I stood, and the way they bounded from crag to crag, and skipped in single file along dangerous ledges, was simply astonishing ... Clipping shears are unknown in St Kilda, and the wool that does not drop off or cannot be pulled off the backs of the sheep is cut away with pocket-knives.

... My friend Mackenzie told me that the people wanted to cross the original breed of Soay sheep with Scotch black-faced one, but that Macleod of Macleod, the proprietor, had very naturally objected, and taken the island over himself.

The Keartons tried to photograph the women milking ewes on Hirta but they always resisted, fearing that anyone who saw the pictures would laugh at them. The brothers concluded that cheese made by mixing cow's and sheep's milk was rather tasteless stuff. They estimated about a thousand sheep on Soay, Boreray and Hirta, with between 25 and 30 cattle.

In 1912, the ornithologist Henry Elwes gave Eagle Clarke a list of questions about the sheep which he had answered by the grounds officer Donald Ferguson, who had succeeded his father in that office some 20 years before. With Ferguson's son Neil acting as interpreter, Donald maintained that there had been no four-horned sheep on Hirta in his time. He also recalled that four rams of the type that preceded the blackfaces were released on Soay by Sir John Macleod probably in the 1860s 'but they did no good'. A few white sheep appeared for a time, but their descendants soon reverted to the original colour. Elwes went on to record what he knew of Soay sheep in captivity on the mainland, the first that he heard of being taken from St Kilda being in the 1890s. But it is indeed fortunate for posterity, as the Keartons confirmed, that Macleod would not let the islanders cross the pure flock on Soay to be out-crossed with blackface.

Interestingly, in 1815, MacCulloch had noted that 'a few goats also wander about, kept chiefly for the purpose of milking'.

MacGillivray (in 1840) added that 'goats are plentiful among the rocks, where they have run wild', while a year later Wilson announced their demise:

Goats were plentiful among the rocks at a recent period, but they were found to disturb the birds in their hatching places, and have been destroyed.

When the inhabitants finally abandoned St Kilda in 1930, they removed all their sheep from Hirta. Approximately 1,200 were sold at Oban mart on 3 September. However, in July 1931, Tom Harrisson encountered no fewer than 12 ewes, at least three of which the expedition despatched for food. No doubt the St Kildans did the same. Alasdair Alpin Macgregor noted that a few days before the evacuation the islanders had gone to Boreray, but so wild were the sheep there that there were insufficient men to round up more than a score. The islanders had not, in fact, bothered to visit Boreray nor Soay for three years or more. Not only did they lack the manpower to gather sheep, but also to stay with the boat.

In 1932, the islands' proprietor, the Earl of Dumfries, decided that a second flock of Soay sheep grazing on Hirta would benefit the island. It would not be an easy task! Only St Kildans could achieve the capture and transfer of sheep from an island as inaccessible and as precipitous as Soay. The expedition was described in 1976 by Malcolm or Calum Macdonald (1908–1979), who had left the island in 1924 as a 16-year-old. Eight years later and only two years after the evacuation, he was enlisted to participate in the operation.

Although the detail is scant, the episode is worth quoting in full for it was a significant ecological event for Hirta. Furthermore, Macdonald's story contains some poignant comments by the exiled islanders, the whole escapade offering a brief moment of nostalgia for them:

At the time of the evacuation in 1930, there were 56 born Islanders alive; today in the year 1976 there are only 24 natives of St Kilda still alive. Our descendants whose numbers are in the hundreds are dispersed throughout the world and to them St Kilda is a word of mouth memory handed down to them by their parents ...

... Still no work was forthcoming. I was beginning to get very apprehensive when I received a letter from A. G. Ferguson, the St Kildan tweed merchant in Glasgow. He asked me if I would care to join him on a visit to St Kilda. The purpose of this visit was to catch wild sheep on the island of Soay; these would be transferred to the main Island of Hirta. The ownership of the Islands had now passed from the hands of MacLeod of MacLeod, who had owned the Islands until the evacuation, to Lord Dumfries who now instigated the trip.

I grasped at this opportunity and replied by return of post my acceptance of the kind offer. So in June 1932 I joined the SS '*Hebrides*' which was lying at anchor in the South of Harris. This ship made annual voyages every year to the Western Isles. On board was A.G. Ferguson, his brother Neil and his wife Annie who in turn was my aunt. Their son Donald John was with them, as was Finlay MacQueen – an uncle, Finlay Gillies, Donald MacDonald, John and his brother Neil Gillies and their sister-in-law, Kirsty Gillies. It was quite a meeting for we had not seen each other for many years. We were all terrible excited to be going back to our dear Island for the duration of that summer. We headed out of the Sound of Harris at 2pm and arrived in St Kilda at 7 pm the same evening ...

All through the night my aunt and myself cleaned out the old homestead and unpacked the stores. When the ship had left we gathered together to plan our stay.

A. G. Ferguson who had a boat stowed away on the island suggested we got her ready to visit the islets. It was like old times with everybody so happy to be back. We caught a hundred wild Soay sheep and transferred them to the main island, and killed three or four of them for our own use.

Fig. 28. Calum Macdonald, Neil Gillies and Finlay MacQueen rowing to Soay for sheep in 1932 (John Macdonald).

In our spare time we wove tweed for A. G. Ferguson who had brought the yarn ready for the loom. This was the first time I ever sat on a loom weaving and as I was going to be paid for this trip all my free time was spent weaving. We feasted on Puffins, Fulmers like the olden days. Everyone slept in their old homes except for me, as my aunt would not let me sleep in my father's home, I had to sleep in her home. She told me on several occasions during these days 'I wish I had never left here, today I feel so happy as if I had never left here.'

At last our stay was near an end the last ship was due to arrive. We packed to leave with each of us to go our separate ways. We went to the church for the last service together ... It was said in Gaelic ... For my part of the expedition and working on the islands, I received a cheque for £20 from A. G. Ferguson with all expenses paid.

Calum Macdonald had impressed Lord Dumfries during the Soay expedition and so was asked to join his Lordship's staff on the mainland. This enabled him to return to St Kilda several more summers before moving on to work in Glasgow, London, and elsewhere. He made his last trip to St Kilda in 1967 with his eldest son John. After he died in 1979, his ashes were buried in Hirta's graveyard.

Against the odds, the Earl of Dumfries had successfully orchestrated the transfer of 107 Soays of mixed age and sex to Hirta – 20 tups, 44 ewes, 22 ram lambs and 21 ewe lambs. Despite this limited gene pool, scientists have since ascertained that the Soay sheep of Hirta still demonstrate a remarkably high degree of genetic variation.

Following the 1932 expedition, an article by George E. Meston appeared in the *Scotsman* in 1934 describing his visit to St Kilda between 18 July and 8 August. His interest was in rock climbing so he took every chance to join the St Kildans who were summering that year and visiting some of the other islands, amongst them Soay. This account implied more sheep were to be taken back for release on Hirta. More likely, however, the islanders were just catching some Soays for eating, which seemed to be a regular event for several summers after the evacuation. Probably they dare not slaughter any of the laird's new flock of sheep on Hirta and doubtless enjoyed the adventure on Soay.

> CATCHING MOUNTAIN SHEEP. Six of us set out in a boat to visit Soay for the lst time this season. We went by way of Ruaival, where one wrong use of an oar would have smashed our boat to pieces. It took four of us nearly two hours rowing to reach Soay's Seal Cave. After taking off our shoes, we jumped to the nearest rock and climbed the famous cliffs with ropes. We did not get back to the boat for five hours and we only managed to catch two of the fifteen sheep. The boatmen then carried the sheep over the slopes until it became necessary to lower them with ropes into the waiting boat.
>
> I consider that to be the thrill of a lifetime.

When David Lack heard of the transfer of sheep to Hirta, he lamented a lost opportunity to study the botanical and other long-term changes on Hirta so recently abandoned. But, as we shall see, it opened up a whole new scientific opportunity. The sheep back on Soay could never have been studied in the detail they have today on Hirta. Hitherto they had been rather dismissed by visiting naturalists and largely neglected by zoologists.

It was a young student from Glasgow, J. Morton Boyd (1925–1998), on the first of countless visits to St Kilda in 1952, who took an initial interest. He undertook a census of the sheep and thus established an effective routine to be repeated virtually every year subsequently:

> The string of little brown sheep that I had sighted from the 'Glas Island' on first arrival were part of a 1,114 strong population which had sprung from the introduction in 1932 of 107 sheep from Soay ... In doing so the owner, the Marquess of Bute, had rather upset the paradigm of the return of St Kilda to a natural state, but had enhanced the scientific interest of the islands in other ways. Where in Europe could another population of large mammals of known history be found in near wild conditions? From the beginning I sensed the importance of the Soay sheep to science and set about laying the foundations of a long-term study. The method of annual census of the sheep on Hirta, which I organised in 1952, has been repeated ever since by successive researchers.

Not only had Boyd recognised the importance of the Soay sheep but in particular he quickly realised their research potential.

St Kilda presents many superb problems in plant and animal ecology, and none would be more rewarding than a study of the wild sheep.

In 1956, Morton Boyd returned to St Kilda accompanied by an Appin shepherd called Malcolm Colthart and his border collie Jim. Morton was keen to examine the sheep at close quarters and recalled:

The behaviour of those sheep on the appearance of 'Jim' was interesting. They proved to be quite unworkable with a single dog, streaming away in all directions instead of flocking. A ram, a ewe and a lamb were on one occasion cornered by the dog, which crouched some 20 yards distant awaiting the next command of its master. Colthart held the dog motionless for a few minutes, and in this short time the adult sheep had started to graze, while the lamb curled up in a ball and proceeded to fall asleep.

The following year Boyd joined the Nature Conservancy as Conservation Officer for North West Scotland, so was able to put his ideas into action, initiating a study that has continued virtually uninterrupted to this day. He first wrote to the National Trust in 1959 with the proposal:

The management of the sheep flocks on St Kilda flocks from a Conservancy point of view is one of scientific management – namely of pursuing a well considered enquiry into the ecology, physiology and anatomy of the sheep. The information obtained from this enquiry will help us to understand the basic factors governing the stability of those wild flocks which are able to maintain themselves in such a remarkable way in rigorous conditions. This understanding will be our key to conserving their numbers if, as happens in many insular habitats, they are drastically reduced by disease or human interference. It is hoped that the enquiry will go some way to explaining the lineage of the Soay breed – one of the most primitive in existence and about which, up until now, we have only been able to hazard a guess.

Boyd sought the support of two research officers from the Hill Farming Research Organisation, Dr John Doney and Dr Graham Gunn. Quite independently and newly appointed to a research fellowship at the Zoological Society of London, Peter Jewell (1925–1998) was developing his interest in archaeology to include the domestication and biology of Soay sheep. They all teamed up together with Dr Cedric Milner, an agricultural botanist with the Nature Conservancy, and in May 1960 made the first of many visits to St Kilda to begin work.

Immediately, the scientists encountered many sheep carcases scattered all over the village. Repeating Morton Boyd's count from the previous year revealed that over half the ewes and three-quarters of the rams had died, with heaviest losses amongst yearlings and the oldest age classes. Realising that this might be a cyclic event known from other mammal species rather than some drastic disease outbreak, the team resolved to continue monitoring the sheep population on an annual and long-term basis.

Since the island of Soay is so difficult of access, Lord Bute's 'young' population on Hirta, established in 1932, has become the focus of the research, especially those sheep living within the Village. Regular counts and round-ups for tagging allowed not only the fortunes of the study population to be followed, but also that of individual sheep within it.

Following the 1960 'crash', the next lambing began earlier and survival was high. Numbers continued to recover until by 1964 another crash was anticipated. This time three veterinary surgeons, I. A. Cheyne, W. M. Foster and J. B. Spence, were on hand to witness the event. Disease was found not to be a mortality factor, rather a shortage of food in late winter combined with the debilitating effects of intestinal worm parasites. The mineral status of the sheep on Hirta was found to be as good as anywhere on the mainland (the pasture probably enhanced by salt spray), while specially imported X-ray equipment revealed tooth structure to be even better.

The research project expanded thereafter with two students recruited to live on Hirta throughout the year. Peter Grubb observed the rut in November, behaviour over winter and the overall population dynamics of the population. David Gwynne studied the botanical composition of the pasture related to the diet of the sheep.

In March 1963, the Nature Conservancy expressed interest in transferring some live sheep to London and Edinburgh Zoos.

> When one is dealing with a population unique in the world, as is the Soay stock, it is always wise to ensure against possible catastrophe and therefore the staff of the NC feel that the maintenance of small flocks of pure Soays on the mainland has much to commend it.

The following month Dr Joe Eggeling (1909–1994), Scottish Director of the Nature Conservancy, attended an Executive Committee Meeting of the National Trust for Scotland where it was agreed that six blackface sheep could be removed from Boreray for the Hill Farming Research Organisation, 12 Soay sheep to London Zoo and 12 to Edinburgh Zoo (Nature Conservancy files).

Scientific research effort peaked when in 1974 Peter Jewell, Cedric Milner and J. Morton Boyd edited their classic book *Island Survivors: The Ecology of the Soay Sheep of St Kilda*.

Since 1985, with the advent of modern demographic and genetic techniques, a new wider study has been supervised by the Large Animal Research Group at Cambridge University under Professor Tim Clutton-Brock, working with Dr Josephine Pemberton from Edinburgh University. Botanical work has been initiated through Professor Mick Crawley of Imperial College London. The project has enjoyed input from many other research students, too many to mention here, but all summarised in Clutton-Brock and Pemberton's seminal book *Soay Sheep*, published in 2004. Most of the following account derives from both these invaluable sources.

Adult male Soay sheep reach 36 kg or more in summer and adult females about 25 kg. About 5 per cent of the sheep have miscellaneous white markings on the face or body. The population is dimorphic with about three times as many individuals having a light brown coat than light fawn. Rather more than half of the ewes are polled, the remainder carrying horns, some of which (10–12 per cent males and 65 per cent females) are small and crumpled horns (scurred). The light coat frequency has remained at about 20–25 per cent, while over the same period the frequency of scurred individuals has fluctuated around 20 per cent. In years of low density the survival of all phenotypes is high. In years of high density the survival of dark and scurred individuals is higher than light and unscurred. Normal horned rams are more successful in the rut so are better equipped for fighting. Scurred rams survive harsh winters better, however, so compensate for a lower annual breeding success by being able to compete in more ruts.

The Hirta population averages 1,200 animals, with crashes every four years or so, supporting a density of some 0.9 ewes per hectare – a relatively low figure with the average mainland sheep being about 2.5 ewes per hectare.

The counts reveal a period of rapid increase to high density, followed by periodic crashes when up to 60 per cent of the population can die in a single winter. These crashes seem to have become more regular in recent years, but this can be obscured by weather effects. 1996 was one of the highest populations ever, but the population declined little the following winter; thus high density does not necessarily trigger a crash. Crashes have also occurred from relatively low populations when the sheep might have been expected to be in good condition. Gales in March seem to be involved, but the overwinter mortality seems to be exacerbated by parasites, particularly gut worms.

Parasite burdens increase as the density of sheep increases, imposing a strong natural selection for parasite resistance. Indeed, Soay sheep demonstrate one of the highest resistances to parasites anywhere in the world. They share the same parasites as blackfaces, but seem to be more effective in dealing with them, which has important implications for commercial sheep husbandry. High parasite loads in domestic sheep can cause heavy stock losses and helminth treatments are costly so this aspect of the Soay study has attracted much interest.

The rut takes place in November, triggered by the shortening days of the northern autumn. The ewes are in oestrous for one or two days only, so there is intense competition amongst rams to mate with them, especially during the mid-month peak. Threats, head butting, etc., have already established a hierarchy so that the most dominant rams will consort with and successfully defend most ewes. Ram lambs are fertile at six months so readily involve themselves in this and, in years following a crash when there is a shortage of older rams, they may be able to score with 'precocious reproductive success'. Undoubtedly though, this contributes to loss of condition and the higher mortality amongst young ram lambs over ewe lambs. Following such intense activity, without much time to feed, adult rams have to enter the winter in poor condition and mortality can be high. There is thus a preponderance of ewes in the population, varying annually from three to every ram, to as much as eight.

Lambs are born after a gestation of 151 days; this is several days longer than modern breeds, which also mature faster. Most births are clumped within 10 days on either side of 20 April. A small number of twins are born, but their survival is poor. There has been at least one instance of triplets and in 1984 the warden Pete Moore reported the birth of one lamb followed by Siamese twins. Lambs weigh about 2 kg at birth and are weaned by July. The ewes can then spend the rest of the summer regaining condition before the rut in November, by which time those that have had lambs that year weigh just as much as those that have not. This is in contrast to red deer where yeld or barren hinds are heavier than mothers with a calf. The better the condition of the mother, the better the birthweight of its lamb and its chances of then surviving to weaning. Males grow faster than females and by late August are about 20 per cent heavier. Obviously this 'fast growth' strategy of the males is costly if the mother is in poor condition, but otherwise the male offspring attain a better weight advantage competing for mates in the rut.

As the population increases so does the number of lambs that die in their first year, with more males dying than females. Males then continue to succumb at a constant rate, while ewes enjoy better survival in the middle years. Young rams grow faster than ewes and lose more body weight over the winter. Those animals that survive population crashes can enjoy a ripe old age; the oldest tagged ewe being 15 when it died; others have lived to be 14, 13 and 12 years of age. For a ram to live to ten is rare on the other hand and most die before they are six. A sample of lambs were castrated 1978–80; without having to participate in the rigours of the rut their survival was high and the last one died one month short of its 17th birthday.

The duration of study of marked individual sheep has enabled their lifetime reproductive success to be documented, backed up by DNA studies to determine their inter-relatedness. This could then be linked to nutrition

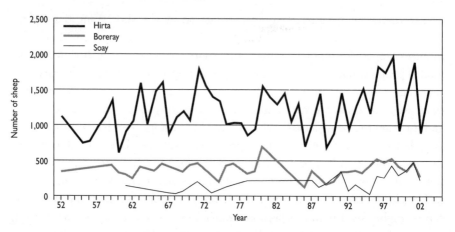

Fig. 29. Sheep counts on Hirta, Boreray and Soay (after Clutton-Brock and Pemberton 2004).

and energy budgets, parasite cycles, vegetation dynamics and weather. Peter Jewell concluded:

> These long-term studies can probe more deeply into the processes of evolution itself and add profoundly to our better understanding of the world we live in ... More than any other feature of the natural history of the archipelago of St Kilda, the Soay sheep are a treasure of surpassing value.

From time to time, following a crash when so many carcases of sheep are scattered over the island, a debate is reopened as to whether they ought to be left unmanaged. Critics naturally assume that the animals have crashed and died because they have eaten themselves out of house and home, a situation that would never be allowed to happen in shepherded situations. It is often forgotten that the sheep population of Soay has not had any management to speak of for some considerable time, hundreds, perhaps thousands, of years. This feral flock seems to behave in a similar manner to the Hirta Soays; and indeed to the sheep on Boreray (Fig. 29). Research has shown that Hirta's sward has a remarkable ability to recover after peaks and crashes and there is in fact little evidence of overgrazing. Some of the rarest plants on Hirta such as gentians occur in the areas that are utilised heavily by the sheep. Without any grazing at all the sward is liable to become overgrown, choking out some species of plants and thus reducing biodiversity.

Morton Boyd concluded that for St Kilda to lose its sheep would not only remove assets of great cultural, historical and scientific interest, but would also:

> ... reduce the diversity of plant life which their grazing sustains on the islands ... The sheep are now adjusted, over centuries, to meet the rigours of their world.

Boreray sheep

In 1920, James Ritchie had commented how 'in some ways more interesting than its wild mammals are the domesticated sheep of the islands'. And St Kilda, of course, still possesses two distinct breeds. Towards the end of the 19th century the ubiquitous blackface were kept on Hirta and Boreray. The islanders cleared Hirta when they departed in 1930, but those on Boreray, some 6 km to the north-east and difficult of access at the best of times, were abandoned to their fate.

With dark collars and white or tan markings the Boreray sheep look like a cross between Soays and blackfaces, but, in fact, they are survivors of a cross between early blackfaces and the old Scottish shortwool sheep that still survive on North Ronaldsay in Orkney and in the Shetland Islands. Their fleece is shed earlier than Hebridean blackface, but not as early as the Soays. Atkinson described the Borerays as:

> ... often striped and mottled in a curious manner, and long in the leg, giving one very much the idea of reverting to Nature.

To some extent, being survivors of an early type of commercial sheep, but having been left to their own devices for so long, they too can now be considered a truly feral flock. It is difficult to believe that the Nature Conservancy contemplated wiping out all the sheep on Boreray when they were first setting up the Nature Reserve in 1957:

> Consideration should be given to the elimination of a flock of Black Faced sheep on Boreray; this operation would give useful control on the development of vegetation when freed of all grazing pressure.

Fig. 30. Boreray sheep (P. Duncan).

The logistics of such an operation would have been formidable, however, given how wild they are, so (fortunately) the Boreray sheep were spared. They are now recognised as a Rare Breed in their own right, presenting another research opportunity for anyone able enough to try. Whenever an opportunity arises, wardens and other casual visitors have attempted a census of the whole island, but the data set remains intermittent. Nonetheless, there is enough information to indicate that the numbers of Boreray sheep seem to cycle in tandem with the Soay sheep back on Hirta (Fig. 29). This is unlikely to happen if the populations increased independently of one another, and overgrazing is unlikely to kick so synchronously on all three islands.

At the end of May 1979, Morton Boyd was afforded an opportunity to spend four days on Boreray while six companions (including Stuart Murray and Mary Harman) were engaged in ornithology, archaeology and filming. He chose to study the sheep, but, having just experienced a round-up to capture five ewes and two ewe lambs for a breeding facility on the mainland, the sheep remained nervous of humans. Notwithstanding, Boyd counted 357 sheep, only 20 of which were mature rams and in addition made some useful observations on their behaviour.

The following year, Dr Dave Bullock from St Andrews University was able to spend longer studying the sheep when he and six others camped on Boreray from 8 to 25 July, probably the longest continuous presence on the island since the islanders had quit St Kilda in 1930. From a boat Bullock tallied 495 sheep, but two land-based counts soon afterwards revealed 653 and 699, indicating just how many animals can remain hidden from an observer at sea. This also suggested that Morton Boyd's 1979 total was underestimated. One of the most interesting conclusions from Bullock's study was that the high density of sheep was probably compacting the soil and thus improving its suitability for burrowing seabirds such as puffins. In contrast, with no sheep, the island of Dun enjoys no such benefit. The fowlers of the Faroes were well aware of such an effect and deliberately released sheep to improve the puffin slopes they harvested.

From studies such as those of Boyd and Bullock we know that Boreray sheep have large curving horns, especially on the rams. The animals have a largely creamy-brown coat coloration; about a quarter of them being grey-brown, a few blackish and the occasional one tan in colour. The face colour varies from black and white to greyish, with a few completely black, tan or white. Both Soay and Boreray lambs withstand cold and wet better than commercial sheep, but freely make use of shelter in the cleits. They are also skilled climbers so the varied topography of the island cliffs offers shelter too. Lambs bond quicker with their mothers than mainland sheep and are quicker to suck, all of which enhances survival in such exposed conditions. Lambing percentages on Boreray can be high, equivalent to hirsels in the Scottish Borders that are regularly shepherded.

Numbers of sheep on Boreray vary, however, probably due to weather, and it has become obvious recently that the Soay sheep on Hirta (and probably on Soay too) cycle in synchrony with the sheep on Boreray (Fig. 29). Counting sheep on Boreray is difficult, however, and land counts are better than those undertaken from a boat offshore. Totals fluctuate from 350 or so to nearly 700, although ram mortality is high, presumably because they expend so much energy in the rut, just before winter sets in.

Only about 60 ha of Boreray's rocky 77 ha can act as pasture for the sheep so the density of animals is high, about 12 per ha, five times the density of hill sheep in the Hebrides; lowland sheep only reach densities of 15 per ha. Although soaked in salt spray, the vegetation of Boreray is well manured by guano from the nesting seabirds. The diversity of plants making up this well-grazed sward have a thick and extensive root system which, together with compaction of the soil by the sheep flock, helps reduce erosion. Thus such a high density of sheep on such steep, wind-swept slopes does not appear to be a problem.

Periodically, the issue is raised as to whether Boreray and Hirta, and indeed Soay, should now be restored to a natural, wilderness state, just as the Nature Conservancy had advocated for Boreray half a century ago. Undoubtedly, grazing has an impact upon the sward, changing its composition and perhaps even reducing its diversity, but we have already mentioned how the sheep are probably benefiting the burrowing seabirds. But the sheep of St Kilda are much more than mere lawn-mowers. As Morton Boyd has concluded they have:

> ... also become part of the cultural and historical interest of St Kilda and provide a surviving biological link with the now extinct native human community of St Kilda. Whatever may be the best formula for the management of [these islands] for nature conservation, it is vitally important that the Boreray sheep remain genetically intact as a unique, rare breed ...

.13.

Marine life

What is special is the visibility, the water is clearer than in any part of Britain ... It is as rugged and grand below the surface as it is above, and with very little sediment to stir up, the visibility remains incredibly good. The waters are also very rich in marine life with brilliant colours, predominantly reds, oranges, yellows, purples and blues. Another peculiar feature is the tremendous wealth of rock structures under the water. Off Stac Lee and Stac an Armin vertical rock walls, in places overhanging, reach down to depths of over 50m. There are huge under water caves and tunnels, some opening at a depth of 30m. Below Conachair, a valley has eroded into the sea and the water is not so deep ... The island is so exciting and romantic above the surface – it is equally so below!

Gordon Ridley (in Quine 1982)

THUS THE DIVER Gordon Ridley summed up the attractions of St Kildan waters.

Yet, surprisingly, the marine life around St Kilda has only really attracted serious study in the last few decades. Previous to this, references were merely anecdotal. One of the earliest was provided by Henry Brougham in 1799. He was fascinated by luminescence on the surface of the sea:

A circumstance occurred which, if you ever were at sea, must add vastly in your mind to the charms of this fine scene. Every stroke of the oars was attended with a vivid and durable stream of fire, throwing out sparks on all sides still more bright.

The naturalist John MacGillivray saw the same thing in July 1840, as did Norman and Evelyn Heathcote round off an epic day climbing Stac Lee as they overnighted in a sea cave under Boreray.

The phosphorescent lights on the water were most beautiful. All round the sides of the cave where the swell washed against the rocks there was an ever-changing row of bright lights. Occasionally a gleam would appear on a wavelet in the foreground, only to vanish instantly and be succeeded by another in some other place, but the principal display was round the edges. Then, as it began to get lighter (it was never absolutely dark), it was interesting to watch the birds getting up. Gannets, fulmars, kittiwakes, guillemots and shags were sleeping either in our cave or just outside it . . .

Where phosphorescence and other plankton are abundant, so too are fish. Despite lying amidst rich and productive fishing grounds, the lack of a suitable harbour always constrained the St Kildans' efforts to benefit. But an anonymous report written for the Crown sometime between 1577 and 1595 probably underestimated the role of fish in the islanders' diet:

Thay make na labour to obtene or slay ony fisches.

Martin Martin listed numerous species caught by the islanders using limpets as bait, with the flesh of 'bowger' or puffins on hooks. Fishing could take place directly off the rocks or sometimes in good weather from small boats.

According to the Reverend MacAulay:

The rocks to which the people of this island have access with their angling rods, are only two, and these abundantly frightful to any other race of mortals. On each of them are ten fitting places, so they call the craigy declivities, where they plant themselves while at the fishing; and on every one of these, two men make a shift to stand or sit. There they catch a variety of excellent fishes, cod, ling, mackerel, turbot, pollocks, perches, lithes, and some other kinds.

In 1815, the geologist John MacCulloch considered that:

The neglect of fishing proceeds from the wealth of the inhabitants. They possess already as much food as they can consume, and are under no temptation to augment it by another perilous and laborious employment added to that to which they seem to have a hereditary attachment; while their distance from a market, and the absence of commercial habits, prevent them from undertaking a fishery for the purpose of foreign sale. Yet the coast abounds in cod and ling . . .

The Reverend Mackenzie did not mention fishing in the 1830s and in 1847 W. M. E. Milner confirmed that fishing was entirely neglected due to the danger amongst the rocks. The risks were brought into tragic focus on 2 October 1906 as described in Quine (1988) by the teacher Mrs Alice Maclachlan, wife of the missionary:

We were finishing our tea, we heard a great shouting, and other confused noises. In a few moments the men were down, and in less time then it takes me to write they launched the boat, The woman were screaming and wringing their hands. It seems that poor [13-year old] Norman Gillies (who had got away from school a little earlier than usual to go to Point of Coll to fish mullet) had fallen from the rocks into the sea. There is a fearful current there and although the only man there had flung him a rope, the current carried him out beyond it. Some of the bigger boys had run off home to give the news. Norman MacKinnon went to the place on foot but only in time to see poor Norman sink. He was clinging to the fishing rod. He never made a sound. The boat was too late even to see him . . .

Back in 1860, Captain Otter recognised that the lack of a good landing place and a secure anchorage for a boat acted as deterrents against fishing. He magnanimously offered 6,000 hooks to try to encourage the activity. John Sands could then play up the islanders' subsequent fishing efforts:

Fish abound on the coast, including ling, cod, lithe, halibut, black-mouths, skate and conger eels. The latter are used for bait. Two boats, with crews of eight and nine men respectively went to sea frequently in the evenings during the time I resided on the island this year (1875) to fish for ling with long lines. Each boat would return in the morning with perhaps on an average about thirty-five ling and a few cod, besides other fish. The ling were all salted and stored up for the factor, who pays 7d each for them. The cod are sold for 3d each. The men provide their own lines, but are supplied with salt. They themselves kept no note of the number of fish exported, but Macleod incidentally acknowledged receipt of '1080 marketable fish'. A number of elderly men were wont to sit on the rocks near the village and angle for bream in the July evenings. For each of these they receive a penny'

In 1887, Henry Evans arrived from Jura with herring nets which the islanders set that same night – although they caught nothing. Robert Connell was there at the time. He knew the St Kildans were notorious for being bad seamen and fishermen so he considered that, even if an effective boat harbour could be provided, any fishing industry would be bound to fail. And it is not surprising that by 1894 Steele Elliott was again commenting on a lack of interest in fishing:

Strange to say, the St Kildans are no fishermen, having neither pots or nets in their possession; and very few fish are taken during the whole year, although the bay is crowded with herring, pollack, and other fish during the seasons.

Without a doubt, rock fishing did occur for, only two years later, Richard Kearton reported on a typical hour's effort in Village Bay when he:

... caught 17 coalfish [which] with another coalfish and a pollack caught by Rev. Fiddes, came to an aggregate weight of nearly 200 pounds.

Yet the Heathcotes could only muse on how the St Kilda economy might be improved:

Take the fishing industry. There are swarms of fish round their shores, but hitherto the greater part of the harvest of the sea has been reaped by strangers. It has been a favourite fishing-ground for steam trawlers for many years.

On 23 May 1914, the trawler *Sealark* dropped anchor overnight alongside the Duchess of Bedford's yacht. Its mate admitted how coming across the Duchess's vessel in Village Bay had come as a severe shock. *Sealark* had been fishing illegally, well within the 3-mile limit, and had caught a vast number of fish. The mate had taken the yacht for an Admiralty boat and thought he was caught. The Duchess added that the St Kildans did not seem to attach any importance to their fishing.

Before leaving, the Duchess was given a written petition from the islanders, through their missionary, Mr MacArthur, asking for her assistance in getting a lifeboat and in improving their landing stage. No action resulted and by 1916 nothing much had changed.

The St Kildan Calum Macdonald recalled when he was eight years old going on a night fishing trip off Dun with his father and six others. They had a good catch which was salted and a halibut over 5 ft long was cut up amongst the families on the island.

After a spate of interest from collectors, naturalists and scientists early in the 20th century, St Kilda attracted comparatively little attention until after the evacuation and World War II. One of the first post-war expeditions took place in 1952. As a natural sciences student, David Gauld first heard about St Kilda from one of his geology lecturers, none other than the geologist Dr Alex Cockburn. Since his survey with John Mathieson in 1927/28, Cockburn's enthusiasm was to rub off on his students. David Gauld later became one of my lecturers in zoology at Aberdeen University.

Gauld graduated PhD in 1947 before taking up a post with the Scottish Marine Biological Association at Millport on the Clyde. Here he met another marine biologist Timothy Bagenal and an algae specialist Harry Powell. Together, in 1952, they decided to organise an expedition to St Kilda, pulling in two undergraduate students at Glasgow, Joe Connell and Morton Boyd, along with two geologists and a non-scientist friend who looked after the logistics. However, their scientific output was severely compromised by the owner, the Earl of Dumfries, refusing them permission to take away any samples.

Britain was still under food rationing, but, undaunted and with a helpful grocery store in Glasgow, the biologists gradually pulled everything together. A puffer *Glas Island* was chartered from Scalpay to provide transport. Chugging into Village Bay they disturbed a suspicious-looking fishing boat which beat a hasty retreat. Unloading their stores and a small dinghy, they made their base in the Manse. During the first week marine biologists Bagenal, Powell, Connell and Gauld surveyed the relatively sheltered shores of Village Bay. Despite one tricky episode, they employed their dinghy to survey the more exposed shoreline of Dun, before turning their attention, on foot, to Glen Bay. They recorded 54 species of algae, and over 100 invertebrates; the latter list has now trebled with later surveys using scuba diving, etc. (Howson and Picton 1985; Ellis *et al.* 1995). In the summary accounts below it will be necessary to use many Latin names or scientific terminology since many marine life forms have no common names.

During the second week the marine biologist students all helped Morton Boyd complete a systematic sheep census on Hirta. When the time came to leave, it was blowing a gale so the puffer skipper eventually had to despatch his son's ring-netter *A'Mhaidean Hearrach* to collect the expedition from their desert island.

It was a further five years before the army became established and could offer scientific expeditions some degree of support and back-up. Fifty years later, having known the island post-evacuation, Tim Bagenal in the *St Kilda Mail* (2003) was highly critical of the army presence. He expressed a hope that all traces might one day be removed, if not by the military themselves then at least by nature.

A comprehensive survey of intertidal and subtidal habitats around St Kilda. was conducted by Scottish Natural Heritage in 1997, involving complete mapping of the intertidal habitats around all the islands and the main stacs, together with broadscale mapping of the seabed using a sophisticated RoxAnn acoustic ground discrimination system with ground truthing provided by scuba diver observations, underwater video and grab samples. A second survey in 2000, carried out jointly by Scottish Natural Heritage and the Fisheries Research Services Laboratory, Aberdeen, mapped the extensive areas of seabed between the islands and a substantial area to the north-west of Soay. This survey employed a range of acoustic survey techniques such as RoxAnn, multibeam swathe bathymetry and side-scan sonar, together with towed video and ROV and extensive grab sampling in the areas of soft sedimentary seabed (Posford Duvivier Environment 2000).

Much of the intertidal zone around all the islands, stacs and skerries is extremely exposed to wave action and influenced by an almost constant oceanic swell. As the 1952 expedition had first realised, less exposed areas such as Village Bay support a slightly different flora and fauna.

Fig. 31. A diver with the Scottish Natural Heritage survey team
(Scottish Natural Heritage).

Typically, at sea level the shoreline is vertical or near-vertical. Only in a few places do small horizontal platforms or ledges occur with some shallow rock pools that can support a more specialised fauna and flora. The classical intertidal zonation pattern of communities reaches higher above high water mark due to the effects of wave splash and swell. This splash zone can extend a further 20 m and, exceptionally, to 50–100 m on the most exposed west- and north-west-facing cliffs. This zonation is remarkably uniform around most of the archipelago and St Kilda thus presents a classic pattern highly adapted to conditions of extreme wave exposure.

The splash zone comprises a very broad band of lichen-dominated rock with extensive crusts of black lichen (*Verrucaria maura*) and various foliose yellow, orange and grey lichens. Where the rock surface is enriched by guano from roosting and nesting seabirds, very dense growths of the tufty green alga *Prasiola stipitata* develop. In other areas the ephemeral red alga called dulse *Porphyra umbilicalis* covers the rock in a band, up to 4 m wide, of glistening, ruby-red sheets. Very few animals are able to survive in these conditions, with only the occasional barnacle and small limpet and various tiny winkles that are able to find some shelter in the small cracks and crevices etched in the rock surface.

The intertidal zone is characterised by different mixtures of a small number of habitat types that reflect subtle variations in the local topography. Nonetheless, they are all typical of the highly wave-exposed nature of the area. Whilst they are relatively species-poor/animal-dominated, they do include some constituent species considered rare in the UK.

The intertidal rocks are colonised by barnacles *Chthamalus montagui* and *Semibalanus balanoides* that form a broad grey-white band. In the more exposed areas can be found a dark blue-black band of small blue mussels, often with a covering of thin clingfilm-like dulse and various small red algae. Limpets are also scattered amongst the barnacles and patches of black tufted lichen *Lichina pygmaea*. Occasional clumps of small red algae such as the carragheen-like *Mastocarpus* (formerly *Gigartina*) *stellatus* and *Osmundea pygmaea* can survive in sheltered cracks or crevices.

At some of the most exposed locations above the main mussel band there is a narrow band of rare, highly specialised algae – *Fucus distichus* and *Fucus spiralis* var. *nana*. These species have very restricted distributions in the UK, being confined to the most exposed areas of the far north and west coasts of Scotland. The specialised, almost bladderless form for bladder wrack *Fucus vesiculosus f. linearis* also occurs in a narrow band in places below the *F. distichus* band.

The constant action of the sea has resulted in the formation of partially exposed caves, tunnels, gullies and overhangs. The ceilings and walls of these are constantly damp from the effects of the swell and spray and support luxuriant growth of animals such as anemones, sponges and the orange hydroid *Tubularia indivisa*, normally only found in the kelp zone.

At the lowest levels of the intertidal zone, barnacles and mussels give way to a dense turf of seaweed *Mastocarpus stellatus*, under which are various other algae such as dulse *Palmaria palmata*, *Corallina officinalis* and *Osmundea pinnatifida*, together with encrusting coralline seaweeds. Such extensive growths of *Mastocarpus stellatus* at St Kilda are scarce elsewhere in the UK. In some places around St Kilda the lower intertidal is characterised by growths of the surge-tolerant brownish-green alga thongweed *Himanthalia elongata* with its characteristic buttons and straps. There is an understorey of red algae and where there is sufficient shelter from the surge, various small animals including anemones and gastropods are to be found.

Below the tidal zone are surge-tolerant kelp species, principally dabberlocks *Alaria esculenta*, ideally adapted to the constant surge of the waves by their narrow midrib and thin wavy fronds. The orange-brown dabberlocks contrast with the startling pink coralline algae encrusting the rock beneath. With a little more shelter, tangle can grow amongst the dabberlocks and numerous foliose red algae amongst the red coralline encrustation. The effects of the surge extend to considerable depths and the dabberlocks communities persist to depths of around 15 m, much deeper than is typical (i.e. 5 m) in other parts of the UK.

Immediately below this fringe of dabberlocks, steeply sloping bedrock cliffs are covered by a rich forest of kelp *Laminaria* which completely surrounds the islands. One of the remarkable features of St Kilda's marine environment is the depth to which this kelp forest extends. This is due to the clarity of the oceanic waters allowing sufficient light to penetrate to a depth of over 30 m. The density of kelp plants begins to reduce below this depth, to form a 'park' of individual plants, but it is not unusual to find them at depths of over 40 m (the deepest recorded was at 45 m). This contrasts with some 15 m in other parts of the west coast and as little as 5 m on the Scottish east coast.

The dense kelp forest that surrounds the islands like a vast protective curtain is dominated by cuvie *Laminaria hyperborea* and supports a rich underflora of red algae together with a variety of encrusting fauna, including various sea anemones, creating vast, colourful carpets over the rock. Other encrusting animals such as various sponges, the colonial sea squirt *Botrylloides leachi* and the corals, *Caryophyllia smithii* and *Alcyonium digitatum* all compete for space. Mobile species are limited, but the large pink topshell *Calliostoma zizyphinum* is widespread, together with a variety of small but colourful sea slugs. Such dense assemblages occur in deeper areas where the kelp is less abundant. In some of the most exposed areas below the dabberlocks, where it is too turbulent for cuvie to develop or where it has been lost due to storms, the kelp forest comprises the opportunistic, fast-growing sugar kelp and furzebellows.

Below the kelp zone, where the light has diminished to levels capable only of supporting encrusting red algae, the rock surfaces are dominated by encrusting animals that themselves support populations of scavenging and grazing organisms such as sea slugs, gastropods and echinoderms.

The walls and ceilings are colonised by dense sponge crusts such as *Myxilla incrustans*, together with hydroids such as *Tubularia indivisa* and sea mats (bryozoans such as *Escharoides coccinea*) and, where there is sufficient light, specialised, surge-tolerant red algae, including *Parasmittina trispinosa* and *Schmitzia hiscockiana*. In areas of reduced surge, anemones such as the *Phellia gausapata* and jewel anemones *Parazoanthus anguicomus* and *Sagartia elegans* are abundant, often occurring in massive monospecific aggregations, along with thin encrusting sponges, and bryozoans and feather stars *Antedon bifida*.

Within the deeper caves there is an apparent wave exposure gradient with species more typically found in more sheltered environments such as the fan worm *Sabella pavonina* and the burrowing anemone *Cerianthus lloydii*. Rarely recorded nocturnal species also occur in the innermost reaches of some caves including the crab *Bathynectes longipes* and the anemones *Arachnanthus sarsi*. The floors of many of the caves are covered in large, rounded boulders that act as massive rock mills, grinding out pits in the bedrock beneath. In more shallow areas these boulders support a sparse fauna of tubeworms, barnacles and seasonally occurring communities of turf-forming hydroids such as *Obelia dichotoma*. In deeper water they also support the Devonshire cup coral, common sea urchins and squat lobsters *Galathea strigosa* and *Galathea nexa*.

Vertical or near-vertical underwater cliffs plunge 40–50 m to reach a more gradual slope covered in massive boulders down to a depth of around 70 m. Below the sea surface, away from the islands, skerries, etc., a remarkable underwater topography is concealed. This rugged boulder landscape is the result of erosion by rain and ice over the last 50–60 million years, before sea levels rose to their current levels.

Extensive areas of gravelly/sandy seabed lie between the main islands, the rippled surface reflecting the effects of the relentless Atlantic swell, even at depths of 70 m or more. These areas lack any conspicuous fauna of note, but the sediments do support a diverse infauna of nematodes, sipunculids, annelids, crustacea, molluscs, bryozoans, echinoderms and tunicates.

Extensive areas of rocky outcrops and boulders are found between 60 m and 80 m that are still affected by surge and complex deep-water eddies and currents. These are highly unusual conditions to occur at such depths and are reflected in the unusual species assemblages found here. The community is characterised by erect sponges such as *Axinella* spp. and *Phakellia* spp., as well as bryozoans, including *Porella compressa*. The erect coral-like bryozoans *Pentapora foliacea* and *Coronapora truncata* are found on these deep rocks and cobbles. Occasionally, at depths in excess of 70 m, there are patches of pink encrusting algae, emphasising the remarkable water clarity. The crevices amongst the boulders are ideal for brittlestars such as *Ophiocomina nigra* and squat lobsters *Munida* spp.

So far we have described the submarine rock faces of the various islands that we know of today as St Kilda. These form the visible part of a circle of rock outcrops traced out on the seabed. This encloses a plateau some 70 m beneath the surface. Beyond the submarine rock walls of St Kilda, the seabed falls away rapidly on all sides to a flat sandy/boulder seabed lying in around 140 m of water.

A number of notable marine species have been recorded in these recent surveys. A jewel anemone which has a predominantly southern and western distribution is superabundant. The rarely recorded snail *Sinnia patula* is a southern species that is intimately associated with the soft-coral dead man's fingers. Other southern species at or about the extreme of their range include the sponges *Tethyspira spinosa* and *Plocamilla coriacea*, the soft coral *Pareryth-ropodium coralloides*, the sea slugs *Crimora papillata*, *Eubranchus doriae* and *Antiopella hyalina* and the brown alga *Carpomitra costata*. In addition, there are a number of northern species reaching the southern limit of their ranges such as the anemones *Parazoanthus anguicornis*, which is particularly abundant, and *Phellia gausapata*, the spider crab *Lithodes maia* and the starfish *Stichastrella rosee*.

Divers admit there are surprisingly few fish to be seen close to the rocks, just an occasional wrasse, pollack, saithe, lumpsucker or conger eel, the latter reaching lengths of 2 m. Shoals of smaller pollack and saithe frequent Village Bay near Dun, while shoals of mackerel arrive in July and August, attracting feeding gannets close inshore. Studies of seabird diet have provided additional opportunities to examine both pelagic and benthic species which may evade scientific collecting techniques. Herring fry and sprats are important prey for fulmars for instance, while sandeels, sprats, whiting and rockling have featured in puffin diet. Nonetheless, I was recently able to make a cursory list of over 40 species of fish recorded around St Kilda, from tiny three-spined sticklebacks to the occasional sunfish and basking shark (Love 2004).

The islanders used to believe that basking sharks in the bay presaged the onset of bad weather. There have been 20 sightings of basking sharks since 1986, up to three at one time. A few have been seen in May and June, but most during July and August. Another large fish, a sunfish, was seen off St Kilda in June 1998 and five more during June and July 2000, with yet another behind Dun in 2003. A fish called the reticulated dragonet *Callionymus reticulatus* was caught in Village Bay in August 1993 and proved to be one of the most northerly records in British waters. The common eel, occasionally seen running up the few streams on Hirta, is the only 'freshwater' fish.

Lacking waterproof skin, amphibians rarely manage to ride rafts of vegetation or driftwood out to offshore islands, nor, of course, have any reptiles managed to establish on St Kilda. Marine reptiles are a different story. There have been seven records of leathery turtles in the waters around St Kilda, all from late July through September. On 9 August 1994 the skipper of the Range Launch spotted one 20 miles south of St Kilda, only to find it dead a couple of days later, upside-down and being eaten by gulls.

Marine mammals are commonly seen around St Kilda. The only seal to frequent its shores is the Atlantic grey seal. David Boddington, however, saw a newborn pup in November 1958 which lacked the characteristic silky coat (Nature Conservancy files). This is a characteristic of the common seal, and it remains the only record, unverified and questionable perhaps since common seals normally give birth in the summer.

Seals provided the islanders with a welcome supplement to their economy. In 1678, Robert Moray, the first President of the Royal Society, mentioned seal hunting expeditions that the islanders undertook to Soay where in fact there is a cleft near the landing place called Geo nan Ron. Heathcote referred to this place as a cave named Uamha nan Ron. David Quine (1982) quoted 'a 1799 report', perhaps Moray's, from a century earlier:

> There is a remarkable creek resorted to by a vast number of seals. The method of destroying them is as follows. The natives approach the mouth of it which is very narrow, in one of their boats with as little noise as possible and leaving the boat at the mouth, they rush in with large clubs with which they knock down the seals. They, however, sometimes perish themselves in the attempt, for as they never make the attempt except when the wind is easterly, so if the wind happens to change before they retire, the sea rolls into the creek with such violence that the boat and all in her inevitably perish. They used formerly to pay a considerable part of their rent in the skins of these animals, which however, are not found in such numbers now.

People used to consider seals to be amphibious since they could live on both land and sea. The Keartons confirmed that this 'amphibian' seldom went near the place now, but added how dried sealskins had been used to contribute towards rent.

Once humans abandoned Hirta and casual hunting, Lord Dumfries promoted it as a Nature Reserve. It might be expected that as a result grey seals would increase in number and commence breeding, but this did not happen immediately. Apparently Lord Dumfries was not averse to the shooting of seals and even had a sealskin sporran made. The St Kildan Calum Macdonald was sometimes asked back to his native island with his Lordship and friends. He reported how everyone had a wonderful time lobster fishing, catching puffins and ringing them and ... shooting seals. The cook even broke his collar bone when firing at a seal in the bay.

When, in late September 1947, James Fisher flew over the islands in a Sunderland, there were quite a few seals in Village Bay but none ashore. This is one of the few localities along the precipitous exposed coastline of St Kilda where seals could haul out, let alone give birth, which they do in the inclement months of October/November.

In 1952, Morton Boyd and his companions discovered seals hauled out below the Manse and just before the Army Base was constructed a few pups were being born on the beach below. In 1957, the first military medical officer Peter Saunby recorded a few seal pups born there, with some 30 more seal pups on Dun. However, on 2 February 1958, the military detachment saw Spanish trawlers killing seals, something they had probably been doing ever since the evacuation.

Over the winter of 1958/59 David Boddington was the medical officer on the Army Base. He had been a keen naturalist since boyhood, having attended the school at which James Fisher's father had been headmaster. He had also been a friend of Ken Williamson and when he was on St Kilda effectively functioned as warden for the Nature Conservancy. During his first autumn he began some interesting observations on the grey seals around Hirta. He found only two places offered them easy access for hauling out on the rocks – a corner of Dun nearest Ruaival in Village Bay and Leacan an Eithein in Glen Bay. At first by autumn there were no more than a dozen ashore, but, as winter storms became more frequent, numbers built up to 250 by 23 October and 312 by 29 November, declining again thereafter to about 50 by the end of 1958 (Nature Conservancy files).

> Pollock and mackerel were being caught during the period, and seals were probably taking both as food. When these shoals appeared in the evening gannets from the Boreray group used to follow them in, but were very reluctant to feed on the crowded mass of bewildered fish being driven towards the shore by the seals.

About 100 pups were born in 1958, a considerable increase on the previous year, and not surprisingly mostly on the flat, sloping rocks of Dun where they experienced less human contact. There are fewer now as a result of increased disturbance by the visitors and traffic to the Base. A few seal pups have also been seen on the boulder beaches at Mol Ghiasgar and at Mol Shoay, and seals may well breed inside the caves, as the old St Kildans discovered to their advantage. Around 300 to 400 adults and juveniles continue to frequent the shores of St Kilda throughout the year, with the main concentrations in Glen Bay, Soay Sound and on both sides of the neck of the Cambir. Their calls echo round the tunnel at Gob na h-Airde and, as they did in the past, at Geo nan Ron.

As a footnote, there is a curious record of a walrus on St Kilda in 1939 which Lord Dumfries wanted shot so Alex Ferguson is said to have taken some pot shots at it (Fleming 2005).

It is more difficult to gain a handle on the status of the most marine mammals of all, the whales and dolphins or cetaceans. One has to rely on casual sightings from the shore, or from boats at sea, and ultimately upon the ability of observers to identify them. In 2004, Stuart Murray summarised the current situation. Records have increased in recent years, probably because of more interest, better data collection and more experienced observers. Sightings were made on 128 days to date, with 37 per cent of records of cetaceans inside or crossing the mouth of Village Bay; 23 per cent of records were made from elsewhere on the Hirta coast and 9 per cent from Boreray; vessels at sea reported cetaceans on 23 per cent of these days and a final 7 per cent could not be assigned. Most sightings are made in the summer months May to August, but some killer whales, porpoises and Risso's dolphins have been seen in the period November to March. Ten species have been sighted from St Kilda so

Fig. 32. Sowerby's beaked whale (J. Vaughan).

far, all but one known to occur regularly off the Scottish west coast in summer. The exception was a rare Sowerby's beaked whale which was washed up in Village Bay on 29 September 1994.

Minke whale is the most commonly sighted species (on 293 days), mostly in ones or twos, but five different individuals were seen in one day, and twice eight; once, on 2 August 1984, no less than 15 were seen from Hirta.

Killer whales are the next most common species, seen on 79 days. Seven animals spending some hours off Hirta on 9 August 1979 were the first recorded instance, though doubtless they had been frequently seen long before this. Since 1984 there have been no more than two reports a year, usually in May to August; there have also been a few sightings in February, March and October. Pods vary in size, with an estimated 40–50 animals being seen in July 1984. Occasional groups may remain around the islands for several days or even weeks. Some have been seen breaching in Village Bay, while in February/March 1996 they were seen lob-tailing close inshore and playing with a freshly killed grey seal.

The smaller dolphins and porpoises have been seen on only 49 days, with groups of up to 15 Risso's dolphins, perhaps the largest and most distinctive species, being the most common (16 days). Groups of white-sided dolphins have been seen on nine days, with 200 off Village Bay on 2 July 1984 and 50–60 actually inside Village Bay on 29 July 1996. Porpoises were first recorded in 1988 and – usually singles – have been seen on nine days. Small numbers of white-beaked dolphins have been seen on seven days, with a maximum of 20 in Village Bay on 21 July 1990. These animals are probably more common further offshore, white-beaked being more prone to bow-riding boats on passage to St Kilda than are the similar white-sided dolphins. Single bottlenosed dolphins have been seen twice, with six off Village Bay once. Common dolphins have been seen on five days. Two sightings of pilot whales were unconfirmed until 19 February 2007 when a long-finned was washed up dead in Village Bay.

There have been a further 23 sightings where the species could not be determined, seven of them involving 'large whales'. Four fin whales were seen east of Hirta on 22 September 2002, including, probably, a mother and calf. Since Stuart's published analysis (1973–2000), reporting of cetaceans around St Kilda has declined somewhat, but the pattern of sightings over the next eight years to 2008 (125 in total) remains essentially the same, with minke whales making up half of them (66 records), harbour porpoises (16) and killer whales with common dolphins (7 each) the next most numerous.

Table 4. Sightings (days) of cetaceans from St Kilda (usually May to August; 1973–2000) (after Murray 2004)

Minke whale	293 (seen all years, mostly 1–2)
Killer whale	79 (1–2 per year, up to 6 per pod)
Risso's dolphin	16 (max. 30 per pod)
White-sided dolphin	9 (max. 200 per pod)
White-beaked dolphin	8 (max. 20 per pod)
Porpoise	7 (up to 2–3 animals)
Common dolphin	5 (max. 50 per pod)
Bottlenosed dolphin	4 (max. 16 per pod)
Pilot whale	2 (both singles)
Sowerby's beaked whale	1 (washed up dead)

Minke whales tend to be an inshore species, at least in summer, so it is not surprising that it is the only whale to be observed from the shores of St Kilda. The Sowerby's beaked whale probably would not have been recorded had it not been washed up dead in Village Bay. All the remaining larger whales are rarely seen since they tend to frequent the rich feeding grounds around the continental shelf well to the west of St Kilda and near Rockall. An exception was four fin whales observed just east of Hirta in September 2002. In earlier centuries the northern right whale, and humpbacks, were the favoured target of whaling ships from Britain and Europe because they were the easiest to pursue and floated after being harpooned. Thus they were depleted early in the North Atlantic whaling era. By the beginning of the 20th century these larger, long-range vessels turned their attentions to the rich waters of the South Atlantic.

By 1907, however, several whaling stations had been established in Shetland, with another in Harris with Captain Herlofsen as the Norwegian manager (Randall 2008). The company paid the owner of St Kilda, Macleod of Macleod, the sum of £401 and, up to 1931, an annual rent of £1. They wished to reserve the right for a whaling station on Hirta on an area of 4 acres near the Feather Store (and marked as Norwegian on a map in Dunvegan Castle), but the plan never actually materialised (Harman 1997). The whaling station at Bunavoneader in West Loch Tarbert was opened in 1908 and operated until 1927, with a further bout of activity in 1950 and 1952. The whalers first appeared in St Kilda in early May and finally departed for home around the end of September. As can be seen from the table below, Fin whales were the most frequently caught in the waters between St Kilda and Rockall, and the catcher boats often moored the inflated carcases in Village Bay until they had enough to justify a boat coming to take them back to the Harris station. Records from the Harris whaling station give a good indication of the cetaceans to be found in the waters off St Kilda early in the 20th century.

Table 5. Whales killed between St Kilda and Rockall and processed in the Harris Whaling Station (Scottish Natural Heritage)

	1908–27	1950–1
Blue whale	310	6
Fin whale	1,492	46
Sei whale	375	3
Humpback whale	19	0
Northern right whale	94	0
Sperm whale	76	1
Northern bottlenose whale	1	0

The St Kildan Lachlan Macdonald recalled the whaling activity (in Quine 1988):

The whalers, Norwegians, used to come in at any time, they had a base in Harris. When they started coming here first there were a lot of whales round about the islands. They used to come round the islands and kill the whales, huge big whales, then they would come in with their catch of one or two whales and tie them on to the buoy in the bay. When they had been lying there for two days or so the whale came up like a huge great balloon – if it burst the smell was terrible – the stink was terrible – but usually they took them away. Then they would go out and see if they could get more: if they were lucky they would have four attached to the buoy and they would go out and get a couple more. Then they would come in, pick up the ones they had there and go with them to Tarbert in Harris. Many a time I have seen them towing six back to Harris. That's the way we got so familiar with the Harris folk, you would get across with the whalers and they wouldn't charge you anything; then you would be able to pick up one of them coming back ... The other time we were well off was when 1914 war was on, when the boats were coming in, warships and destroyers at first, later trawlers with guns.

On Wednesday 13 July 1927, the botanist John Gladstone witnessed the smell for himself:

The two whales left last night in the bay have swelled out enormously and have completely changed their shape. Every moment we expected them to burst and to send out an awful smell. This happened about 7 o'clock just as the island was coming from its prayer meeting.

The St Kildan Calum Macdonald added:

The stench was vile and lingered over the whole bay for a long time. People in the village street often went around holding their noses after such an occurrence.

No wonder the whalers were so keen to be helpful in so many other respects to the long-suffering islanders!

Although the whales had been depleted by the whalers, the small minkes not being worth catching. Thus they may now be the most numerous species in these waters. Sperm whales needed processing separately so were not a favoured quarry for the whalers.

White-beaked dolphins like to approach boats to bow-ride, so feature quite highly in the sightings from St Kilda itself, contrasting with the many more white-sided dolphins seen from ships further out to sea. Risso's dolphins tend to be an inshore species so also feature highly in the St Kilda list, as do killer whales which are quite conspicuous from the shore while they are hunting seals and fish.

Whaling apart, human impact upon the water around St Kilda has been negligible so its waters remain pristine. Besides the clarity, the geographical position of St Kilda, the depth of its surrounding waters and the high degree of exposure, also conspire to make St Kilda one of the premier marine sites in the British Isles – surely worthy of Marine Nature Reserve status? It is already a World Heritage Site for its diverse marine interests, 23,346 ha of sea around the archipelago's 854.6 ha, coincident with Special Protection Area status under the European Community's Birds Directive. This area is also a Special Area for Conservation under the Habitats Directive. The land area of the archipelago is also a Site of Special Scientific Interest coincident with its National Nature Reserve status.

Of course, all the designations in the world will not protect St Kilda from oil spills. On 9 December 1981 the 100,000-ton tanker *Maersk Angus* was under ballast on the way to Shetland. She lost power and drifted helplessly for 24 hours, perilously close to Hirta and Boreray. During the night 16 of her crew were taken off by Sea King helicopter as a precaution. Fortunately, the ship carried no oil and she was eventually taken in tow for Glasgow. However, the incident did bring home the awful possibility of disaster from fully laden tankers going to and from the oil terminal at Sullom Voe in Shetland. So, in order to divert the risk of oil pollution within the confines of the Minch, a deepwater route west of the Hebrides is recommended for laden tankers. While this gives sea room to resolve problems, it does bring increased tanker traffic past not just St Kilda but also other important seabird breeding stations like Sule Skerry, Rona, Sulaisgeir, the Flannans, Mingulay and Berneray.

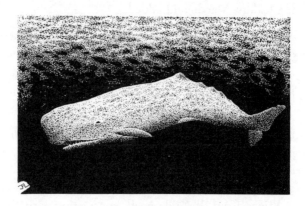

.14.

Visitors

T<small>HUS FAR WE HAVE SEEN</small> how incredibly rich St Kilda is in wildlife and scenery, which, for several centuries now, have attracted a succession of naturalists, scientists and tourists. It is now time to consider the human presence on St Kilda and the effect such visitors have had on the resident community.

Although the St Kildans would have had periodic contact with the 'outside world' from a priest, or from the Factor and his entourage coming to collect rents, etc., it was Martin Martin who in 1697 might be considered their first 'tourist'. He offered the first detailed account of fowling along with descriptions of the breeding habits of the seabirds they were hunting. Much has been written subsequently on seabird fowling, but, as the habit died out elsewhere, it became something of a peculiarity of the St Kildan way of life. This, together with the attraction of a community living at the very edge of the British Isles and leading an apparently Utopian existence, encouraged a spate of travellers and travel books in the 19th century.

Many travellers were naturalists, some of whom we have already encountered. Others were ordinary tourists, a few of whom were to leave us with classic accounts of St Kilda. It is worth dwelling upon some of these noteworthy visits since tourism, and natural history in particular, was to play a significant part in the island economy and play a not insignificant part in its decline and ultimate abandonment. We owe much of what we know about the demise of the St Kilda community to visitors, and to naturalists.

Although tourism began with Martin Martin, it was not until exactly a century later that we learn of another tourist. The eminent naturalist Thomas Pennant (1726–1798) had never reached the Outer Hebrides, so when a young Sussex geologist Edward Daniel Clarke (1769–1822) contacted him for advice on his intended voyage north, Pennant suggested St Kilda would prove of particular interest. Clarke's companion was a son of Lord Uxbridge who managed to arrange a revenue cutter for him. With fine weather and favourable wind, Clarke departed Barra to find St Kilda in fog amidst a very, heavy rolling sea. Although some of the islanders took to the hills in fright when the cutter appeared, others plucked up courage to meet the landing party. Clarke noted:

> I shook hands with all of them, and began to distribute my little parcels of tobacco and snuff.

Clarke showed little interest in the geology of the island, being diverted instead by the islanders. He slowly won their confidence so that they invited him – and him alone – inside their houses. Later they treated him to a display of their climbing prowess on the cliffs, soon to become standard fare for visiting tourists. Some of the young men wished that Clarke had come earlier for a wedding:

> You would have the whole island dancing, and the whole island drunk.

They persisted with their attentions, however, so that Clarke chose to ignore a summons from his ship:

> They kissed my hands, running sometimes before, and sometimes after, me, saying, 'Come, we dance and sing: you eat and drink!'

The alcohol apparently came in quantity with the Factor on his annual visit, but the St Kildans seemed pretty abstemious for most of the year.

Finally, in the Manse some of the older men began to open up to the visitor with general grievances, but, for some reason, Clarke chose not to record this in his journal. Finally taking leave, his vessel sailed past Boreray on its way north. Clarke went on to discover the element cadmium and became Professor of Mineralogy at Cambridge.

The next visitors gave a diametrically opposite account of the community. Henry, Lord Brougham (1778–1868) was a member of an expedition organised by a rich Irishman called John Joseph Henry. Another of the expedition's aristocratic members was Charles Stuart, a grandson of the third Earl of Bute. In early August 1799, they were *en route* to Iceland but ran out of time and made St Kilda the goal of the voyage instead. Perhaps this disappointment was why Brougham was so cynical and left such a brief, facetious account of his visit, but then at Edinburgh University he had a reputation as a bit of a hooligan. The ship was mistaken for a French privateer and the inhabitants – or 'savages', as Brougham insisted on calling them – nearly took to the hills in fright. His unbelievable arrogance is typified by comments such as this:

A total want of curiosity, a stupid gaze of wonder, an excessive eagerness for spirits and tobacco, a laziness only to be conquered by the hope of the above-mentioned cordials, and a beastly degree of filth, the natural consequences of this, rendered the St Kildian character truly savage.

Brougham also accused them of stealing everything they could lay their hands on and claimed he had to storm a suspect's house with drawn sword in order to recover a stolen cloak! But then as students in Edinburgh 'Hooray Henry' Brougham and his friends were reputedly a pretty wild bunch!

On 17 July 1812, a wealthy Devonshire baronet called Thomas Dyke Acland (1787–1871) arrived at St Kilda in his private yacht, with his wife Lydia and their three-year-old son. Reputedly Lydia was the first Lady to set foot *voluntarily* on St Kilda – presumably a reference to the incarceration of Lady Grange there from 1734 to 1742. Acland made a dozen or so fascinating watercolours of Hirta, showing the old village and the seacliffs, which are now of great historical interest.

One of the earliest scientists to study St Kilda was geologist John MacCulloch who visited in 1815, noting that there had not been anyone else on the island for at least a year. His survey has already been described in Chapter 3. MacCulloch was met at the pier by the minister's wife and a host of islanders who eagerly pulled his boat up the beach. He discovered that if the islanders' 'curiosity was great, their civility and good humour were still greater'.

In 1834, Acland was back. Now a Member of Parliament, he had just bought a two-masted schooner, fitted it with steam as a pleasure yacht (complete with Lady Acland's piano), and named it *The Lady of St Kilda* after his wife. Appointing Fairfax Moresby as Captain, they immediately embarked upon a circumnavigation of the British Isles. Ever the philanthropist, Acland donated some money to the island's minister, the Reverend Neil Mackenzie, towards improving houses on St Kilda (see Chapter 2). Later in her history *The Lady of St Kilda* ended up in Australia, where in 1842 she gave her name to the city of St Kilda near Melbourne. Coincidentally, Captain (later Admiral) Moresby's son was to give his name to the capital of Papua New Guinea, just to the north of Australia.

At the end of July 1834, St Kilda received another notable visit, not as grand as the *Lady of St Kilda* perhaps. It was the 120-ft steamship *Glen Albyn* on her maiden voyage. The 60 passengers included an Edinburgh geologist James Torrie. By now the islanders had become used to visitors though never before with quite such frequency. One anonymous account of the occasion appeared in the *Glasgow Free Press* on 2 August, anticipating the impact such visits ultimately may have upon the islanders:

Fig. 33. A party of tourists on St Kilda (National Trust for Scotland).

At length the party took leave of that simple-minded and warm-hearted, little community, with feelings of deep interest and commiseration, hoping that the visit might be remembered in their annals as the commencing point in the era of improvement. Yet they could not altogether suppress their fears, that if a visit to St Kilda should become a common occurrence in parties of pleasure, it might unfortunately happen that the vices of civilised life would be imparted to them sooner than its virtues and blessings.

Within four decades 'parties of pleasure' became commonplace and, as this pioneering reporter had feared, began changing that 'simple-minded and warm-hearted' community for ever. They arrived aboard private charters or in steamships, commercial or otherwise – naval vessels, fishing boats and whalers. The St Kildans were quick to exploit every opportunity.

One of the first recorded boat charters to reach St Kilda was the well-to-do young naturalist George Clayton Atkinson (1808–77) who arrived with his brother in 1831. He too saw the best side of the islanders, but again feared impacts upon their innocence and where it might lead:

It would indeed have been a pity if their hospitality had brought on them an acquaintance with the social vices, and been the means of corrupting the most innocent and unsophisticated people in the universe.

... as no fermented or spirituous liquor is made on the island, and they only receive a trifling half yearly supply from the Tacksman, they are of necessity sober ... they are kind and hospitable in the highest degree: observe the most scrupulous regard for truth; and are obliging and attentive to strangers to a most pleasing extent. They are celebrated for the goodness of their singing, and for cheeses ...

The islanders took Atkinson on several boat trips around St Kilda during his short stay. For a chance to visit Boreray, Atkinson rewarded the crew with some tobacco since:

> ... their idea of the value of money is so vague that Mr Mackenzie thought they would be more pleased with tobacco than with any reasonable sum of money.

In exchange for the remainder of Atkinson's tobacco supply, two courageous young men were landed on Stac Biorach and climbed to the top of this so-called 'inaccessible pinnacle', the ultimate test of a St Kildan's skill. The islanders were said to be more content with this settlement than the three guineas they had received from a yacht owner two weeks earlier, as Atkinson recorded, 'without eventually seeing a tenth part of what we saw'. They also collected some birds' eggs for Atkinson, along with two live peregrine falcon chicks.

Another steam yacht, the *Vulcan* arrived with a half-complement of 30 tourists in 1838, all who responded to newspaper advertisements in the *Glasgow Herald*. They loosed a cannon off Boreray to panic the gannets and then took pot shots at them. With smoke belching from her funnel, another cannon shot and a brass band in full swing on the deck, the islanders fled to the hills again. One of the passengers, a Free Church minister, fell into the water as they were leaving.

It was two years after the *Vulcan* that John MacGillivray arrived in 1840 and gained early indications of how exploitative the islanders were becoming:

> Intercourse with strangers has created many artificial wants and previously unknown luxuries, as well as encouraged an avaricious spirit, shewn by the value they place upon articles offered for sale to strangers ...
>
> When exhibiting before strangers, which they are easily induced to do, they generally choose for the display of their agility a precipice about 600 feet in height, overhanging the sea, at a short distance from the village. One of them will then suspend himself about mid-way down the cliff, and, striking his feet against the rock, shoot himself out some ten or twelve feet more, rebounding from it several times, and increasing the distance with each rebound; performing this, and many similar feats, with all the agility of a professional performer upon the tight rope.

The following year, the Reverend James Wilson arrived, the brother of a noted Paisley critic and essayist of the day who styled himself 'Christopher North'. Since the first National Census of Scotland had omitted to include St Kilda altogether, Wilson undertook one of his own. He listed 28 families including two old widows and a widower, totalling 96 people, while the Factor's family added another nine individuals. Wilson concluded that the whole male population who had 'attained to or passed the prime of life are what we may call practised ornithologists, or cragsmen'. He also noted a change in the islanders, from once happily celebrating their culture to a more serious outlook on life:

> The singing of psalms and hymns is even a favourite spiritual recreation of the people, and is resorted to frequently and voluntarily in their own houses, independent of the more formal meetings which may be occasionally called for the express purpose. These spiritual songs ... have in a great measure superseded all ordinary vocal music of a worldly character. The Irish melodies are unknown. Dancing is also now regarded by them as a frivolous amusement, and has ceased to be practised, even during their more joyous festivals, such as marriage or baptism.

This strict religious observance had consolidated during the Reverend Mackenzie's tenure on the island, but probably had been inspired by several visits between 1822 and 1830 from the charismatic Reverend John Macdonald of Ferintosh, known as 'the Apostle of the North'. Macdonald's fourth and final visit had been to accompany Mackenzie to begin his charge at St Kilda in 1830. Mackenzie noted:

> I soon found that they were only charmed by his eloquence and energy, and had not knowledge to follow or understand his argument.

While Mackenzie may indeed have been responsible for reinforcing Macdonald's evangelism, the strictest regime the islanders would have to endure was undoubtedly under the charge of the Reverend John Mackay (*c.* 1816–1901). A native of Jeanstown in Easter Ross, he was nearly 50 years old when he went to live amongst them and he was to remain for 24 years from 1865 to 1889 without a single break away (see later). Mackay was much less 'hands-on' than Mackenzie and left no detailed account of his experiences.

Despite his religious orthodoxy, the Reverend Neil Mackenzie did take down many of the old Gaelic songs, as did the folklorist Alexander Carmichael (1832–1912) in May 1863. While some of the islanders, notably 84-year-old Euphemia MacCrimmon, seemed willing to give of their traditions, Carmichael later judged that 'People seem to be spoiled. Not polite.'

Carmichael bought 10 yards of cloth for 14 shillings, and a bottle of fulmar oil for one shilling; he also watched a climbing display on the cliffs.

By 1844, the Reverend Neil Mackenzie felt that his job on St Kilda had been completed. The year before, the Church of Scotland had been split by the Disruption and the breakaway Free Church was formed. Mackenzie returned to St Kilda for one final visit in June 1847, with a colleague. He had met up with two ornithologists in Harris, one of whom was Sir William M. E. Milner and together on 12 June they set out. Not far from their destination they were overtaken by a storm and for four hours were beaten about helplessly before finding shelter and respite in Village Bay. Milner found the people:

> ... hospitable, most anxious to serve us, and, unlike their brethren in the mainland, we had great difficulty in persuading them to take what we considered they were entitled to for two hard days' work among the cliffs and rocks. [Several pounds-worth of tobacco however] delighted them not a little.

Three or four days later the party took their leave, and not least the Reverend Mackenzie for whom:

> ... there was not a dry eye in the island. So much had this good man made himself beloved, that the people would have obeyed him in everything except leaving their barren rock, to which they are most deeply attached.

On Monday 30 May 1853, Mary, Lady Mackenzie of Gairloch, and her 11-year-old son Osgood hired the *Jesse* to take them to St Kilda. Lady Mary seemed somewhat disappointed that none of the islanders bowed or curtsied, although she did concede that they:

> ... were kind and gentle in speech and obliging and friendly in action. Yet this does not prevent them from being keen for money and still more for tobacco. They would part with any of the commodities of the island for half their value if paid in tobacco.

Mother and son were taken over to view Boreray and Stac Lee in the islanders' boat. Lady Mackenzie left an interesting account of the visit which is reproduced in Osgood's book *A Hundred Years in the Highlands*, published in 1921.

After a pleasant voyage of 14 hours Thomas Smyth Muir (1802–1888) and the crew of the trading sloop *Foey* reached Village Bay at midnight on 9 July 1858. Next morning they went ashore and immediately had a bath in the stream – much to the consternation of the islanders. Muir's interest was in ancient church and chapel architecture, but time was precious. He endeavoured to see as much as possible and even witnessed a demonstration of cliff-climbing by the islanders – for a fee of course (Muir 1888):

> In the years 1697 and 1758, their transactions with the steward appear to have been altogether in the way of barter; consequently, at these periods, their disregard of money would, in all likelihood, be just as profound as their disregard of anything of which they could make no use. But, in later times, money having become to some extent the medium of traffic, a thirst for it is now as keen in

lonely St Kilda as it is in quarters where its acquisition is a matter of hourly concern.

There were some ten or fifteen minutes of wrangling before three or four of them could be prevailed upon to accept each a good day's wages for the hour's work of letting us see one of their number go down the face of a precipice at the end of a rope. They once got as many pounds as we were offering shillings for doing the same thing for a Lady Somebody, and what was there to hinder us from giving a like sum?

After attending church, and a meal with the catechist, Muir was given a lightning tour of the ecclesiological remains on Hirta before he left, concluding 'we had got our glimpse of Hirt'.

John Morgan and a friend managed to reach St Kilda for six hours on a 25-ton yacht *Falcon* on 17 June 1860. They failed to entice the islanders to give them a demonstration of fowling, since the fowlers were reluctant to disturb the birds at the height of the breeding season.

In 1851, Charles Kelsall of Southampton left £700 to be used to purchase articles of benefit to the inhabitants of St Kilda. In 1859, the residue – some £600 – was transferred to the Royal Highland and Agricultural Society of Scotland for future administration. That year it was decided to spend the bequest on the construction of new houses on the island (the cottages that are still there today) and a slipway for hauling up the island boats.

We know only, of course, about the visitors who published an account of their visit to St Kilda; many others would have gone unrecorded. Naval survey ships were for a short time vital links for the islanders and Captain (later Rear Admiral) Henry Otter was to become involved in various useful projects from 1859 to 1864, including the installation of a crane to help getting the island boats ashore.

With this early succession of visitors the islanders had discovered an income, although they still seemed to prefer recompense in kind. Gradually too they were receiving gifts or acts of benevolence. Their age-old self-sufficiency was becoming undermined. Nonetheless, the archipelago remained extremely inaccessible and in 1869 Henry Elwes highlighted the difficulties:

> It is not the distance which makes St Kilda so difficult of access ... but the want of a good anchorage, and the never-ceasing swell which beats on its precipitous shore, even in the calmest weather, form such serious impediments to effecting a landing, that, in many seasons, it would be impossible to get there before the middle or end of June.
>
> An intending visitor to St Kilda must take his choice of two evils; either to go in a small boat, which, on his arrival, can be hauled up on the rocks, though most people would hardly venture three-score miles into the Atlantic in such a craft; or

to go in a larger vessel, which can lie in the bay at anchor so long as the wind is light, but would be obliged to put to sea immediately if the weather became bad, as the anchorage is very exposed and dangerous. I had made arrangements for a smack to take me there but the spring and summer of 1868 were so unusually stormy that I should have failed in the expedition if it had not been for the kindness of Capt. Bell of HMS 'Harpy', a paddle-steamer which was going to see how the St Kildians were faring, since they had been cut off from communication with the other islands, for nearly nine months.

About one o'clock, a.m., on the 22nd May the 'Harpy' got under way from the Sound of Taransay ... Soon after we entered the bay the people began to appear; and some of the men came off to the steamer in a large, clumsy boat, the only one, however, they have in which to go to the adjacent isles. On landing were met by the minister, Mr Mackay ...

After visiting a few of the houses, and examining all the objects of interest, I returned to the 'Harpy' to deposit my birds and eggs, and found most of the older men collected on board begging for tobacco, sugar, and other things, though they did not seem very anxious to give us anything in exchange.

Some of the man-of-war's men had been collecting eggs on shore; and this excited the indignation of the older men, who considered it in the light of stealing their property. After we had pacified them with some small presents of tobacco and sugar, I showed them the pictures in my 'Yarrell' [a popular bird book at the time], among others pointing out the Fork-tailed petrel. This, however, they did not seem to distinguish by any peculiar name from the stormy Petrel, which is common enough, and is here called 'Assilag'. The petrels are too small to be any use for food, and are probably not much seen by the natives, especially as they only come out at night.

We had much difficulty in getting into the boat, owing to the increasing swell, and after arriving on board ship were obliged to take leave of the people and put to sea without loss of time. Before long it was blowing a gale from the south-east, and the weather continued so bad for five weeks that no boat could possibly have landed; so I was obliged to content myself to what I had already seen, and leave a more thorough examination of the group to some future observer.

In 1877, a major initiative presented a world of new opportunities for St Kilda. The steamship company Martin Orme advertised a cruise from Glasgow on the *Dunara Castle* to take place on 28 June for a fare of £5. One of its first 40 passengers was the advocate George Seton, who was to write a long-winded but well-researched volume about St Kilda, all on the strength of his most brief of visits. That same year John Sands, an Edinburgh lawyer and journalist, noted how no fewer than five steamers and two other vessels called at St Kilda, 'more than in any other previous year', indicating that the *Dunara Castle* was not in fact the first tourist vessel to have made the voyage. It made only a single trip the following summer, but would achieve several every year after that.

The full story of the shipping services has been told by the postal historian James Mackay in his *The St Kilda Steamers: a history of McCallum, Orme & Co.* (2006), published not long before he died. Mackay had been an officer on St Kilda around the time the military base was established, overlapping with David Boddington. In 2002, Mackay wrote of these experiences in *Soldiering on St Kilda*.

There have long been two opposing views of St Kilda and its islanders. What some refer to as 'the sublime' is encapsulated in Martin Martin's description from as long ago as 1697:

> The inhabitants of St Kilda are much happier than the generality of mankind as being the only people in the world who feel the sweetness of true liberty.

Martin was by no means the only visitor to adopt this view. The arcadian myth about St Kildan society persisted. Some observers, however, would adopt the opposing view. This was first expressed by the young, aspiring novelist Anthony Trollope who, on the *Mastiff*, called in at St Kilda on his way to Iceland in 1878. He concluded that the archipelago was:

> ... a most picturesque point in the ocean at which to land and at which to marvel at the freaks of nature. But it is an atom of land hardly intended by nature as a habitation for man.

The reality lay in between perhaps, but no outsider who lived there for any length of time could possibly appreciate the island as the St Kildans themselves saw it. First and foremost to them it was home, probably the only one they would ever know, with little prospect of experiencing anything different. John Sands was marooned on Hirta for eight months in 1876, the first outsider to 'overwinter' on St Kilda. He brought to public attention the harsh reality of the St Kildans' isolation, and indeed helped fuel interest in this strange community on 'the edge of the world'.

The following year, John MacDiarmid, Secretary of the Highland and Agricultural Society, who administered the Kelsall Bequest, was sent to St Kilda on HMS *Flirt* with a cargo of emergency supplies, but he found that the islanders were in less dire straits than the world had been led to believe.

We will return to Sands's description shortly. His rebellious nature also instilled in the community a desire for independence from the monopoly of Macleod's Factor. Although Sands was no admirer of the minister, the Reverend John Mackay also began to involve himself in local politics. As Mackenzie the Factor wrote to his employer in August 1882:

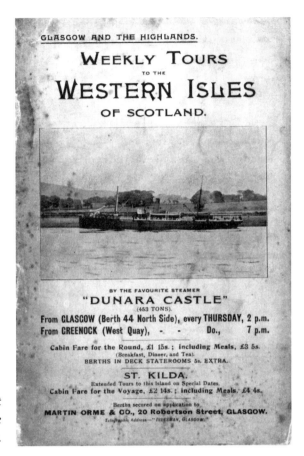

Fig. 34. An advertisement for weekly tours on the Dunara Castle.

For some time past I have been noticing that he [Mackay] has been losing ground with the people, and to recover his influence with them he has all of a sudden taken up the position of pleader and sympathizer, and he has become just as low, and as great a beggar as any of them, that the people like and admire.

The passengers on board the 'Dunara' were very much disgusted with him . . . The people are so elated with the number of trips the steamers have made to the Island this year that they are difficult to hold.

The summer steamer service was proving highly popular. After 1882, a rival company, MacCallum and Co., tapped into the market with their vessel the *Hebridean*, later replaced by the *Hebrides*. Like the *Dunara Castle*, these initially made two voyages each summer; indeed, the *Hebridean* made three trips in 1882. Along with two visits from the Factor, the St Kildans were now enjoying six mail deliveries (weather permitting of course) in each four-month summer season. But they received none for the remainder of the year.

It would be interesting to know what the islanders thought of the steamers regularly blasting their hooters at the gannets, as they passed under the cliff colony on Boreray and its stacs. The resulting panic might have enhanced the visitor experience, but probably caused havoc to eggs and young as the parent birds took flight. In 1896, Richard Kearton aboard the *Dunara Castle* described one such demonstration:

> As the boat came abreast of the towering rock, some members of the crew loaded and ran out a small brass cannon. The tip of a red-hot poker applied to the touch-hole of the gun produced a deafening explosion, which seemed to be instantly flung back at us by Stac Lee, and then thundered and reverberated from crag to crag along the rocky shores of Borrera sending a great white cloud of startled gannets into the air above us.

On board the *Dunara Castle* on 24 May 1880 was a rather unpleasant lowland farmer, R. Scott Skirving (see Chapter 7). His fellow passengers graciously distributed tobacco, tea, oranges, illustrated papers, pictures and so on which the islanders received – according to Skirving – 'most unthankfully'. He wanted the out-of-date habit of handing out gifts to be discontinued, but he was impressed by the islanders' demonstration on the cliffs, cynically adding how it was:

> … the only manly thing the natives of St Kilda are capable of.
> … On bringing the Fulmars to the top the St Kildens [*sic*] showed themselves to be quite civilized so far as the practice of extortion goes. They demanded 2s 6d each for the Petrols [*sic*] but ultimately were glad to get 6d when they found no more could be got.

On Saturday 2 June 1883, HMS *Lively* brought Lord Napier (1819–1898) and five Royal Commissioners of Inquiry to St Kilda and, without any prior warning, they held a meeting in the church immediately on arrival. Their first witness was the minister who admitted that the islanders were better off both materially and morally than they had been when he had arrived 18 years before. He admitted that the steamers did not introduce alcohol to the islanders, but some of the passengers coming ashore were drunk and would peer rudely in the windows or strike the dogs. They were an especial nuisance when they were put ashore during the Sabbath. When the Commissioners went on a tour of Hirta, they immediately recognised the need for a pier to encourage more local fishing and were, of course, treated to the obligatory demonstration of fowling on the cliffs. The *Lively* departed later that same night.

In June 1884, the Inverness architect and geologist Alexander Ross (whom we met in Chapter 2) was able to visit St Kilda in the company of the Jura sportsman Henry Evans on his yacht *Erne*. Evans was to sail St Kildan waters on at least nine occasions. Where Skirving had been brutal about the St Kildans,

Ross – on an equally short encounter – found them 'good-looking, healthy and intelligent'. He also had a rather coloured impression that they were well fed, one shared with certain other casual visitors. Again, he was to notice that:

> The people have learned the value of money, and to enjoy many of the luxuries of civilised life ... they are learning to depend too much on their visitors, and really look on as their rights what the kindness of yachtsmen may lead them to give up ... Indeed, they run a great risk of being spoiled by visitors who go there in considerable numbers annually.

J. A. Clarke published a newspaper article about his voyage to St Kilda on the *Dunara Castle* on 23 June 1885. He too considered that the islanders appeared healthy, which he thought surprising when intermarriage must have been so prevalent. Indeed he thought them:

> ... rather pleasant-looking ... some of the younger women are even pretty, with sparkling eyes and expressive countenances; [a few of the older people however] did not impress one so favourably.

Clarke and his fellow passengers bought cloth, stockings, socks, eggs, live and dead birds, and 'a curious native brooch made out of a halfpenny beaten thin'. The local fowlers gave a demonstration on the cliffs and sold the birds they had caught before asking:

> ... a collection be made by way of payment for the exhibition of daring of which we had just been witnesses ... An impression prevails in the minds of many that the St Kildians know not the value of money, and they would be just as well pleased to receive a penny as a shilling, but from personal experience we can positively affirm the contrary.

Clarke attended the local church, but, at odds with some others, formed a favourable impression of the Reverend Mackay.

There followed a great storm in September 1885 which destroyed the island's corn and potatoes and one of their boats. Mailboats were set adrift in the hope of contacting the outside world. The *Hebridean* was despatched with supplies from the Clyde on 15 October, with Robert Connell, a correspondent from the *Glasgow Herald*. Connell was critical of everyone, commented how dirty the islanders were and viewed with trepidation the prospect of having to shake hands with them. A week later HMS *Jackal* landed on an identical mission of relief. Connell was to return for a fortnight the following summer with the Factor and the new schoolteacher, George Murray, on the 60-ton smack *Robert Hadden*. On seeing so many gloomy countenances, Connell joined Sands in a slightly unfair condemnation of the Reverend Mackay and his autocratic religious regime:

There can be no manner of doubt that for much of the unhealthy moral atmosphere pervading the island at present the ecclesiastical authority in the person of Mr Mackay is mainly responsible ... Men are enjoined to two hours devotions every week day, and eight on Sunday, when they must also wear a sad face and speak an octave under their usual voice. Whistling and singing are at all times tabooed ...

In 1887, Connell pulled his various journalistic efforts into a frank, informative but generally unsympathetic book entitled *St Kilda and the St Kildians*. Like Sands, Connell was vexed about the vulnerability of the islanders:

If nothing is done and things remain as they are, the condition of the Islands will go from bad to worse, and destitution periods will recur oftener ... One cannot be long on the island without discovering the great moral injury, that tourists and sentimentalists and yachtsmen, are working upon a kindly and simple people. They are making the St Kildian a fibreless creature ... The best gift that can now be made to the St Kildian is to teach him to help himself.

A strange little book was published by Robert Thomson in 1891 about his cruise aboard the *Hebridean* some years earlier; it kept alive the character assassination of the Reverend Mackay. The minister had, however, finally lost all respect in the community by 1889 so, having spent as long on the island as a distinguished predecessor, the Reverend Alexander Buchan, Mackay was asked to retire. His place was taken by another Gaelic-speaker from Easter Ross, Alexander Fiddes (born about 1843), who was on St Kilda as missionary, minister and teacher from 1889 to 1902. While he tended the community's spiritual welfare as zealously as Mackay, Fiddes would go down in island history as the man who helped eradicate the devastating infant tetanus.

Towards the end of the century, a third boat, Hutcheson's *Clydesdale*, was also undertaking cruises. We have seen from the various accounts already described in this chapter that St Kilda had indeed become a popular tourist attraction. Six steamers landed over 300 passengers each summer, while other yachts, private charters, naval ships, fishing boats and whalers dropped anchor in Village Bay. Indeed, in 1900, the folklorist Miss Ada Goodrich Freer (1857–1931) was moved to comment that while the more accessible Isle of Eriskay in the Outer Hebrides had only two visitors in two years, over 300 people had set foot on St Kilda in a single fortnight! She complained:

St Kilda, like Iona, has become the happy hunting ground of the Lowland tourist, and nearly every year some irresponsible book or magazine article, founded on a week's observations plus a Kodak camera, is added to the 'literature' on the subject ... The natives are deteriorating under the foolish treatment of those who 'take an interest' in them; who bring them presents of silver teaspoons, confectionery, silk aprons, mantelpiece ornaments, and silk handkerchiefs of tartans belonging to no clan in the island. A lady on her return showed me with much delight an old Celtic brooch she had 'picked up' for five shillings. It was made, doubtless, in anticipation of such purchasers, out of a brass safety pin and a penny key-ring (both new). Such an incident, I venture to say, could occur in no other island, not even in Iona ... The birds of St Kilda are its most interesting feature, but even they can be more than paralleled elsewhere in lovelier spots, and where the hand of man is less violent against them. We can remember with far more interest than St Kilda can invoke in us, at least half-a-dozen islands which, if geographically nearer to the world, are at least much more 'far from the madding crowd's ignoble strife.'

Why she should be so disparaging about St Kilda and disapproving of its inhabitants is not clear. Perhaps it was because she never got there. So presumably all she wrote was secondhand, which may not be surprising since she was to plagiarise the folksongs and folklore of Eriskay from its priest, the good Father Allan Macdonald. Curiously, she was an active investigator for the Society for Psychical Research, whose Vice-President was the third Marquis of Bute, grandfather of the Lord Dumfries who was later to buy St Kilda.

In 1697, Martin observed how the inhabitants made no distinction between a guinea and a sixpence, while half a century later MacAulay still asserted that they had no desire for either gold or silver. It is strange then that from 1800 or so the St Kildans were making ingenious wooden locks for their doors. Quite why such a close-knit and inter-related community should have felt the need for such security is a mystery. It tends to be a characteristic of island communities even today not to lock doors. I find it hard to accept Fleming's assertion that they were safeguarding their own little 'nest-eggs' of cash, or that they were striving to maintain a modicum of privacy. When I moved to South Uist to live, I only locked my door to stop the gales blowing it open in the middle of the night. Perhaps the St Kildans were doing the same!

Without a doubt though, with increasing visitors during the 19th century, the St Kildans now had a ready market for their wares – tweed, knitwear, some local crafts such as bronze brooches, wooden locks, or stone lamps, but especially stuffed birds and blown eggs. They also charged for ferrying passengers ashore from the steamer. A visitor in May 1907 put this at a shilling and it still remained at this level in 1931. But it was to prove a bone of contention between a grudging David Lack and the island warden Neil Gillies:

> The boat loads of trippers now came ashore, the St Kildans duly exacting from the first boat load one shilling per person. Finding this easily paid they exacted two shillings per person from the second boat. They presented us with a bill for

one pound five shillings for landing, but after much subsequent arguing we made this pay for our return journey as well. We were thus early introduced to the craving of the inhabitants for money ... [Neil] was incredibly mean with regard to money, charging for everything he did for us and several times as heavily as his services deserved. He took an intense dislike to us from the first, because we refused to pay the price he charged for landing us, so we saw him at great disadvantage ...

Tom Harrisson summed it up thus:

The islanders knew the value of money much better than we did. They were after every penny they could get out of us, but as there weren't any pennies to get, they didn't do very well. We found them difficult people to live with, on the whole ...

One day Lack and some of his party wanted to go to Dun, but Neil Gillies wanted ten shillings for himself and Finlay MacQueen to row the 20-minute journey – in a boat that was not his, but belonged to Alex Ferguson! Finlay was not party to this arrangement but Lack made sure he got his share of the fee – 'at which he was very surprised and pleased'. Gillies wanted a further two shillings if he found them a Leach's petrel nest. Lack thought this fair enough and in fact they were shown three petrel nests.

The Oxbridge students always seemed to be haggling with the islanders, but there were lighter moments too. One Sunday John Buchan astonished everyone – visitor and islander alike – by turning up to church in a smart lounge suit which he had packed for the steamer journey. Lack, a staunch Christian, rather admired Finlay MacQueen's adherence of the Sabbath and his conduct at Sunday worship. But the young scientist and his colleagues were constantly impressed by MacQueen's boldness in scrounging food and tobacco from passing ships and fishing boats.

Lack's party should have been fully provisioned for all eventualities. Anyone who visits an island, especially one as inaccessible as St Kilda, should know to take extra supplies in the event of delays by bad weather. There seemed to have been a slight difference of opinion within Lack's expedition about their provisions. John Buchan reported:

Our food was excellent. Breakfast consisted of porridge, bacon and egg, biscuits, butter, marmalade and tea. Lunch was handed out cold – a hard-boiled egg, an orange, two cabin biscuits, some dried prunes, figs or raisins, and some chocolate. Dinner was corned beef, potatoes and porridge, also biscuits and tea.

But after a week he had changed his mind:

We were all getting somewhat tired of the food and there had never been quite enough, even though we capped supper with huge quantities of porridge to make ourselves imagine we had eaten an enormous meal.

Harrisson was more frank:

We brought some food, mostly rice, porridge and oranges, with us. For the rest we relied largely on the island.

They tried killing sheep with the gun they had brought, and the islanders gave them mutton, puffins and fulmars. The expedition had no vegetables except a few plants they picked on the island. Fish was plentiful, even lobsters, bought from the three French fishing boats that came into the bay. The foreign crews seemed more generous and helpful than the Fleetwood boats. Not surprisingly, the young scientists were very concerned when the Fishery cruiser *Norna* arrived and arrested the French boats for fishing illegally. Lack pleaded with the captain of the cruiser to be lenient with them 'as those lobsters and claret meant a lot to us'. The boats were back to resume their illegal activities three days later! But at the end of the day, and somewhat unreasonably, the expedition seemed to expect the islanders to share in any handouts they got of fish and other provisions from the visiting fishing boats.

The disagreements that Lack and his privileged companions had with the

Fig. 35. Finlay MacQueen with a stuffed puffin (National Trust for Scotland).

islanders over food and money were at complete odds with the experience of Robert Atkinson seven years later, with the same individuals. Being a seasoned Hebridean traveller, Atkinson exhibited a much more sympathetic attitude to the St Kildans. Neil Gillies had become a rather disinterested bird warden for the proprietor, still a bit grudging. Sure, Finlay MacQueen was still scrounging tobacco at every opportunity, but Atkinson was happy to tolerate this for the privilege of their company and their stories, and for endless cups of tea. He was only too willing to share his own meagre supplies of food and whisky, considering it a small price to pay for enhancing his own enjoyment of the place.

A young Sutherland schoolteacher John Ross had been more measured, and probably wholly accurate, in his assessment when he taught for a summer at the St Kilda school in 1889:

> On a steamer day [the St Kildans] are seen in one sense to the best advantage, and in another to the worst advantage. Let me explain. They are seen to the best advantage in this way. A great part of the clothes is cleaned up in readiness for that occasion and some of them may put on a little extra in honour of the visitors, as they like to appear externally as decent as possible. Then their houses get a little bit of a turn to harmonize with their persons.
>
> Again, they are seen to the worst advantage in the way they generally act on such a day. Parties are very often if not always led to take an entirely wrong view of a St Kildan's character during a stay of a few hours. In fact the St Kildans are spoiled children, and as such must be dealt with. This is the only opportunity afforded them of 'turning a penny', and they use just overpressing in taking advantage of it . . .
>
> . . . Possibly you may at times make a Glasgow merchant reduce his price but the St Kildan stands to his price firm as the rocks that surround his island home . . .
>
> A few years ago visitors there used to scatter money right and left, and they [the islanders] expect that it should flow a little more freely now. This makes them actually look greedy, and when money is concerned this is only a failure common to many people, although it is more noticeable in such a small community, especially when so many eyes are eagerly watching to find some fault . . .
>
> The best and only way to remove this difficulty in St Kilda is to put the income of an honourable living within their reach, in the shape of a proper landing place for boats, and give them at least quarterly steamer calls to enable them to send their labour to, and bring goods direct and regularly from the market.

In 1884, Alexander Ross commented:

By the frequent visits of tourists and yachtsmen, and the liberal gifts of wine and clothes of the latest fashion, the St Kildian has ceased to be the simple unsophisticated mortal he was 30 years ago, and though by no means spoiled or importunate in his demands, he is, I believe, degenerating like some other of the Highlanders, and is not ashamed to accept gifts, if not to beg them.

This assessment was shared by Steele Elliott in 1894:

You are not long on the island before you learn that you are expected to have tobacco and several pounds of sweets about you, which you have to distribute among them for nothing. Strange as it may seem, sweets are the greatest weakness of the people; both man, woman and child are ready to render you any small service for a handful of sweets – especially peppermint – bestowed upon them.

Despite his brief sojourn on Hirta, the teacher John Ross took away with him a strong affection and sympathy for the islanders, offering this very pertinent retrospective:

They are as nice civil kind and honest a people to live among as can be found anywhere. Especially as to strangers, though at first sight, from their strange behaviour when under excitement, one is very apt to form quite a different opinion of them. But the better one gets acquaint with them, the more one is convinced that at heart they are a well enough meaning people. They are very determined in their own way however ...

The children are exceedingly nice and clever, and ... they have made wonderful progress. The older ones can speak the English nicely, and the younger ones are well on the road. Intermarriage has not weakened their intellect in the least. They are as bright as the children on the mainland.

While there is inconsistency amongst visitors about how they perceived the islanders, and indeed what they thought of their minister Reverend Mackay, there does emerge a trend in attitudes. Most short-term visitors – unless of romantic bent – saw the St Kildans as grasping. Their published accounts, often based on the briefest of encounters, then enshrined this view for posterity. We have seen how some visitors, probably encountering the islanders on a bad day when alcohol was suddenly available, would condemn their drinking habits. It probably would not take much to get a mostly dry community inebriated. Other visitors maintained that alcohol was not an issue on St Kilda. Attitudes very much depended upon circumstances on the day of a visit. Visitors who stayed any length of time invariably experienced the St Kildans' better side. Sands and Ross, for instance, acquired a distinct empathy towards the islanders in their unforgiving situation. The Heathcotes and the Keartons too struck up some firm friendships.

Richard and Cherry Kearton described their time on St Kilda in 1896 in their book *With Nature and a Camera*, published the following year. They arrived off the *Dunara Castle* in June and lodged in the Factor's House. They found the islanders fearfully inquisitive but scrupulously honest. They considered St Kilda to be:

> ... the only place in Scotland where drunkenness is unknown, although it is said that all the inhabitants keep a supply of whisky by them for use in cases of illness, Such admirable self-restraint is worthy of all praise ... In addition to enjoying a unique character for sobriety, St Kilda can also boast the distinction of being the only inhabited part of the British Isles which has not been officially surveyed by Her Majesty's Ordnance Department.

As we have seen, this latter task was not accomplished until John Mathieson's visit in 1927. The Keartons went to hear the Reverend Fiddes preach, but, where Sands had described the islanders on their way to church as 'the troop of the damned being driven by Satan to the bottomless pit', the Keartons found the churchgoers cheerful and quite ready to chat as they made their way home. Indeed, the brothers won the friendship of the islanders and, after their visit, continued to correspond with one or two of them.

The Keartons accompanied Finlay Gillies, Finlay MacQueen, Neil Ferguson and other skilled fowlers to Soay, Dun and Boreray. Back home from his business in Glasgow, another St Kildan, Alex Ferguson, also accompanied them and posed for photographs on a rope over the cliffs. Richard watched as his brother got into a very hazardous and awkward situation 'from which he managed to take a photograph of the ex-fowler in the holiday war-paint of Buchanan Street'.

On 20 March the following spring, Neil Ferguson sent Richard a letter, via a mailboat from Hirta, recalling the event:

> ... thinking of the day I was with you and Cherry photographing, when a big stone fell from your feet and nearly killed Cherry.

On their departure on 24 June, Richard Kearton concluded:

> We had endeared ourselves to [the islanders] by frank dealing and readiness to go where they went, endure what they endured, give tobacco and sweets, or accept whey and bannock in the same simple spirit.

Other steamer passengers who took time to get to know the St Kildans were Norman Heathcote and his sister Evelyn, friends of the Laird, who stayed for ten days in July 1898, and then a whole summer in 1899. Heathcote considered there to be a regular invasion of visitors, the island population often being 'temporarily augmented by something like 20 souls, some on pleasure, some on business bent'.

The visitors on business were masons and carpenters employed in building a new school on to the church. Like Sands and the Keartons, the Heathcotes' sensitive approach to the islanders in turn earned them friendship and respect, and thus they were able to provide in their book a rare insight into the issues that the islanders themselves wished to highlight. Indeed, having spent the winter attempting to become fluent in Gaelic, Miss Heathcote was asked in 1898 to lay the foundation stone of the new school.

Norman Heathcote's account is a delightful read. He apologised for producing yet another book about St Kilda, but emphasised how he had exceptional opportunities for studying the people. He preferred Martin's work to that of MacAulay and expressed relief that Dr Johnson was no longer around to criticise his own first literary effort! Armed with a theodolite, Heathcote also produced (and published through the Royal Geographical Society) what he himself thought was the best map yet of St Kilda – which was true.

After a brief summary of the island and its history, Heathcote went on to assess the islanders' character, an affectionate but probably quite truthful summary:

> Some writers have accused them of being grasping. Possibly the fact that so many people have given them presents, and that they have been paid liberally, often too liberally, for anything they have done, has tended to make them so, but we certainly did not discover it. They have been presented with boats, nets, ropes, furniture, food and all kinds of things at various times, and I am afraid it is a trait of human nature, not so much to be grateful to the people who give, as to be annoyed with those who don't ... I dare say that their limited knowledge of the value of money has been partly responsible for their reputation of greed. Until quite recently, when pedlars have taken to visiting the island, and have made it possible for the women to spend 3s 6d on a coloured handkerchief worth perhaps 4d, they have had no use for money. Rent was paid in kind, and all their wants were supplied by the factor in exchange for cloth, oil, etc. It is hardly to be wondered at that the gentleman who asked the natives to get him a fulmar's egg, and was told that the price was a sovereign, should form the opinion that they were greedy for money; but the explanation is that, a short time before, a wealthy yachtsman had asked for the same article, and had generously, but, from an ethical point of view, wrongfully, given them a sovereign for their trouble. They were absolutely ignorant of the true market value of the egg, and, not unnaturally, assumed that, if it was worth 20s to one man, it would be so also to another.
>
> I find it difficult to make up my mind as to whether they are lazy or not. There is no doubt they waste a lot of time; but I am inclined to think that this is because they are as ignorant of the value of time as of the value of money

... If there is some doubt as to the laziness of the men, there is none as to the energy of the women.

Where even the Keartons had failed to photograph the women milking ewes at the shieling, Norman Heathcote managed it. Summing up his experiences, he wrote:

I should say they are the most truly religious people I have ever come across, not merely because they go to church a great deal and have daily prayers in their houses morning and evening, but because they seem really devout and honestly believe their religion to be the most important part of their life ...

... I have done my best to give a fair picture of the lonely island and its people; I have not slurred over their faults, but I hope I have also made clear their virtues; I have dilated upon the charms of the scenery and the fascination of the mode of life; but I trust that I have also laid sufficient stress upon the difficulties of getting there, and the discomforts and dangers of the place, to deter most people from going thither.

He could not resist adding:

I admit that this smacks rather of the dog-in-the-manger; indeed, that this is the feeling that prompted the remark. There is not room for more than a few outsiders to enjoy themselves in St Kilda at the same time; and as I hope to spend many more pleasant holidays in 'the last of the sea-girt Hebrides', I don't want to find my happy hunting-grounds invaded by a host of Sassenachs!

But visitors continued to arrive. A pioneer in bird photography, called Oliver Pike (1877–1963), lugged hefty camera equipment with him to make one of the classic early cine films of St Kilda and the St Kildans (still available today on DVD). On this his first visit Pike wanted a shot for his film of a woman spinning. She demanded half a crown and would only pose behind the house where her neighbours would not see her. It was all over in 30 seconds. Afterwards her daughter appeared with two shillings, saying that her mother thought she had asked too much. On another day he tried to film the women milking in Gleann Mor, but they preferred not to appear until it was too dark for him to film. One woman slipped and sprained her ankle, blaming the accident on the cine camera. But the resourceful Pike was able to turn this to advantage by telling her it actually was because they had refused to be filmed.

On 29 March 1949 he wrote to James Fisher from Leighton Buzzard, Bedfordshire:

My first visit to St Kilda was the first fortnight of [June] 1908. On this occasion I went alone and had rotten weather, there were really only three days that we could use a boat. My visit to Stac Lee was on my last full day and I had to bribe the natives heavily to launch a boat ... My second visit to St Kilda was in 1910 [with two friends] We had wonderful weather the whole time. This was the first fortnight of July ... I climbed to the top of Stac Lee on both visits. If you should be visiting the islands again, take great care if you attempt to climb Stac Lee, it's a desperate job: I have made some rather dangerous climbs in my time, but nothing could touch this. There is only one track up, and I doubt if it would be possible to climb it without a guide. Most of the climb is fairly good, but just over halfway up, there is a horrible corner where you are practically back downwards with the sea beneath. I couldn't have done it without a rope fore and aft!

Pike's words only strengthen one's admiration for Evelyn Heathcote's earlier conquest of Stac Lee. A few months later Pike wrote to Fisher again:

I enclose an additional shot of Stac Lee with our track marked in red. If you go there again it might be useful, but take care, it's a hell of a climb, and I advise anyone attempting it to make chalk marks on the rocks in ascending to help in the descent, for if you miss the one and only track you will be a fixture for life! Also you should ascend in three, roped together. Wish I was young enough to have another shot at it.

The islanders had been reluctant to take Pike to Stac Lee the first time. They rowed for three solid hours and managed to get ashore despite the swell. It proved a strenuous climb, but at the top Pike was able to film the gannets, including the one occupying the very highest point, as he described in one of his books:

Imagine the scene ... It was a wild pandemonium – like a panic amongst a crowd – a screaming, terrified panic, with beautiful birds for the actors, and the helpless fluffy youngsters as the spectators. It was a great avalanche of living birds, rolling down to the edge of the cliff, and I stood transfixed with the tremendous novelty of the scene ... The descent of Stac Lii was even more difficult than the ascent. Again roping ourselves together in Alpine fashion, we crept and climbed slowly down, while all around us the birds shuffled from our path. At last, with torn clothes and tired limbs, we found ourselves half-way down, and we rested on a narrow ledge crowded with talkative guillemots. 'There's worse to come,' said one of the St Kildans. 'Just round the corner there's a very dangerous place.' I thought that if the plucky natives said it was dangerous, it certainly must be a very desperate place, and so it proved to be ...

The next morning I left St Kilda and the kind natives heaped little presents upon me, such as gloves and socks which they had made themselves. Altogether they were not exactly the kind of things one could wear in society, yet I valued them very much, for they were given in a real spirit of friendship. Nearly every one of the natives, men, women and children, insisted on shaking hands many times as I walked down to the shore, and I look forward to the time when I shall again have the pleasure of meeting them.

But three of these brave men I shall never see again, for on 18 April 1909, I received a sad letter from one of the islanders which was brought over by a fishing trawler. It appears that five men went out on a bird-catching expedition, and soon after the boat left the shore it capsized, and three of its inmates were drowned, namely Donald Macdonald, Norman MacQueen, and John MacQueen, three men who helped me in my work several times during my stay on the island. This tragedy was a terrible blow to the little village, and it was long before the gloom passed away.

Pike returned two years later in July 1910 with two friends, both keen naturalists: Dr Donald Hutchinson, who did early work with colour photography, and E. Richmond Paton, the nature artist. It was their intention to live for a fortnight in tents, notwithstanding that they had been warned that it was impossible to get a tent to stand on the windswept island. Pike was critical of the islanders' apparent laziness, or unwillingness to do anything unless they were paid, and especially about their cruelty to animals, whether birds or sheep:

> The St Kildans must learn that even if birds and sheep are killed for food there is a humane way of killing them. But apart from these faults, and if any of the natives should see these enumerated here, let them remember that I have mentioned them simply for their own good, so that they may learn to be more kind. The people of St Kilda are exceedingly interesting, and with these faults missing it would be a fine race.
>
> All the men are magnificent climbers, and I would trust myself on a cliff with a St Kildan for my guide. In my travels I have never seen one to equal any of the St Kildan cliff men.
>
> We had remarkably good weather during our stay on the island. Not a drop of rain fell in the fortnight, although on the mainland it was very wet. And so each day we tried to get out amongst the birds with our cameras. Dr Hutchison was very successful with his colour photography, and secured some wonderful instantaneous photographs taken by the autochrome process. On the first calm day we made a trip to Stac Lii ... Not many strangers have succeeded in reaching the top, and at all times it is a difficult and nerve-trying ordeal; but of this I am certain; the Doctor was the first man who ever went to the top of that rock, six hundred feet above the sea, with a broken rib! But he did it and had the satisfaction of standing on the topmost rock.

Most steamer passengers viewed St Kilda as little more than any other far-flung outpost of the Empire and treated the islanders as mere objects of curiosity. In June 1883, one of the islanders told the Napier Commission:

> Some of them are drunk when they come ashore, but the people avoid them as far as they can. They are very annoying when they remain here over the Sabbath.

But he did admit:

> ... they leave a good deal of money among the people.

Heathcote was moved to lament:

> Many tourists treat [the islanders] as if they were wild animals at the zoo. They throw sweets at them, openly mock them, and I have seen them standing at the church door during service, laughing and talking and staring in as if at an entertainment got up for their amusement.

An obligatory presence on the steamship was the commercial photographer who would pose cameos of any islanders who were willing and sell them to the passengers as souvenir postcards condescendingly labelled 'The natives of St Kilda'. But such postcards brought custom to the island Post Office, which also came to stock its own postcards. Clearly, they were a useful contribution to the island economy. The ex-National Serviceman and historian James Mackay in his *Postal History of Harris and St Kilda* (1978) quoted the postmaster in Lochmaddy:

> Every trip this season (1903) there has been posted at St Kilda an average of 600 pictorial post cards. These post cards of St Kilda were for sale on the steamer and nearly all the passengers have them written ready for posting.

It seems the islanders quickly realised that posing for postcards could be just as lucrative. In 1896, the photographer Richard Kearton heard how the islanders demanded money to be photographed, which was not his own experience:

> The men never objected to our photographing them, nor, so far as I could gather, expecting anything for allowing us to do so, though had they done, we could not have had serious reason for complaint ...
>
> Before passing judgement on these poor creatures, it is only fair to them to take evidence on both sides of the question of their selfishness, and then throw in a little consideration for the influence of their utter isolation and the folly of tourists and other visitors who have done much towards the destruction of that ideal state of unwordliness which characterised them only as far back as 1697, when they 'condemned gold and silver as below the dignity of human nature'.

It is clear from the Keartons and Heathcotes that the more one got to know the St Kildans, the better impression one formed. A few short-term visitors were just as touched by their whole, albeit brief, St Kildan experience as long-term visitors. As early as 1834, Sir Thomas Dyke Acland left £20 to purchase windows and furniture for each household. In 1851, Charles Kelsall left a handsome bequest for the islanders, which eventually led to new housing. One Miss Macleod covered the cost of the first resident nurse on the island between 1879 and 1880.

Captain Otter was particularly kind to the islanders. In 1876, John Sands had delivered a boat which he deemed big enough to ply between St Kilda and Harris, thus attempting to cut out the middleman (the Factor) from local economic transactions. Acts of benevolence were, however, relatively rare.

Alongside the growing cash economy, such well-meaning attempts to bring the St Kildans into the 19th century actually contributed to the community's slow decline, as well as increasing its dependence upon largesse from outside. The new houses were said to be the most modern in the Hebrides at the time, but were never as comfortable as the St Kildans' own design which had been perfected over generations to cope with the harsh conditions they endured. The old houses, with rounded corners, sensibly presented their gable ends to the elements, while the door and windows of the new ones faced the sea. The new zinc roofs were soon replaced by tarred felt roofs, which at least were not quite as noisy. Attempts at providing a landing stage and then a pier never fulfilled expectations and were highly vulnerable to winter storms.

Providing the islanders with a boat of their own that could maintain contact with civilisation, reducing dependence upon the Factor for disposal of their produce, only led to disaster. Two years after Captain Otter delivered the 30-ft *Dargavel*, she disappeared in April 1863 on a voyage to Harris, with the loss of seven men and a woman – Betty Scott from Lochinver who had come as housekeeper for the Reverend Neil Mackenzie and married an islander. Many more boats, often paid for by the Kelsall Fund, were to be wrecked as they lay ashore, but fortunately with no more loss of life, that is until three men were drowned taking sheep to Dun in March 1909 – the tragedy to which Pike had referred to earlier.

Where the islanders once dealt with occasional privation and tragedy in their own way, they were now becoming reliant on goodwill from beyond. Even the vital necessity of securing enough crops and seabirds to last overwinter was being eroded. Despite the worthy efforts of Captain Otter and his naval colleagues, successive governments repeatedly failed the St Kildan community. It was largely left to visiting shipping to provide the most basic of public services. After 1877 the steamers provided a safer means of communication with the outside world, but for only four months in summer, and even then weather-dependent. But the unsung heroes of the St Kildans were the fishing boats and whalers, especially the Fleetwood trawlers, as Alexander Macleod, the son of the missionary and teacher John Macleod, attested:

> The trawlers, mainly from Fleetwood, frequently sheltered in Village Bay transforming the night into a twinkling Fairyland of lights. How indebted we were to those intrepid mariners. They ferried our mails to and fro, they gave us generous gifts of fish and they gave us their time and their company by coming ashore and visiting our houses.

The St Kildan Lachlan Macdonald told how they would often see trawlers in the bay in the wintertime, not so often in the summer. Some would be from Fleetwood, others from Hull or Aberdeen. The teacher from 1906 to 1909, Alice Maclachlan, recalled no fewer than 17 boats sheltering in the bay during a storm. One of the kindest of skippers, Captain Walker of the *Knowsie*, was arrested in April 1907 and imprisoned in Aberdeen for fishing illegally. Mrs Maclachlan, her husband the minister, and some of the prominent islanders, wrote a letter to the Scottish Office pointing out how dependent the community was upon such men and that they were petitioning for his release. It must have proved successful for the bold captain arrived back in St Kilda in early May to great rejoicing.

Ironically, World War I and the presence of the naval attachment brought a host of benefits to the St Kildans, as the St Kildan Donald John Gillies, latterly a church minister in Canada, recalled in Quine (1988):

> When the War came we were never so well on St Kilda. You were even working sometimes and being paid for it, and you were getting mail every week or twice a week. You would start building for the Gun and get 2/6 a day. There were four [islanders] engaged during the War itself ... They were on a watch and they built a place on Mullach Mor and were round the clock there watching the North Bay.

The steamers of course brought essential supplies in the summer months with handouts of sweets and tobacco from visitors. They generated an even more lucrative opportunity for commerce. Ultimately, as everywhere else in the kingdom had already done, St Kilda was fast developing more of a cash economy than a self-sufficient one.

The islanders quickly realised that steamer passengers and other visitors to St Kilda wanted souvenirs to remind them of their intrepid voyage. In July 1890, Robert Thomson came off the *Hebrides* and observed:

> Several purchases of stockings, cloth, birds, and eggs were made, and very good prices indeed were paid in current coin of the realm for all such articles, but here as in many places elsewhere, a few were more forward and greedy than others, and would have taken all the visitors had in fact, some of them had no hesitation

in asking point blank for anything which took their fancy, and very persistent they were in their demands. The trail of the serpent in this and various ways is seen in St Kilda, where one would expect to find every inhabitant pure and good, and the village a little heaven below, without stain or sin.

Understandably, the islanders relished and exploited the opportunity to sell tweed, woollens and souvenirs. Norman Heathcote felt that the islanders could have introduced improvements further to develop the manufacture of cloth:

> The wool of the St Kilda sheep is beautifully soft, and the cloth made from it is first-rate stuff. Personally I habitually wear it in the country, but many people object to it because, being made of undyed wool, it is rather light in colour. The St Kildans use indigo for their own clothes, in fact you hardly ever see a native wearing a suit made from the natural wool, but for export they never use any dye. When they take the trouble to collect the wool from the Soay sheep, which is even finer and softer than the rest, they mix the brown wool with the white and produce a rather darker cloth, but they are always rather slack about getting it, and some years do not bother about it at all. The Harris tweeds are more popular, because the use of dyes introduces variety. There is no reason why the St Kildans should not produce a similar cloth, they have crotal on the island and indigo is easily imported. They say it is expensive, but their method of using it makes it much more expensive than it need be. Instead of having a common dyeing pot for the whole island, each family dyes its wool separately, obviously a very wasteful process.

In 1887, Robert Connell described how every St Kilda man had five or six distinct occupations – crofter, cragsman, fisherman, tailor, cobbler and weaver:

> His loom is in operation for only about two months of the year, when the nights are at their longest and outdoor work is suspended . . . The work is carried on with astonishing zeal [and] . . . certainly proves the capacity of the people for work.

In 1927, John Mathieson noted how the islanders exported 1,000–1,200 yards of tweed annually. John Gladstone added that the St Kildans sold tweed to tourists at five shillings a yard, while the whole of 1927's output had been acquired by mainland buyers to be made up into 124 men's overcoats and sold in America. He noted that few shawls and gloves were being made at that time as there had not been much demand.

A not inconsiderable part of the islanders' trade was in souvenirs and particularly in specimens of the local natural history, some of them obtainable nowhere else in the country. Eggs were blown and birds stuffed for sale, not just to naturalists and collectors but also the run-of-the-mill tourists. Joseph Wiglesworth (1903) noted that the eggs of raven, hooded crow, peregrine, shag,

*Fig. 36. The Duchess
of Bedford.*

gannet, eider, great black-backed gull, guillemot, puffin, shearwater and storm petrel were all on offer, while the St Kildans had the British monopoly on the eggs of fulmar, Leach's petrel and St Kilda wren. Most eggs of the common species sold for a penny each, while those of Manx shearwater fetched a shilling, and a clutch from the wren as much as £5. In 1890, John Ross noted that 'some of them send boxes of these [seabird eggs] away by Parcels Post to collectors'.

Undoubtedly, eggs and skins of Leach's petrel were particularly valuable. Since 1818 it was known that St Kilda was one of its few British breeding stations. Such was the demand from museums and collectors that both eggs and old birds were being taken by the natives. According to Elliott (1895) the petrels were 'kept in stockings till the arrival of visitors, when these once beautiful little birds, now starved and mauled, are offered for sale'.

When dealers on the mainland began placing orders for any number of rare species, the market began to escalate to a worrying extent. Acts for the preservation of seabirds had been passed as long ago as 1869 and 1880, but due to the dependence of the St Kildans on fowling, these islands had always been exempt. In a new Act of 1904 this exemption for food species such as fulmars, gannets, puffins and razorbills still applied, but Leach's petrels and St Kilda wrens, and their eggs, had to be given special protection.

Mary, Duchess of Bedford, arrived in her yacht on 23 August 1910:

> St Kilda at last! After spending a whole week in almost birdless wastes waiting for a favourable wind for St Kilda, I have at last managed to get there ... I came to land some stores for Mr Eagle Clarke, who hopes to spend a month here, and not with the hope of studying birds on this much-described and visited island. Migration seasons, however, when tourists are quiescent, would be very interesting if one were able to live on the island.
>
> I was lucky enough to arrive just at the time that the cliff climbers were catching young fulmars. Anything so foolish as the conduct of these birds, which, though apparently able to fly, sit still to have their necks wrung, can hardly be equalled in the avian world. Their only attempts at defence is the squirting of oil, which has no terrors for the St Kildaite.
>
> The inhabitants told me that there was great excitement when the yacht arrived, as some of them guessed it was mine, because they had heard that I was going to buy the island. It is the first that I have heard of it.

She returned on 23 May 1914:

> Went on board at Tarbert, Harris for breakfast and left for St Kilda. There was rather a heavy swell, but fortunately from the west, and we arrived and anchored about 1.30 pm.
>
> The islanders swarmed down to the pier as usual with tweed and other things to sell, and then followed me in procession. The adults soon tailed off, but some of the boys are an appalling nuisance. In spite of repeated requests to clear off, they follow close at one's heels, and if one stops or sits down, stand and stare for an unlimited time.
>
> I have bought nothing from them and do not intend to do so, as they have been quite sufficiently demoralised by tourists already. It is a great pity, as these people are naturally kind-hearted and hospitable, like those one meets in lonely parts of the Outer Hebrides, but now they have degenerated into a race of beggars.
>
> As an example of the ways of St Kildans, as taught them by tourists, I was asked 2s 6d for a razorbill's egg; the owner's reply, when asked the price, being 'I've been getting 2s 6d for this colour.' One woman insisted upon giving me a pair of knitted gloves and refused to take payment for them, but afterwards asked me to help her father buy a new boat – price £20. I should have refused the gloves at all costs, had I not brought them three sacks of flour, and for the moment had allowed myself to believe the present was an act of gratitude. I only know one place in the world where the people behave worse with tourists, and that is on the Island of Maarken, in Holland. I daresay if one can stay in the place some

time and settle down amongst them as Mr Eagle Clarke did, their natural good qualities may reveal themselves.

Before leaving I received a written petition from the islanders through their missionary, Mr MacArthur, to assist them in getting a life-boat and to improve their landing stage. I took the opportunity of telling him what I thought of my reception, with the result that, having expressed a desire to buy three or four fulmar eggs for Henry, I found 9 placed in the dinghy on my return, with no donor forthcoming and none to accept payment for them.

For all her moral high ground, the good Duchess was going to buy some birds' eggs after all! In the *Scotsman* of 15 May 1907 a 'Medical Inspector' recorded:

> On board the steamer the St Kildians did a fair trade in guillemot's eggs, at 6d per egg; and each person was charged a shilling for the privilege of being rowed ashore.

Such trade quickly developed into a cottage industry. That same year, 1907, saw one Manchester dealer make 'a short but successful collecting trip to St Kilda' and the following summer he sought subscribers for a return visit to the Hebrides including St Kilda:

> The abundance of bird life in these islands enables me to guarantee for the sum of £15 the large and representative collection of which I append full particulars, but the arduous nature of the work compels me to limit the number of my subscribers to ten. The specimens would be delivered in the form of first-class cabinet skins with full data attached to each. Apart from the educational value of such a series of British birds, many are likely to greatly increase in value owing to their growing scarcity, and to the increasing stringency of the Wild Bird protection laws.

Of course, his 'guaranteed series of birds' included the St Kilda wren and the Leach's petrel, both specifically protected by Act of Parliament. The *Annals of Scottish Natural History* printed the offending circular (Brazenor 1908), but only with the intention of bringing the proposed raid to the attention of the appropriate proprietors and the Society for the Protection of Birds.

Perhaps this Manchester dealer had inspired a 'rewarding little hobby' for Calum Macdonald's father William:

> This was catching wild birds and stuffing them in the tradition of a taxidermist. He sold the finished product to the Manchester Museum in return of cash which helped to pay for the little extras that most families enjoyed.

Not surprisingly, the distinctive St Kilda mice were of interest only to specialists and museums and were never in any great demand.

Undeterred by the law, the islanders continued their lucrative, if illicit, market in eggs and skins. In addition to regular tourist vessels, specialist naturalists and obsessive collectors such as J. A. Harvie-Brown and W. Eagle Clarke were doubtless good customers, while others, such as the Duchess of Bedford and Henry Evans, made repeated visits in their own private yachts. Evans, for instance, made no fewer than nine visits in total in the *Erne*, and many other wealthy tourists and naturalists must go unrecorded. In 1931, Tom Harrrisson recorded that 400 Leach's petrel eggs were still being sold by the St Kildans every year.

Since most visitors arrived outwith the fowling season, the islanders could also be paid to stage special demonstrations of their climbing skills. Heathcote noted:

> Very few writers on St Kilda have spent more than a few days there, some only a few hours; and though most of them saw exhibitions of the prowess of the natives on the cliffs, such as any tourist who visits the island may see, no-one, as far as I can make out, has been an eye-witness of the serious business of the St Kildan fowling expeditions, and most of these accounts are written from hearsay.

George Seton noted how convenient sheer cliffs, such as at the Gap in Hirta, tended to be used for climbing displays so as not to disturb the young fulmars on their nest ledges. However, many of the photographs taken of these

Fig. 37. A bird collector on St Kilda (David Clugston collection).

*Fig. 38. St Kildan boys blowing eggs with Alex Ferguson to sell to tourists
(National Trust for Scotland).*

summer exploits do show adult fulmars and puffins being caught which was not a healthy situation for the longer-term sustainability of the seabird harvest. Furthermore, as the human population of St Kilda diminished along with the number of able-bodied men, visits to other islands and stacs to harvest seabirds became less frequent. So the pressure on Hirta's colonies must have increased.

Thus we can see that, up until 1939, and at least in the brief summer months, St Kilda was not at all as remote or isolated as it is today. Furthermore, the islanders were by then deriving a considerable income from birds' eggs, skins, tweed, knitted garments and other souvenirs, cliff-climbing demonstrations or even just posing for photographs. The economy that built up around this trade had become an important part of the islanders' very existence and life-style, and one that they had come to depend upon. The extent of this might compare to that operating upon St Kilda today. As part of their duties, successive summer wardens and rangers on St Kilda note the number of vessels and visitors that reach the islands. Fig. 39 shows the number of visitors each year from 1986 to 2008.

It is immediately obvious that nowadays as many visitors come by private yacht as by charter boat (about 400 each), almost all during the months of June, July and August. Visitors rarely exceeded a thousand per annum, until the 1990s when larger cruise boats began to include the archipelago on their

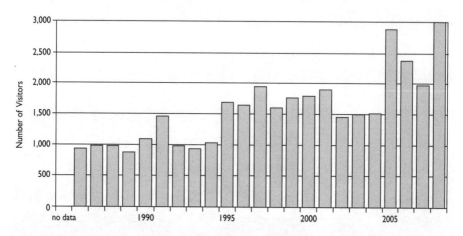

Fig. 39. Annual visitor numbers on Hirta 1986–2008.

itinerary. Thereafter annual numbers increased by several hundred but still fall short of 2000. In 2001, the *Black Prince* alone (one of three cruise ships that July) landed 374 tourists, more than compensating for the restrictions in access that operated earlier in the season due to the Foot and Mouth outbreak. Its passengers were unable to land in the next three years due to bad weather, but 400 were ashore in 2005. That year 14 cruise ships were able to land a total of 1,382 passengers. I was a Lecturer with the National Trust for Scotland cruise aboard the *Spirit of Adventure* on 4 June 2008 when nearly 350 passengers were landed.

Furthermore, in 2005, day trips began on a regular basis from Harris, no more than 12 passengers on three or four days of each week through the summer, weather permitting of course. That first year 677 day-trippers were landed and it is expected that in future years this will exceed 1,000, trebling the annual visitor numbers. In 2006, visitor numbers were down 18 per cent, largely because of fewer cruise ship visits, only nine putting 853 people ashore. Only now perhaps is St Kilda approaching the accessibility and exceeding the visitor numbers it once enjoyed over a century ago.

From 1877 to 1939, at least one steamer carrying up to 60 passengers arrived in St Kilda every ten days or so during two or three months each summer. Thus, together with private charters, fishing boats and naval patrol vessels, it is likely that visitor numbers a hundred years ago may have been little different from those of the 1980s and 1990s. (We might recall Ada Goodrich Frier's estimate of 300 visitors on Hirta in one single fortnight!) Currently, the takings from books, postcards and other souvenirs being sold in the St Kilda Club shop on the island peaked at £32,000 in 2005. This might indicate, taking into account the exchange rate, that in peak years the St Kildans themselves with their birds' eggs and skins, tweed, woollen goods and other souvenirs were indeed able to derive a not-insubstantial income from tourism.

Charles Maclean (1972) considered that the introduction of money into the lives of the St Kildans introduced a dependence upon it and upon its acquisition. The islanders lost interest in seeking sufficient food for themselves, preferring to buy in supplies (and indeed luxuries) from the mainland. Notwithstanding, the season was short.

By the beginning of the 20th century, the attractions of St Kilda for tourists were beginning to wane. Deliveries by steamers in the summer, and by whalers and fishing trawlers in winter, were limited and erratic, only to be disrupted totally by World War I.

A small naval attachment was stationed on Hirta between 1915 and 1919 and some of the islanders gained employment as watchers, labourers or radio officers. (Two of them were to see military service in the Forces.) Sixteen arrived by armed trawler on 12 January 1915, the personnel being changed every four months or so.

In reality, St Kilda's real war began and ended on 15 May 1918 when a German submarine surfaced in Village Bay. Finlay MacQueen was about to row out to scrounge some tobacco when the U-boat shouted out a warning to the islanders by loud hailer, before it shelled the village. Seventy-two rounds demolished the Feather Store and severely damaged the church, the manse, two cottages and the wireless station. The islanders had fled for shelter in the Dry Burn and fortunately no one was injured. The radio was quickly repaired. In October a 4-inch gun (bearing the date 1896 on its breech) was installed just beyond the Feather Store; it was never fired in anger and remains the sole relic of St Kilda's Great War.

For a short time at least, with the naval supply from Stornoway, along with patrolling armed trawlers and whalers, the island enjoyed a near weekly boat service. Some of the men had even been receiving wages, but when peace came that standard of living could not be maintained. One of the islanders, Alex Ferguson, had left St Kilda to become a successful businessman in Glasgow and was acting as an independent agent for the sale of the St Kildans' products. The *Hebrides* and *Dunara Castle* had resumed four sailings each in the summer months. The naturalist Seton Gordon (1886–1977) arrived off the *Dunara Castle* on 26 June 1927 and stayed six days, long enough to visit Boreray and, with Mathieson and Cockburn, landed on Soay. Seton Gordon contributed an account of St Kilda birds for Mathieson's report in the *Scottish Geographical Magazine*. He also included an account of his visit in *Islands of the West* (1933), one of 27 books he wrote in his long and illustrious life. He was also a piper, a lifelong hillwalker with a deep love of the Hebrides and the Cairngorms, but he was also a renowned photographer, most famous perhaps for his work on golden eagles. He was in error however in *Islands of the West* when he said his St Kilda visit took place in 1928; it actually took place the year before.

But such visitors do not seem to have been all that frequent in the first decades of the 20th century. The Great War was to offer a few opportunities for islanders, and even an income for some, but the impacts upon the island economy must have been very influential in the St Kildans' decision to quit.

In June 1929, amateur naturalists Frank and Betty Lowe married at home in Bolton, but were determined to honeymoon on St Kilda. Frank (1904–85) was a passionate photographer of wildlife and, with his brother, ran a small textile manufacturers in the north of England. He would write a *New Naturalist* monograph on the heron in 1954 and served as the wildlife correspondent for the *Bolton Evening News* for 59 years. His interest in St Kilda had been inspired by the Keartons' book and he was encouraged in his passion by Richard Kearton himself. Little did the new bride suspect what was in store for her!

> To take some of the pictures, my wife will be lowered down steep cliffs by a rope and will have to hang there motionless for indefinite periods until the birds are in the right poses for the pictures. It is a great strain but it is the work she loves. She is a tremendous help to me.

They found lodgings with a widow in No. 13, sharing their room with St Kilda mice, which had been known to nest in the bed! These would, of course, have been house mice, doomed to extinction within a few years. In the main room was an open grate, over which a cauldron hung, Nearby was a spinning wheel or loom, also a gannet wing used as a sweeping brush. For lighting, fulmar oil was kept in the stomach of a gannet and gannet quills served as wicks.

By that time the human population had dwindled to 37 and the islanders appeared shy and treated the visitors rather coldly until they were offered sweets. Surprisingly, one old man refused an offer of tobacco, but pounced on boiled sweets. Lowe admired the way the islanders waged what he called 'a long, dour conflict with the forces of nature'. He was led to believe that no naturalist had landed on the island for 20 years – but this cannot have been true. As Pike had done, Frank too shot some movie film, which for years would augment his popular lantern slide shows back home. But by then, of course, nobody was living on St Kilda.

The observation made by Anthony Trollope in 1878, and others before and since, was about to become reality:

> Who shall say that these people ought to be deported from the homes and placed recklessly upon some point of the mainland? I have not the courage to say ... But yet their existence cannot be good for them, and certainly not for their posterity;

and as far as we can judge a time will come when that posterity must die out unless the people be removed.

On the first trip of the *Hebrides* on 31 May 1930 the purser recorded how the islanders had anticipated their fate:

A favourable passage and excellent landing attended our first call of the season at St Kilda, The cargo landed consisting mostly of foodstuffs, no doubt will supply the needs of the inhabitants, which according to the Public press, were so urgent. The request by the natives for leaving the island seems to be genuine, for they have not planted either potatoes for themselves or corn for their cattle as formerly.

Alasdair Alpin Macgregor (1899–1970), alone amongst journalists, was finally given permission to travel to St Kilda – in the *Hebrides* – to cover the event for *The Times*, filing reports also to the *Daily Express* and the *Quarterly Review*. The following year he published *A Last Voyage to St Kilda*, consciously echoing Martin Martin's *Late Voyage*. Macgregor even indulged in a lengthy subtitle – though not as long as Martin's – which in Macgregor's case seems to tell a story all of its own:

... being the observations and adventures of an egotistic private secretary who was alleged to have been 'warned off' that island by Admiralty officials when attempting to emulate Robinson Crusoe at the time of its evacuation!

All of which says more about the author than it does the Admiralty officials. Behind the title page we have to endure six chapters (more than a third of the book) before Macgregor finally tells us anything about St Kilda. As with Seton, he utilised previous accounts and it is only at page 213 of 316 that we hear how the author finally stepped ashore on 23 August. Without doubt, his eye-witness account, and in particular his poignant photographs, constitute a historic record. But then, given that the islanders would have had so much else on their minds, I am amazed that they managed to spend any time with him at all. He did make himself useful on 27 August by acting as postmaster for the 30 tourists arriving on the *Dunara Castle* and with whom he departed at noon the next day. The islanders meanwhile got on with the business of loading their belongings. They themselves were to leave on the Fishery cruiser HMS *Harebell* on the morning of 29 August.

During the 1920s the population had been ageing, and deaths were outnumbering births. There were now only eight able-bodied men on the island. Launching the island boat alone required considerable manpower, as did loading and offloading stores, tending livestock and other communal tasks. Fowling on Boreray and its stacs had become very difficult and, with humanitarian aid from the mainland, it was no longer an essential part of their life-style anyway. It had become merely a dying tradition and a tourist attraction.

One child was drowned whilst fishing off the rocks in 1906, three men drowned off Dun in March 1909, two able young men were killed on the cliffs in August 1916, and four islanders died of influenza in a single week in May 1926. Mothers feared the worst if their children ever fell sick, as Mrs Anne Gillies testified in 1930:

> We all want to leave the island. My daughter has been ill for a long time and will never get well here. We can get the doctor very seldom during the winter and we could not face another winter here. My husband died from appendicitis out on Boreray when a doctor, if one had been available, could have saved his life by operating. One of my daughters died young, and another was taken to Fleetwood by trawler … The young men of the island are going, and we cannot stay alone.

In February 1930, Mary, the wife of John Gillies, had to be taken to hospital in Glasgow by the Fishery cruiser *Norna*, but died soon after. The American folksong collector and photographer Margaret Fay Shaw (1903–2003), then living in South Uist, was aboard the first steamer of the season, which bore the sad news to the island. Under these circumstances Margaret was reluctant to bother the locals, but she was invited into one house for a cup of tea. On admiring a faded tartan headscarf worn by her host, the woman took it off and handed it over. Only reluctantly did she accept half a crown in return. On talking to the resident Nurse Barclay, Margaret was told a distressing tale:

> The people were close to starvation. She had been there a couple of years and she told me that five of the men had duodenal ulcers and hardly one was able to do hard physical work … They had no sugar, no soda and no potatoes. The nurse did have some jam, and the children came every day for a spoonful to give them some energy. The islanders had become such beggars that the trawlermen would not give them anything. The deep sea trawlers would go in to shelter and if the St Kildans went out in their small boats to ask for food, they turned their hoses on them.

Families, especially young folk, were leaving. Another family with eight children were about to quit when the decision to evacuate was ultimately agreed. Thus only 36 people boarded HMS *Harebell* on 29 August 1930, effectively ending several thousand years of human inhabitation.

Dr A. Pomfre, the Surgeon of HMS *Harebell*, recorded the dying moments of the community (Mackay 2006):

> All the houses were locked and the people taken on board. Shortly afterward

they were looking their last at St Kilda as the '*Harebell*', quickly increasing speed, left the island a blur on the horizon. Contrary to expectations they had been very cheerful throughout, though obviously very tired, but with the first actual separation came the first signs of emotion, and men, women and children wept unrestrainedly as the last farewells were said.

The islanders were settled on the mainland, some of the men being given jobs in the Forestry Commission, though most had never seen a tree in their lives. The Morvern historian Iain Thornber has told me that the islanders got their own back in a manner of speaking. Being such skilful cragsmen they planted trees in places where no one dared venture when they were mature enough to be harvested! Sadly Margaret Fay Shaw later discovered that the boy who had helped her with her heavy camera, along with two of his sisters, had died of tuberculosis.

But perhaps the last word should go to a St Kildan, Neil Ferguson (1876–1944) the postmaster, younger brother of the Glasgow tweed merchant Alex:

> I was the last to leave the island, all the rest were aboard the steamer early in the morning. I was in charge of the post office and made every excuse to remain as long as I could. I was threatened and pleaded with, but I always made the excuse that I wasn't ready yet, but excuses were of no use. I went for a last walk round the village. It was weird passing the empty houses, it was just like looking at an open grave.

.15.

Conservation

Here ends the story of a last voyage to St Kilda, and of the removal of the remnant of a race that has struggled to maintain an existence upon it for a thousand years. Hirta will now be devoid of human interest ... In a long struggle for the supremacy of St Kilda, Nature has outwitted man; and man now retires from the fight. The removal of this small community means that, ethnographically at any rate, Scotland has contracted and the Atlantic gained by about forty miles. St Kilda is now one with North Rona; and the likelihood is that in the near future this precedent may result in a further shrinkage in the area of peopled Scotland. Men may return to Hirta with the summer; but the people will have gone ... The loneliest of Britain's island-dwellers have resigned their heritage to the ghosts and the seabirds; and the curtain is rung down on haunted homes and the sagas of the centuries.

Alasdair Alpin Macgregor 1931

THE AGE-OLD CULTURE HAD GONE, and so much more with it that is irreplaceable. But, as we have seen, a historic landscape, an array of artefacts, and a huge corpus of written material remains to tell what St Kilda used to be like. However, its story does not end there. The steamers continued to call, and a few islanders kept coming back. But since the evacuation the public had largely lost interest in the island and it tended to be only naturalists who came, until World War II intervened. Then came the Cold War with a military presence on St Kilda, and the islands entered simultaneously both the atomic age and the age of conservation. Suddenly, too, sociologists, historians and archaeologists realised the value of the culture that had now gone. The island became a fertile field for research by all manner of specialists.

The Fergusons were amongst the first St Kildans to return in the first summer after the evacuation. The *Glasgow Herald* on 1 June 1931 reported how Alex Ferguson, his wife and son, and his brother Neil Ferguson the Postmaster had just failed to reach St Kilda on the *Hebrides* due to bad weather. The full party of islanders, including Finlay Macqueen and Neil Gillies, were finally landed on 19 June. Sad to say, they found that their houses had already been broken into and looted, believed to have been by the crew of a Belgian trawler.

Alexander G. Ferguson (1872–1960) was the son of Donald Ferguson (1833–1918), who as Ground Officer was the islander responsible to the Factor for rents and management on the island. Alex's mother was Rachel Gillies (1839–1891) and the family lived in No. 5. His parents are both buried in Hirta's circular graveyard. In 1892, the 20-year-old Alex moved to Glasgow where he became a successful tweed merchant. He retained a deep love for his native island and frequently returned home, being photographed as a young man by Cherry Kearton in 1896 – 'an ex-fowler in the holiday war-paint of Buchanan Street'. Ferguson acquired his own yacht *Colonsay* which Seton Gordon saw in the bay in 1927:

> None but a native would, I think, have ventured on the long passage from the Outer Hebrides in a craft of her size.

Ferguson's daughter later recalled how he would take a few friends, two of a crew and an engineer because he knew nothing about engines. He even sailed to St Kilda during the war, but after a bad experience approaching the island on one voyage he largely gave up taking his own boat.

That first post-evacuation group of St Kildans overlapped with the Oxbridge expedition. On their departure that first summer of 1931, David Lack was touched by how depressed Finlay MacQueen was on leaving the island. On the long voyage home Lack tried to cheer him up by giving him tobacco. But the only thing that seemed to divert him was the visit to Dunvegan Castle, where the steamer stopped to offload at the pier. The expedition called in to thank Sir Reginald Macleod of Macleod, still the owner of St Kilda, for granting permission for their visit. Macleod was over 80 by this time and was dressed in a kilt. Alex Ferguson invited himself along and seemed subservient and obsequious in the presence of his former landlord. Finlay MacQueen, however, proudly marched in to introduce himself, fully confident that Macleod would know exactly who he was!

In November 1927, Sir Reginald had put St Kilda up for sale for the sum of £3,000, but it was not until September 1931 that the 23-year-old Honourable John Crichton-Stuart, Earl of Dumfries, acquired the islands for £5,000. Lord Dumfries (1907–56), later to become the fifth Marquis of Bute, liked to promote St Kilda as a Nature Reserve. Neil Gillies was appointed summer warden. Each summer Gillies would arrive by steamer, usually accompanied by his mother, by Finlay MacQueen, Finlay Gillies and a few other St Kildans. At the end of one season, waiting for the last steamer to arrive, Neil spent three weeks on the island totally alone. Curiously, when one of David Lack's party approached Lord Dumfries for permission to revisit St Kilda and assess ecological changes in the absence of the people, permission was refused.

A devout Catholic and a keen ornithologist, Lord Dumfries visited the islands for a few weeks each summer using the steamer. The Manse was fitted out as a base and referred to as 'Oiseval House', a name to be stamped on headed notepaper. In June 1932, Lord Dumfries gathered some islanders on Hirta to help bring sheep over from Soay as recounted in Chapter 12.

That year we know that the *Hebrides* called at St Kilda on 22 June, 21 July, 15 August and 20 August, while the *Dunara Castle* also called on at least three other occasions. The purser on the *Hebrides* was particularly conscientious about sending telegrams to the press and on 18 July 1934, for instance, he reported transporting the Earl of Dumfries and friends, on the *Dunara Castle*. She duly arrived on 21 July to pick up the Earl's party (his second visit of the summer), leaving only two St Kildans on the island until the end of August. Meanwhile the *Hebrides* was next due on 2 August.

In 1934, the Earl's party included his wife and his brother, along with ornithologists Father John Morell McWilliam, Niall Rankin and his wife Lady Jean. Rankin was to return again the following year. The 1934 party overlapped with George Meston who described his arrival in the *Weekly Scotsman* a few months later:

> When the SS 'Hebrides' anchored in the Village Bay (often called Hirta Loch), St Kilda, it was such a lovely morning that I could not refrain from swimming

Fig. 40. *The Dunara Castle.*

*Fig. 41. Back, left to right: Jean and Niall Rankin, Lord Dumfries,
Lady Dumfries (?), Alex Ferguson, Mrs McWilliam (?), Rev. McWilliam.
Front, left to right: Neil Gillies, unknown, Calum Macdonald (John Macdonald).*

ashore. That same evening, when I had the experience of seeing a 30 foot shark one yard from my harpoon, and of taking part in the spearing of 30 dogfish within an hour, I vowed I would never swim in these waters again.

For the first three days of my three weeks' stay on St Kilda, Hirta had ten inhabitants – nine men and one woman. After that there were but three of us.

In the afternoon of the day I arrived on St Kilda, eight of us rowed across the three-quarter mile stretch to Dune Island. We jumped ashore one by one, near a cave, as the boat rose on the wave, and landed at the spot where three St Kildans lost their lives on March 22 1909.

Irish-born Father McWilliam (1883–1968) was a founder member of the Scottish Ornithologists' Club, and a passionate collector of books and also of birds' eggs. He wrote a book on Bute's birds (in 1927), followed by another on the birds of the Firth of Clyde (1936). Many years later he sent a letter to James Fisher about his visit in 1934:

An article by a Glasgow schoolmaster called [George] Meston, I think, deals with our visit there. He was on the island at the same time, and we took him out with us one day. I was only on St Kilda from July 18, 1934 till July 21, when we left early in the forenoon. And one of the days was wet and misty. I was on Doon on the 18th. On the 20th we went to Soa, where I did not land, and then rowed round the outside of Hirta going completely round the island ... One time [Lord Dumfries] sent off from St Kilda by the little 'St Kilda mailboats' three letters simultaneously in three boats, one to his father, one to J T Gordon of Corsemabrie, and one to me [Tyron Manse, Dumfriesshire]. The three boats arrived together on the coast of Norway some months later and got columns in the Norwegian papers. I still have my letter somewhere. I have a set of the twelve little photographs of St Kilda issued by McCallum, Orme & Co, the shipping people … Michael [Powell]'s mother lives in the next house to my manse, and he and she are friends of mine, but I did not know him when the St Kilda tussle occurred. In fact it would not have been right, in my opinion, to have the St Kilda church and cemetery overrun by film stars. They lifted the roof off the Foula church. But certainly Michael would have made something remarkable in a St Kilda film. He still mourns over that affair.

The 'tussle' to which McWilliam refers is an interesting story in itself. Michael Powell (1905–1990) was a young director who in 1936 had lobbied Lord Dumfries to make a film *The Island on the Edge of the World* on St Kilda. He had read Alasdair Alpin Macgregor's reports in *The Times* about the evacuation in August 1930, and then found his book *A Last Voyage to St Kilda*. Powell was hooked. Immersing himself in the works of George Seton, the Keartons, Martin, Johnson and Boswell, he soon came up with an outline script. He proposed a full-length film, or drama-documentary as it would be called nowadays. So, early in 1936, he met Macgregor in London, whom he described as very lean, very brown, very clean-shaven with stiff wiry hair; he was a Gaelic-speaker, a climber, a vegetarian and teetotal, 'a bit of a crank, but so are lots of nice people'. Macgregor felt he could assist, so Powell took him on as technical advisor.

Powell described in his book *200,000 feet on Foula* (1938) how he then set about seeking permission – but St Kilda's new owner Lord Dumfries refused outright. Undaunted, Powell then made contact with Niall Rankin who was a close friend of Lord Dumfries. Young, rich, and an enthusiastic wildlife photographer, Rankin was supportive and so phoned Dumfries there and then. The noble lord agreed to meet to discuss Powell's proposal.

The window for filming was fast closing so Powell arranged an early appointment at Lord Dumfries's country house near Cumnock in Ayrshire. A thin young man sporting a Guards moustache and wearing a kilt answered the door; it was the Lord himself. The film director set out his plans: the company were to buy their own ship to act as supply vessel and operational base, and they were to employ the labour force locally who would then spend the summer on St Kilda servicing the infrastructure necessary for actors and camera team.

But Lord Dumfries was adamant. He had bought St Kilda as a bird sanctuary, and was passionate about the native sheep. The Factor's House had been refurbished so that he and his friends could visit for a month each summer. Not only would Powell's project disrupt this rural idyll of his, but it would cause serious disturbance during the bird breeding season. Every time their supply ship blew the siren thousands of birds would panic, sending eggs and chicks hurtling off the ledges to their death. If only Powell had been aware of his Lordship's seal shooting escapades! Dumfries did not seem attracted by a fee, but Powell, conscious that time was pressing, was prepared to offer the generous sum of £500 anyway.

Lord Dumfries reluctantly agreed to discuss the matter with his Factor and to meet Powell again the next day at the solicitor's office in Glasgow. Dumfries arrived wearing kilt and bonnet and carrying a knobbly stick. The whole £20,000 enterprise hung upon a nod from him. The peer set out the same arguments from the day before, but Powell stuck to his guns, confident that the solicitor cum Factor would not resist the idea of making a tidy profit on such a 'feckless hobby' as a bird sanctuary. So they met again after lunch, but it was all over in five minutes: permission was refused.

Devastated, Powell then had to find another island that might serve as a convincing alternative. He was told that no one knew St Kilda better than John Mathieson who had surveyed it so thoroughly a few years earlier. He found Mathieson in his Edinburgh home, a small, shy and personable man with blue eyes, white hair and a rosy face. Asked to suggest a location that could fill St Kilda's shoes, Mathieson paused 'while his soul hovered like an eagle over the Hebrides', as Powell so eloquently put it. Then Mathieson said 'Mingulay'.

Powell pressed him for one more island as a second string to his bow. When Foula was suggested, Powell at once knew that his pet project might proceed after all. Foula was still inhabited. Mathieson had recently been there. Having

Fig. 42. Michael Powell and Seton Gordon (Seton Gordon collection).

determined the height of Conachair on St Kilda, he had been keen to see the Kame of Foula for himself so, in his own time and at his own expense, he did so and found it 14 ft lower than its St Kildan rival. There was little in it, he admitted, but in fact the Kame is broken by a broad, grassy shelf halfway down. So nowadays Conachair is usually described as the highest *sheer* cliff in the British Isles.

The new owner of Mingulay lived in Essex, but Alasdair Holbourn, who had Foula, lived right there in Edinburgh. The next day Powell had his agreement and had even signed him up as technical advisor in Macgregor's stead. He then took Mathieson and Holbourn to dinner where the two guests squabbled over the relative heights of the Kame and Conachair! The film proved to be a resounding success and the rest of the story is cinematic history.

The postscript was that Alasdair Alpin Macgregor was so offended at being replaced as technical advisor that he tried to sue Michael Powell for breach of copyright over the use of his book and was laughed out of court. In his comic novels Compton Mackenzie was to base one of his characters, Hector Hamish Mackay, upon Macgregor.

Powell's go-between to Lord Dumfries, Lieutenant-Colonel Arthur Niall Talbot Rankin (1904–1965), was a wildlife photographer of some renown himself. He had wished to marry Lady Jean Courtenay, the daughter of the Earl of Stair, but her family had other ideas. Rankin's parents had separated soon after Niall was born, so he had never met his father. When he finally tracked him down, Sir Reginald Rankin took an instant liking to his son's fiancée. In the end he bequeathed his long-estranged son all his money. And so Niall and Lady Jean were wed in 1931. They bought the estate Treshnish Point, Calgary, on Mull. In 1951, Niall wrote and illustrated *Haunts of British Divers* in 1947, closely followed in 1951 by *Antarctic Isle* about his voyage round South Georgia. He died when only 61, although Lady Jean lived to the ripe old age of 96.

Having visited St Kilda with their friend Lord Dumfries, Niall described his impressions in the Royal Society for the Protection of Birds' magazine *Bird Notes* (October 1935):

> It is indeed fitting that this, the loneliest outpost of the British Isles should become (as indeed it has) the finest seabird haunt and sanctuary to be found anywhere round our shores. Other famous places, such as ... the towering cliffs of Foula in the Shetlands, may claim the distinction for themselves and may actually possess a greater number of species; but for sheer isolation, magnitude, and grandeur of scenery, there is no other place in the whole kingdom even to approach this lonely island group. One has to see it to believe it ...
>
> The ordinary traveller who first sees St Kilda from a steamer in Village Bay, has no real conception of the place, and he probably thinks that the wonders of the island have been grossly exaggerated, for more often than not there is hardly

a bird to be seen in the bay. Also he appears to be enclosed in an amphitheatre of grassy slopes, and there is absolutely nothing to show that the skyline forms the edge of one of the most staggering precipices in our country, falling more than 1200 feet sheer into the sea. To understand what has made St Kilda famous the world over, the ascent to the top of Connachair must be made ...

It was on the side of Connachair that I was initiated by one of the natives into the mysteries of fowling. In the days when the population were almost entirely dependent on the birds for food, the snaring of fulmars and puffins was brought to a fine art.

St Kilda is now uninhabited, and no longer are the sea fowl hunted for food. Its very inaccessibility makes it impossible for egg thieves to raid it except on the few occasions when the steamers call, and then the resident Watcher makes it no easy matter. St Kilda may therefore be called Britain's greatest seal and seabird sanctuary.

As an interesting aside, the Glasgow school teacher George Meston, who was there at the same time as the Rankins, recorded how he had found 'the nose of a German shell near house No. 5' just before he left Hirta. Immediately after, on 20 July, the *Glasgow Herald* reported:

According to a report unofficially circulated after the steamer '*Hebrides*' arrived in Glasgow yesterday, an explosion occurred on St Kilda last week during demolition operations. The windows of the church and manse were broken, but, fortunately, a native of the island who was engaged in the work escaped injury. Mr Neil Gillies, who is remaining on St Kilda until the last sailing of the season, was destroying the remains of Government huts erected during the war on Hirta and burning the debris when there was a sudden explosion. The theory has been advanced that it was caused by the bursting of a shell fired from a German submarine early in the war.

There were to be nine steamer visits in 1935, with five more in 1936, the last being delayed for several days by storms. In 1937, there were at least five visits, the last trip of the *Hebrides* being cancelled, leaving Neill Gillies and his cousin Alastair, Alex Ferguson's son, stranded until the *Hebrides* diverted from its Outer Isles run on 30 August to rescue them. Although eight visits were advertised in 1938, only four voyages succeeded in reaching St Kilda.

Robert Atkinson (1915–1995) arrived on board the *Dunara Castle* on 24 July 1938, astonished that it should be the exact same vessel which had transported the Keartons in 1896! Indeed, the ship was to remain in service for a further ten years. Atkinson left Hirta on 9 August aboard the *Hebrides* (which remained on cargo duty until 1952).

Even before he came down from Cambridge in 1936, Atkinson had been determined to visit the Hebrides, in search of the Leach's petrel. He reached

Rona in a Buckie drifter and then visited the Shiants. His accounts of these and other expeditions – and of his stay on St Kilda in 1938 – were published in the popular *Island Going* in 1949. Having spent the war in the Royal Navy, Atkinson was then able to spend more time in the Hebrides with his own boat, *Heather*, purchased in 1939. After the sad death of his wife in 1973, Atkinson brought up their three children on his fruit farm near Reading. But he never lost his love of the islands, managing to publish *Shillay and the Seals* in 1980.

The St Kilda steamer service finally came to an end at the outbreak of World War II. But first James Fisher was to land on St Kilda with fellow naturalists Julian Huxley and Max Nicholson aboard the ocean-going ketch *Escape* on 31 May 1939. There they met Lord Dumfries who was on his last visit before the war. Fisher and Nicholson (1949) summarised their activities:

> Although the party's visit lasted only from the early hours of May 31st to the evening of June 2nd it was possible, owing to the possession of a yacht with an auxiliary engine and two dinghies, to the exceptionally fine weather and the long daylight, and also to some curtailment of sleep, to put in as much ornithological work as might ordinarily have been expected in a full week. The party's special thanks are due to the Earl of Dumfries, who in addition to affording every facility and much generous hospitality gave valuable guidance on ornithological matters and personally led a midnight expedition to the Petrel breeding place on Dun.
>
> On May 31st, in the early morning, a census was taken of the village of Hirta, followed by an examination of Conachair and the north-eastern cliffs. The rest of the day was spent in a long expedition to Boreray, on which the ornithologists landed and visited most of the commanding positions, afterwards cruising closely under the cliffs and examining Stac Lee and Stac an Armin. On June 1st the Ruaival, Village Bay and Oiseval sections of Hirta were examined and a long expedition to the closely adjoining island of Dun led to very satisfactory results. Towards midnight the party again landed on Dun, located a number of Leach's Fork-tailed Petrels and Manx Shearwaters in their breeding burrows, and did a little ringing. On June 2nd a morning expedition reconnoitred the west and north-west of Hirta, one party investigating Gleann Mor and the other pushing along the coast to the Cambir. Later, still in the most brilliant and calm weather, the whole party went round Dun, the west and north coast of Hirta and Soay in the yacht, keeping close under the cliffs most of the way, and finally in the evening a further reconnaissance was made of Boreray and its adjoining stack before returning eastwards. Thus the lonely part of the group wholly unvisited was the small outlying islet of Levenish.

The party noted various changes in some bird populations, black guillemots having decreased for instance, while starlings, eider, snipe, and pipits had increased. Eider were probably benefiting from the cessation of egg-robbing now that the people had left, the others from a lack of cats. Fisher and Nicholson noted too how the spread of snipe into the dry village meadows, was a new, atypical habitat. Later Nicholson and Huxley busied themselves investigating all the old buildings for wrens' nests. Huxley thrust his head through the window of one of the best-preserved cottages to be met with a flood of Gaelic oaths from one of the St Kildans living there for the summer. Huxley turned to Nicholson who was making a tally of the birds and calmly reported '*Homo sapiens*, one!'

According to one of Fisher's party, as soon as Lord Dumfries had left the island, the St Kildans took a boat over to Dun and came back with 'baskets' of eggs – razorbills, guillemots, puffins, etc. – and about 100 fulmars. According to Fleming (2005), a naturalist called Davie protested to Neil Gillies, and later sent a letter to his Lordship:

> [the St Kildans] are not playing the game. Apparently they make the holiday at St Kilda a purely business trip . . .

John Buchan and Tom Harrisson had always suspected as much. In 1931, they had known of a clutch of St Kilda wren eggs being sold for £5. Only the previous year, their informant had been offered a single egg for seven shillings and sixpence; furthermore, he had claimed to know of a dozen or so nests being robbed annually. Harrisson and Buchan acknowledged that Lord Dumfries employed a bird warden during the summer, but they considered the position 'far from satisfactory'. They obviously had their suspicions as to who was marketing the wrens' eggs!

During World War II St Kilda lay deserted and largely forgotten. Three aircraft crashed with tragic loss of life. A Beaufighter with two of a crew crashed into the side of Conachair in June 1942. Almost exactly two years later a Sunderland flying boat hit the ridge between Glen Bay and Village Bay with the loss of all ten crew.

But St Kilda's second war had not ended there. In the summer of 1955, Morton Boyd was viewing sheep on the face of Soay from the Cambir when he spotted some wreckage. The following year, his Glasgow University expedition managed to land John Wilson on Soay, the first person ashore since the war, and he confirmed the wreckage was an aeroplane hitherto unrecorded. Boyd himself managed to land in May 1959 and having done his national service in the RAF could conclude it to be a Warwick or a Wellington. He found a human rib amongst the wreckage.

Various brief landings were made on Soay subsequently, but it was not until 12 July 1978 that the warden Wally Wright went ashore with some RAF personnel and found some human bones in the wreckage. Two more visits, one with the Procurator Fiscal, recovered 30 lb of human bones. The plane was confirmed as a Wellington bomber and subsequent research by John Barry (1980) determined that it could only have been one of two that went missing in the area around that time – one in September 1942 (the most likely candidate) and another the following February. The issue remains unresolved to this day. A memorial plaque was dedicated in the church in 1979, with a place for the names of the Wellington crew should they ever be known.

There were no known visits by German U-boats to the island during the war, although, remarkably, the indomitable Alex Ferguson went out in his own yacht *Colonsay* in 1942 and found a swastika flying from a flagpole near the pier. Norwegian whalers apparently kept to their own grisly quest during the hostilities. No sooner had peace been declared than James Fisher was back on the case.

Fisher accompanied Robert Atkinson and John Naish in Atkinson's *Heather*. This was an 8-ton converted fyfie fishing boat, with 30 horse-power Kelvin paraffin engine and ketch rig. On the evening of 9 June 1947 the trio left Leverburgh in *Heather*. They enjoyed calm weather for the next few days, landing on Hirta, Dun and Boreray before a south-east wind forced them to return to Harris. They were back on 16 June so that Fisher could complete his bird counts. That evening Atkinson had to take the boat round to Glen Bay for shelter where he picked up Fisher next morning. There they safely sat out the south-easterly for a couple of days before finally limping back to Harris, having had to leave their anchor behind in Glen Bay – perhaps it had snagged on the wreck of the Fleetwood trawler.

A month later, on 30 July and in exceptional conditions, Fisher, Atkinson and the bird photographer Eric Hosking were able to commission an RAF Sunderland to fly around and photograph St Kilda, having flown via Islay, Skerryvore Lighthouse, Barra head and the Monach Isles. It took an hour and 20 minutes to reach Rockall 170 miles beyond, before returning via the Flannans, Sulaisgeir, Rona, Handa, the Summer Isles, the Shiants, Treshnish and Ailsa Craig. It must have proved a totally breath-taking flight. Between 27 and 30 September that same year, Fisher, Max Nicholson, R. M. Lockley and Fraser Darling were able to fly all the islands from Pembrokeshire to Orkney, Shetland, Sule Skerry, Rona, Sulaisgeir, the Flannans, St Kilda (29 September) and the Inner Hebrides to complete a historic aerial census of grey seals (Fisher notebooks via David Wilson).

Around 21st May 1949, Fisher was able to land briefly at St Kilda on his return from a voyage to Rockall in the *Petula*; in the short time available he managed some counts of fulmars and gannets to supplement the aerial counts from the year before.

That same year, 1949, the Nature Conservancy was established as the government's conservation agency. Scotland was given its own Wildlife

Conservation Committee which recommended that the St Kilda archipelago become a National Nature Reserve.

> [St Kilda] is of exceptional scientific interest. [It] has an interesting and unique fauna ... including the Soay Sheep, the wren and the field mouse ... [and] provides a first class field for the investigation of sub-oceanic island conditions. It is essential that this unique island group should be maintained as a reserve for all time.

However, the Conservancy considered the islands in no immediate danger under the ownership of Lord Dumfries (Nature Conservancy files).

Meantime, a young Morton Boyd had been reading the Keartons' book *With Nature and a Camera*. And then, as a student in Glasgow he came across a rare copy of *St Kilda Papers 1931* which was the published record of David Lack's Oxford-Cambridge University expedition. Morton then resolved to visit for himself, so he assembled a group of eight students from Glasgow and Edinburgh Universities, including the marine biologists David Gauld and Tim Bagenal (see Chapter 13). Lord Dumfries gave his permission, with the express proviso that nothing, not even scientific samples, was to be removed from the island. The steam collier *Glas Island* from Scalpay was chartered and they finally reached their goal on the late evening of 24 July 1952. Two hours after dropping anchor they were ensconced in the only two houses still with roofs – the Manse and the Factor's House. Eiders were nesting in the roofless houses along the street, with fulmars on the chimney heads, wrens singing amongst the old walls and a corncrake rasping in the iris bed in front of No. 8. While the geologists and marine biologists set about their work, Morton began a bird census until, during the second week, he could enlist them into helping with a sheep count.

By 1954 the Air Ministry were looking at Hirta as a radar backstop for their proposed rocket range on the Uists. This Inter Services guided missile project proposed the establishment of radar installations on St Kilda, one on top of Conachair, a larger one on Mullach Mor, another on Mullach Sgar, and a low-level one near Ruaival. However, the deep peat and other unfavourable conditions rendered the site of Conachair itself impracticable, while difficulties of communication invalidated Ruaival. Planning therefore was to be concentrated on Mullach Mor and Mullach Sgar.

The Conservancy, as a government agency, speedily involved themselves to monitor and mitigate developments. They also realised that now would be an appropriate time to revisit an earlier proposal for St Kilda to become a National Nature Reserve. At first they looked into the purchase of the archipelago from Lord Dumfries, now the fifth Marquis of Bute, on the basis that the family could continue to enjoy full access. The Nature Conservancy would then lease to the Air Ministry the areas of land they required for their installations.

Meanwhile, Morton Boyd was now a post-graduate student at Glasgow (studying earthworms on the machairs of Tiree). He was able to visit St Kilda in 1955. Morton then returned again the following year with an expedition from Glasgow University to study the sheep flocks on Hirta, Soay and Boreray. He had hired a 15-ft rowing boat in Harris, but deficiencies in this frail little craft were compensated by a Fair Isle man in the party, John Wilson, who in his role as coxswain had brought a trusty Seagull outboard. Blessed with unusually calm weather, the party were able to visit both Boreray and, as we have already seen, Soay.

In the summer of 1956, as the military made a reconnaissance of the facilities to be erected on Uist and Benbecula, HMS *Bridport* visited the deserted islands offshore to see which might be suitable for radar installations. Aboard were James Fisher and Max Nicholson, with St Kildans 83-year-old Alex Ferguson and his nephew Neil Ferguson. They landed on Hirta on 11 June and over the next three days, while the RAF surveyors were confirming the suitability of the island for their purposes, Fisher and the St Kildans walked the cliff tops.

On 14 August 1956, Lord Dumfries, now the Marquis of Bute, died suddenly, aged only 49. He had decided to offer the islands to the National Trust for Scotland, having considered them more likely than the Conservancy to give equal prominence to both the natural and cultural heritage. The Trust decided to accept in December 1956, but, without funds to run the property, they prudently entered into discussions with the Nature Conservancy. Early in 1957, the Air Ministry met with the Trust and the Conservancy to set out their plans for St Kilda.

Under the National Parks and Access to the Countryside Act of 1949, St Kilda was declared a National Nature Reserve on 4 April 1957, at the same time as the Isle of Rum, and Caerlaverock on the Solway. This brought the Conservancy's holding of reserves in Scotland to 15. It now stands at about 60, including Rona and Sulaisgeir, the Monach Isles and Loch Druidibeg as St Kilda's nearest neighbours in the Outer Hebrides.

The Conservancy would bear the costs of wardening and managing St Kilda, yet involve the Trust directly when it came to the cultural monuments. A Joint Standing Committee was set up between the Trust and the Conservancy to advise on the general administration of the islands. The Trust would organise work parties to undertake restoration work on the buildings, etc. In July 1957, Morton Boyd became the first Regional Officer in the West Highlands and Islands for the Nature Conservancy and St Kilda came under his remit.

The military operation was code-named 'Hardrock' after a simple quotation from Martin Martin about St Kilda: 'The island is one hard rock.' It proposed first to establish the beach head area and temporary camp and then make roads up the hill so that the radar sites could be constructed. The permanent domestic buildings were to be built in the following year. 5004 Airfield Construction Squadron would commence that summer, with completion in the spring of 1958. The intention was to route their road from the Manse, through the meadows behind the Factor's House to Tobar Childa, and thence via Lag Aitimir and Creagan Breac to the lowest part of the ridge at Am Blaid, and finally to the summit of Mullach Mor. The military engineers considered the necessary 'hard rock' was in abundance in the form of the old buildings – the cleits, the cottages and the adjacent enclosure walls! This would save time and labour involved in opening a quarry.

This had become the accepted working plan when the Hardrock advance party arrived on 16 April 1957. The force was commanded by Wing Commander W. M. Cookson and consisted of some 30 military personnel landed from HM Army Vessel *Ageila* (LCT No. 4002). Accompanying them were Bob Hillcoat of the National Trust for Scotland, Roy Ritchie of the Ministry of Work Inspectorate of Ancient Monuments, Dr J. Morton Boyd and Ken Williamson from the Nature Conservancy. They reassessed the working plan on the ground. Williamson was to remain throughout the construction period to represent the interests of the Conservancy and the Trust.

Needless to say, it was immediately obvious that the working plan would cause untold damage to the Village area, not to mention destroying an interesting geological morraine. But before refusing permission the Conservancy/National Trust for Scotland/Ministry representatives had to formulate an alternative. This involved a more permanent beach head on more suitable terrain and a more direct route for the road that was shorter and more convenient than that originally proposed. It was accepted that a dozen cleits outwith the Village area would have to be sacrificed, but an accurate record would be made first:

> Since the change was a major one it would require to be agreed at a high level between the Air Ministry and the Nature Conservancy; a signal was despatched asking that the proposed change be considered and confirmed (as it immediately was).

Although it was the Easter weekend, wires hummed all the way to Edinburgh and London and, with the full understanding of the Wing Commander in charge on Hirta, this act of national vandalism was successfully averted. The road was rerouted along the shore, utilising a minimum amount of material from the storm beach. Unfortunately, this would open up an ugly quarry on the hill above, but at least it avoided the Village altogether and retained its structures intact. This was undoubtedly one of the most significant contributions that conservationists made to the preservation of St Kilda's cultural heritage (Nature Conservancy files; Love 2004).

Heavy equipment and personnel continued to arrive at fortnightly intervals, with all precautions taken to avoid the introduction of rats on the supply ships. By June, some 300 airforce personnel had begun work on the radar station. Soon every available piece of level ground below the Village was being taken up by all the military personnel and their kit – 90 domestic tents, 6 marquees and 11 Nissen huts in total. Heavy plant slowly gouged a route up to the radar installations being erected on Mullach Mor and Mullach Sgar. A young journalist Magnus Magnusson (who later became Scottish Natural Heritage's first Chairman) chartered a boat so that he could cover the story.

Work progressed apace. In rare idle moments the island's church doubled as a cinema, while the crack of willow on leather and the genteel patter of applause, albeit mingled with the wayward cries of kittiwakes, superimposed an English village green on to this alien meadow. Such is the vivid description given by Ken Williamson and Morton Boyd in their fascinating book *St Kilda Summer* (1960). They pointed out that as long ago as 1697, according to Martin Martin, the islanders used to play a game on the beach involving sticks and a wooden ball. This would not have been cricket but probably an early form of shinty.

Ken Williamson had left the Bird Observatory on Fair Isle (another National Trust property) to serve as the first Conservancy warden on St Kilda. He returned to Fair Isle for the month of June 1957, to be relieved on Hirta first by Morton Boyd and then by Tim Bagenal. In early September, Williamson attended a meeting in Edinburgh to discuss arrangements on Hirta for the winter months, when he was relieved by Crispin Fisher, son of James Fisher. Other visitors during the year were Dr Joe Eggeling of the Conservancy and the journalist/climber Tom Weir from 3 to 13 May. A party of National Trust representatives arrived on board MV *Turquoise* on 14/15 July. This included the Earl of Wemyss (Chairman of the National Trust for Scotland), Jamie Stormonth Darling (Secretary), James Fisher and the film-maker Christopher Mylne. Williamson was back from his Edinburgh meeting for a fortnight before finally departing on the last tank landing craft of the season on 26 September (Nature Conservancy files). The first phase of Operation Hardrock was over, leaving a caretaker garrison of 30 men to face the harsh St Kilda winter.

Ken Williamson moved on to become Migrations Officer with the British Trust for Ornithology, and editor of their journal *Bird Migration*. His role on St Kilda in 1958 was covered by numerous Conservancy staff, including Morton Boyd, also the bird artist Donald Watson. The first two National Trust Work Parties arrived in June 1958, led by George and Irene Waterston, and then Alex Warwick, the Trust's Buildings Officer. They repaired collapsed walls, tidied the village, retrieving sundry artefacts of historical interest (National Trust for Scotland archive).

Fig. 43. Operation Hardrock, 1958 (Scottish Natural Heritage).

On completion of Phase 2 that year, the Air Ministry handed over control of the entire military establishment to the army in September 1958 . The facilities operated the Base on St Kilda as a radar 'back stop' for the Royal Artillery Range in South Uist and Benbecula which commenced firing their Corporal missiles in June 1959. One of the first test rockets turned back on itself and hit the military camp, but fortunately damaged nothing but pride. David Boddington recalled that the officers had told the attendant press that the incident had been deliberate, in order to show how efficiently the rocket could be detonated if something went wrong.

One of the last missiles of this design was fired from South Uist on 10 May 1966, before it veered south and crashed into Loch Druidibeg National Nature Reserve a few miles to the south of the launch pad. The incident was immortalised in a Gaelic poem by a local Uist bard, Donald John Macdonald, who lived nearby.

The military installation on Hirta, which maintained a detachment of some 30 military personnel, was on a few acres near the Manse, and at the summit of Mullach Mor, land which was sub-leased from the Conservancy. While he was writing his novel *Atlantic Fury*, Hammond Innes failed to visit St Kilda by landing craft in mid-September 1959, but he did manage to fly over a few days later on an air drop.

On 10 May 1959, the first of the annual National Trust cruises arrived, with 150 passengers on the 29,000-ton luxury liner *Meteor*. Before it departed next day, the ship gingerly circumnavigated Boreray and the stacs, with a cutter sent ahead to take soundings. On 13 May, Morton Boyd, Derek Ratcliffe and David Boddington made a landing on Stac an Armin. The first Trust Work Party of the season arrived on 21 May 1959, followed by National Trust dignitaries and pressmen in HMS *Adamant* on 7 July. The first helicopter, a Dragonfly from Lossiemouth, landed in front of the Manse on 7 September to evacuate one of the last Work Party, whose wife was dangerously ill in Inverness. On 8 October 1959, the *Daily Mail* chartered a De Havilland Rapide biplane to St Kilda to drop newspapers – bringing the results of the General Election! This paved the way for a regular air drop by fixed-wing aircraft of mail, newspapers and emergency supplies thoughout the winter months. One pilot chose to gauge the crosswinds on each sortie by dropping a teddy bear with its own little parachute, until one day it failed to open, so now the toy, in a neat little coffin, lies in state in the Puff Inn.

Not everything hit the target, however. More than one mailbag ended up in the sea and one ignited on impact because of a large box of matches inside. One of the most lamented of early disasters was the total loss of a pack of tinned beer. One of the most amusing in retrospect – but potentially the most serious – occurred on 27 March 1982. On its sixth and final pass the plane dropped a heavy bag containing some frozen chickens, which smashed the windscreen of a waiting Land Rover and then hit the officer standing beside it. He was knocked unconscious and suffered serious injury to his arm which necessitated him being taken to hospital by helicopter. He was never to regain full mobility in his elbow again (Spackman 1982).

This antiquated mode of supply had long ceased by the early 1990s when the warden Jim Vaughan recovered an old, unopened mail bag from a dangerous cliff face. Amongst the soggy letters inside was a box of slides in a return envelope which the cautious photographer had marked emphatically 'Do not Air Drop!'

The army officer and postal historian James Mackay recalled the visit of Queen Elizabeth the Queen Mother to Benbecula on 7 September 1960, where she opened the North Ford causeway. She was accompanied by her close friend and Lady-in-Waiting, none other than Lady Jean Rankin who had of course visited St Kilda in 1934 with her husband Niall and Lord Dumfries. Lady Jean went on to serve the Queen Mother for over 40 years.

On 12 August 1971, on the Royal yacht *Britannia*, Queen Elizabeth II visited St Kilda, where she and her family were shown around by Lord Wemyss of the National Trust for Scotland and Morton Boyd. This was not St Kilda's first encounter with a reigning monarch, however, for the indefatigable Finlay MacQueen had shaken hands with King George VI and Queen Elizabeth (later the Queen Mother) at the 1938 Empire Exhibition in Glasgow. On the Royal yacht's final cruise in August 1997, Queen Elizabeth II and Prince

Philip returned again to Hirta, while Princess Anne landed off the lighthouse ship *Pharos* in July 2003.

Brigadier 'Tony' Spackman recorded many other interesting events in his useful publication *Soldiers on St Kilda*, published in 1982, while the late James Mackay's *Soldiering on St Kilda* (2002) is rather more self-indulgent and anecdotal. Twenty-two-year-old Mackay arrived in April 1959 as second-in-command, overlapping with the naturalist David Boddington who had been army medical officer since the previous August. The two became friends, but otherwise Mackay did not have a high opinion of the official conservation presence. This may have been coloured by the fact that he did trap and kill some mice around the Base, and had also undertaken an illicit excavation of Calum Mor's house, much to the dismay of the Trust and the Conservancy. Another naturalist, Estlin Waters, was medical officer during 1961 and 1962, studying wrens, petrels and much else besides.

The history of the Army Base, wardening and work party experiences is a long and colourful one, which remains to be written one day. Brigadier Spackman began the process with his book, but only as far as 1982. There is not the space here to take up the challenge, it remaining now to summarise events as far as they impinge upon the recent conservation history of St Kilda.

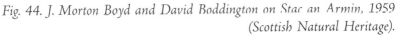

Fig. 44. J. Morton Boyd and David Boddington on Stac an Armin, 1959 (Scottish Natural Heritage).

312 A Natural History of St Kilda

In 1959, the Nature Conservancy commissioned a sturdy 18-ft clinker-built dinghy to be based on St Kilda and named her *Fulmar*. In 1960, Murdo Macdonald of Tiree, and then the shark fisher Tex Geddes, acted as coxswains. They successfully nudged the vessel into the rocks of St Kilda, enabling landings on most of the islands and stacs. Morton Boyd described some of these adventures in another book with Ken Williamson, entitled *A Mosaic of Islands* (1963). When Zodiac rubber dinghies became the preferred mode of transport, to be later replaced by a modern rigid-hulled inflatable, the *Fulmar* was retired to the Conservancy's National Nature Reserve on the Isle of Rum. There she was maintained by the island's boatman/shipwright Ian Simpson. In the 1970s I spent many a happy evening's mackerel fishing rowing her around Loch Scresort, sometimes with one of Ian's daughters, Gail, taking an oar.

Morton Boyd was appointed Scottish Director of the Nature Conservancy in 1971; two years later the government reinvented it as the Nature Conservancy Council. He became not only my boss but also a good friend. John Morton Boyd (1925–98) retired in 1985 and just before he died he wrote a delightful book about his astonishingly productive and colourful life called *The Song of the Sandpiper* which his family saw into print in 1999. In the meantime, the Nature Conservancy Council became Scottish Natural Heritage in 1992.

From the outset these government advisory bodies have liaised with the National Trust to maintain on St Kilda a summer warden from April to September inclusive, based in the Factor's House. Since 1957, over 25 successive wardens have worked closely with the army, the staff at the Base, research workers, cruise ships, charter boats and the public. They have submitted detailed monthly reports on management, visitor numbers and biological records which provide a valuable account of the Nature Reserve. Records have been supplemented by valuable observations from Base staff during the winter months and are lodged with both Scottish Natural Heritage and the Trust.

From 1996 the National Trust for Scotland was able to appoint a resident archaeologist on Hirta for the summer months, first Lorna Johnstone until 2000, followed by Marcia Taylor and then Susan Bain, who is now the National Trust for Scotland Manager in charge of the Outer Hebrides, and St Kilda in particular. 2005 was the first year that the Trust was able to appoint a dedicated Seabird and Marine Ranger, reflecting the importance of the marine environment around St Kilda. Dr Sarah Money has since been undertaking vital monitoring of seabird breeding success.

The St Kilda Club was formed in 1959, with Alex Warwick as first President. The qualification for membership is to have spent 24 hours on the islands. Its first reunion, involving the first two work parties, was held in Trust Headquarters in Edinburgh on 3 April 1959, followed by a public meeting chaired by Seton Gordon. The speakers included Morton Boyd, Bob

Hillcoat of the Trust and Tom Weir. Annual reunions have taken place every November since, with a huge array of popular speakers. The club journal *St Kilda Mail* first appeared in January 1977 and has been produced annually ever since, full of interesting snippets, reports and accounts about St Kilda (though mostly about history rather than nature). The club has supported all manner of initiatives on St Kilda, its members – many of whom have returned to the islands over many years – maintaining a healthy interest in all that goes on there.

From time to time, in the interests of health and safety, the wardens have had to make decisions regarding access. In 1963, for example, the warden stopped visitors walking over the half of Dun that is riddled with puffin burrows, estimating that 600 may be trampled each year. It would be many years though before the bold but unpopular decision was made to cease the obligatory trips to Dun for each work party and other tourists. Nor did visitors like being advised to avoid one particular area of the ridge on Hirta where the great skuas nested – despite the warden himself having been concussed twice that season by dive-bombing birds. It has always been an unwritten policy that, in their own interests, visitors should not venture alone outwith the Head Dyke and on to the slippery cliff tops. Tragically, on 1 August 1999, one lone Belgian walker chose to ignore the warnings and his body had to be recovered by staff the next day from the sea below Oiseval. Nowadays, paradoxically, strict health and safety policies have removed the obligations to maintain a safety boat on the island so the options of accessing Dun and the other islands or stacs (or even recovering bodies after an accident) is now a thing of the past.

The Foot and Mouth outbreak of 2001 resulted in the cancellation of all work parties that season. Some charter boats complained bitterly about loss of livelihood, though it has to be said that the longest-established skippers fully understood the necessity of restricting access. The fear was that if the Hirta flock of Soay sheep became infected, it would have to be destroyed, as was the policy of government vets at the time. Furthermore, it would have been all too easy for the infection to be carried by air currents across the narrow gap to Soay itself, which supported the only other feral flock in the world. In the end a compromise was reached whereby a strict programme of bio-security was instigated, together with a vetting of everyone landing. No one from within the infected areas on the mainland would be allowed to step ashore, but one person who should have known better slipped through the net. She was a vet living and working within the infected zone in Northumberland, who failed to admit her background in order not to compromise her holiday of a lifetime!

Another contentious issue is rock climbing. I feel strongly that it should not be allowed anywhere or at any time within the St Kilda archipelago. Climbers appreciate their impact upon nesting seabirds (and naturally avoid spitting fulmars). They worthily set up an online code of conduct. However, this maintained that the seabird breeding season lasted from February to mid-July inclusive. Any experienced ornithologist knows, as did the old St Kildans, that some seabirds are present on the cliffs for most of the year (see earlier chapters).

Some might maintain that the St Kildans themselves had been amongst the very first cragsmen. However, they were hardly sports climbers. What they did was out of necessity for survival. St Kilda has been designated a Special Protection Area for its nesting seabirds, with all interested parties being charged with minimising human impact on breeding colonies. The islands' vegetated seacliffs (which could be subject to 'gardening' by rock climbers) are similarly protected as Special Areas for Conservation under the European Habitats Directive.

It is not unreasonable that remote places with Nature Reserve status, and especially World Heritage status, should impose access restrictions, whether for conservation reasons or those of health and safety. Galapagos is a good example. These islands are much more extensive than the archipelago of St Kilda. Both island groups enjoy World Heritage status. The Galapagos National Park limits tourist landings to only some 50 localities around the coast, and even there – accompanied by Park wardens – they must confine themselves to marked paths. There are few places in Galapagos where one is at liberty to wander at will. In East African National Parks tourist vehicles are restricted to established tracks, and visitors are not even allowed out of their car.

That is not to say that St Kilda should be out of bounds. For 40 years St Kilda had its own set of byelaws, empowered through the National Trust for Scotland Orders of 1935 and 1961, and approved by the Secretary of State for Scotland on 21 April 1971. Their aims were to protect against vandalism of the buildings, to minimise undue disturbance to the flora and fauna and to reduce the risk of injury or accident to visitors. There were 20 of them, posted at the door of the Factor's House where the warden lived. Although some might view the wording as authoritarian, wardens did find them useful to help deal with awkward visitors. Some yachtsmen, for instance, did not like to be told they could not bring dogs ashore, a measure instigated to protect the sheep and nesting birds, and also to prevent the introduction of sheep parasites from mainland flocks. Under the new management arrangements the stakeholders have recently had to review the byelaws, with the emphasis now being on responsible access. An access leaflet, available through the boat operators, tourist information centres and the websites, carefully explains any restrictions in a more user-friendly manner.

Anyone who has endured a rough boat journey to reach St Kilda should be given an enjoyable experience ashore. The wardens will offer advice and a leaflet on walks around the immediate sites of interest on Hirta and its village, and groups are free to wander at will. Even if landing on the other islands was easy, weather and the ability of the visitor usually rule it out. But in my opinion the finest experience on offer at St Kilda is a cruise by boat around its awe-inspiring coastline, in particular Boreray and the Stacs. It is just a pity that weather conditions cannot always ensure this can take place.

We saw in Chapter 14 how the St Kildans, while anticipating an income, could find the arrival of visitors disruptive, and on rare occasions, even unpleasant. So it is today amongst the staff operating the Base. They have to live and work there so their needs have to be respected. In summer water can be in short supply, and public toilet facilities are virtually non-existent. The busiest days in their week are during resupply and, as anywhere, the staff value their weekends. Care needs to be taken not to disturb breeding birds or sheep, and not to introduce alien plants or animals, and of course not to endanger life and limb.

Any remote tourist attraction like St Kilda is a matter of a compromise between the various parties. The owners (the National Trust for Scotland) and the occupiers (Scottish Natural Heritage, the Ministry of Defence or QinetiQ, work parties, research workers) should be allowed to fulfil their particular aims without impairing the enjoyment of visitors, nor impinging on the best interests of the wildlife. The Range Facility only leases a tiny fraction of Hirta for its use. But the staff provide a permanent, if constantly rotating, human presence and are largely responsible for the infrastructure that allows everyone else to be there. Furthermore, the staff fulfil a very important monitoring function in winter, when no National Trust Ranger is present.

The summer wardens were appointed and line managed by the Nature Conservancy Council through their warden based at Loch Druidibeg National Nature Reserve in South Uist. Since 1992, when Scottish Natural Heritage was created from the Nature Conservancy Council, this role was performed by Area staff (myself included] still based at Stilligarry on the Druidibeg Reserve. Towards the end of each year a tri-partite meeting was held, hosted in turn by each of the three partners involved in St Kilda – the Trust, the Nature Conservancy Council or Scottish Natural Heritage – and the army. Being based in the Uists and so close to the Range facility, Scottish Natural Heritage staff were able to maintain excellent relationships with the military, mainly through a succession of military Conservation Officers, and latterly with DERA and QinetiQ.

When I first visited St Kilda in 1979, the army maintained a continual presence of some 25 squaddies, three sergeants and an Officer Commanding. Supply was by fortnightly army landing craft from Rhu on the Clyde or Loch

Carnan, South Uist, from April to October, with mail drops by plane at regular intervals through the winter. Latterly, the landing craft was making fewer visits, while supply was effected at fortnightly intervals throughout the year by a hired 18-seater helicopter.

In recent years and in line with the Range in the Uists, the Base on St Kilda has become increasingly civilianised. The army finally withdrew from St Kilda on 1 April 1998, with the last remaining soldier leaving on 31 July that year. Weapons Research and Development passed from the Royal Artillery to a civilian wing of the Ministry of Defence known as DERA, now a totally private company called QinetiQ. They maintain a staff of 15 at the Hirta Base, often augmented by additional contractors, etc.

The last army landing craft left St Kilda in September 1998. Since then heavy supplies have been delivered several times each summer by the chartered Norwegian landing craft *Elektron*. Helicopters now run twice weekly throughout the year (weather permitting of course), but with a seating capacity of only six.

Pursuing their interest in the cultural heritage and monuments, the National Trust have been sending out work parties and archaeologists to St Kilda every year since 1959 (missing only one year during the Foot and Mouth outbreak in 2001). They undertake maintenance or restoration of some of the buildings and have refurbished six of the old Village houses, repaired *cleitean* and other monuments, as well as undertaking valuable excavation work.

Scottish Natural Heritage were always keen to acknowledge the ability of owner/occupiers to manage their Nature Reserves as 'Approved Bodies'. The National Trust for Scotland have successfully managed other National Nature Reserves such as St Abb's Head and Staffa. So, recently, while negotiations on a new lease with the Ministry of Defence were being finalised, it was decided that this should be directly with the owners, the Trust. As an Approved Body, they would also manage the National Nature Reserve on Scottish Natural Heritage's behalf. Scottish Natural Heritage continue to fund the warden's post, but as one of the National Trust's own Rangers. A National Trust for Scotland Property Manager is currently based in Inverness, with additional responsibilities for a blackhouse on Lewis, and the islands of Mingulay, Berneray and Pabay which recently came into Trust possession (with a modest financial contribution from Scottish Natural Heritage).

So, on 26 August 2003, just about the time that a Gaelic version of the popular St Kilda website went on-line (www.kilda.org.uk and www.hiort.org.uk), the new lease for the Base was signed at QinetiQ in Balivanich, between the Ministry of Defence and the Trust.

On 9 October 2003, the St Kilda National Nature Reserve was re-declared at Balnain House in Inverness, in the presence of Dr Ian Jardine,

Chief Executive of Scottish Natural Heritage, and Dr Robin Pellew, Chief Executive for the National Trust for Scotland. A new Management Plan had been agreed between the Trust and Scottish Natural Heritage, which will serve to focus future strategies on the World Heritage Site, and by all other parties involved. To the public or visitors to St Kilda, little will change, but both new arrangements confirm the various organisations' commitment to St Kilda, while streamlining the successful management of St Kilda as a National Trust property and a National Nature Reserve. Scottish Natural Heritage will continue to fulfil their statutory role, not just in monitoring the National Nature Reserve and Site of Special Scientific Interest, but also in the National Scenic Area, the Special Protection Area and the Special Area for Conservation.

Scientists continue to visit, mainly to study the seabirds, or the sheep. The sheep study is now one of the longest running studies of a large mammal anywhere in the world. Dr (now Professor) Mike Harris (with assistant Stuart Murray) studied puffins on Dun during the 1970s and 1980s. The seabird numbers and breeding success are still monitored annually for the Joint Nature Conservation Committee's Seabirds at Sea Team through the National Trust for Scotland Seabird Warden, while the nesting gannets are counted by aerial survey on a roughly ten-year cycle. Smaller short-term research projects are undertaken from time to time.

It is not surprising, and entirely justified, that the archipelago should have attracted a host of conservation designations and accolades in the last 50 years. And as such, particularly as a World Heritage Site, St Kilda, its culture, surrounding seas and wildlife attract global interest and concern.

While there may be as few as a dozen people based on St Kilda in winter, numbers in summer can at times reach 50 or more. The continued presence on the Base provides a valuable off-season presence on the Nature Reserve. Indeed, without the radar station, it is unlikely that the present range of conservation management, archeological activities and visitor facilities could be sustained. In addition to regular transport service for staff, there is a public water supply, constant electric power, a twice-weekly mail service and even a pub. This is engagingly called the 'Puff Inn' and it was former medical officer cum naturalist David Boddington who designed and painted its first logo! Long a diversion and distraction for staff and visitors alike, the Puff Inn is no longer open to the public.

In conclusion, we have dipped into but a fraction of what has been documented about the human history of St Kilda, and indeed its natural history. To summarise either of these disciplines adequately is a huge task. We may recall James Fisher's eloquent comment quoted at the beginning of this book:

Whatever he studies, the future observer of St Kilda will be haunted for the rest of his life by the place, and tantalised by the impossibility of describing it to those who have not seen it.

One need not have visited St Kilda though to understand that it is a place of superlatives. We began this account with a venerable quote from the geologist John MacCulloch, who recognised the islands' worth:

I trust that St Kilda may long yet continue the Eden of the Western Ocean. It is a state of real opulence.

Through the subsequent chapters we have ourselves come to appreciate how St Kilda possesses some of the most spectacular coastal scenery in Britain, the highest sheer cliff and the highest sea stack in the British Isles. Once it supported the most remote community in the country with its own highly specialised history and culture. Furthermore, St Kilda has its own races of mice and wrens, the largest gannetry in the world, the largest puffin colony in the country, Britain's oldest fulmar colony, the most primitive flock of domestic sheep in the world. It carries a host of designations at national and international levels, including a National Scenic Area, a National Nature Reserve, and is Britain's only dual World Heritage Site both for its cultural and natural interests, and so on.

It is no wonder that this remote little archipelago has been drawing interested

Table 6. Conservation designations accorded to St Kilda

1957	Ownership to National Trust for Scotland (leased to the Nature Conservancy)
1957	National Nature Reserve
1963/72	Buildings scheduled under Ancient Monuments Act
1976	Biosphere Reserve (delisted 2000)
1981	National Scenic Area
1984	Site of Special Scientific Interest
1987	Scotland's first World Heritage Site for its Natural Heritage
1992	European Community Special Protection Area (for nesting seabirds)
2002	The boundaries of all four Scheduled Areas were extended and rescheduled.
2004	Marine interest added to the World Heritage listing
2005	European Community Special Area of Conservation (for sea caves and cliff vegetation)
2005	Cultural interest added to World Heritage listing (only 25 such dual sites out of 878 in world)

visitors for over three centuries. Amongst them were, not surprisingly, naturalists and scientists who would play a key role in documenting not just the geology and wildlife but also the people. Some names have become familiar with anyone who delves into the island 'library', but they themselves are seldom celebrated and remain shadows in St Kilda's story. Quite rightly the islanders figure prominently in their experiences, but lamentably few visitors endeavoured to commit much to paper, and, if they did, it was mostly in romantic retrospect.

Given the archipelago's rich natural heritage, it is hardly surprising that many authors were naturalists and scientists. At the risk of adding yet another volume to the numerous shelves already devoted to St Kilda, this book has attempted to tell their story, against that of the islanders themselves. Naturalists have done us a valuable service in studying the islands' rocks, scenery, plants and animals, while also unwittingly witnessing the islanders' decline and fall. But it has to be admitted they, and other tourists, have also played their own role in that story.

The issue has been less what visitors brought to the island but what they took away with them, generating a lucrative and important trade in natural history specimens for instance, and in souvenirs. For countless generations the St Kildans had successfully relied upon their own natural resources and their resourcefulness to survive. If their natural harvest failed and the elements conspired too much against them, they risked starvation, not a pleasant prospect of course and one that must have remained with them constantly.

Over the last couple of centuries, easier access to the outside world at last offered a buffer against deprivation, so it is understandable that the islanders reached for it. Initially, a few visiting benefactors introduced the idea that St Kilda might dip into foreign resources. By 1877, so many more tourists were arriving by steamer that not only was commercial opportunity available for the islanders, and sometimes even handouts, but they became an expectation. For all that the islanders came to be accused of scrounging whatever they could from outsiders, the British public and successive governments can take some responsibility for generating feelings of helplessness, hopelessness and abandonment amongst St Kildans. No other community on the mainland would have been, or indeed would now allow themselves to be, ignored quite as blatantly as the St Kildans. Alongside this, the church, its missionaries and ministers, may also take some responsibility for introducing elements of fatalism to the islanders' outlook.

The outside world had treated St Kilda little different from primitive outposts of the Empire on the other side of the world. A very few of the most intrepid travellers made a supreme effort to see Hirta for themselves, thus creating the modest tourist industry. Islanders were introduced to a cash economy which they came to exploit to maximum advantage – if somewhat clumsily. Visitors, on the other hand, were unwittingly damaging the very thing that they had come to see. These interactions were to present a brief respite however, but one that the St Kildans came to depend upon to a fatal degree.

Once more the outcome proved to be two-way. Regular communication in the summer brought tourists but also introduced the facility for islanders to leave Hirta altogether for greener pastures on the mainland or abroad. This happened from time to time in the past, notably in 1852 when 36 left for Australia: 18 of them died on the voyage. But by the end of the 19th century, emigration seemed a more attractive prospect. As the population diminished, such events had a greater impact upon those left behind, eroding their self-sufficiency, self-confidence, even their health. For two centuries, fulmars, for instance, contributed to the high infant mortality, whether through their oil, or even a disease like ornithosis as I described earlier. Margaret Fay Shaw recorded the nurse's opinion of the islandmen's poor state of health just prior to the evacuation. When it reached the point that there were barely enough able-bodied souls to perform even the most basic – yet vital – of community tasks, St Kilda's ancient race was doomed. That ultimate misfortune has already been well documented elsewhere.

It is a cruel irony that these self-same tourists, naturalists and now conservationists have inherited the Nature Reserve and World Heritage Site that is St Kilda. Their presence would hardly be possible without government input – an intervention that had appeared all too late, and for less charitable reasons. The Cold War introduced the need for early warning systems and missile-testing facilities in the Hebrides, in which St Kilda plays a role. The military infrastructure on Hirta has since been privatised, but still permits the owner – the National Trust for Scotland – and its partner organisations to fulfil research, management and conservation commitments. St Kildans would have been astonished at the services that have developed since the army arrived in 1957! If only their little community had managed to hang on for three more decades, their evacuation may never have been necessary.

Bibliography

Acland A. 1981 *A Devon Family: The Story of the Aclands* Phillimore & Co, Chichester

Anderson A. 1957 A count of fulmars on Hirta, St Kilda in July 1956 *Scottish Naturalist* 69: 113–16

Anderson A. 1962 A count of fulmars on Hirta, St Kilda, in July 1961 *Scottish Naturalist* 70: 120–25

Armstrong Rev. E. A. 1955 *The Wren* Collins, London

Armstrong Rev. E. A. 1959 The history, behaviour and breeding biology of the St Kilda wren *British Birds* 52: 136–8

Atkinson G. C. 1832 Notice of St Kilda *Transactions of the Natural History Society of Northumberland* 2: 215–25

Atkinson G. C. 1838 An account of an expedition to St Kilda in 1831 *Transactions of the Natural History Society of Northumberland, Durham and Newcastle* 2: 215–25

Atkinson R. 1947 Studies of species rarely photographed VI The St Kilda wren *British Birds* 40: 145

Atkinson R. 1949 *Island Going* Collins, London (Reprint 1995, Birlinn, Edinburgh)

Bagenal T. B. 1953 The birds of St Kilda, 1952 *Scottish Naturalist* 65: 19–24

Bagenal T. B. 1958 The feeding of nestling St Kilda wrens *Bird Study* 5: 83–7

Bagenal T. B. 2003 The rape of St Kilda? *St Kilda Mail* 27: 27–8

Baldwin J. 1974 Sea bird fowling in Scotland and Faroe *Folk Life* 12: 60–103

Barrett-Hamilton G. E. H. 1899a On the species of the genus *Mus* inhabiting St. Kilda. *Proceedings of the Zoological Society, London* 77–88

Barrett-Hamilton G. E. H. 1899b On two recently described mice from St Kilda *Annals of Scottish Natural History* 31: 129–140

Barrett-Hamilton G. E. H. 1900 On geographical and individual variation in *Mus sylvaticus* and its allies *Proceedings of the Zoological Society, London* 387–428

Barrett-Hamilton G. E. H. 1906 On a collection of mice (*Mus hirtensis* and *M. muralis*) from St Kilda *Annals of Scottish Natural History* 57: 1–4

Barrett-Hamilton G. E. H. 1910 *A History of British Mammals* London

Barrington R. M. 1866 Notes on the flora of St Kilda *Journal of Botany* 24: 213–16

Barrington R. M. 1884 The St Kilda wren *Zoologist* 8: 383–5

Barrington R. M. 1913 Ascent of Stack na Biorrach, St Kilda *Alpine Journal* 27:195–202

Barry J. 1980 Aircraft wrecks of St Kilda *After the Battle* 30:28–43

Baxter J. 1998 Spectacular underwater secrets of St Kilda *Heritage Scotland* 15: 22–5

Beare T. H. 1908 Notes on the Coleoptera from St Kilda *Annals of Scottish Natural History* 17: 30–5

Beare T. H. 1916 Notes on Coleoptera from St Kilda *Scottish Naturalist* 258–60

Bedford, Duchess of 1914 Spring bird notes from various Scottish islands *Scottish Naturalist* 1914: 173–81

Berry R. J. 1969 History in the evolution of *Apodemus sylvaticus* (Mammalia) at one end of its range *Journal of Zoology* 159: 311–28

Birkhead T. 1993 *Great Auk Islands* Poyser, London

Boddington D. 1958–9 St Kilda, Outer Hebrides *Bird Migration* 1: 24–5, 72–3

Boece Hector 1527 *Scotorum Regni Description f xiiii: part of: Scotorum Historiae Prima Gentis Origine cum aliarum et rerum et gentium illustratione non vulgari* Paris

Bones M. 1992 The Garefowl or Great Auk *Pinguinis impennis Hebridean Naturalist* 11: 15–24

Bones M. 1994 Notes on the flora of St Kilda *Hebridean Naturalist* 14: 37–59

Booth A. 1996 *A National Vegetation Classification Survey of Hirta and Dun* Report to Scottish Natural Heritage

Boswell J. 1786 *The Journal of a Tour to the Hebrides* (Reprint 1974, Oxford University Press)

Boyd J. M. 1952 St Kilda in 1952 *Scottish Field* October 1952

Boyd J. M. 1953 The sheep population of Hirta 1952 *Scottish Naturalist* 65: 25–8

Boyd, J. M.1954 The St Kilda Wren in the village area, 1952 *Scottish Naturalist* 66: 47–9

Boyd J. M. 1956a The St Kilda field mouse (*Apodemus sylvaticus hirtensis* Barrett-Hamilton) population in Village area, Hirta, May 1955 *Oikos* 7: 110–16

Boyd J. M. 1956b The sheep population of Hirta, St Kilda, 1955 *Scottish Naturalist* 68: 10–13

Boyd J. M. 1956c The Lumbricidae of Hirta, St Kilda *Annual Magazine of Natural History* 9: 129–33

Boyd J. M. 1957a Animals and humans at St Kilda *Discovery* 344–8

Boyd J. M. 1957b Ecological distribution of the Lumbricidae in the Hebrides *Proceedings of the Royal Society of Edinburgh* 66B: 311–38

Boyd J. M. 1957c Lumbricidae at Boreray, St Kilda *Glasgow Naturalist* 17: 280–1

Boyd J. M. 1959 Observations on the St Kilda Field Mouse *Apodemus sylvaticus hirtensis* Barrett-Hamilton *Proceedings of the Zoological Society, London* 133: 47–65

Boyd J. M. 1960 Distribution and numbers of the Kittiwake and the Guillemot at St Kilda *British Birds* 252–64

Boyd J. M. 1961 The gannetry of St Kilda *Journal of Animal Ecology* 30: 33–54

Boyd J. M. 1979 The natural environment of the Outer Hebrides *Proceedings of the Royal Society of Edinburgh* 77B: 561

Boyd J. M. 1981 The Boreray sheep of St Kilda, Outer Hebrides, Scotland: the natural history of a feral population *Biological Conservation* 20: 215–28

Boyd J. M. 1986 *Fraser Darling's Islands* Edinburgh University Press

Boyd J. M. 1999 *The Song of the Sandpiper* Colin Baxter, Grantown-on-Spey

Boyd J. M., Munns D. J. and Whitehouse A. A. K. 1956 Birds in St Kilda, May 1955 *Scottish Naturalist* 68: 14–22

Boyd J. M., Tewnion A. and Wallace D. I. M. 1957 Birds in St Kilda, midsummer 1956 *Scottish Naturalist* 69: 94–112

Brathay Exploration Group 1972 Field studies on St Kilda, 1971 *Field Studies Report No. 20* Brathay Hall, Ambleside.

Brazenor H. 1908 Proposed dealers' raid on the birds of St Kilda and the Outer Hebrides *Annals of Scottish Natural History* 17: 35–6

Bristow W. S. 1927 The spider fauna of the Western Isles of Scotland *Scottish Naturalist* 88–94, 117–122

Brougham, Lord 1871 *Memoirs of the Life and Times of Lord Brougham Written by Himself* London and Edinburgh

Buchan A. 1727 *A Description of St Kilda* Lumsden and Robertson, Edinburgh (reprinted with substantial alterations by Miss Buchan, 1752)

Buchan J. N. S., Harrisson T. H. and Lack D. 1932 Early autumn migration in 1931 *Scottish Naturalist* 3–8

Buchan, J. N. S. 1953 *Always a Countryman* Robert Hale, London

Bullock D. J. 1983 Borerays, the other rare breed on St Kilda *The Ark* August 1983

Buxton B 1995 *Mingulay: An Island and its People* Birlinn, Edinburgh

Cadman P., Ellis J., Geiger D. and Piertney S. 1993 A survey of the marine fauna of the St Kilda archipelago *Report of Department of Marine Biology University of Wales, Swansea*

Campbell R. 1799 *An Account of the Island of St Kilda and Neighbouring Islands, Visited August 1799* National Library of Scotland, MS. 3051

Campbell R. 1945 Obituary: John Mathieson FRESE FRSGS *Scottish Geographical Magazine* 61: 71

Carmichael A. 1928–71 *Carmina Gadelica* vols 1, 2, 4, 5 & 6 Oliver and Boyd, Edinburgh and London

Cartier J. 1534 Quoted in Biggar H. P. 1924 *The Voyages of Jaques Cartier* Publications of the Public Archives of Canada No. 11

Castro P. M. and Keppie J. L. 1981 A note on the St Kilda flora *St Kilda Mail* 5: 30

Clarke Edward Daniel 1824 *The Life and Remains of Edward Daniel Clarke* Ed. W. Otter, London

Clarke W. E. 1911 Birds of St Kilda *Annals of Scottish Natural History* 51–2

Clarke W. E. 1912a Baird's sandpiper at St Kilda *Scottish Naturalist* 9–10

Clarke W. E. 1912b *Studies in Bird Migration* 2 vols, Edinburgh

Clarke W. E. 1913 Song thrush of Outer Hebrides *Scottish Naturalist* 124–8

Clarke W. E. 1914 Notes on mice of St Kilda *Scottish Naturalist* 124–8

Clarke W. E. 1915a The wren of St Kilda, its status, plumages and habits *Scottish Naturalist* 291–6

Clarke W. E. 1915b Corncrake at St Kilda *Scottish Naturalist* 333

Clarke W. E. 1916 Notes on some Scottish birds observed in 1915 *Scottish Naturalist* 75–9

Clarke W. E. 1919 Starlings of Shetland, Fair Isle and St Kilda *Scottish Naturalist* 183–5

Clegg E. J. 1977 Population changes in St Kilda during the 19th and 20th centuries *Journal Biosc. Science* 9: 293–307

Clegg E. J. 1984 Some factors associated with island depopulation and the example of St Kilda *Northern Scotland* 6: 3–11

Clutton-Brock T. and Pemberton J. 2004 *Soay Sheep*. Cambridge University Press

Cockburn A. M. 1934 The geology of St Kilda *Transactions of the Royal Society of Edinburgh* 35: 511–54

Collacott R. A. 1981 Neonatal tetanus in St Kilda *Scottish Medical Journal* 26: 224–7

Collacott, R. A. 1985 Medical and nursing services to St Kilda, *Scottish Medical Journal* 30: 181–3

Connell R. 1887 *St Kilda and the St Kildians* Adams & Co., London

Corbet A. S. 1945 The lepidoptera of St Kilda *Entomologist* 78: 166–8

Cott H. B. 1951–2 The palatability of the eggs of birds. *Proceedings of the Zoological Society, London* 121: 1–41; 122: 1–54

Cott H. B. 1953 The exploitation of wild birds for their eggs. *Ibis* 95: 409–49, 643–75

Crawley M. J. 1993 *The Flora of St Kilda* Imperial College, Silwood Park

Dale C. W. 1884 Captures in North Uist and St Kilda *Entomologist's Monthly Magazine* 20: 213–14

Dale C. W. 1884 Capture of insects in the Hebrides and in St Kilda *Scottish Naturalist* 7, 284

Dale C. W. 1889 The insect fauna of St Kilda *Entomologist* 22: 12–13

Dampier William 1927 *A New Voyage Round the World 1697* Argonaut Press, London

Darwin C. R. 1839 *Journal of Researches into the Natural History and Geology of the Countries Visited during the Voyage of HMS Beagle round the World* Colburn, London

Darwin C. R. 1859 *On the Origin of Species by Means of Natural Selection* Murray, London

Davies L. 1981 Additions to the list of Diptera for Hirta, St Kilda Group, Scotland *Entomologist's Monthly Magazine* 116: 216–18

Davies L. and Richardson J. 1973 Occurrence of the two *Petrobius* spp.(Thysanura) in different habitat types on Hirta, St Kilda *Entomologist* 106: 16–22

Dixon C. 1885 The Ornithology of St Kilda *Ibis* 5: 69–97, 358–62

Dixon C. 1888 *Our Rarer Birds* London

Dresser H. E. 1886 On the wren of St Kilda *Ibis* 4: 43–5

Duffey E. A. G. 1959 *Spiders taken on St Kilda with Extracts from a Field Notebook* St Kilda Nature Reserve Record: The Nature Conservancy (Unpublished)

Duncan N., Bullock D. and Taylor K. 1981 *A Report on the Eecology and Natural History of Boreray, St Kilda* Department of Zoology, University of Durham.

Edwards F.W. and Collin J. E. 1932 A revised list of Diptera for St Kilda *Entomologist's Monthly Magazine* 68: 263–6

Elliott J. S. 1895 St Kilda and the St Kildans *Journal Birmingham Natural History and Philosophical Society* 1: 113–35

Elliott J. S. 1895 Observations on the fauna of St Kilda *The Zoologist* 19: 281–6

Ellis J. R., Cadman P. S., Piertney S. B. and Geiger D. L. 1995 The marine fauna of the St Kilda archipelago *Scottish Naturalist* 107: 53–70

Elwes H. J. 1869 The bird stations of the Outer Hebrides *Ibis* 5: 20–37

Elwes J. 1912 Notes on the primitive breeds of sheep in Scotland *Scottish Naturalist* 10: 1–7, 25–9

Evans W. 1906 Some Invertebrata, including *Ixodes borealis* from St Kilda *Annals of Scottish Natural History* 15: 93–8

Evans W. 1912 Some Lepidoptera and other insects from St Kilda *Scottish Naturalist* 262

Evans W. 1921 Some moss records from St Kilda *Transactions and Proceedings of the Botanical Society of Edinburgh* 28: 67–9

Ewart J. C. 1913 Domestic sheep and their wild ancestors *Transactions of the Highland and Agricultural Society Scotland* 5, 25: 160–91

Ferguson C. 1995 *Hiort; far na laigh a'ghrian* Acair, Stornoway

Ferguson C. 2006 *St Kilda Heritage* Acair, Stornoway

Ferguson T. 1958 Infantile tetanus in some Western Isles in the second half of the nineteenth century *Scottish Medical Journal* 3: 140–6

Fisher J. 1948 St Kilda: A natural experiment *New Naturalist Journal* 1: 91–108

Fisher J. 1952 *The Fulmar* Collins, London

Fisher J. and Lockley R. 1954 *Sea Birds* Collins, London

Fisher J. and Vevers H. G. 1943 and 1944 Breeding distribution, breeding and population of North Atlantic gannet *Journal of Animal Ecology* 12: 173–213 and 13: 49–62

Fisher J. and Waterston G. 1941 Breeding distribution, history and population of Fulmar in British Isles *Journal of Animal Ecology* 10: 204–72

Fleming A. 2005 *St Kilda and the Wider World* Windgather Press, Cheshire

Fleming J. 1828 *A History of British Animals* Bell and Brad Fute, Edinburgh

Fordun, John of 1871 *Chronica Gentis Scotorum* ed. W. F. Skene. Edmonston and Douglas, Edinburgh

Forrester R. W., Andrews A. J., McInerny C. J., Murray R. D., McGowan R. Y., Zonfrillo B., Betts M. W., Jardine D. C. and Grundy D. S. (eds) 2007 *The Birds of Scotland* 2 vols. Scottish Ornithologists Club, Aberlady

Freer A. G. 1903 *Outer Isles* Constable and Co., Westminster

Fuller E. 1999 *The Great Auk* Errol Fuller, Southborough

Gauld D. T., Bagenal T. B. and Connel J. H. 1953 The marine fauna and flora of St Kilda, 1952 *Scottish Naturalist* 65: 29–49

Gauld D.T. 1992 Memories of St Kilda *St Kilda Mail* 16: 33–5

Geikie Sir A. 1897 *The Ancient Volcanoes of Britain* Macmillan, London

Geikie Sir A. 1904 *Scottish Reminiscences* Maclehose, Glasgow

George R.S. 1959 A collection of fleas (Siphonaptera) from St Kilda *Entomologist's Gazette* 10: 54–7

Gibson A. H. 1891 The phanerogamic flora of St Kilda *Transactions of the Botanical Society of Edinburgh* 19:155–8

Gibson G. 1928 The tragedy of St Kilda *Caledonian Medical Journal* April 1928: 50–62

Gilbert O. 2004 *The Lichen Hunters* The Book Guild, Sussex

Gilbert O.L., Watling R. and Coppins B. J. 1979 Lichen ecology on St Kilda *The Lichenologist* 2: 191–202

Gillies N. 1988 Autobiographical notes in: Quine, D.A. *St Kilda Portraits* Ambleside 37–9

Gladstone J. 1928 Notes on the flora in St Kilda (ed. J. Mathieson) *Scottish Geographical Magazine* 44: 77–9

Gordon S. 1933 *Islands of the West* Cassell, London

Gordon S. 1937 *Afoot in the Hebrides* Cassell, London

Gray R. 1871 *The Birds of the West of Scotland* Murray, Glasgow

Grieve S. 1885 *The Great Auk or Garefowl* Thomas C. Jack, London

Grimshaw P. H. 1907 On the Diptera of St Kilda *Annals of Scottish Natural History* 16: 150–8

Gurney J. H. 1913 *The Gannet: A Bird with a History* Witherby, London

Gwynne D., Milner C. and Hornung M. 1974 The vegetation and soils of Hirta. In Jewell, P. A., Milner C. and Boyd, J.M. (eds) *Island Survivors; The Ecology of the Soay Sheep of St Kilda* Athlone Press, London

Harding R. R., Merriman R. J. and Nancarrow, P. H. A. 1984 *St Kilda: An Illustrated Account of the Geology* HMSO, London

Harman M. 1997 *An Isle called Hirte* Maclean Press, Isle of Skye

Harris M. P. and Murray S. 1977 Puffins on St Kilda *British Birds* 70: 50–65

Harris M. P. 1984 *The Puffin* Poyser, Calton

Harris M. P. and Murray S. 1989 *Birds of St Kilda*, Institute of Terrestrial Ecology & Natural Environmental Research Council, UK

Harris M. P., Murray S. and Wanless S. 1998 Long term changes in breeding performance of puffins *Fratercula arctica* on St Kilda *Bird Study* 45: 371–4

Harris M. P. and Rothery P. 1988 Monitoring the puffin burrows on Dun, St Kilda 1977–87 *Bird Study* 35: 97–9

Harrisson T. H. 1932 Numbers of grey seals on North Rona and St Kilda *Journal of Animal Ecology* 1: 83

Harrisson T. H. 1933 Counts of gannets in Scottish islands *Journal of Animal Ecology* 2: 116

Harrisson T. H. and Buchan J. N. S. 1934 A field study of the St Kilda wren (*Troglodytes troglodytes hirtensis*), with especial reference to its numbers, territory and food habits *Journal of Animal Ecology* 3: 133–45

Harrisson T. H. and Buchan J. N. S. 1936 Field study of wren, its nesting habits and song *Scottish Naturalist* 9–21

Harrisson T. H. and Moy-Thomas J. A. 1932 House mouse *Nature* 129: 131

Harrisson T. H. and Moy-Thomas J. A. 1933 The mice of St Kilda, with especial reference to their prospects of extinction and present status *Journal of Animal Ecology* 2: 109–15

Harrisson T. H. and Lack D. 1934 The breeding birds of St Kilda *Scottish Naturalist* 1934: 59–69

Harvie-Brown J. A. 1912 Fulmar, its past and present distribution as breeding-species in British Isles *Scottish Naturalist* 97–102, 121–32

Harvie-Brown J. A. and Buckley T. E. 1888 *A Vertebrate Fauna of the Outer Hebrides* Edinburgh

Harvie-Brown J. A. 1902 and 1903 Avifauna of Outer Hebrides *Annals of Scottish Natural History* 83–92, 136–51, 199–217 and 1–22

Heathcote E. 1900 A night in an ocean cave *Wide World Magazine* August 1900: 91–6

Heathcote E. 1901 A Summer Sojourn in St Kilda *Good Words* 42: 460–7

Heathcote J. N. 1900 On the map of St Kilda *Geographical Journal* 15: 142–4

Heathcote J. N. 1901 Climbing on St Kilda *Scottish Mountaineering Club Journal* 6: 146–51

Heathcote N. 1900 *St Kilda* Longmans, London

Hewitt C. G. 1907 Some Arthrostraca and other invertebrata from St Kilda *Annals of Scottish Natural History* 219–21

Howson C. M. and Picton B. E. 1985 *A sub-littoral survey of St Kilda: 7–20 July 1984* Report to the Nature Conservancy Council

Hudson W. H. 1894 *Lost British Birds*. RSPB pamphlet

Huxley J. 1939 Birds and men on St Kilda *Geographical Magazine* 10: 69–82

Innes H. 1962 *Atlantic Fury* Collins, London

Innes H. 1967 *Sea and Islands* Collins, London

Jewell P. A., Milner C. and Boyd J. M. 1974 *Island survivors: the ecology of the Soay sheep of St Kilda* Athlone Press, London

Johnson S. and Boswell, J. 1930 *Journey to the Western Islands of Scotland and Journal of a Tour to the Hebrides with Samuel Johnson* (Reprint 1978, Melven Press, Inverness)

Joy N. H. 1908 Notes on Coleoptera from St Kilda, mainly collected from birds' nests *Annals of Scottish Natural History* 33–5

Kearton R. 1897 *With Nature and a Camera* Cassell, London

Lack D. 1931a Diary, Oxford University Library

Lack D. 1931b Coleoptera on St Kilda in 1931 *Entomologist's Monthly Magazine* 67: 276–9

Lack D. 1932 Further notes on insects from St Kilda, including the orders Thysanura, Dermapetra, Hemipetra, Lepidoptera, Coleoptera (supplement) and Hymenoptera *Entomologist's Monthly Magazine* 68: 139–45

Lack D. 1931 Effect of exodus from St Kilda on the island's flora and fauna *Illustrated London News* 26 December

Lack D. 1932 Notes on the Diptera of St Kilda *Entomologist's Monthly Magazine* 68: 139–45

Lack D. 1937 *St Kilda Papers* Oxford

Lack D. 1959 Some British pioneers in ornithological research *Ibis* 101: 71–81

Love J. A. 1982 Harvie-Brown: a profile *Scottish Birds* 12: 49–53

Love J. A. 1983 *The Return of the Sea Eagle* Cambridge University Press

Love J. A. 2001 *Rum: A Landscape without Figures* Birlinn, Edinburgh

Love J. A. 2004a SNH and St Kilda *Hebridean Naturalist* 14: 1–6

Love J. A. 2004b Marine creatures of St Kilda *Hebridean Naturalist* 14: 34–6

Love J. A. 2004c The lepidoptera of St Kilda *Hebridean Naturalist* 14: 22–7

Love J. A. 2005a *St Kilda: A World Apart* Scottish Natural Heritage, Battleby

Love J. A. 2005b Seabird resources and fowling in Scotland. In Randall J. (ed.) *Traditions of Sea-bird Fowling in the North Atlantic Region*. Islands Book Trust, Stornoway

Love J. A. 2007 Natural history and the St Kilda Library. In Randall J. (ed.) *St Kilda: Myth and Reality* Islands Book Trust, Port of Ness.

Love J. A. 2008 *Three Centuries of Highland Naturalists Island Notes*, Islands Book Trust, Stornoway.

Lawson W. M. 1993 *Croft History: Isle of St Kilda* Northton, Harris

Lowe F. *The Heron* Collins, London

MacAulay D. 1728 SSPCK archive Quoted in Robson M. 2005 *St Kilda: Church, Visitors and 'Natives'* Islands Book Trust, Stornoway

Macaulay K. 1764 *The History of St Kilda* Beckett & Dettondt, London

MacCulloch J. 1819 *A Description of the Western Isles of Scotland* Hurst, Robinson and Co., London

MacCulloch J. 1824 *The Highlands and Western Isles of Scotland* Longman, London

MacDiarmid J. 1878 St Kilda and its inhabitants *Transactions of the Highland and Agricultural Society* 10: 232–54

MacDonald C. (or M.) 1988 Visit to St Kilda to transfer Soay sheep in 1932, also the visits in 1933 and 1936. In Quine D. A. 1988 *St Kilda Portraits* 171–3 Downland Press, Frome

MacDonald J. 1811 *General View of the Agriculture of the Hebrides* Phillips, Edinburgh

MacDonald L. 1988 Autobiographical notes. In Quine, D. A. 1988 *St Kilda Portraits* Downland Press, Frome 115–47

MacFarlane W. 1908 *Geographical Collections* 3 vols. Scottish Historical Society, Edinburgh

Macgillivray J. 1842 An account of the island of St. Kilda, chiefly with reference to its natural history; from notes made during a visit in July 1840 *Edinburgh New Philosophical Journal* 32: 47–178

MacGillivray W. 1830 The birds of the Outer Hebrides *Edinburgh Journal of Natural and Geographical Science* 142: 245–50; 401–11; 87–95; 161–5; 321–34

MacGregor A. A. 1931 *A Last Voyage to St Kilda* Cassell, London

MacKay J. A. 1978 *Islands Postal History: Harris and St Kilda*. James A. Mackay, Dumfries

Mackay J 2002 *Soldiering on St Kilda* Token Publishing, Devon

Mackay J. 2006 *The St Kilda Steamers: A History of McCallum, Orme & Co* Tempus, Stroud

Mackenzie J. B. 1911 *Episode in the Life of the Rev. Neil Mackenzie at St Kilda from 1829 to 1843* (privately published)

Mackenzie O. H. 1853 *A Hundred Years in the Highlands* Edward Arnold, London

MacKenzie N. 1905 Notes on the birds of St Kilda *Annals of Scottish Natural History* 14: 75–80, 141–53

MacKenzie N. 1906 Bardachd Irteach *Celtic Review* 2: 328–42

MacKenzie, Sir George of Tarbat 1681–4 An Account of Hirta and Rona. In MacFarlane, W. *Geographical Collections Relating to Scotland* 1908, vol. 3, 28

MacLachlan Alice 1906–9 Typescript copy of diaries in National Trust for Scotland Archive

MacLean C. 1972 *Island on the Edge of the World: The Story of St Kilda*. Tom Stacey Ltd (Revised edition Canongate, Edinburgh 1996)

MacLean L. 1838 *Sketches on the Island of St Kilda* McPhun, Glasgow

MacTaggart F. 2001 *St Kilda (Hiort) Site of Special Scientific Interest (Part II Geomorphology)* Earth Science Site Documentation Series, Scottish Natural Heritage, Edinburgh

McVean D. N. 1961 Flora and vegetation of the Islands of St Kilda and North Rona 1958. *Journal of Ecology* 49: 39–54

Manson-Bahr P. 1959 Recollections of some famous British ornithologists *Ibis* 101: 53–64

Martin M. 1697 *A Late Voyage to St Kilda* London (Reprint 1986, James Thin, The Mercat Press, Edinburgh)

Martin M. 1698 *Description of the Western Isles of Scotland* Andrew Bell, London

Mathieson, J. 1928 St Kilda *Scottish Geographical Magazine* 44: 65–90

Mathieson J. 1928 The antiquities of the St Kilda group of islands *Proceedings of the Society of Antiquaries of Scotland* 62: 123–32

Mathieson J. 1928 *Map of St Kilda or Hirta and Adjacent Islands and Stacs* Ordnance Survey

Mathieson J. and Cockburn A. M. 1929 St Kilda *Transactions of the Edinburgh Geological Society* 12: 287–8

McVean D. N. 1961 Flora and vegetation of the islands of St Kilda and North Rona in 1958 *Journal of Ecology* 49: 39–54

McWilliam J. M. 1929 Some considerations on bird fluctuation *Scottish Naturalist* 1929

Miles W. T. S. and Money S. 2008 Behaviour and diet of non-breeding snowy owls on St Kilda *Scottish Birds* 28: 11–18

Millais J. G. 1904–06 *The Mammals of Great Britain and Ireland* 3 vols Longman, London

Milner C. and Gwynne D. 1974 The Soay sheep and their food supply. In Jewell P. A., Milner C. and Boyd J. M. (eds) *Island Survivors: the Ecology of the Soay Sheep of St Kilda* Athlone Press, London

Milner W. M. E. 1848 Some account of the people of St Kilda, and of the birds in the Outer Hebrides *The Zoologist* 1848, 2054–62

Mitchell I., Newton S. F., Ratcliffe N. and Dunn T. E. 2004 *Seabird Populations of Britain and Ireland* Poyser, London

Mitchell W. R. 1990 *St Kilda: A Voyage to the Edge of the World* Oban Times Publishing

Mitchell W. R. 1999 Honeymoon on St Kilda *Scots Magazine* (Feb) 150: 165–8

Mitchell W. R. 1992 *Finlay MacQueen of St Kilda* Oban Times Publishing

Money S., Söhle I. and Parsons M. 2008 A pilot study of the phenology and breeding success of Leach's Storm-petrel *Oceanodroma leucorhoa* on St Kilda, Western Isles *Seabird* 21: 98–101

Monro D. 1961 *Description of the Western Isles of Scotland* R.W. Munro (ed.) Oliver and Boyd, Edinburgh

Moran Stephen 1994 *A Preliminary Report on the Invertebrates Collected in Pitfall Traps by SNH Staff on Hirta, St Kilda, July–September 1993* Scottish Natural Heritage, Stornoway

Moray R. 1678 A Description of the island of Hirta *Philosophical Transaction of the Royal Society of London* 12: 927–9

Morgan J. E. 1861 The falcon among the fulmars; or six hours in St Kilda *MacMillan's Magazine* June 1861: 104–11

Morgan J. E. 1862 The diseases of St Kilda *British and Foreign Medico-Chirurgical Review* 29: 176–91

Muir T. S. 1858 *St Kilda: A Fragment of Travel* Privately printed, Edinburgh

Muir T. S. 1861 *Characteristics of Old Church Architecture etc in the Mainland and Western Islands of Scotland* Edinburgh

Muir T. S. 1885 *Ecclesiological Notes on Some of the Islands of Scotland* David Douglas, Edinburgh

Murray J. 1905 Microscopic life of St Kilda *Annals of Scottish Natural History* 94–6

Murray S. 2002 *Birds of St Kilda* Scottish Birds Supplement to vol. 23

Murray S. 2004 Cetacean records from St Kilda *Hebridean Naturalist* 14: 28–33

Murray, S. and Wanless, S. 1986 The status of the Gannet in Scotland 1984–5 *Scottish Birds* 14: 74–85

Napier Commission 1884 Highland Crofters: Report of her Majesty's Commissioners of Enquiry into the Conditions of the Crofters and Cottars in the Highlands and Islands of Scotland, Parliamentary Accounts and Papers 34

Newson S. E., Mitchell P. I., Parsons M., O'Brien S. H., Austin G. E., Benn S., Black J., Blackburn J., Brodie B., Humphreys E., Leech D. I., Prior M. and Webster M. 2008 Population decline of Leach's Storm-petrel *Oceanodroma leucorhoa* within the largest colony in Britain and Ireland. *Seabird* 21: 77–84

Newton A. 1907 *Ootheca Wolleyana* Porter, London

Nicholson E. M. and Fisher J. 1940 A bird census of St Kilda, 1939 *British Birds* 34: 29–35

Nicolson J. 1937 John Sands *Shetland Times* 3.7.1937

Nørrevang A. 1977 *Fuglefangsten på Faerøerne* Rhodos, Torshavn

Olsen B. and Nørrevang A. 2005 Seabird fowling in the Faroe Islands. In Randall, J. (ed) *Traditions of Sea-bird Fowling in the North Atlantic Region* Islands Book Trust, Stornoway

Pankhurst R. J. and Mullin J. M. 1991 *Flora of the Outer Hebrides* Natural History Museum, London

Pennie I. D. 1964 Scottish ornithologists: 1 Sir Robert Sibbald *Scottish Birds* 3: 159–67

Pennie I. D. 1966 Scottish ornithologists: 2 Martin Martin *Scottish Birds* 4: 64–73

Pennington M., Osborn K., Harvey P., Riddington R., Okill D., Ellis P. and Huebeck M. 2004 *The Birds of Shetland* Chistopher Helm, London

Petch C.P. 1932 Additions to the flora of St. Kilda *Journal of Botany* 70: 169–71

Petch C.P. 1933 The vegetation of St Kilda. *Journal of Ecology* 21: 92–100

Phillips R. A., Bearhop S., Thompson D. R. and Hamer K. C. 1999a Rapid population growth of Great Skuas at St Kilda: implications for management and conservation *Bird Study* 46: 174–83

Phillips R. A., Thompson D. R. and Harmer K. C. 1999b The impact of Great Skua predation on seabird population at St Kilda: a bioenergetics model *Journal of Applied Ecology* 36: 218–32

Pickard-Cambridge O. 1905 Spiders of St Kilda *Annals of Scottish Natural History* 14: 220–3

Pike O. G. 1910 *Through Birdland Byways with Pen and Camera* Jarrold, London

Pike O. G. 1946 *Nature and My Cine Camera* Focal Press, London

Pomfret A. A. 1931 The evacuation of St. Kilda *Journal of the Royal Naval Medical Service* 17: 1931

Poore M. E. D. and Robertson V. C. 1949 The vegetation of St. Kilda in 1948 *Journal of Ecology* 37: 82–99

Posford Duvivier Environment 2000 *Broad Scale Survey and Mapping of the Seabed and Shore Habitats and Biota: St Kilda SAC* Scottish Natural Heritage Commissioned Report F97PA01

Powell M. 1990 *Edge of the World* Faber and Faber, London

Praeger R. L. 1897 Flora of St. Kilda *Annals of Scottish Natural History* 1897, 53

Praeger R. L. 1937 *The Way I Went* Methuen, London

Quine D. A. 1982 *St Kilda Revisited* Dowland Press, Frome. (Revised edition 1989)

Quine D. A. 1988 *St Kilda Portraits* Dowland Press, Frome

Quine D. A. (ed.) 2001 *Expeditions to the Hebrides By George Clayton Atkinson in 1831 and 1833* Maclean Press, Isle of Skye

Randall J. (ed.) 2005 *Traditions of Sea-bird Fowling in the North Atlantic Region.* Islands Book Trust, Stornoway

Randall J. (ed.) 2008 *Whaling and the Hebrides* Islands Book Trust, Stornoway

Rankin N. 1935 Notes from St Kilda *Bird Notes and News* 16: 105–8

Ratcliffe D. 1959 *The Vegetation of St Kilda*. Report to the Nature Conservancy, Edinburgh

Ridley G. 1983 *St Kilda – A Submarine Guide* G. Ridley, Glasgow

Ritchie J. 1920 *The Influence of Man on Animal Life in Scotland* Cambridge University Press, Cambidge

Ritchie J. 1930 St Kilda and the significance of some of its animal inhabitants *Scottish Naturalist* 1930: 69–74

Robinson A. J. 2004 St Kilda Seasons 1999–2001 *Hebridean Naturalist* 14: 7–21

Robson M. 2005 *St Kilda: Church, Visitors and 'Natives'* Islands Book Trust, Stornoway

Robson R. 2001 *St Kilda (Hiort) Site of Special Scientific Interest (Part 1 Geology)* Earth Science Documentation Series Scottish Natural Heritage, Edinburgh

Ross A. 1884 A visit to the island of St Kilda *Transactions of the Inverness Scientific Society and Field Club* 3: 72–91

Ross J. C. 1890 *St Kilda* MS. National Trust for Scotland, Edinburgh, Bute Box

Rothschild M. 1958 Fleas from the nest of the St Kilda wren (*Troglodytes troglodytes hirtensis* Seeb.) *Entomologist* 91: 76

Rothschild N. C. 1907 A new British flea *Entomologist* 43: 11

Royal Highland and Agricultural Society of Scotland Papers (Collection of letters, receipts, etc., relating to Kelsall Fund for St Kilda)

Ryder M. *Sheep and Man* Duckworth, London

Sands J. 1878 *Out of the World; or, Life in St Kilda* Maclachlan & Stewart, Edinburgh

Scottish Executive 2003 *Revised Nomination of St Kilda for inclusion in the World Heritage Site List* HMSO, Edinburgh

Seebohm H. 1884 On a new species of British wren *Zoologist* 8: 333–5

Seton G. 1878 *St Kilda Past and Present* (Reprint, Mercat Press, Edinburgh)

Sharp D. 1888 Entomological Society of London meeting notice *Entomologist's Monthly Magazine* 25: 117

Shaw M. F. 1980 St Kilda: The last summer *Scots Magazine* August 510–14

Shaw M. F. 1957 *Folksongs and Folklore of South Uist* Routledge and Kegan Paul, London

Sibbald R. 1684 *Scotia Illustrata sive Prodromus historiae naturalis* 3 vols, Jacobi Kniblo, Edinburgh

Skirving R. Scott 1880 *MS Journal* quoted by Robson M. 2005 *St Kilda: Church, Visitors and 'Natives'* Islands Book Trust, Stornoway

Smith M. 1963 *A Collection of Invertebrates from St Kilda between 1961 and 1963* The Nature Conservancy (Unpublished)

Smith R. A. 1875 A visit to St Kilda in 1873 *Good Words* 141–4, 264–9

Smith R. A. 1879 *A Visit to St. Kilda in 'The Nyanza'* Robert MacLehose, Glasgow

Spackman R. A. 1982 *Soldiers on St Kilda* Uist Community Press, Uist

Steel T. 1975 *The Life and Death of St Kilda* Fontana, London

Stewart, M. 1937 Bibliography of St Kilda. In D. Lack (ed.) *St Kilda Papers* Oxford University Press, Oxford

Stewart M. 1938 Natural History notes on Scottish Islands *Scottish Naturalist* 10: 107–14

Stone J. C. 1988 The St Kilda archipelago *St Kilda Mail* 12: 4–7

Sutherland Dr 1887 Flora of St Kilda *Transactions of the Inverness Scientific Society and Field Club* 3: 218–22

Svensson R. 1954 *Lonely Isles* Raben & Sjogren, Stockholm

Thomson R. 1891 *A Cruise on the Western Isles* Glasgow

Thornber I. 1990 St Kildans no more *Scots Magazine* December 278–88

Trollope A. 1878 *How the 'Mastiffs' went to Iceland* Virtue and Co., London

Turrill W. B. 1927 The Flora of St. Kilda *Bot. Exch. Club Report* 8: 428–44

Vaughan J. and Love J. A 1994 St Kilda Summer 1993 *Hebridean Naturalist* 12: 59–64

Votier S. C., Crane J. E., Bearhop S., De Leon A., McSorley C. A., Minguez E., Mitchell P. I., Parsons I., Phillips R. A. and Furness R. W. 2005 Nocturnal foraging by great skuas *Stercorarius skua*: implications for conservation of storm-petrel populations *Journal of Ornithology* 147: 405–13

Walker J. 1980 *Report on the Hebrides* Margaret M. Mackay (ed.) John Donald, Edinburgh

Walker M. J. C. 1984 A pollen diagram from St. Kilda, Outer Hebrides, Scotland *New Phytology* 97: 99–113

Wanless S. and Murray S. 1996 A census of the St Kilda gannetry in May 1994 *Scottish Birds* 18: 152–8

Waters W. E. 1964a St Kilda winter *Scots Magazine* March 543–5

Waters W. E. 1964b Observations on the St Kilda wren. *British Birds* 57: 49–64

Waterston A. R. 1981 Present knowledge of the non-marine invertebrate fauna of the Outer Hebrides *Proceedings of the Royal Society of Edinburgh* 79B: 215–321

Waterston J. 1905 Notes on the mice and birds of St Kilda *Annals of Scottish Natural History* 14: 199–202

Waterston J. 1906a On some invertebrates from St Kilda *Annals of Scottish Natural History* 150–3

Waterston J. 1906b On some Scottish Siphonaptera *Annals of Scottish Natural History* 15: 211–14

Waterston J. 1923–24 St Kilda *Proceedings of the South London Entomological Natural History Society* 1–11

Waterston, J. 1926 A note on *Allomyia debellator* Fab. *Entomologist's Monthly Magazine* 62: 98

Waterston J. and Taylor J. W. 1906 Land and freshwater molluscs of St Kilda *Annals of Scottish Natural History* 21–4

Werham C., Toms M., Marchant J., Clark J., Siriwardena G. and Baillie S. 2002 *The Migration Atlas: movements of the birds of Britain and Ireland* Poyser, London

Wiglesworth J. 1903 St Kilda and its birds, Reprinted from the *Transactions of the Liverpool Biological Society* Liverpool

Williamson K. and Boyd J. M. 1960 *St Kilda Summer* Oliver & Boyd, London

Williamson K. and Boyd J. M. 1963 *A Mosaic of Islands* Oliver & Boyd, Edinburgh

Williamson K. 1948 *The Atlantic Islands* Oliver & Boyd, London

Williamson K. 1951 Wrens of Fair Isle and St Kilda *Ibis* 93: 599–601

Williamson K. 1957a The St Kilda wren *Scottish Field* September 1957

Williamson K. 1957b Notes on the breeding of the Faroe snipe (*Capella gallinago faeroensis*) at St Kilda File note to the Nature Conservancy, Edinburgh

Williamson K. 1957c Living on St Kilda *Scottish Field* June 1957

Williamson K. 1958a Population and breeding environment of St Kilda and Fair Isle wrens *British Birds* 51: 368–93

Williamson K. 1958b Menace of the gulls at St Kilda *Bird Notes* 28: 330–4

Williamson K. 1958c Life on St Kilda *Scots Magazine* October 1958

Williamson K. 1959 Snipe at St Kilda *Bird Notes* 29: 5–8

Wilson J. 1842a *A Voyage round the Coasts of Scotland and the Isles* 2 vols Adam & Charles Black, Edinburgh

Wilson J. 1842b Additional Notice Regarding St Kilda *Edinburgh New Philosophical Journal* 32: 178–80

Wynne Edwards V. C., Lockley R. M. and Salmon H. M. 1936 The distribution and numbers of breeding gannets (*Sula bassana* L.) *British Birds* 29:262–76

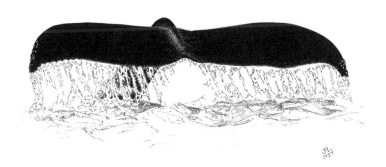

Index

Page references to illustrations are in **bold**.

access 313–14

Acland, Sir Thomas Dyke 20–1, 257, 280

acoustic survey 242

aircraft wrecks 54–5, 303–4

algae 48, 60, 73, 242–7

alien predators 160, 211–18

Alpine swift 170

American golden plover 168–9

American robin 169

amphibia 13, 247

amphipods 74

Anderson, Sandy 97

anemones 244–6

antler moth 67, 71

ants 67, 68, 74, 80

Aeolus 215

Arachnids   *see* harvestmen, mites *and* spiders

archaeology 11, 22–3, 44, 56, 311, 312, 316

Armada, Spanish 38, 216

Armstrong, Rev. E. A. 193–4, 197

army base   *see* radar base

army withdrawal 316

asphodel 64

ashilag *or* assilag   *see* storm petrel

Atkinson, George Clayton 4, 20, 85–8, 91, 127, 132, 176, 185, 258

Atkinson, Robert 4, 90, 193–4, **197**, 207, 209, 235, 272, 301–2, 304

augite 28

auks 70, 161

Australia 3, 320

Avocet 215

Bagenal, Timothy 182, 194, 196, 241–2, 305, 308

Baird's sandpiper 168–9

ballooning 66, 68

barley 12, 17, 55, 56, 60, 70

barnacles 243–4, 246

barred warbler 167

Barrett Hamilton, Gerald E. I I. 201–4

Barrington, Richard Manliffe 57–8, 59, 92, 185–7

basalts 29, 33

basking shark 247, 297

Bass Rock 99–100, 102, 104

bats 53

bathymetry 25, 28, 73, 242

beach 45, 49, 53, 306

beans 56

Beare, T. Hudson 75–6

Bedford, Mary Duchess of 84, 100, 180, 241, **283**, 284, 286

bees 67, 68, 73

beetles 66, 68, 71–3, 75, 76, 78, 79, 81, 180

Berry, Professor R. J. 'Sam' 5, 205

biogeography of islands 52–4, 65–8, 76, 82

biosecurity 201, 212, 215, 313

Biosphere Reserve 318

bird colonisation of islands 82

bird's foot trefoil 63

bird list 167
Birkhead, Professor Tim 135–6
blackcap 167
black guillemot 82, 89, 110, 112, 161, 164, 302
black redstart 181
Blasket Islands 2–3
Blezard, Ernest 180, 212
bluethroat 167, 169
blue whale 252
Blythe's reed warbler 170
boats 145, 200, 212–18, 227, 239–40, 262, 263, 277, 280, 291
boat accidents 141, 145, 214–18
bobolink 169
Boddington, Dr David 45, 47, 174, 197, 213, 247, 248, 264, 309, 310, 311, 317
Bonaventure Island 104
bonxie   see great skua
Boreray party marooned in 1759   141
Boreray sheep 78, 222   see also sheep
    appearance 235, 236
    crashes 237
    density 237
    at evacuation 226, 235
    impact on vegetation 237
    lambing 236
    management 235, 237
    number 222, 234, 236–7
    population cycles 237
botanical changes 229
bottle-nosed dolphin 251
boulder clay 41
bougir/bowger   see puffin
Boyd, J Morton 4, 5, 45, 61, 103, 110, 119, 173, 194, 208, 210, 229–31, 234, 236, 237, 241–2, 248, 303, 304, 305, 307, 308, 310, 312
brachyptery 81–2
bracken 51
breccias 27, 32, 33, 34
breeches buoy 105–6
brent geese 166
Briarlyn 217
brittlestars 246

bristletails 80
Brougham, Lord Henry 57, 238, 256–7
Brunnich's guillemot 111
bryophytes 49
bryozoans   see sea mats
Buchan, Rev Alexander 14–16
Buchan, John 61, 77, 78, 191–4, 206, 303
Buchanan, Rev Alexander 17
bugs 67, 68, 74
Bullock, Dr Dave 80, 236
Bullock, William 115–16, 125, 132
buff-bellied pipit 169
Bute, Marquis of   see Dumfries, Lord
buttercups 54
butterflies 67, 68, 71, 72, 73, 75, 78, 79, 80
byelaws 314

cabbages 82
caddisflies 67, 68
calandra lark 170
caldera 25
calendar, Gregorian/Julian 95–6, 122
Campbell, Sandy 187
Campbell of Shawfield, Robert 56–7
Canna, Isle of 155
cannons 38
Carmichael, Alexander 124, 137–8, 260
carrion crow 170
carrots 56
cats 68, 192, 205–7
cattle 11, 12, 17–18, 68, 70, 226
centipedes 67, 68
cephalopods 114
cestodes 74
cetaceans 249, 251, 252
Ceutorhynchus 6, 65, 66, 79, 81
chaffinch 170
chiffchaff 167
Chlamydia psittaci 159   see ornithosis
Chlamydophila abortus 159   see ornithosis
Clarke, W. Eagle 75, 76, 112, 149, 168, 169, **171**, 170–1, 174, 182, 188–9, 203–4, 208, 209, 226, 284, 285, 286

Clarke, Edward Daniel 26, 149–50, 255
cleg 71, 72
cleits or *cleitean* 139, 141, 209, 316
climate 44–50
clover 63–4
Clutton-Brock, Prof. Tim C. 232
Clydesdale 268
Cockburn, Alexander 29, 30–3, 38, 44, 48, 58, 59, 77, 180, 289
cockroach 73
cod 239–40
Coleoptera   *see* beetles
Collacott, Dr Richard 159
collared flycatcher 170
collectors 163, 180, 186, 189, 191, 241, 263, 283, 285, 286, **286**, 297, 319
collembolans 66, 68, 74
colonisation by plants and animals 6, 43, 48, 49, 52, 65, 82
common crane 170
common dolphin 251
common gull 110, 120
common seal 247
Compositae 52, 53, 54
Conachair, height of seacliff 35, 42, 91, 300
conger eel 240, 247
Connell, Robert 144, 147, 240, 267–8, 282
coral 246
coralline algae 244
cormorant 76, 112, 138, 139, 161
corn 12, 17, 38, 44, 60
corn bunting 174–5
corncrake 174, 305
corn marigold 60
corn spurrey 60
Cott, Hugh 151, 152
cotton grass 50
coulterneb   *see* puffin
crabs 245
Crawley, Professor Mick 54, 232
cross-leaved heath 62
crowberry 64
cruise ships 112, 288, 309, 312
crustaceans 114, 115, 117

cultivation 17, 21, 37, 38, 56, 60, 61–2, 174, 175, 182
cup coral 246
curlew 167
currents 40, 42, 49, 52
cuvie 245

dabberlocks 244–5
daisy 52, 60
Dale, C. W. 73
Dampier, William 8
dandelion 52, 54, 56
Dargavel 280
dark arches moth 67
Darling, Dr Frank Fraser 61–2, 90, 304
Darwin, Charles 5, 52, 53, 71, 76, 198, 199
Darwin's finches 76
dead man's fingers coral 246
deer 11–12
density dependence 160–1
density independence 160
desmids 73
diatoms 53
Diptera   *see* flies
disharmonic flora 54, 60
disharmony of species 67
dispersal of seeds 53
disturbance by ships 112, 159, 259, 266, 299
diversity of species 53, 66, 68
Dixon, Charles 84, 89, 100, **101**, 129, 133, 164, 169, 174, 175, 176, 178, 180, 181, 186–7, 200
DNA 5, 82, 233
dogs 68, 137, 149–50, 153, 205, 207, 314
dogfish 53, 297
dolerite 26, 27, 28, 29, 33
dolphins 68
dragonflies 67, 68
drainage 56
Dresser, Henry E. 188–9
drift migration 171
drifting 48, 52, 53, 66
drowning 141, 145, 214–18, 240, 278, 280, 292, 297

dulse 55, 243–4
Dumfries, Lord 4, 30, 61, 62, 77, 78, 191, 192, 210, 227–8, 229, 231, 241, 248–9, 269, 295, 296, **297**, 297, 298–300, 302, 303, 305
Dunara Castle 28, 58, 59, 78, 94, 132, 263, **265**, 265, 266, 267, 274, 289, 291, 296, **296**, 301
dung/guano enrichment 50, 51–2, 54, 55, 60–3, 64, 82, 243
dunlin 167, 174, 175
Dunvegan 93, 95, 295
dusky warbler 170
dykes 29, 33

echinoderms   *see* starfish
eagles 175
earwigs 67, 68, 74
earthworms 60, 67, 68
ecological equilibrium 66
Edge of the World 298, 300
eel 247
egg collecting 88, 115, 152, 163, 180, 263, 282–7, 297, 302–3
eggs 89, 98, 115, 142, 151–3, 161, 163, 190, 191, 282–7, 303
egg tasting 152
Eggeling, Dr Joe 231, 308
eider duck 181, 283, 302–3, 305
Eigg, Isle of 155
Eldey 129–31
Elektron 214
Elliott, J. Steele 101, 104, 133, 165, 170, 175, 176, 178, 190, 201, 202, 208, 240, 283
Elwes, Captain Henry John 95, 132, 178, 224, 226, 262
enzootic abortion 159
Eriskay 268
erosion 38–42,
exposure 50, 63
extinction 66,
Evans, Henry 40, 101, 127–9, 133, 202, 240, 266, 286
evening grosbeak 169
eye-browed thrush 170

Factor 10, 11, 14, 69, 70, 93, 123, 141, 143–4, 152, 166, 188, 200–1, 221, 240, 255–6, 258, 261, 264, 265, 267, 295, 299
Fair Isle 92–3, 115, 170–2, 182, 184, 189, 194, 205, 306, 308
falk   *see* razorbill
Falkland Islands 142
Fan worm 245
Faroes 4, 92, 130, 131, 139, 141, 146, 154, 157–9, 161, 173, 178, 182, 200, 207, 220, 236
fathach 100, 154
feathers 141, 142, 143–4, 147, 157–9
feather stars 245
feldspar 28, 33
Ferguson, Alex G. 77, 133, **140**, 143, 227–8, 249, 274, **287**, 289, 295, **297**, 301, 304
Ferguson, Calum 3, 57,
Ferguson, Donald 133, 226, 295
Ferguson, Neil 226, 227, 274, 293, 295
ferns 52, 53, 54, 59, 68
fertilisation 50
fescue 50, 63, 209
Fiddes, Rev Alexander 44, 159, 165, 166, 170, 175, 241, 268, 274
fin whale 251, 252
fish 12, 53, 68, 108, 110–12, 114, 115, 117, 119, 153, 239–40
fishing 239, 241, 242, 271, 281
fish nets 240
Fisher, James 6, 35, 61–2, **86**, 87, 89–91, 94, 97, 102, 103, 111, 121, 139, 143, 157, 158, 162, 172, 181, 182, 194, 248, 276, 297, 302–3, 304–5, 308, 317
Flannan Isles 170, 191, 254
fleas 67, 68, 79–80, 209
Fleming, Andrew 22, 23, 249
Fleming, Rev Dr John 126, 131, 132,
flies 66, 67, 68, 71, 72, 73, 75, 78, 80, 166
flightless 67, 81, 123,
fog 70
foot and mouth 313, 316

Fordun, John of 220
fowling 301
  allocation 146, 154, 157
  archaeology 139, 142
  bait boards 146, 148
  demonstrations 260–2, 266, 267, 274,
    286–7
  dogs 148, 149–50
  eggs 142, 151–3, 155
  fatalities 139–40, 154, 292
  harvesting adults 146–7
  harvesting young 153–8
  impact on numbers 162
  management 151, 161, 236
  marooned in 1759 on Boreray 141
  marooned in 1727 on Stac an Armin
    15, 16, 23, 141
  nets 146, 149
  oil 142–3, 157
  other fowling communities 138–9,
    149–50
  plucking 157
  poles 146, 148, 155, 161
  preserving seabirds/eggs 139, 152
  role of women 148, 150, 155–6,
    157–60
  ropes 137, 138, 140–1, 145–6, 154
  salting carcases 157
  snares 141, 146, 148
  sustainability 151, 153, 160–2, 236
  trampling 151, 161, 236
Foula, Isle of 30, 35, 91–3, 115,
  298–300
founder effect 205
Freer, Ada Goodrich 268, 288
freshwater 48, 54, 80, 142
frost 41, 42, 45
fulmar **12**, 50, 64, 70, 74, 78, 80, 82,
  85, 87–98, 104, 110, 138, 161, 164,
  283–4, 301, 303
  arrival/departure dates 95–6
  distribution 91, 97
  eggs 87, 92, 95, 151, 152, 155, 284,
    285, 303
  feathers 144, 155–60
  as food 147, 150, 155, 228

  harvesting 94–5, 96, 146, 155–8, 162,
    284
  harvesting illegal in Faroe/Iceland 158
  nesting inland 98, 305
  numbers harvested 162
  oil 80, 143, 155, 157, 159, 260, 284,
    290
  origin of name 95
  population 96–8, 110
  predation by raptors 179
  rate of spread 93, 97
  reason for spread 93–4
  re-laying 152, 155
  survey 90, 92, 97
  young 95, 155–7
fungi 48, 52, 68
Funk Island 135, 142

gabbro 26, 27, 28, 29, 33, 34, 41
Galapagos 5, 6, 7, 8, 43, 52, 76, 197–8,
  199, 314
gales 40, 45, 47, 48, 98, 168, 215, 217,
  263
gannets 40, 55, 62, 70, 78, 87, 89, 90,
  98–104, 110, 120, 138, 139, 139,
  161, 249, 283–4
  aerial survey 103, 317
  arrival/departure 98–100, 147–8
  distribution 100–4
  disturbance 112, 266
  diet 98–9, 99–100
  eggs 98, 100, 102, 104, 151, 283, 317
  eggs as food/medicine 152–3
  eggs protected on Stac Lee 151
  feathers 144, 157–9
  harvest 94, 102, 104, 147–8, 153, 162,
    163
  human uses 142–3, 152, 290
  laws 163, 283–4
  mortality 104
  numbers harvested 162
  oil 142
  origin of name 98–9
  population 100–4, 110
  range 99, 100
  rate of increase 104

gannets *continued*
  re-laying 151–2
  stomachs 159, 290
  young 100, 153–4
garden warbler 167
garefowl *see* great auk
gastropods 244
Gauld, Dr David 241–2, 305
Geikie, Professor Archibald 26, 28, 29, 34, 35
Geirfulglasker 48, 124, 130
geology 24–42
geomorphology 6, 35
germination 53
Gibson, Alexander 58
Gilbert, Dr Oliver 54, 105
Gillies, Donald 31, 57, 59
Gillies, Rev. Donald John 281
Gilles, Mary (Mrs John) 292
Gillies, Mrs John (nee Anne Ferguson) 4, 77, **197**
Gillies, Finlay 77, 227, 274, 296
Gillies, Murdoch 141
Gillies, Neil 4, 77, **182**, 193, **197**, 227, **228**, 269–70, 272, 295, 296, **297**, 301, 303
Gillies, Rachel 295
glaciations 28, 41–2, 43, 60
Gladstone, John 30, 31, 58–61, 205, 253
Glenalbyn 20, 257
gneiss 25
goats 138, 221, 223, 226
goldcrest 167
Golden Chance 215
golden eagle 155, 178–9, 290
golden oriole 170
golden plover 167, 168–9, 181
Gordon, Seton 31, 289, 295, **299**, 312
goshawk 176
granite 33, 34
granophyre 26, 27, 29, 32, 41, 51
grasses 52, 53, 56, 59, 60, 63, 68
grasshoppers 67, 73
Gray, Robert 91, 123, 125, 126, 128, 131
grazing impact 50, 54, 61–3, 79, 229, 235

great auk 40, 48, 89, 115, 121–36, 162, 176
  appearance 122
  archaeology 135, 139
  breeding 135–6
  eggs 121, 122, 134, 135–6, 151, 152
  Eldey incident of 1844 129–31, 134
  extinction 124, 128–9, 135, 139
  flightlessness 123, 135–6, 139, 162
  fowling 123, 151
  Gaelic song 123–4
  persecution 124–5, 135
  placenames 133
  re-laying 152
  Scalpay incident of 1821 125–6, 127, 131, 132–3
  skins 134–6
  Stac an Armin incident of 1840 127–9
great tit 170
great skua 64, 110, 116–18, 161, 167, 181
  dive-bombing 313
greater black-backed gull 110, 117, 119–20, 162, 283
green-veined white butterfly 75
grey-cheeked thrush 169
grey seal 247–9, 250
  distribution 247–8
  numbers 248–9
  pupping 248–9
Grieve, Symington 125
greylag geese 164, 181
Grimshaw, Percy 75
groundsel 60
Grubb, Peter 231
guga 91, 100, 139, 148, 153, 162
guillemot 70, 74, 85, 89, 95, 109–11, 138, 139, 283
  breeding 109–11
  bridled 111
  diet 110
  disturbance 112
  eggs 109, 151–3, 283, 285, 303
  as food 147, 152–3
  harvesting 88, 109, 146–7, 152–3, 162
  numbers of eggs taken 162
  population 110

gulls 84, 85, 118, 139, 161, 164
Gurney, John Henry 101–2
Gwynne, David 63, 213, 231
gyr falcon 168

hairy bittercress 60
halibut 240, 241
Handa, Sutherland 139, 303
Hancock, Dr Geoff 67, 75, 80, 81
harbour 239–41, 262
Harebell 291–3
harlequin duck 169
Harman, Dr Mary 22, 129, 140, 236
Harris, Professor Mike 97, 106, 167, 317
Harrisson, Tom 76–8, 96–7, 102, 110,
    175, 189, 191–3, 194, 204, 206,
    208, 209, 226, 270, 286, 303
Harry Melling 217
harvest 12, 17, 51, 70
harvestmen 68
Harvie-Brown, John Alexander 28, 40,
    58, 91, 92, **93**, 94, 127, 133, 170,
    186, 286
hawksbit 54, 56,
hay 60, 76, 209
Heathcote, Evelyn 3, 36, 60, 238, 274,
    275, 277
Heathcote, Norman 3, 36, 60, 111, 124,
    133, 238, 247, 273–5, 279
heather 62, 64
Hebridean 265, 267, 268
Hebrides 58, 77, 227, 265, 289, 291, 295,
    296, 301
heavy metals 51–2
Heddle, Professor Matthew Forster
    Heddle 28, 35
helicopter 310, 316
Hemiptera   *see* bugs
hens 68
heron 166
herring 98–9, 104, 110, 111, 148, 240,
    247
herring Gull 110, 118, 163
Hewitt, C. Gordon 74–5
honeysuckle 59, 60
hooded crow 180, 181, 282

hooded warbler 169
hooks 98, 240
hoopoe 170
Hornung, M 63
horses 12, 18, 68, 70, 72
house martin 167, 181
house sparrow 170
houses 17, 21, 215, 257, 280, 295, 336
Hudson, W H 190
Hugh-Jones, Philip 111
humidity 48, 54
humpback whale 251–2
Huxley, Sir Julian 35, 36, 76, 90, 97,
    103, 111, 302–3
hydroids 244–5, 246
Hymenoptera   *see* ants, bees *and* wasps

ice action 32, 41–4, 246
Ice Ages 6, 41–2, 43, 44, 51, 60, 83, 199,
    205, 246
Iceland 5, 23, 24–5, 48, 65, 80–2, 89,
    90, 111, 116, 124–5, 129–31, 142,
    157–9, 167, 169, 189, 205, 225, 256,
    264
ichneumons 67, 74
igneous rocks 32, 33, 34
infant tetanus 16, 159–60, 268
Innes, Hamond 309
insects 70, 73
intertidal zonation 242–3
invertebrates 65–83, 242–6
irises 51
isolation 48, 164

jack snipe
jewel anemone 246
Jewell, Prof. Peter 220, 230–1, 234
Johnson, Samuel 13, 18, 19, 275, 298
Joy, Dr Norman 76
Judd, Professor John Wesley 27

Kearton, Cherry 193, 273, 274, 295
Kearton, Richard 16, 22, 58, 84, 141,
    193, 193, 225–6, 240, 266, 273–5,
    290, 298, 305
kelp 244–5

Kelsall bequest 262, 264, 280
kestrel 176
killer whale 249, 250, 253
king eider 169
Kingsley, Charles 121
kittiwakes 82–3, 85, 89, 110, 118, 119,
    139, 150–1, 163, 164
knot 167
Kumu 217

lacewings 67
Lack, David 59–61, 65, 76–9, 81, 96,
    102, 110, 171, 172, 174, 175, 194,
    198, 199, 229, 269–70, 295, 296,
    305
lair flora 64
land bridge 52, 199–200, 203, 205
landing by boat 11, 17, 19, 26, 29, 31–2,
    39, 40, 41, 49, 71, 77, 87, 144, 240,
    262, 263, 269–70, 291
landing craft 212, 307, 315–6
Lapland bunting 167, 169
large heath butterfly 72
Lauder, Sir Thomas Dick 21
lava 25, 26, 33, 48
lavy   *see* guillemot
laws 163, 190, 283–5
Leach, William Elford 115
Leach's petrel 78, 89, 110, 114–17,
    163, 209, 263, 283–4, 301, 302
    see also petrels
  breeding 116, 117, 209
  eggs 115, 116, 283, 284, 286
  laws 163, 190, 284, 285
  longevity 116, 117
  population 110, 116–17
  scientific name 115–16
  skua predation 116–17
leaching 50
least carpet moth 75
leathery turtle 247
Lepidoptera   *see* butterflies and moths
lesser black-backed gull 110, 118, 163
Levenish 1, 17, 33, 34, 41, 42, 45, 59, 67,
    97, 105, 110, 111, 116, 118, 120
Libhinish   *see* Levenish

lice 67, 68, 79
lichens 48, 52, 54–5, 60, 68, 243–4
lifeboat 241, 285
limpets 71, 239, 243–4
ling 239–40
lithe 240
Litla Dimun, Faroe 220
little egret 170
little grebe 170
little stint 167
liverworts 54, 55, 63, 68
lobster fishing 248
Loch Lomond Readvance 41, 42, 44
Lockley, Ronald 90, 304
locks 269
Lofoten Islands 149–50
longevity 114, 116, 167
Lowe, Frank and Betty 290
Lucas, F. A. 135
lumpsucker 247
lundehund or puffin dogs 149–50
Lundy 126
Lunga, Treshnish Isles 207–8
Lyster, Ian 134

MacAulay, Rev Donald 15, 16
MacAulay, Rev Kenneth 16–19 *et seq.*
MacCrimmon, Euphemia **124**, 124,
    137–8, 260
MacCulloch, John 26–7 *et seq.*
MacDiarmid, J 224
MacDonald, Calum 3, 227–8, **228**, 241,
    248, 253, 285, **297**
MacDonald, Donald 278
MacDonald, Ewen 31
MacDonald, John 88
MacDonald, Lachlan 185, 217, 252, 281
MacDonald, Malcolm 128, 129
MacDonald, Roderick 88
MacDonald, William 285
MacGillivray, John 4, 21, 57, 59, **69**,
    69–72, 73, 87, 96, 127, 128, 129,
    132, 168, 175, 176, 178, 185, 200,
    238, 259
MacGillivray, William 57, 69, 86, 125,
    127, 177

MacGregor, Alastair Alpin 38, 80,
    205–6, **207**, 221, 226, 291, 294,
    298, 300
mackerel 104, 239, 247, 249
Mackay, James 47, 264, 279, 310, 311
Mackay, Rev John 44, 132, 200, 260,
    264–5, 267–8, 273
Mackenzie, Lady Mary of Gairloch
    261
Mackenzie, Osgood 142, 261
Mackenzie, Sir George of Tarbat 121,
    123, 221
Mackenzie, Rev. J. B. 21, 44, 115, 128,
    170
MacKenzie, Rev Neil 19–22 *et seq.*
MacKinnon, Lachlan 127–8, 129, 133
Maclachlan, Mrs Alice 239–40, 281
Maclean, Lachlan 140
Maclennan, Rev Roderick 16
Macleod, Alexander 32
MacNeill, Roderick 138
MacPherson, Rev John 18
MacQueen, Donald 126, 127, 133
MacQueen, Finlay 4, 31–2, 77, 78, **197**,
    210, 227, **228**, 270, **271**, 272, 274,
    289, 295, 296
MacQueen, John 278
MacQueen, Malcolm 3
MacQueen, Norman 278
magma 33
maildrop 310, 316
mallard 166, 170
Manor 217–18
Manx shearwater 89, 110, 113–14, 138,
    283, 302
    eggs 88, 283
    harvesting 149, 154–5
    population 110
    Rum colony 154–5
marine life 42, 48, 238–54
Marine Nature Reserve status 253
Martin, Martin 3, 8–14, 122 *et seq.*
Maersk Angus 254
Mastiff 264
Mathieson, John 30, 35, 44, 48, 58, 274,
    282, 289, 299–300

mayflies 67
mayweed 56
McVean, Dr Donald 62
McWilliam, Father John Morell 94,
    296–8, **297**
meadow pipit 164, 167, 169, 181
medicinal plants 55
Mediterranean gull 170
Meharg, Professor Andy 51
merganser 166, 174
merlin 167, 175–6
mermaid's purse 53
Meston, George 229, 296–7, 301
mice 68, 74, 78, 79, 81
migrants 165, 167–74, 181, 182, 284
Miles, Will 117, 167
Millais, John Guille 220
millipedes 67, 68, 74
Milner, Cedric 63, 230–1
Milner, Sir William 111, 112, 128, 132,
    176, 178, 239, 261
Mina Stack 38
minerals 28, 33, 48, 51, 231
Mingulay 91, 138, 153, 154, 254,
    299–300, 316
mink 215, 218
minke whale 250, 251, 253
mites 66, 74
molluscs 68, 74, 180
Monach Isles 2, 7, 16, 304
Moore, Pete 39, 233
Moran, Stephen 80–1
Money, Dr Sarah 116, 117, 167, 312
Monro, Dean 143, 220
Moray, Robert 140, 144, 247–8
More, Alexander Goodman 185
Morgan, John 262
Morrison, Marion 57
Morrison-Scott, T 210–11
moss campion 59, 62
mosses 48, 49, 52, 54, 55, 60, 63–4, 68,
    73
moths 66, 67, 68, 71, 72, 73, 75, 78,
    79
Moy-Thomas, James Allan 76–7, 204,
    206, 208, 209

Mullach Sgar Complex 34
Muir, Thomas Smyth 261
Murray, George 267
Murray, Sir John 73
Murray, Stuart 38, 40, 80, 97, 98, 103,
    105, 167, 170, 216, 217, 236, 249,
    317
mussels 244
mustard 56
myriapods   *see* centipedes *and*
    millipedes

Napier Commission 266, 279
National Census 259
National Nature Reserve 4, 7, 45, 46, 62,
    90, 166, 172, 173, 235, 254, 305,
    316, 317, 320
National Scenic Area 317, 318
National Trust for Scotland 4, 5, 7, 62,
    107, 112, 194, 215, 217, 230, 306,
    308, 310, 311, 312, 315, 317, 320
National Vegetation Classification 63
Naturalists 6, 65, 69, 73, 80, 163, 166,
    177, 189, 191, 200, 203, 206, 241,
    248, 255, 290, 302, 319, 320
Nature Conservancy (Council) 4, 5, 44,
    54, 62, 63, 81, 90, 103, 106, 172,
    174, 213, 215, 230, 235, 237, 249,
    304, 305, 306, 307, 311, 312, 315
Nature Reserve (Lord Dumfries) 248,
    295, 298–9, 301, 305
naval vessels 258, 262, 263, 264, 266,
    267, 268
nematodes 73
neonatal tetanus   *see* infant tetanus
Ness, Lewis 138–9, 163
nettles 51
Newton, Professor Alfred 101, 102, 121,
    127, 128, 130, 132, 134–5
niche expansion 54, 211
Nicholson, Sir Max 90, 97, 103, 172,
    181, 191, 194, 302–3, 304
Norway 89, 142, 149–50, 205, 216,
    223
Northern Lighthouse Board 125–6
North Ronaldsay 223, 235

northern bottlenose whale 252
northern right whale 251–2

oats 12, 55, 56, 60, 70
oil spills 254
onions 56, 59
Operation Hardrock 45, 306–9, **309**
orchids 60
Ordnance Survey 30, 274
Orkney 97, 115, 125, 132, 139, 182, 223,
    235, 304
ornithosis 157–60
Otter, Captain Henry 35, 216, 240, 262,
    280
otters 13, 215
overfishing 100, 108, 153, 160, 163
oystercatcher 167, 181

painted lady butterfly 67, 75, 78
Papa Westray 125
parasites 74, 79, 80, 314
parrots 158
partridge 53, 170
passerines 167, 181
peas 53, 56
peat 43, 50, 61, 63, 64   *see also* turf
pectoral sandpiper 168–9
Pelham-Clinton, E. C. 80
pellets 167, 180, 212
Pemberton, Dr Josephine 232
penguin 74, 121, 135, 142
Pennant, Thomas 18, 124, 255
peregrine 88, 174, 175, 176–7, 179–80,
    259, 282,
Petch, Charles Plowright 59–61, 65, 76,
    78
petrels 41, 115, 139, 161, 311
phosphorescence 238–9
Pickard-Cambridge, Rev O 74
pied flycatcher 167
pied wagtail 181
pier 49, 213–14, 215, 262, 272, 285
Pike, Oliver 276–8
pilot whale 251
pipefish 108
plankton 239

plantain 63
plantation 172
plants, flowering 17, 48, 53, 56, 57, 58, 68, 70, 185
pollack 247, 249
pollen analysis 43
pollination 67
pollutants 51–2, 104, 106–7, 114, 160, 177
Poore, Duncan 61–2
Poplar Diver 217
porpoises 249, 250
potatoes 17, 32, 56, 60
Powell, Harry 241
Powell, Michael 30, 298–300, **299**
Praeger, Robert Lloyd 58
primroses 62
Protection of Birds Act 163
Protection of Birds at Sea Bill 163, 283
psittacosis   *see* ornithosis
ptarmigan 165
puffin 12, 41, 63, 70, 74, 78, 84, 85, 95, 104–8, 110, 138, 139, 239, 283–4, 317
   ageing puffins 161
   arrival/departure 105
   breeding success 107–8
   colonies 88–9, 105
   diet 108
   distribution 105
   eggs 87, 105, 151, 283, 303
   effect of lights 106–7
   feathers 144
   as food 147, 148, 153, 228
   harvest 104, 146, 148–50, 151, 153, 161–2
   longevity 167
   moult 108
   predation 167, 180
   population 105, 108, 110
   survey 105
   trampling 161, 236, 313
   young 106–8, 148, 153, 167
puffinet   *see* Manx shearwater
puffling   *see* puffin, young

puffin dogs   *see* lundehund
purple saxifrage 44, 59, 62

quartz 33

radar base 2, 5, 6, 46, 49, 107, 114, 172, 211, 248, 305, 311, 315–17, 320
radar migration studies 172, 174
radiocarbon dating 44
rafting 66, 247
rainfall 44–8, 52, 69–70
raptors 168, 175
Rankin, Lady Jean 296, **297**, 300, 310
Rankin, Niall 296, **297**, 298, 300–01
rats 211
   1959 scare 212
   1967 scare 212–13
   Elektron incident 214–5
   Leverburgh observation 214
Ratcliffe, Dr Derek 62–3, 180, 310
raven 164, 179–80, 181, 282
raven pellets 180
razorbills 85, 89, 95, 110, 111–12, 138, 139, 151, 153, 284, 303
red admiral butterfly 67, 78
red algae 243, 245
red-backed shrike 167
red-breasted flycatcher 169
red-necked phalarope 181
red grouse 170
redpoll 167
redwing 82, 167
reed bunting 169
reed warbler 167
reintroduction 178
reptiles 68, 83, 247
reticulated dragonet 247
rhizopods 73
Ridley, Gordon 42, 238
Ring-necked duck 169
ringed plover 167
Risso's dolphin 249, 250, 253
Ritchie, Professor James 58, 75, 94, 184, 206, 210, 235
robin 167
Robinson, Andy 51, 80, 168–9

Robson, Michael 16, 19, 22
Rockall 58, 90, 251, 304
rockfall 39–42
rockling 247
rock climbing 313–14
rock dove 174, 175
rock pipit 167, 181
rock thrush 169
roller 165
Rona, North 7, 46, 47, 54, 61, 76, 92,
        115, 116, 117, 139, 191, 254, 294,
        302, 303
rooks 90, 170
rosefinch 167, 169
roseroot 59
Ross, Alexander 27, 266, 272
Ross, John 272, 273, 283
Røst   *see* Lofoten Islands
Rothschild, Hon Miriam 79
rotifers 73
royal visits 310–11
RoxAnn marine survey 242
Rum, Isle of 25, 28, 29, 54, 154–5, 205,
        306, 312
rushes 59, 64
rustic bunting 169
Ryder, Michael 219–20, 223

saithe 247
saltspray 48–50, 51, 55, 63, 231, 237
sandeels 108, 110, 111, 119, 153, 160,
        247
sanderling 167
Sands, John 3, 72, 110, 181, 200–1, 208,
        263, 264, 267, 273, 274, 275, 280
sandstone 41
scorpion flies 67
Scottish Natural Heritage 5, 7, 33, 61,
        63, 80, 81, 242, 315, 316, 317
Scalpay 125–6, 242
school 275
scraber   *see* Manx shearwater
scree slopes 41
scrub 22, 43–4, 185
scurvy 142
scurvy grass 55, 56, 66, 79, 81, 209

seabed habitats 242–6
seabirds 12, 29, 50, 51, 68
    adult survival 161
    attracted to lights 106–7, 114
    as bait 142, 239
    as bedding/clothing 141, 142, 155
    changes in abundance 160
    deferred maturity 161
    disturbance by ships etc 112, 159, 259,
        266, 299
    exploitation 163
    feathers 144, 155, 290
    as fertiliser 147
    fidelity 161
    as food 78, 89, 98, 143, 144, 147,
        150–60
    harvesting 87, 89, 93–4, 104, 137–63,
        142–4, 155–9
    for implements 142, 290
    juvenile survival 161
    longevity 114, 116
    as medicine 155, 290
    for oil 142–3, 153, 155, 157
    population dynamics 160–3
    predation by gulls 119, 162–3
    productivity 161
    protection 163
    as rent 143, 154
    research 317
    sexual maturity 161
sea campion 50, 51, 62
sea caves 37, 38, 40–1, 243–4
sea cliffs 35–42
sea depths 25
seals 13, 68
sea mats 245–6
seamount 28
sea pink 50, 51, 62
sea plantain 50
sea rocket 49
sea slug 245
sea squirt 245
sea urchin 246
sea water 53
seal hunting 247–8
seal shooting 248

sealskins 248
seaweed *see* algae
sedges 53, 56, 59, 64
Seebohm, Henry 185–6, 187–8, 201
seeds 53
sei whale 252
seismic survey 112
self heal 63
Seton, George 3, 72, 224, 263, 286, 291, 298
sgrobir *see* Manx shearwater
shag 89, 110, 112–13, 138, 139, 150, 161, 180, 282
Shaw, Margaret Fay 141, 292, 293, 320
sheep 12, 18, 50, 67, 68, 70, 72, 78, 141, 150, 183
    appearance 221, 224
    blackface sheep 61, 223–4, 226, 232, 235
    on Boreray 78, 222, 223
    counts 242
    as dairy animal 221, 223, 226
    on Dun 224
    at evacuation 226
    fleece 225
    foot and mouth 313
    for meat 224–5
    lambing 222–3, 225
    lamb predation 177–8, 180, 212
    management 225
    milking 226, 276, 276
    numbers 221, 224, 226
    as rent 221, 222
    Scottish shortwool 223, 235
    Stac an Armin 142
shellfish 12
shepherd's purse 60
Shetland 30, 35, 91–3, 115, 139, 160, 182, 189, 194, 200, 235, 252, 254, 304
shipwrecked sailors 200
Sibbald,Sir Robert 10, 13, 98, 122, 221
silverfish 67
silverweed 55
silver Y moth 66, 67, 71
siskin 167

Site of Special Scientific Interest 254, 317, 318
skate 53, 240
skins 134–6, 163, 182, 190
Skirving, R Scott 132, 266
skylark 167, 174
slugs 74
smallpox epidemic 15, 16, 23, 141
small heath butterfly 71, 72
small tortoiseshell butterfly 75
Smith, Malcolm 80, 81, 106
snails 74
sneezewort 63
snipe 181–3, 302–3
snow 45–7
snow bunting 53, 82–3, 164, 167, 169, 181
snowy owl 167–8
Soay sheep 61, 62, 63, 68, 79, 183, 219–234, 305 *see also* sheep
    appearance 220
    archaeology 220, 230
    in captivity 226
    colour morphs 232
    crashes 231, 232, 234
    disease 231
    density 232
    on Dun 224
    fleece 220, 226
    gathering 225
    genetics 228–9, 231, 233
    grazing impact 231, 234
    on Hirta 227–9, 234
    history 219–222
    lambing 222, 231, 233
    longevity 233
    management 230, 234, 237
    mortality 231, 233
    number 222, 224, 225, 229, 231, 232, 234
    parasites 231, 232
    purity of breed 226
    reaction of dogs 230
    rerproduction 233
    research 229–32, 234, 317
    rut 231, 233

Soay sheep   *continued*
  scurred rams 232
  on Soay 234
  transfer to Hirta 227–9
  transfer to the mainland 231
  weight 232
soil 12, 48, 50–2, 63
solan goose   *see* gannet
song thrush 171, 174
songs 57, 123–4, 137, 219, 260, 269
sorrel 64, 96, 113
Sowerby's beaked whale 250, **250**
Spackman, Brigadier Tony 46, 311
Special Area for Conservation 314, 317,
  318
Special Protection Area 254, 314, 317, 318
sperm whale 252, 253
speciation 198
species lists 68, 167, 185
Spinningdale 215, **216**
spider crab 247
spiders 67, 68, 73, 74, 79, 80
splash zone 243, 245
sponges 244–6
sprats 247
springtails   *see* collembolans
squat lobster 246
squid 114
sprats 110, 111
Stac an Armin 1, 15, 31, 36, 40, 41, 42,
  63, 97, 102, 103, 105, 110, 111, 116,
  119, 120, 127–9, 133, 139, 141, 310
  party marooned in 1727 15, 16, 23,
  141
Stac Biorach 38, **39**, 42, 58, 88, 110,
  145, 185, 259
Stac Dona 38, 41
Stac Lee 1, 32, 36, 40, 42, 97, 100, 102,
  103, 110, 111, 112, 119, 133, 139,
  151, 238, 277–8
  gannet eggs protected on 151
starfish 245, 247
starling 181, 302
steamer service 73, 93, 180, 257, 263, 265,
  268, 279, 281, 285, 289, 295, 301
Stewart, Malcolm 76

St Kilda
  as a bird observatory 172–3
  emigration 16, 320
  evacuation 2, 3, 60, 62, 174, 226, 227,
  235, 236, 290–3, 298
  human population 11, 16, 70, 259–60,
  290, 291, 292, 320
  mailboats 200, 267, 274, 297
  mail deliveries 265, 281, 289, 310,
  316, 317
  maps 8, **9**, 30, 275
  post office 206, 291, 293
  relief missions 200–1
  sale 62, 78, 295, 306
  seabird station 89, 110
  survey 30, 33, 61, 62, 78, 112, 274, 275
  wartime detachment 289
  work parties 308, 316
St Kilda Club 312–13
St Kilda Complex 34
St Kilda field mouse 5, 23, 37–8, 67, 78,
  80, 167, 180, 199–218, 305
  appearance 201–2
  biosecurity on Boreray 201, 298
  colonisation 203, 205
  distribution 201
  genetics 205
  habits 208–10
  to mainland 210
  with petrels 209
  size 204, 213
  subspecies 202, 204, 205
  trapping 203, 204, 311
  with wrens 209
St Kilda house mouse 5, 78, 200–8,
  208, 290
  appearance 202
  co-existence with field mice 207–9
  colonisation 200
  distribution 203
  on Dun 208
  extinction 207
  habits 205, 208, 209
  to mainland 206
  size 204
  trapping 204

St Kilda mice 199–218   *see also* mice
   in salt barrel 210–11
St Kilda wren 5, 67, 79, 82, 84, 163, 167,
   283–4, 305, 311
   Act of Parliament 190, 284, 285
   breeding 189, 192–4, 196–7
   collecting specimens 185, 187, 283–4,
      285, 303
   distribution 191–2, 194–5
   habits 186–7, 192, 195–7, 209
   MacAulay on wrens 5, 184, 200
   migration 184
   mortality 192, 194–5
   numbers 194–5
   size 189
   status 190, 194–5
   subspecies 185–9, 194
St Kildans
   alcohol 256, 258, 266, 272, 273, 274,
      279
   attitudes of visitors 264, 266, 267,
      272–3, 274, 275–6, 278, 284
   climbing ability 29, 31, 57–8, 87–8,
      137–8, 144, 154, 177, 259, 261,
      266, 274, 278, 286–7, 314
   collecting specimens 163, 180, 190,
      263, 264, 269, 274, 282–6, 289,
      303, 319
   as fishermen 240–1
   food supply 200, 239, 264, 267
   fowling 123–4, 135, 137–63, 177
   income 287, 289, 319
   medicines and diseases 15, 16, 23,
      55, 71–2, 80, 98, 143, 152, 155,
      157–60, 292, 320
   money 261, 266, 267, 269–71, 272,
      274, 275–6, 279
   occupations 282
   physical features 16
   relief 257, 262, 264, 267, 275, 280,
      319
   religion 260, 268, 270, 274, 276,
      319
   souvenirs 267, 269, 275, 279, 281–2,
      284, 289, 319
   at time of evacuation 227, 291–3

   treatment by visitors 273, 275, 279,
      284
   use of seabirds 142–44, 152, 155–9,
      162
   with tourists 259, 266, 268, 276,
      279
   with whalers 252–3
stonechat 181
stoneflies 67
Stora Dimun, Faroe 130
storm petrel 89, 110, 113–1, 263,
      283   *see also* petrels
   population 110
storms 32, 34, 40, 160, 215, 217, 245,
      261, 267, 301
Stout, George Wilson 170, 204
strawberry clover 63
Sub-Alpine warbler 165
submarines 289, 301, 304
subspecies 171, 182
Sulaisgeir 7, 254, 304
Sule Skerry 45, 46, 254, 304
sundew 64
sunfish 247
sunshine 44–6
Surtsey 5–6, 24, 25, 34, 43, 48, 49, 53,
      65, 66, 67, 81, 82–3, 130, 164–5,
      189
sustainability 152–3
swift 167
syenite 26, 27, 28

tacksman   *see* Factor
tape response census of burrow-nesters
      113–14, 116–17
tardigrades 73
teal 181
temperature 44–8
Tennessee warbler 169
terns 139, 161, 163, 164
Tertiary activity 25, 26, 34
Tewnion, Sandy 80
The Lady of St Kilda 20, 257
thistles 51
Thomson, James 177
Thomson, Robert 268, 281

thongweed 244
thrift   see sea pink
tidal range 40, 42, 49
ticks 67, 74
tormentil 142
toxicity in soils 51–2
tourists 6, 20, 255, **258**, 259, 268–9,
    276, 279, 281, 287, 291, 319
traditions 3, 14, 20, 22, 23, 26, 71–2,
    123–4, 137, 141, 151–2, 219, 260,
    269
Traill, Professor James W H 125
trawlers 78, 94, 217–18, 258, 268, 269,
    281, 289, 292
tree cover 22, 43–4, 53
tree pipit 167
tree sparrow 174
Trollope, Anthony 264, 290–1
Trollval, Rum 154
tweed 260, 282
tubeworms 246
tufted duck 166
turf 12, 18, 50–1, 70
turnips 56
Turrill, William Bertram 59
turnstone 167
turtle dove 82
turtle, leathery 68
twite 174, 175
tystie   see black guillemot

Uist, North 2, 7, 16, 73, 91, 167, 168,
    175
Uist, South 47, 90, 141, 167–8, 175,
    219, 292, 309, 316
umbilicus 159

Vaerøy   see Lofoten Islands
vagrants 68, 75, 82, 165, 167
Vaughan, Jim 80, 111, 119, 166, 169,
    170, 197, 31
vegetables 56
vegetated sea cliffs 314
vegetation 43–64
vetches 53
vikings 5, 23, 154, 205, 216, 220, 225

visitor numbers 46, 268, 274, 276, 87–8,
    288, 291
visitors 313–14, 317, 319
    fatality 313
volcanic activity 25, 28, 33, 48, 49, 81,
    82, 164
Vulcan 259

waders 167, 168–9
walrus 249
wasps 54, 68
Waters, Dr W. Estlin 45, 47, 106, 196,
    197, 311
Waterston, George 92, 171, 179, 308
Waterston, Rev James 74, 75, 78, 79,
    180, 203, 208, 209
Waterston, Andrew Rodger 74, 79
wave action 40, 42, 48, 243–4
wave-cut platform 42
website 316
weevil 5, 65, 66, 79, 81
wells 48, 71–2, 142
Wells, Charles Henry 190
Westmann Islands 5, 24, 48, 116, 157,
    159
whaling 31, 58, 65, 94, 95, 252, 258,
    268, 281, 289, 304
whaling station 252
whales 29, 68
wheatear 167, 181
whimbrel 167, 180
whinchat 167
White's thrush 167, 169
white-beaked dolphin 251, 253
white-sided dolphin 250, 251, 253
white-tailed sea eagle 174, 175,
    177–9
white wagtail 164
whiting 247
whooper swan 165, 167
wigeon 166
Wiglesworth, Dr Joseph 94, 102, 175,
    181, 282
Wild Birds (Gannets on Sula Sgeir)
    Order 163
wildfowl 166

Williamson, Kenneth 4, 5, 79, 142, 162,
    171, 173, 182–3, 184, 191, 194,
    196, 212, 249, 307, 308, 312
willow, creeping 58, 64
willow, dwarf 44, 57, 58, 64
willow warbler 167
Wilson, George Washington 27
Wilson, Rev James 4, 21, 44, 56, 72–3,
    123, 128–9, 131, 141, 165, 174, 175,
    176, 178, 180, 185, 200, 211, 224,
    226, 259
wind 40, 43–8, 52, 53, 60, 66, 70, 75,
    81, 98
wingless 67, 81
winkles 243
Wolley, John 130, **131**

woodlice 74, 80
wood mouse 199   *see* St Kilda field
    mouse
woodrush 62, 64
World Heritage Site 5, 6, 33, 253–4,
    314, 320
World War I 282, 289, 290, 301,
World War II 2, 4, 54, 302, 303
wrasse 247
wrecks 38, 54, 214–18, 303–4
Wright, Wally 54, 303
wryneck 167

yellow-breasted bunting 169
yellowhammer 169
yellow wagtail 167, 181